A Family of His Own

🔖 *A Family of His Own*
A Life of Edwin O'Connor

Charles F. Duffy

The Catholic University of America Press
Washington, D.C.

To Sara

Charles Duffy

January 2004

Copyright © 2003
The Catholic University of America Press
All rights reserved
Printed in the United States of America

The paper used in this publication meets the minimum requirements of American National Standards for Information Science—Permanence of Paper for Printed Library materials, ANSI Z39.48-1984.
∞

Library of Congress Cataloging-in-Publication Data
Duffy, Charles F., 1940–
    A family of his own : a life of Edwin O'Connor / by Charles F. Duffy.
      p. cm.
    Includes bibliographical references and index.
    ISBN 0-8132-1337-1 (alk. paper)
      1. O'Connor, Edwin. 2. Authors, American—20th century—Biography.
   3. Fathers and sons in literature.   4. Irish Americans in literature.
   5. Irish Americans—Biography. I. Title.
PS3565.C55 Z64 2003
813'54—dc21

                            2002014871

*For Ivy,
Ariane, and Tara*

Contents

⚛ *List of Photographs*

❧ Preface

My first awareness of Edwin O'Connor coincided with a memorable introduction to literary commentary and controversy. One afternoon in the late winter of 1956 our French class at Boston College High School was treated to an inspired performance by Father Robert Sheridan, who was affectionately known to generations of students as "Mon Pere." Often imbued with spiritous influences—in the several senses of that term—the aging Jesuit was a character out of Dickens, or Edwin O'Connor for that matter. On this day he glowed with unusual excitement as he launched into one of his captivating digressions. In time-honored Jesuit tradition he read us a favorable and an unfavorable review of a newly published novel called *The Last Hurrah*. I forget everything about the favorable review, but I do remember the other one because it was written by another French teacher at the school who later regretted his sophomoric critique.

Only in college did I actually read the novel, even though it had been pointedly dismissed by some professors at Boston College. This "trolley car" school for early generations of Boston Irish used to display Gaelic script and Irish murals in a handsome Gothic lecture room in Gasson Hall. But by the late 1950s, B.C. had become an assimilating university determined to shed all traces of that Gaelic past. Nary a course in Irish history or literature existed. When the lecture room became the Treasurer's Office, lowered ceilings, flourescent lighting, and office walls covered up the Gaelic script and Irish murals—since restored, now that Boston College has one of the world's best Irish studies programs. In some ways *The Last Hurrah* was instrumental in inaugurating this and other important rediscoveries of Irish America.

In the early 1960s, our grad student car pool used to read favorite excerpts from *The Last Hurrah* to fortify ourselves for our much duller courses in law, history, and Victorian prose. And that was pretty much my last contact with Edwin O'Connor until the late 1990s. As I was preparing my course in Modern Irish Literature, I decided to include some Irish American literature for the first time. Figuring that Edwin O'Connor would loom large in that segment of the course, I reread *The*

Last Hurrah and then looked around for a biography of the author. To my surprise, no such book existed. When I mentioned this odd fact to a colleague who had grown up in Edwin O'Connor's home town, Mario DiNunzio, he pointed an authoritative finger at me and declared, "You do it." Thus commissioned, a few weeks later, when O'Connor was inducted at last into the Rhode Island Heritage Hall of Fame, I introduced myself to his sister. The rest is this biography.

In many unexpected ways it was a pleasure to research and write a book about a good man. I received so many delighted responses from people who wanted to remember Edwin O'Connor fondly. Put simply, he was not like most authors. When Mary McCarthy once admitted that yes, Ed O'Connor was a nice man—"almost too nice"—the acerbic author only pointed up the cynicism of her literary set.[1] By no means, however, do I wish this book to be hagiography. O'Connor was conscious of his reputation, literary and otherwise. But he would have been the first to agree a biography should not be the first step in a push for canonization, in the two senses of that term; I leave those crusades to others. O'Connor's fundamental decency, generosity, and tolerance coexisted with other less than saintly traits, and I do not expunge them. But when the agnostic Edmund Wilson, no mean interpreter of people and letters, declared that Edwin O'Connor was one of the few people he knew who strove for a sincere Christian life, his judgment has some force.[2]

According to many people, Edwin O'Connor was not an easy person to know. This challenge to a biographer recalls what that other Irish American novelist, F. Scott Fitzgerald, said somewhere: "There never was . . . a good biography of a good novelist. There couldn't be. He's too many people if he's any good."[3] Discouraging news for a biographer, if Fitzgerald was right. Some people found O'Connor disarmingly simple, like Harvey Breit in his column for *The New York Times Book Review:* "There is no side to him, no overtones or undertones."[4] But those who knew him for more than the interviewer's hour knew differently, as when Robert Taylor, one of his oldest friends, said of him: "He was a simple man—and enormously complex."[5] Marian Schlesinger wrote a year after his death that this merriest of men nevertheless possessed "an inner core which was forever under heavy

---

1. Quoted in *BL,* 34.
2. *BL,* 367.
3. Quoted by Robert Rogers in *A Psychoanalytic Study of the Double in Literature* (Detroit: Wayne State University Press, 1970), 3.
4. March 18, 1956: 8.
5. Review of *BL* in the *Boston Globe,* January 28, 1970.

guard."[6] His own confessor divulged that "Ed was not one who revealed himself easily even to his friends; he was a shy man of great interior depth and he guarded himself against intrusion in a firm if light-hearted manner."[7]

The coexistence of playful gregariousness and extreme retirement in this man accounts for his ability to render a flesh-pumping Frank Skeffington in *The Last Hurrah* and follow with an intimate portrait of a troubled priest's soul in *The Edge of Sadness*. A few people have tried to detect Edwin O'Connor in his works—always a hazardous enterprise, but not an impossible one. Just as the novelist's works guided Norman Sherry as he wrote his biography of Graham Greene, so too O'Connor's works, hermetically sealed though they might appear to be, do yield themselves to considerable biographical analysis. Shaun O'Connell came close to realizing this when he called O'Connor's three major novels his "oblique spiritual autobiography," in which the author worked out his stance on Boston and the Irish experience.[8] This biography will examine O'Connor's writings not so much to interpret them but to illuminate them with material from the author's life; in turn, the writings will be examined for patterns that reflect the man, most especially his extended treatment of the family. Biography does not replace critical commentary, and there is much more to say about O'Connor's works than is contained in this book. But if it helps readers to understand better what O'Connor wrote, then this book will have served its purpose.

Others have touched on Edwin O'Connor life. Arthur Schlesinger Jr.'s introduction to *The Best and the Last of Edwin O'Connor* (1970), which included important brief memoirs by John V. Kelleher and Edmund Wilson, was the first biographical account of the author. Hugh Rank's 1974 book for the Twayne United States Authors Series contained a biographical chapter. The time is long past for a full-length life of the author.

A note on method: I have not summarized *The Last Hurrah* and *The Edge Sadness;* these books are still fairly well known. For most of his other work, especially and most obviously his unpublished work, I have tried to keep summaries brief.

The title of this book is taken from the closing words of Edwin O'Connor's last novel, *All in the Family:* "And so, the next morning, I left Ireland again, to go back to the city I had always loved, to the house which had been my home, but now, for the first time, with my dear Jean, to a family of my

---

6. "That Rarity—A Merry Man—Remembered," *Boston Sunday Globe*, March 23, 1969: A6.

7. Monsignor Francis J. Lally, review of *BL, Boston Sunday Globe*, February 22, 1970.

8. *Imagining Boston: A Literary Landscape* (Boston: Beacon Press, 1990), 110.

own." Going back: to Ireland, to America, to the Boston he loved, to house and home, and above all to family. That is the world of Edwin O'Connor.

Toward the end of my researches I made a visit to Edwin O'Connor's grave in Brookline, Massachusetts. Before I left, I looked around for a small stone to place on his tombstone, but when I found one I realized that the unusual tombstone is banked at a forty-five-degree angle, and so any small stone would simply slide off. Then something made me turn over the one I had found, which I had assumed to be smooth all around. To my surprise, the other side had a long beveled groove that allowed my stone to fit perfectly on the top edge of the tilted gravestone: an Irish moment. I only hope that this book fits as well as that stone.

Providence, Rhode Island
April 2002

❧ Acknowledgments

For its generosity in providing a grant for travel and research, I am most grateful to the Committee on Aid to Faculty Research at Providence College. In addition, I would like to thank so many people at Providence College for their help, skills, and time. First, my colleagues on the faculty, especially Brian Barbour, Rodney Delasanta, Mario Di-Nunzio, and John Hennedy; also, Terrie Curran, Suzanne Fournier, Bruce Graver, Rev. Robert Hayman, Rev. Nicholas Ingham, O.P., Richard Murphy, Paul O'Malley, John Scanlan, and Yinsheng Wan. Also, thanks to the staff at the Phillips Memorial Library, especially Linda Alijian, William Anger, Constance Cameron, and Francine Mancini; and for the expert skills of Phyllis Cardullo, Roger Desautels, Vilma Gagnon, Jane Jackson, Janet Masso, and Diane Wilks. And, not least, I thank my students Brian Daley, Mary Finucane, Kerry Gardner, and Julianne Hertel for those Monday afternoon discussions of Edwin O'Connor's world that always seemed to pass too quickly.

I owe a huge debt to Edwin O'Connor's sister, Barbara O'Connor Burrell, who, with her husband, William, provided me with information, materials, and connections during three extended interviews and countless ensuing telephone conversations, letters, and E-mails. Without their generous and gracious help at every stage of this project, the book simply could not have been done. Edwin O'Connor's stepson, Stephen Weil, was also an important help for the last six years of the life. And to all those others whom I interviewed, a big thank you: the late Phoebe-Lou Adams, Virginia Albee, Ruth Bourke, Jason Burrell, Francis and Lucille Carroll, Peter Davison, Eleanor Rogers DeCoste, Jean DeGiacomo, John Kenneth Galbraith, William Gilbert, Edward Giobbe, Anna Hamburger, Louise Barry Hogg, Nina Holton, Ati Johansen, John V. Kelleher, Owen Laster, Mimi McConchie, Vincent P. McGinn, Robert Manning, James Montgomery, Elliot Norton, Rose Mary O'Brien, Beatrice O'Connor, Michael O'Sullivan, Vita and Gustav Petersen, James H. Reilly, George E. Ryan, Arthur M. Schlesinger Jr., Marian Schlesinger, John Skeffington, Rev. Matthew J. Strumski, Rev. Francis Sweeney, S.J., John Taaffe, Robert Taylor, Arline Tehan, Pat

Greene Thibodeau, John F. Tosi, Aileen Ward, Helen Miranda Wilson, and Esther Yntema.

Of that wonderful community of librarians and archivists, always so diligent and patient, I wish to thank especially the staff of the Department of Rare Books and Manuscripts at the Boston Public Library for their untiring help with the Edwin O'Connor Papers, particularly Eugene Zepp, and also William Faucon, Beatrice Greene, and Roberta Zhonghi. Many thanks also to Henry Scannell and the Microtext Department of the Boston Public Library; Aaron Schmidt of the Print Department of the Boston Public Library; *Atlantic Monthly;* Charles Hogan, archivist of La Salle Academy; William Kevin Cawley and Sharon Sumpter of the University of Notre Dame Archives; Veronica Primrose, transcript coordinator at the University of Notre Dame; James H. Gallagher of the Beebe Communications Reference Library at Boston University; Marlene Lopes of the Adams Library at Rhode Island College; David Maslyn and Serina Wyant of the University of Rhode Island Archives; Ronald Patkus, head librarian of archives and manuscripts at the Burns Library of Boston College; Robert Johnson Lally, archivist and records manager of the Archdiocese of Boston; *The Boston Globe;* Rev. Monsignor Peter V. Conley, editor of the Boston *Pilot;* Michael Brown, editor of the Providence *Visitor;* Chris Duffy of the Woonsocket *Call;* Pat Pothier of the *Providence Journal* library; Lauren Dixson and Dr. Milton Hamolsky of the Rhode Island Medical Licensing Board; Richard W. Peuser, Old Military and Civil Records, Textual Archives Services Division of the National Archives and Records Administration; Joel Wells, formerly with the Thomas More Association; Pamela T. Wilson, archives coordinator at the Research Center of Time Inc.; the Woonsocket Harris Library; the Rhode Island Historical Society.

And thanks to Betsey Burrell, Nancy Carlson, Patrick Conley, Heyward Cutting, Jim Dedman, William Donnelly, P. Albert Duhamel, Brother Dominic Fontaine, F.S.C., David R. Godine, John Graby, James Harkin, Margo Howard, Herbert Kenny, Rev. Paul Lippert, Lawrence McCaffrey, David Meskill, Jenny and Michael Neff, Conor Cruise O'Brien, Carroll O'Connor, Edwin O'Connor (nephew), Hugh Rank, Jean Ricoux and the staff of the Shelbourne Meridien Hotel, James Rogers, Bruce Stewart, and Andrew Wilson.

For their abundant help, I wish to thank the staff at the Catholic University of America Press, especially David McGonagle, Susan Needham, and Beth Benevides. And a special thanks to Ellen Coughlin for her copyediting mastery.

If I have failed to mention anyone, please accept my apologies.

Finally, I thank my wife, Ivy, who has been a constant help and encouragement from the beginning.

❧ Abbreviations

B	*Benjy*
BL	*The Best and the Last of Edwin O'Connor*
"CG"	"Coast Guard" Manuscript
D	*I Was Dancing*
EOCP	Edwin O'Connor Papers, Boston Public Library (MS. ACC. 1600)
ES	*The Edge of Sadness*
F	*All in the Family*
LH	*The Last Hurrah*
O	*The Oracle*
"TB"	"The Traveler from Brazil"
"YMP"	"A Young Man of Promise"

A Family of His Own

A Life of Edwin O'Connor

CHAPTER ONE

❧ *Rhode Island*
(1918–1935)

Woonsocket sits on Rhode Island's northern border with Massachusetts, close to the corner of the state that points toward Boston.[1] The precise meaning of the Native American place name is disputed, but the one most favored by the city's later settlers is the dramatic "Thunder Mist," which refers to a substantial waterfall of the Blackstone River. That river flows southeast from central Massachusetts, through Woonsocket and Pawtucket, where in the 1790s the newly arrived English millwright Samuel Slater built the textile mill that began the Industrial Revolution in America. At Providence the river empties into Narragansett Bay. As testimony to industrial Woonsocket's vital dependence on the river's water power, the seal of the city displays a waterfall surmounted by gaunt mill buildings.

Long before it became a city, much of present Woonsocket was a scattering of New England hamlets. In fact, a main street and adjoining section of the city is still called Hamlet, and in some ways the neighborhoods of the later factory city retained the small town flavor often reflected in the fiction of Edwin O'Connor even when he was writing of a much bigger city. It was only in 1867 that the present Woonsocket gathered up these villages to become a separate township. Two decades later, it had its first mayor.

Irish immigrants began appearing in New England in some numbers in the 1820s and 1830s. Mostly men at first, they came as ditch diggers on projects like the Blackstone Canal (opened in 1828), remnants of which can still be discerned in Woonsocket. Shortly afterwards they helped build railroads like the Providence and Worcester, which ran through Woonsocket. In the mid-1840s, southern New England was

---

1. For this chapter I am indebted to Marcel Fortin, ed., *Woonsocket, Rhode Island: A Centennial History 1888–1988* (Woonsocket, R.I.: Woonsocket Centennial Committee, 1988), especially the first five chapters, written respectively by Raymond H. Bacon, Nancy E. Hudson, Robert C. Mulcahy, N. David Bouley, and Phyllis H. Thomas. Additionally, I have learned much from my Woonsocket-raised colleagues Rodney Delasanta and Mario DiNunzio.

overwhelmed by tens of thousands of refugees from the Irish potato failure who gravitated toward seacoast cities like Boston and Providence and inland mill towns like Woonsocket. However, with the possible exception of the blue-collar Fairmount section, the Irish of Woonsocket never developed distinctively Irish American neighborhoods as did nearby Providence and Boston. Woonsocket was a city where Irishness could be quickly shed.

The sudden immigration of French Canadians after the American Civil War is the most important event in Woonsocket's ethnic history.[2] Many of the Irish who had recently preceded them moved north across the Massachusetts state line to Blackstone, where they became the largest group. As the textile industry boomed for the next sixty years, waves of Québécois families left their desolate rural homes for tenements in the Social district and long, dreary shifts at the factory spindles. They brought with them a strong sense of cultural identity, unified by family, language, and Catholicism. Whereas the Irish had quickly joined the welcoming Democratic party, French Canadians gravitated toward the Republican party in order to gain their own political power. Religious and labor friction with the Irish would exacerbate their political differences. Shortly before O'Connor's birth in 1918, French Canadians were the largest ethnic component of the population, with 44 percent, while the Irish hovered around 20 percent. Among southern New England cities with large Québécois populations, Woonsocket laid easy claim to the highest percentage. In fact, French was still widely heard on its streets well into the mid-twentieth century, so much so that outsiders to this day jokingly refer to the city as "Woonso*quette*," although no one in the city pronounces it that way.

When O'Connor was born, Woonsocket had reached its historic high point: factories were roaring with war orders, and population growth was outstripping the state's pace. At its height around 1920, Woonsocket had over 40,000 people crammed into a relatively small six square miles. The tight urban topography of his home town may contribute to the distinct sense in O'Connor's novels that the cities he delineates, even if they are mostly modeled on much bigger Boston, are compact and knowable—and also in decline. For the rest of the century, Woonsocket was beset by swift and seemingly unstoppable economic deterioration, violent labor turmoil, political

2. For the history of French Canadians in Woonsocket, see Gerard Brault, *The French-Canadian Heritage in New England* (Hanover, N.H.: University Press of New England, 1986) and Claire Quintal, ed., *Steeples and Smokestacks: A Collection of Essays on the Franco-American Experience in New England* (Worcester, Mass.: Assumption College, Institut francais, 1996). Woonsocket's new interactive Museum of Work and Culture is devoted largely to the French Canadian experience in industrial Woonsocket.

corruption, ethnic tensions, natural disasters including a devastating flood in 1955, and even open strife within the Catholic Church. As O'Connor grew up in a comfortable upper-middle-class environment in the 1920s and 1930s, the sense that the city had seen better days induced a looking back. That mood would overshadow the future writer as he cultivated the eccentricities of nostalgia.

As O'Connor readily admitted, most of Woonsocket was not attractive: "Woonsocket has a way of coming coldly against the alien eye. Let us face it at once: Woonsocket is not one of those fortunate communities in which every prospect pleases. To see it is not to love it. No stranger, walking down Main Street . . . has ever stood in danger of perishing before beauty." [3] Much of the industrial city's twisty layout was dictated by the all-important river and the large stone and brick factories that angled alongside it. As with many New England cities, the streets seem haphazardly laid out, and lumpy hills only contribute to the undistinguished appearance.

Nevertheless, the city developed its own quirky civic pride even as many sought to flee the place, and there were redeeming features. Some factories incorporated the occasional touch of a period-revival tower, and many handsome churches added their distinctive roofs and spires in their own national styles, such as Quebec Gothic. The title of Claire Quintal's book on French Canadians in New England, *Steeples and Smokestacks,* aptly images the skyline of the city. Downtown boasted a decent courthouse and a dark stone city hall, which was possibly a partial model for City Hall in *The Last Hurrah.* A special point of civic pride was the Opera House, completed for Woonsocket's incorporation as a city in 1888. It was done in Romanesque manner with boldly recessed round-arch windows and OPERA HOUSE rendered in "P.T. Barnum" lettering under the frieze. Its theater, which held 1,500 people, could host plays, provide lecture space for fiery orators like William Jennings Bryan, and finally alternate as a movie house and a showplace for vaudeville acts as late as World War II. Even in his early teens O'Connor was fascinated by the dying world of small-time vaudeville, and whenever he had the chance he would go to these performances by old troupers at the Opera House (then called the New Park Theater) and other establishments in Woonsocket and Providence. His writings show a recurrent interest in this bygone world. His novel *I Was Dancing* even puts a vaudevillian at center stage.

The city bustled during the decades 1880–1920. An extensive trolley car

3. Edwin O'Connor, "A Love Letter to Woonsocket," *Providence Sunday Journal Magazine,* October 7, 1951, 12.

system of twenty-three miles was somehow inlaid on its congested streets, and the city even made space for a series of varied and pleasant parks. The city boasted two daily newspapers, an older Republican paper and a newer Democratic one, founded in 1892. The factories diversified somewhat: leather, rubber, and wooden products joined textiles as French and Belgian companies invested. Small groups of Poles, Jews, Ukrainians, Syrians, and Italians settled in. The city fielded a baseball Hall of Famer in Napoleon "Larry" or "Nap" Lajoie, who still holds the American League record batting average of .422, set in 1901. O'Connor, a baseball fan, must surely have boasted about that.

However, life for most people was onerous. In 1910 work weeks of fifty-six hours were the norm for factory workers, most of whom were not unionized. One mill was paying $7.50 a week for sixty hours of work. Child labor laws were still being debated when a survey done in 1907 found 709 laborers aged fourteen to sixteen years out of a work force of 8,000. There were few social services for injured or laid-off workers, and no OSHA to muffle the pandemonium of the factories or to safeguard life and limb around dangerous machinery. Families tended to be large, and although public and parochial schools systems were extensive, high school graduation rates were low. Young people often married early or moved away.

After the 1888 incorporation as a city, local politics became important in Woonsocket. Elections were frequent and often frenetic as older Yankees, brash Irish upstarts, and determined French Canadians vied for City Hall. The first mayor, a Yankee Republican, won by five votes. By O'Connor's time the mayors were usually French Canadian. In something of an anomaly in urban politics in the Northeast, the smaller Irish community could boast of only one mayor by 1918; he closed the city's five brothels in 1909. When Prohibition started in 1920 in a state that voted "wet" and whose Narragansett Bay became a haven for rum-running, Woonsocket became infamous for flouting its provisions. Some thirty legal saloons carried on a brisk business serving weak beer. In an indirect way, the city's notoriety during the Prohibition years 1920–33 may have been a contributing factor to O'Connor's early determination never to drink alcohol.

The notoriety of the city's corruption matched or exceeded the state's in general, and the young O'Connor heard many tales of political shenanigans. This was the state, after all, whose centuries-old nickname of "Rogues' Island" was earned by a succession of colonial outcasts that started with the religiously unorthodox Roger Williams and Anne Hutchinson, and was later confirmed by a more nefarious line of pirates, privateers, and slave traders who planted both genetic and monetary seeds for many of the state's old-money families. When that colorful era passed, state politics kept alive a spirit of blatant roguery practiced by all parties and always coated with a patina of appeals to independence. Not for nothing does the Rhode Island State House sport a ten-foot gilded statue of the Independent Man on its dome. In *The Last Hurrah* Nathaniel Gardiner, a judicious old Yankee at odds with most of his cronies, sums up Mayor Frank Skeffington thus: "'He's a rogue. A complete rogue. And yet the most engaging rogue I've ever met'" (105). He might almost be from "Rogues' Island."

In that most Catholic state, an unusually active religious culture, which is to say largely French Canadian Catholicism, flourished in Woonsocket. Many parishes had become centers for *"foi et langue,"* and therein were planted the seeds of an extraordinary series of events just after O'Connor's birth. By 1920 Franco-Americans had adopted a widely held nationalist outlook termed *survivance.* Catholic faith and French language were seen as indispensable to maintaining cultural survival in the adopted land. During the 1910s there had been some friction with the overwhelmingly Irish Catholic hierarchy, but by far the most serious conflict was the Sentinellist Movement of 1923–28, which has been called the most "traumatic, rending, and divisive" event in the city's history.[4]

The details of the Sentinellist Movement are complex, but it was essentially an eruption by the French Canadian laity against the financial and educational policies of the Irish-led diocese. Elphege Daignault, an attorney, pitted his large Woonsocket-based movement against Bishop William Hickey of Providence in a struggle that involved mass outdoor rallies, a newspaper called *La Sentinelle* ("The Guardian") from which the movement got its stirring name, moral support from around New England and even Quebec, fierce internecine feuding with a vocal minority of compatriots who opposed Sentinellism, growing involvement by clergy on both sides, and eventually unusual action in the Rhode Island courts in 1927, where the Sentinellists lost their legal battle. To compound their defeat, in early 1928 the still-defiant Daignault and sixty-two supporters were stunned by an excommunication which had the full backing of the Vatican. *La Sentinelle* was placed on the Index. Within a year Daignault and his followers capitulated and were readmitted to the Church, but the scars would remain for at least half a century.[5]

4. Fortin, *Woonsocket,* chapter 4 by N. David Bouley, 86.
5. It is perhaps no accident that a devotional cult surrounding Marie Rose Ferron, known as "Little Rose," sprang up during this time among Franco-Americans in Woonsock-

Although O'Connor was just a young boy during this strange episode in American religious history, he keenly attended adult talk and at the very least absorbed from this drawn-out conflict the seriousness with which Catholics, especially in the midst of disputes, took their institution. However, it seems curious that in all O'Connor's writings Franco-Americans rarely show up, and then only in bit roles. Three explanations can be offered. First, O'Connor's upbringing largely sheltered him from Franco-American neighborhoods barely a mile away. Later, when he launched himself as a serious writer, it was the Boston Irish and Yankees who intrigued him. Finally, interest in Franco-Americans might have advertised his Woonsocket roots unnecessarily. As a postscript, though, it is curious that his one veiled reference to the Sentinellist Movement occurs in the last piece he was writing, an unfinished and unusually autobiographical work, the early chapters of a novel tentatively called "The Boy," where a discussion by Irish cronies develops. It is worthy of Joyce at his satirical best:

"A very primitive people, the Canucks," he said. "They're not at all like us."

"Not too much culture there, would you say, P.J?" said Mr. O'Donnell. . . .

"No, no, none at all," my grandfather said. "Even their language is a queer jabber that nobody but themselves can understand: part French, part English, and part squirrel for all I know. And their priests are no better than the rest of them. I yield to no man in my respect for the clergy, you all know that, but the Canuck priests are a poor lot. Trouble makers, you know."

"They're apt to go into business for themselves quite a bit, isn't that it?" Mr. O'Donnell said. "*Skismatics,* I believe they call them" (*BL* 444).[6]

Labor strife hit the city particularly hard with the onset of the Great Depression, when "Y'er workin'?" was a common Woonsocket street greeting. Intransigence by some factory owners to union organizing, especially by the moderate Independent Textile Union, led to a series of strikes and clashes culminating in serious rioting by 10,000 people, or nearly one-quarter of the city, on the night of September 12, 1934. The rioters, many of whom were in a party mood at first, looted most of the downtown businesses, overturned cars, and vandalized factories. A quickly mobilized but ill-trained National Guard used tear gas and finally bullets to quell the roving mobs. Two people were shot dead and many more wounded in one of the worst civil distur-

---

et. Reputed to be a stigmatic and mystic, she was a consolation to her community as their public battles were lost. She died at age thirty-four in 1936, but efforts by her devotees to advance canonization (including an exhumation in 1947) have been consistently discouraged by ecclesiastical authorities. Although busloads of visitors come to her house to this day, that kind of private Catholic devotion held little appeal for O'Connor.

6. Consult the list of abbreviations used in this book for O'Connor's longer works.

bances in Rhode Island history. Fairly or not, many Woonsocket Irish at the time blamed French Canadians for being scabs. Thus, ethnic economic strife only stressed the fault lines caused by recent religious tensions.

This then was Edwin O'Connor's Woonsocket. In three of his novels he obliquely refers to it as "Deerford" or "Derrford," a city of 40,000 with a mostly French Canadian population. This city is, however, only at the margins of his customary setting. O'Connor may have grown up sheltered from his city's turmoil, but at the very least hometown history would impress upon him two passionate human activities: religion and politics. Those two, and family.

Edwin Greene O'Connor was a third-generation Irish American.[7] Both parents were born in the United States and were of that assimilation-minded generation which seldom looked back to the "old sod," and which in fact often looked down on anyone playing the professional Irishman. The family took little interest in genealogical searches. In his late novel *All in the Family,* O'Connor has the narrator's father say, "neither your mother nor myself ever went in much for family trees" (46–47). O'Connor's mother, Mary (May) Greene, was descended from John and Mary Ryan, who had emigrated from Templemore, County Tipperary, in the mid-nineteenth century. Their daughter Mary, Edwin's grandmother, was born in 1863 and married James F. Greene, whose surname would become Edwin's middle name and whose exceptional tallness contributed to O'Connor's own. In turn, their own daughter Mary, Edwin's mother, was born to them in Woonsocket in 1894. About O'Connor's father's family even less is known and the family today has trouble locating their grave sites in Woonsocket. John V. O'Connor was born in 1884 in adjacent Blackstone, Massachusetts.

John V. O'Connor was one of nine children. His father had been a reporter for the *Woonsocket Call* daily newspaper. A brother, Thomas, became a Woonsocket city alderman. Journalism and politics—twin early occupations for those ambitious Irish Americans who came over with the advantage of knowing English—were part of family history and would become some of Edwin O'Connor's favorite subject matter. Many of his father's siblings never married and it appears that John, the only one to get a college education, was

---

7. For much of the family history in this chapter I am deeply indebted to Edwin O'Connor's sister, Barbara O'Connor Burrell, and her husband, William, who shared their recollections in a series of personal interviews in the summer of 1998, and in many subsequent follow-up conversations in person and by telephone and E-mail. An obituary of Dr. John V. O'Connor in the *Woonsocket Call,* September 15, 1956, was also helpful.

financially responsible for some of them from time to time. John was a determined, no-nonsense man who worked hard and became very much the O'Connor patriarch. After attending a Boston preparatory school and graduating from Woonsocket High School, he studied at a Baltimore pharmacy college, the fourth oldest in the country and quite respected, that would become part of the University of Maryland in 1904, in time for his degree to be from that institution. He worked for a time at pharmacies in Woonsocket and Newport before deciding on medical school. Then it was back to Baltimore, but curiously enough he spent his first term at Johns Hopkins studying English literature. Although his formal study of literature was brief, it reveals an unexpected side of this self-made man and forecasts his son's bent.

John O'Connor next enrolled in the College of Physicians and Surgeons, which was loosely associated with the Johns Hopkins Medical School.[8] He quickly became an honors student. The College of Physicians and Surgeons was one of many proprietary medical schools in the country, most of which were fly-by-night outfits that were eventually shut down. Fortunately, John's college was in fairly good standing and was spared the ax. Nevertheless, during his years as a practicing physician rumors circulated in Woonsocket that Dr. John O'Connor was only a glorified pharmacist. These rumors can be easily laid to rest. In those years it was common for pharmacy to be a legitimate route to the practice of medicine; the medical school he graduated from in 1911 was decent enough; and finally and most importantly he passed the Rhode Island and Massachusetts medical exams upon his return. The Rhode Island oral exams were quite thorough for their day and he passed all seven sections. No doubt his son heard the rumors about his father and was probably more than upset by them. Indeed, as we shall see, he not only alludes to such rumors in developing some of his characters, but more importantly he weaves these rumors (and much more besides) into complex portraits of one of his most enduring subjects—fatherhood itself.

An episode from his father's medical student days reveals another trait and talent that intrigued the son. To earn some money and probably also to indulge in a little madcap medical school fun, John O'Connor tried his hand at vaudeville in Baltimore. It seems he had notions of himself as a potential song-and-dance man. At an important audition, however, he was literally given the hook of a cane when fellow students whooped it up too boisterously on his behalf. Years later he told his daughter-in-law that were it not

---

8. For some details about Dr. O'Connor's education I wish to thank Dr. Milton Hamolsky and Lauren Dixson of the Rhode Island Medical Licensing Board.

for that incident he might have had a career in vaudeville.[9] Even allowing for the doctor's tongue-in-cheek spin on this tale, it shows a fun-loving side of him, not usually in evidence, that the son would always ponder. (Well into his advanced years Dr. O'Connor enjoyed singing and playing the harmonica on Sunday afternoons—another lingering bit of show biz.) John O'Connor's first son received his name from Edwin, John's brother, who did in fact have a successful career in vaudeville on the West Coast. Uncle Edwin would come back east occasionally for visits and for medical checkups from his brother. Apparently his namesake took a fancy to him. Dozens of people still vividly remember that for decades the author's signature entrance was a brief soft-shoe routine and hammy quip. This little scrap of vaudevilliana may seem a short peg to toss a hypothesis onto, but the peg seems sturdy enough when O'Connor's lifelong fictional quest for the ideal father is explored.

His 1911 medical school yearbook, *The Clinic,* noted that "John O'Conner" [sic] was president of his graduating class: a politician resided inside the physician. The entry goes on to say that "John is a good student and is always pushing to the front. . . . He has a stern look, but a gentle heart." Already the determined ambition and strict demeanor of O'Connor's father were much in evidence, making his benevolence not always easy to detect. For his first son there would be a lifelong quest to probe that gentle heart inside the stern outer man. The politician and the vaudevillian that resided somewhere in his father were for Edwin O'Connor two of the most important elements in his many portrayals of fathers and their surrogates.

In 1911, at age twenty-seven, Dr. O'Connor set up his practice. For the next forty-four years he practiced medicine in Woonsocket, a successful and widely known general practitioner and internist who developed something of a specialty in heart diseases by taking additional medical courses at Harvard and Johns Hopkins. During the terrible influenza plague of late 1918 he won special laurels. Dr. O'Connor worked hard during most of his career before heart problems in middle age slowed him down. The meticulous discipline of his daily schedule was something that O'Connor would take with him and put to different use.

John O'Connor was of average height. He had a bulbous nose, blue staring eyes, and a dour expression that masked a witty but sometimes mordant personality. His tightly ordered daily life could occasion petty outbursts—a late delivery by a paper boy was cause for public wrath. All remember him as

9. Beatrice O'Connor, telephone interview, September 10, 1999.

a stern family disciplinarian, especially with regard to his two sons, from whom he expected much. Some detected a kindness underneath that would only reluctantly show itself.[10] His pattern of firm outer mien and private inner life would become O'Connor's as well, though with a markedly different arrangement of contents. Throughout much of his writing, O'Connor wrestled with fathers and their stand-ins who often resembled his own. Although it became an obsession only in *I Was Dancing* (O'Connor was too level-headed for the modern American sport of mindless father-bashing, and in fact in *The Edge of Sadness* Father Kennedy specifically warns against it), this recurring motif becomes inescapable to anyone who meticulously reads all his published and unpublished work (where often it is even more on display).[11] To be sure, this subject nearly amounts to a cliche in contemporary biography. And in any case, there was no open rebellion by O'Connor against his stern father. Nonetheless, the evidence from the fiction remains: fathers and sons, that age-old preoccupation of literature, loomed large in O'Connor's career as well.

Mary Greene was quite different from her husband. She inherited the Greene trait of being big-boned, although she was not especially tall. She had a large head with a prominent brow which Edwin inherited. In fact, his top-heavy physique is largely his mother's. Mary Greene was raised in a substantial white Victorian known as the Henry Darling House, built in 1865. She graduated from the old Woonsocket High School (later the Harris Public School, which her children would attend) in 1912. Her class picture shows her in a long white dress of the era when hems were beginning to rise a few inches. She has a kindly look, and her head is tilted noticeably to her right, as if its size made her self-conscious. That same year she enrolled in the old Rhode Island College of Education, a normal school founded in 1854 as the state's first public college, and since 1958 called Rhode Island College in its more suburban reincarnation. After the standard two years of courses and a semester of practice teaching, Mary graduated in 1915.[12] She taught for a couple of years in the Woonsocket school system.

John O'Connor and Mary Greene met at a dance during this time, and after a conventional courtship they married on June 25, 1917, at Sacred Heart

10. William Gilbert, personal interview, summer 1999; Beatrice O'Connor, interview; Pat Greene Thibodeau, telephone interview, August 2, 1999.

11. In preparing his study of O'Connor, Hugh Rank left inconclusive notes on this subject in the Notre Dame Archives. He told me that he did not wish to play armchair psychiatrist, and so decided not to use the material for his book. Hugh Rank, letter to author, April 16, 1999.

12. My thanks to Marlene Lopes, Rhode Island College Special Collections.

Church in Woonsocket. In keeping with a custom widely practiced well into the century, Mary resigned her teaching position when she married. The O'Connors found their first house through an ecumenical gesture unusual for the times. Samuel Hudson, publisher of the *Woonsocket Call* newspaper and a prominent citizen, told the young doctor that the St. James Episcopal Church rectory on Hamlet Avenue was available. It was a good location for a doctor, and the couple was pleased with their substantial, somewhat boxy house. A year later they bought their first house, a large simplified Victorian with a wrap-around porch, also on Hamlet Avenue, where they moved in on July 28, 1918. The very next day Mary O'Connor gave birth to her first son.

Edwin's birth was a long and difficult one. Doctor O'Connor insisted that his child be born in the up-to-date Providence Lying-In Hospital not far from the State House. Because of his Providence birth, many people to this day erroneously assume that Edwin O'Connor grew up in that city and are surprised to learn otherwise; the error has also appeared in print several times. Her first son became something of his mother's favorite. Three more children followed: in 1922 a sister, Barbara, who died a few days after birth; a second son, John, in 1923; and a sister also named Barbara in 1928. In 1935 a five-year-old orphaned cousin, Pat Greene, came to live with the O'Connors, but was never formally adopted. She has sometimes been incorrectly identified as Edwin's other sister, an understandable error because he occasionally alluded to her as such.

Edwin's name at baptism, taken from the vaudeville uncle, was an English saint's name. In 1918 the Irish American vogue for Seans and Meghans was a long way off. Indeed, most Irish families of the day, in their eagerness for Anglo-American assimilation, had little hesitation about picking English names—even while, ironically enough, the struggle for independence from Britain was turning into a guerrilla war in Ireland. Furthermore, in O'Connor's novels, which are populated by scores of Irish American characters, few Mc's and even fewer O's can be found, and they are never main characters. Instead, for his important Irish American characters O'Connor usually selects surnames that do not appear immediately Irish. His most famous Irish American, Frank Skeffington, has an English name.[13] Many other principal surnames do not immediately appear Irish, even though they are thoroughly so: Sugrue, Carmody, Considine, Kinsella. (Conversely, "heavies" of various kinds often get dubbed with Mc's and O's that faintly suggest denseness or

13. In fact, a Sir William Skeffington was sent from England to Ireland to suppress the revolt of Silken Thomas in 1534.

buffoonery; Skeffington's wooden opponent Kevin McCluskey is the best example.) A gloss on this pattern occurs in *All in the Family,* when Phil Kinsella talks about the advantages of the Irish family name. The novel's narrator, another Kinsella, then recalls:

> I remembered: it was a family joke. When I was a boy in school I had often bitterly regretted having one of those names—Costello was another—which was subject to mortifying misinterpretation. In a way proud of my name because it was my father's, my mother's, I nevertheless longed for something clearcut: Sullivan, Murphy. But now, years later, ambiguity apparently paid off (*F* 204).

In this late novel, O'Connor seems to have finally become aware of the pattern of non-Irish-looking names in his stories, which were supposed to be so much about the Irish. But the "ambiguity apparently paid off," as Jack Kinsella said, though for a different reason: in the 1950s, when O'Connor became famous and before the renewal of ethnic pride in America, having his main characters not look too Irish could help sales of his books.

Mary O'Connor supervised her growing family with firmness but in a soft and quiet manner. She is remembered for her many kindnesses, rapt devotion toward her children, and considerable if occasionally naive charm. Early on she accepted her husband's workaholic demands on family schedules, and she became particularly adept at making sure meals went by the clock. She excelled at baking treats of various kinds. More importantly, the former teacher patiently introduced her children to reading at an early age. Like so many other writers, O'Connor knew he owed a large debt to a parent who opened Keats's magic casement windows. Many of his later friends would note his devotion to his mother; he seldom spoke of his father, although they seemed to get along well enough, albeit uneasily on both sides.

To assist O'Connor's mother, the family usually employed some domestic help, even some live-ins on occasion, especially when the family moved to the fashionable North End of the city. They served as cooks and general housekeepers. Such help was still readily available for middle-class professional people through the 1930s, an era when wages were low and before electric appliances were widespread. In O'Connor's novels domestics as characters begin to appear quite easily and naturally once he became affluent himself; they are found in *The Edge of Sadness* (1961) and even more so in his last novel, *All in the Family* (1966), at a time when he and his wife did in fact employ a housekeeper, and at considerably greater expense than was the case during his boyhood. In O'Connor's intensely autobiographical unfinished novel "The Boy," the narrator remembers his testy Irish Catholic grandfather's demand that all domestic help must emphatically not be Irish: the

The house in the fashionable North End of Woonsocket where Edwin O'Connor was raised. *Photo taken by author, 2000.*

Irish gossip too much about the family (always an important O'Connor family concern) and bolt for church just when you need them. Better, he says, to hire a "good homely Swamp Yankee" (Rhode Islandese for low-bred Anglo native) like Alma in "The Boy" (*BL* 434). The vignette has the ring of fact. The inclusion of various domestics in his later novels also served as aids to reconstituting an ideal and orderly family—part boyhood memory, part Victorian novel (his favorite kind), part Evelyn Waugh pretension (another favorite)—which ideal by 1966 far surpassed the social scale of his own family in Woonsocket.

By 1923 Dr. O'Connor was ready for a move to Woonsocket's North End, the most fashionable section of the city.[14] Ever since the mid-nineteenth century this area abutting the Massachusetts line had become a haven from the city's factories, which are invisible from the North End even though downtown is only a mile distant. This suburban insularity helps explain the sense

14. The name "North End" even today leads some people to think the neighborhood is gritty and run-down.

of quiet refuge conveyed by so many of the large city houses and their neighborhoods in O'Connor's fiction. The North End first attracted the city's industrialists, who built modestly showy Victorian houses in various French and English revival styles. These mini-mansions hardly approached the scale of Newport's to the south, but they were clearly meant to display wealth and privilege. By the 1920s the first affluent Irish Americans—doctors, lawyers, businessmen—were beginning to move into newer but somewhat smaller colonials. Today the North End is still pleasant, with many handsome houses, and has been rediscovered as an upscale community. For a few months in 1923 Dr. O'Connor's family, now grown to four with the recent arrival of son John, lived in a rented apartment on Meadow Road in Woonsocket while their new house was being built. By 1924 the family had moved into a substantial brick colonial at 247 Gaskill Street, which runs northeast to the state line, as if pointing the way to Boston. Two large shade trees, sometimes remembered in his novels, stood on the front lawn; one is still there. This was the house and neighborhood that O'Connor would fondly remember all his life, and whose memory helped shape not a few of his fictional ones. O'Connor even had the staff photographer of *The Providence Journal* take a picture of the house, which was unidentified, to accompany his 1951 Sunday magazine article, "A Love Letter to Woonsocket." The house remained in the O'Connor family until 1958. A small historical plaque now reads "The O'Connor House, ca. 1926," but without mention of the author who grew up there.

For some years the house stood largely by itself on its side of the street. Behind the house was a large expanse of still undeveloped land which contained a smouldering dump for factory ashes; access was informally called Dump Road. A long stone wall ran along the opposite side of Gaskill Street where a few recessed Victorian houses stood, among them the house of Samuel Hudson, the city's newspaper publisher. The O'Connors were only the second Irish American family on that part of the street and for at least one of the older Yankee dwellers, this apparently was too many. One evening in the mid-1920s, during the height of a nationwide resurgence of the Ku Klux Klan, which was then including among its targets all immigrants and especially Catholics and Jews, the newly arrived O'Connor family was startled to see a small burning cross beside their house. The perpetrator was widely believed to be a deranged neighbor.[15] For the most part, however, relations with their Yankee neighbors was cordial and even friendly, although

15. Gilbert, interview.

few neighbors, especially children, went inside the O'Connor house. The O'Connors no doubt felt they were brave, successful settlers in somewhat alien territory. O'Connor would experience similar sentiments when he moved into Boston's Beacon Hill, where few Irish Americans lived. To attain this status was for him an important victory.[16]

Family tradition, his mother's training, and his maternal grandfather's insistence all dictated that the boy attend public schools, this in spite of the fact that Catholic parochial schools were well established in the city. Although the O'Connors were dutiful Catholics, they were independent in matters like education, something that did not always make for comfortable relations with some rectories of the day. Although in "A Love Letter to Woonsocket" O'Connor claimed, "No kindergarten product I," for a few months he did attend an informal kindergarten run by a Catholic women's club. He was the only boy among six girls, and was differentiated from them only by his sailor suit.[17]

For the next seven years, 1924–31, O'Connor attended public schools in a somewhat confusing manner typical of Woonsocket at the time; these schools are echoed in the "The Boy." For grades one to three he attended the Summer Street School. Looking like an enlarged version of a little red schoolhouse, cupola and porch included, this wooden building was built in 1895 and is still in use as a day-care center. It may very well be the model for the schoolhouse attended by the insufferable Benjy in O'Connor's one children's story. It also appears that Mary O'Connor had her son move up during second grade into the third, possibly as part of a tacit competition with another doctor's child who had done the same. This leapfrogging resulted in O'Connor's always being about a year ahead of most children his age, a situation his large size could always handle. An incident at this school puts him, by his own admission, in some bad company. It seems that on one afternoon he and some young hooligans were apprehended by a teacher as they were gleefully stuffing warm ashes inside the clothing of an obviously distressed classmate. "'You are such VERY destructive little boys,'" she scolded.[18] For the fourth grade he went to the Boyden Street School, now gone. Grades five and six were in the squat, red brick Harris Street School, which still stands. Finally, for seventh and eighth grades he attended the Junior High School, which had "Faith," "Hope," and "Wisdom" carved in stone above its three main doors. Classes were large in those years before unionization, but some-

---

16. Peter Davison, conversation with author, July 1, 1999.
17. Louise Barry Hogg (of that kindergarten class), telephone interview, August 31, 1999.
18. "Love Letter," 13.

how order was kept and truancy was generally low. O'Connor was a bright and eager pupil: "I was neither beaten, humiliated, nor physically disturbed; as I remember it, I had a fine time."[19] He may also have been something of a teacher's pet because of his young age and eagerness to learn, but apparently not an annoying one. His eighth grade English teacher remembers how O'Connor always finished his class work ahead of the others so that he could begin reading a favorite book.[20]

By most measures Edwin O'Connor had a contented boyhood. His family nickname of "Sonny" may even have been a pun on "sunny." (He is still known in the family as simply "Sonny"; a nephew and niece who never knew him refer to him as "Uncle Sonny.") He certainly did not suffer material want, and this fact makes his decade of privation before the success of *The Last Hurrah* all the more remarkable. Whenever he wrote or talked about his boyhood, he always looked back upon it fondly. In this regard two documents are important: "A Love Letter to Woonsocket" from 1951, and "The Boy" from the last weeks of his life in 1968. (The more problematic *Benjy* of 1957, his "children's" book that is actually a parable for adults, is a loaded special case to be examined later in its turn.)

At the center of "A Love Letter to Woonsocket" is a faded Eden informally called Hoyle's Field. Not a public playground at all, it was two acres of a long narrow field ending at an apple orchard. It belonged to a kindly Yankee who oversaw a large family in an adjacent Victorian diagonally across from the O'Connor house. Joseph Hoyle and his wife enjoyed letting North End children play sports there, and they also offered it to groups like the Boy Scouts. Apparently he had even refused offers to sell the land to developers. Hoyle was a man of remarkable patience. Several times during the summer an errant foul ball would sail over some small pine trees and break one of his windows. A hasty collection of pennies, along with apologies, would be presented to the composed Mr. Hoyle, who would gravely but politely thank the boys. These halcyon days ended when a nervous neighbor, a Mrs. Doherty according to another neighborhood recollection,[21] called the police, who then posted the field, and all games stopped. Hoyle's field was planted as a Victory Garden during World War II, and later reverted to an overgrown hayfield.

And yet, in spite of O'Connor's glowing tribute to this playing field, he

---

19. Ibid.

20. Jim Winn, "O'Connor Always Remained Down to Earth Despite Fame," *Woonsocket Call*, March 29, 1987, D4.

21. Gilbert, interview.

was not in fact one of its more vigorous athletes. He played baseball and a little mostly solitary golf, but the boy was steered away from contact sports by his protective mother. There are memories of Edwin sitting on the sidelines, rather aloof and too dressed up for roughneck games.[22] This dapper standoffishness led some to dub him Lord Fauntleroy, a label he would exorcize in *Benjy* many years later. The relatively safe and bucolic game of baseball was clearly his favorite sport, and would remain so throughout his life. One old friend, William Gilbert, remembers being knocked unconscious during a baseball game, and waking up to see a concerned Ed O'Connor peering down at him—a combination of his father's professionalism and his mother's compassion.[23] Throughout his life O'Connor had a strong instinct for coming quickly and unstintingly to the aid of others—whether it involved rescuing drowning swimmers or supervising funeral arrangements for distraught widows.

Much of "Love Letter" is devoted to more solitary pursuits, however. O'Connor relates his excursions along the Dump Road nearby and to a pond further off where he would overturn rocks to look for snakes and listen in the swampy sections for legendary rats, frogs, lizards, and turtles. Half a mile to the northeast he could cross a narrow wooden bridge into "terra incognita, known to the adults as Massachusetts."[24] Here the woods were thicker, and O'Connor, like a budding Thoreau, delighted in identifying wild flowers with quaintly descriptive names like the lady's slipper and jack-in-the-pulpit. To be sure, O'Connor became primarily an urbanite in both life and fiction; his novels show little interest in natural phenomena. Nevertheless, for most of his adult life he would cherish extended retreats from the city, as long as they were within easy reach of good company and not too far from Boston and Rhode Island.

The three and a half chapters of "The Boy," written some seventeen years after "Love Letter," present a different Woonsocket. Although the city is never named (true of almost all his cities), the fragment's opening establishes Woonsocket beyond doubt: "When I was a boy, growing up on what were then the outskirts of the small and rather ugly mill city . . ." (*BL* 425). In this work the emphasis is on family and the wider social structure of the city, items barely touched on in the earlier article. Here the hand of the mature novelist is more in evidence. Most notable is the young boy's fascination with adult conversation. This trait, often found in the oldest child in a fami-

22. Eleanor Rogers DeCoste, telephone interview, April 19, 1999.
23. Gilbert, interview.
24. "Love Letter," 15.

ly, was unusually strong in O'Connor and helps explain why so many of his novels and short stories portray older people being observed by younger ones. It may even explain the curious graveness of large stretches of O'Connor's fictional dialogue: lacking the spontaneity of more youthful banter, his characters sometimes talk as if delivering orations.

In "The Boy" some mostly Irish American cronies gather in the back room of the drugstore owned by the boy's loudly self-righteous grandfather. (This establishment may be modeled on a drugstore run by a relative in Blackstone; O'Connor told his friend John Kelleher that this relative once actually charged him five cents for an ice cream cone and was altogether the stingiest man he ever knew.)[25] Talk consists of male gossip and amateurish Catholic theology that is barely above the Baltimore Catechism level and practiced by not overly charitable adherents. Woonsocket appears now as mean and unforgiving, like Joyce's Dublin. The narrator recalls: "I would just sit there and listen while all of them talked. It was pretty nice, being there, especially on summer days, because even though the front part had two big fans in the ceiling that were always going around slowly, here in the back it was always kind of dark and cool and full of a good drug store smell" (*BL* 440). There the big-eared boy slowly gets his initiation into dark secret-mongering, including mysterious hints about the Quebec seminary education of an albino soda jerk named Onesime (modeled on a Woonsocket drugstore clerk known as "Bois")[26] and the even darker insinuations about a local priest, old Father Sheridan. However, at home the boy's more compassionate father dismisses "that Old Sod pharmacy talk" as he endeavors to make his son skeptical of gossip and more understanding of human failings (*BL* 455).

In his teens O'Connor became friends with Ted Kennedy, son of a Rhode Island politician, Ambrose Kennedy (no relation to the Massachusetts Kennedys). Ambrose Kennedy was half Irish, half French, and pure Woonsocket. He rose through Rhode Island State House politics to serve briefly as house speaker, and then served five terms, from 1913–23, as a Republican Congressman, back when the state could boast three congressional districts. According to O'Connor's sister, Edwin enjoyed listening to political lore at the Kennedy home; the origins of *The Last Hurrah* go back that far. (Rhode Island lost one of its Congressional districts after the 1930 census and O'Connor, a connoisseur of bygone days, must have mused upon the dwindling political fortune of his home state.)

25. John Kelleher, personal interview, May 29, 1999.
26. Gilbert, interview.

The O'Connors were communicants at St. Charles' Church, half a mile distant in the direction of downtown. The oldest Catholic church in northern Rhode Island, it had long been one of the two "Irish" churches in a city where ethnicity usually determined parish membership and also engendered strong loyalty. Although always rendered simply as St. Charles' by O'Connor's time, the full name was St. Charles Borromeo, after the sixteenth-century Italian ecclesiastical reformer. When O'Connor's parish celebrated its centennial in 1928, during the most intense period of the Sentinellist controversy when the Irish American hierarchy stood fast, the parish strenuously emphasized its Irish identity. A twenty-five-page hardbound booklet, *St. Charles'—Old and New,* published for the occasion, contains not one mention of the full, official title of the parish. The historical section luxuriates in the kind of Hibernian triumphalism that O'Connor always found obnoxious. The single one-line allusion to the church's Italian patron saint refers to him simply as St. Charles, but five lines get devoted to stained glass windows honoring St. Patrick and St. Bridget.[27] Indeed, the church was known locally as the "Irish cathedral." (O'Connor excoriated the complacent pieties of comfortable Irish Catholic parishes through the embittered outburst of Father John Carmody in *The Edge of Sadness.*

Father Cornelius Holland, pastor of St. Charles', became a family and personal friend. Edwin always admired his quiet dedication and his ethic of hard work. Holland was also the author of several books that popularized Catholic beliefs and practices with some imaginative flair; he also had his own amateur plays performed. O'Connor was unusually fortunate in having in his pastor an encouraging man of letters. Monsignor Holland died in 1956; the next year O'Connor would begin *The Edge of Sadness,* and it may very well be that Holland was one source for its protagonist, Father Hugh Kennedy.

Such was Edwin O'Connor's Woonsocket and these were some of his memories. A city with sharp class distinctions, it seriously wounded itself through class warfare, especially on that one terrible night of rioting. Its ethnic tensions were equally taut and often were reflected in city politics. And finally its predominant Catholicism could erupt into bitter in-house battles that seem overblown today. Class, ethnicity, religion—all were taken seriously there.[28] Although the young O'Connor never enlisted as a combatant in

27. *St. Charles'—Old and New* (Woonsocket, R.I.: n.p., 1928), 17–18.
28. Music also did well by Woonsocket, which produced soprano Eileen Farrell of the Metropolitan Opera, liturgical composer C. Alexander Peloquin, and jazz pianist Dave McKenna. Aside from show tunes, however, music held few charms for O'Connor.

these frays, and although even his political novels are notable for their general avoidance of topical issues, the turbulence of his city during his first two decades impressed upon him that politics and religion are matters of utmost importance. If you were Irish, there was a lot to talk about.

The O'Connors took annual summer vacations of several weeks. His mother liked the Rhode Island seashore, while his father liked the woods and mountains of northern New England. Seashore usually won out. Dr. O'Connor never bought a summer house because he did not like to be tied down to one place. (When his son became suddenly wealthy in 1956, his first big purchase was his first house—a summer vacation place.) Rhode Island's many bays and islands make the seacoast remarkably extensive for such a small state. Over the years the O'Connor family vacationed at several different summer houses, some of which were swept away in the great New England hurricane of September 1938, when over 400 Rhode Islanders were killed. On those beaches O'Connor felt his first intense attraction to the seashore.

Sometimes the family stayed for a month at the Red Mill Inn in East Jaffrey, in southwestern New Hampshire. In September 1934, for an English class in senior year of high school, O'Connor wrote a short composition entitled "Summer Leftovers," on the well-worn topic of summer vacation.[29] This is the earliest piece of formal writing that survives, the only writing from high school he saved, and the first item in his archives. The subject is the Red Mill Inn, and especially its manager, Mr. Charles Holden, whom O'Connor vaguely depicts as an eccentric but endearing Yankee. He may be the first of O'Connor's many portraits of eccentricity in older people. O'Connor goes on to record his own feats at the nearby Peterborough Golf Club, where he claims his record was an impressive eighty-one. The composition received an A/B, and, except for one sentence fragment, it is maturely if stiffly written. Notable at the outset is his confession of strong nostalgia for summer, which was always his favorite season. The slightly roundabout, vaguely apologetic opening would become an O'Connor signature in his nonfiction writings.

O'Connor's most memorable boyhood trip took him across the country with his father in the summer of 1929, when he was almost eleven. Dr. O'Connor's brother Edwin, the former vaudevillian, was now in the movie industry, as was Mary O'Connor's brother, James Greene, who worked as a sound engineer for the Hal Roach Studio. Father and son kept accounts of

---

29. Edwin O'Connor Papers, Boston Public Library (MS. ACC. 1600), 1. Hereinafter referred to as EOCP.

this trip in the same small diary, now in the possession of Edwin's sister. After only four days, however, Edwin's entries stop. This early boredom with travel diaries would be repeated on adult trips to Nova Scotia and Ireland, when his diary entries also cease before a week is out. His father had more endurance and makes diary entries from the start of the trip, June 24, to near the end of their Los Angeles stay on July 16. The diaries show a fairly close father-son relationship. Edwin's four small entries dutifully record times and places from Woonsocket to Colorado; the only interesting person he describes was a sheep rancher. Dr. O'Connor's entries, hastily jotted down in prescription-like scrawl, are notes for future elaboration, as he reminds himself to relate or describe such and such later on. He records precise times of departure and arrival as the train passed through the Massachusetts Berkshires, upstate New York, the bleak farms of southern Ontario, and on through Michigan and into Chicago where they changed for the Sante Fe railroad. After a one-day stop in Kansas City to visit relatives, they passed through Colorado, New Mexico, and Arizona (with a stop at the Grand Canyon), and finally arrived in California after almost a week of traveling.

Throughout the trip the father notes his son's easy friendliness with adults several times. Edwin had already formed a lifelong manner of confidently approaching total strangers to engage in easy conversation. Whether it was with railroad workers, a woman professor, or Hopi dancers in Arizona, the boy was not at all shy about making acquaintances. This trait would stay with him for life and accounts for the wide and varied range of O'Connor's friendships.

Once in Los Angeles the pair stayed in an apartment building named Das Palmas. They were shown a great time by the relatives. Excursions took them to nearby Santa Barbara, San Diego, Tijuana, and Catalina Island. They toured movie studios, where they saw Laurel and Hardy in person and had pictures taken with the young cast of *Our Gang*. They also went to Grauman's Chinese Theater and took in some vaudeville, which the father especially enjoyed. Throughout their stay they were frequently guests at relatives' houses, where Dr. O'Connor was impressed by his son's lengthy performances involving jokes, magic tricks, and songs—a budding vaudevillian in the very city that was destroying the trade. Most of all, the father was astounded and even exasperated by Sonny's nonstop chatter: "Sonny talking like the devil," "Talk, Talk, Talk, Sweet Mulligan." Later in his life, others also noted O'Connor's volubility, which to some bordered on garrulity. His fictional characters, at any rate, are seldom at a loss for words by the long paragraph.

Dr. O'Connor talked to his wife by telephone once, while his relatives all lined up behind him waiting to speak. He was impressed by the sound quality in those early years of long distance calls. One letter home by Sonny—his earliest known—survives. Dated July 8, 1929, it begins formally, "Dear Mother." He thanks her for sending shoes he had apparently forgotten, and goes on to describe the Franciscan mission at Santa Barbara, where the priest showed them old relics and vestments. Sonny took a boy's interest in Indian arrowheads and the "Indian worshiping place made of old stones." Once they felt an earthquake which rattled furniture. "Dad told me to stand still, and when I did I shook all over." He misses Jack, his younger brother by five years, and one-year-old "Bobby," as his kid sister Barbara would always be known.[30]

Father and son were back in Woonsocket in time for Sonny's birthday on July 29. They left no descriptions of the trip home, and O'Connor never returned to Hollywood, even when invited. But clearly, as Hugh Rank says, the entertainment industry remained a fascination for life.[31]

When it came to high school, the family decided that public schools would no longer do, and that it was time for some serious Catholic schooling beyond the weekly Sunday school conducted by the parish. (Many years later O'Connor recalled that one nun in that school said that one of Saint Peter's tasks was to hang up the stars every night and then take them down in the morning.)[32] Furthermore, the high school would have to be the best available—a pattern repeated many times in O'Connor's life. Locally there was Mount St. Charles Academy in Woonsocket, but it was considered too new and, because of its Quebec connections, too Francophone in the immediate post-Sentinellist years. The only serious alternative was La Salle Academy in Providence, some fifteen miles to the southeast. O'Connor was enrolled there on September 14, 1931, at age thirteen.

La Salle Academy had been established as a boys' school in downtown Providence in 1871 by the De la Salle Christian Brothers (not to be confused with the Christian Brothers from Ireland).[33] By O'Connor's time this French order had become heavily Irish-American in its make-up, unlike the French Canadian Brothers of the Sacred Heart at Mount St. Charles. By the 1920s the overcrowding at La Salle Academy and other schools led to diocesan-

30. Edwin O'Connor, letter to Mrs. J.V. O'Connor, July 8, 1929, courtesy of Barbara O'Connor Burrell. Sometimes the family spelled "Bobby" as "Bobbie."

31. Hugh Rank, *Edwin O'Connor* (New York: Twayne Publishers, 1974), 18.

32. Edwin O'Connor, "A Meeting on Sunday," in *The Best and the Last of Edwin O'Connor*, ed. Arthur Schlesinger Jr. (Boston: Atlantic Monthly Press/Little, Brown, 1970), 387.

33. For information on the history of La Salle Academy, I am indebted to the school archivist, Charles Hogan.

wide fund-raising for education, which in turn sparked the Sentinellist reaction. In 1925, La Salle Academy moved from downtown Providence to the residential Mount Pleasant section where it still thrives. It has been coed since 1984.

When O'Connor enrolled there in 1931, he saw a new, imposing, well-built structure of brick, concrete, and stone, with flourishes of diocesan baroque in the trimmings, that had cost a princely one million dollars. Today the interior looks much as it did in O'Connor's time: wooden floors in classrooms, ample daylight from tall windows, long silver radiators, a small cafeteria (where in O'Connor's time one ate standing up), a good-sized gym even though located in the basement, and an auditorium big enough to seat the whole school for assembly. Above the stage is inscribed "One Flag, One Country, God Over All," an echo of the "Pro Deo" and "Pro Patria" mottoes carved in stone above the school's entrance. Both sets of mottoes, typical of the day, highlight the Catholic display of patriotism still thought to be so necessary. The less strenuously patriotic official school motto is "Religio, Mores, Cultura"—religion, morals, culture.

At the rear of the building expansive grounds, now somewhat reduced, lent the school a rural air enhanced by tall bordering trees. Even today as one enters from the busy streets, there is an unusual sense of an enclosed rural retreat. Here the spreading acres contained landscaped walkways, tennis courts, a duck pond (now gone), and a football stadium with bleachers. There was even talk of a small golf course some day.

To get to La Salle Academy O'Connor first had to walk a mile from 247 Gaskill Street to the downtown Victorian-era train station, now a Blackstone Valley Park ranger station, where he would board the aging cars of the old New Haven Railroad. The antiquated milk run with its seven stops was usually crowded with commuters to Providence, and the steam engine's smoke and cinders are still remembered less than fondly.[34] For his first three years this was his transportation to Providence; when train service was curtailed in 1934, he took the bus for his senior year. Once he arrived at downtown Providence's Union Station, the young O'Connor was presented with a striking view. From the high platform of the old station, whose elevated city-bisecting tracks earned the nickname "Great Wall of China" before their demolition, he could see Providence's Second French Empire City Hall a couple of hundred yards behind him, and in front of him the gleaming white marble of Rhode Island's classically domed State House, a quarter of a mile away on

34. Francis Carroll, personal interview, July 15, 1998.

Smith Hill. Whether the proximity of state and local government in the smallest state impressed the boy is unknown, but it is worth noting that in his two political novels Frank Skeffington and Charles Kinsella move easily back and forth from City Hall to State House. Indeed, O'Connor's political landscapes sometimes have the feel of the notoriously cozy Rhode Island brand of politics.[35] La Salle Academy itself was already nurturing a significant share of the state's politicians. Assistant football coach Dennis Roberts would be governor of the state twenty years later. A favorite educational route for many state politicians was La Salle Academy, nearby Providence College, and Suffolk University Law School in Boston.

From the train station it was a short walk to a trolley car which took him to La Salle. This was his regimen for four years. One day he even walked the fifteen miles home; though never a hiker, O'Connor did enjoy leisurely walks all his life.

The incoming class of 1935 was almost four hundred strong. The school's 1,200 students were taught by a faculty of eighteen brothers and ten laymen, mostly young Irish Americans, resulting in a roughly 42:1 student-teacher ratio, large by today's standards. O'Connor's freshman section, 1A, had thirty-nine students. While Irish Americans were the biggest ethnic group among the students, there were sizable percentages of Italians and French Canadians as well, and sprinklings of other groups. There was one black student three years ahead of O'Connor. A small contingent of Woonsocket boys traveled down with O'Connor, among them two brothers from the North End, his good friends Charles and Francis Carroll. Charles attended the Moses Brown School on Providence's East Side, while Francis continued on to La Salle with O'Connor. Other students commuted from even more distant Westerly in Rhode Island and Fall River in Massachusetts. Coat and tie was mandatory, and some students were still wearing knickers. Almost all the students at La Salle were Catholic. There were frequent religious observances, including a mandatory annual retreat.

In sophomore year students chose the classical, scientific, or commercial track. O'Connor opted for college-prep classical. He took four years of Christian doctrine, English, and Latin; three years of Greek, which he enjoyed more than Latin; two of history and algebra; one of French, biology, and geometry; and a half year each of civics and free drawing. He did exceptionably well in all his English classes, and almost as well in his Latin and Greek ones, while he trailed off somewhat in French. He did very well in al-

35. One wonders what O'Connor, always on the prowl for quirks, thought of the fact that the smallest state has the longest official name; however, I have found no instance of his views on "The State of Rhode Island and Providence Plantations."

gebra and geometry, even though he disliked them, and did especially well in biology, as befitted a physician's son. There are no obvious weak points in O'Connor's high school academic record. O'Connor was a B+ to A- student with a remarkable degree of consistency in all subjects over his four years. If there was anything like a weak period, it might be a small dip toward the end of junior year. He earned a "silver" academic letter. Allowing for some apparent grade inflation at the school where many received a "silver," O'Connor's record is still an honorable one.

James Reilly, one of O'Connor's classmates in his second year, remembers him quite vividly as an impulsive, eager student who would leap out of his chair to answer questions. O'Connor would raise his hand vigorously, almost irascibly. There was no shyness about the gregarious but somewhat reserved, well-dressed boy with the tousled, reddish blond hair and tall, erect stance. James Reilly also found O'Connor to be serious, though hardly introverted. He minded his own business—a useful quality for a teenager.[36]

A retired La Salle teacher who taught during those years, Vincent McGinn, says corporal punishment was occasionally administered by some teachers; it was considered a normal counterpart of home discipline. Others refrained from it. He remembers that during lunch recess the boys had permission to roam the grounds—an intense freedom to anyone lucky enough to have attended such a school. On schedule the ducks would waddle out of their pond to be fed by the students. Then the first whistle called everybody in; the second whistle formed lines; the third whistle called for a silent filing back in for the afternoon session.[37] Francis Carroll recalls that this same Mr. McGinn once found O'Connor acting suspiciously at a goldfish tank in a biology lab. Although O'Connor was actually trying to save the goldfish from harmful bits of blotter paper mischievously thrown in by other students, the teacher thought that O'Connor was the culprit and ordered him to write an essay in Latin entitled "The Elephant Remembers."[38]

La Salle was a boisterously high-spirited school that placed great emphasis on sports, fund-raising activities (raffle winners got a day off), pep rallies, and assemblies in the auditorium. Unfortunately, in O'Connor's senior year funding for yearbooks in diocesan-supported schools was cut off for five years as a Depression economy. A school paper, called *The Maroon and White*, did continue publishing and tried to make up for the lack of the yearbook.

Athletics got top billing as an extracurricular activity for the muscular

36. James Reilly, personal interview, June 30, 1998.
37. Vincent McGinn, personal interview, December 5, 1998.
38. Carroll, interview.

Catholicism of the day. O'Connor participated in some track and basketball in his first years, but lost interest quickly. After coming in sixty-second and eighty-third in state cross-country meets for freshmen, he turned in his track suit. "I could never see any sense to chasing another man around a track," he told an interviewer years later.[39] He also played a little intramural basketball, but in spite of his height he took little interest in the sport. In two yearbook photos of intramural basketball teams, O'Connor is easily half a head taller than those around him.

O'Connor joined several of the more active clubs. While only a sophomore, he was elected president of the Latin Club. In a Latin Club debate O'Connor once took the affirmative on whether Caesar had a right to invade Gaul. An interesting minor crisis occurred when the club moderator, Brother Charles (the brothers were customarily known by their first names only), decided on a play depicting Roman life. O'Connor was to wear a toga while singing "Fit as a Fiddle and Ready for Love." Many years later O'Connor told a *Maroon and White* newspaper interviewer that he "violently, but vainly" protested his part in the Roman farce. Getting nowhere with Brother Charles, O'Connor went boldly over his head and appealed to Brother Raymond, the principal, who promptly canceled the skit after observing a rehearsal, much to O'Connor's relief.[40] Although the skit may have been an innocent enough bit of fun, O'Connor's strong reaction is an early example of a certain Irish American squeamishness he exhibited at public displays of anything remotely sexual. Although this episode was hardly of the scale or quality of Stephen Dedalus's protest to the rector against personal injustice in Joyce's *A Portrait of the Artist as a Young Man*, O'Connor's action does show bold determination when he thought the occasion demanded.

O'Connor joined the French Club in his junior year, but held no office in a group dominated naturally enough by Franco-Americans. More to his taste, he joined the Debating Club. In junior year he defended the negative side on whether the United States should adopt the features of the BBC. The juniors defeated the seniors in this debate. Years later, O'Connor would repeat for real his dim view of the BBC when on assignment for *Life*. In another debate in November 1933, the month when the new Roosevelt administration recognized the Soviet Union, O'Connor again was given the negative position: "Resolved: that the United States should recognize Soviet Russia." The 1934 yearbook summarized O'Connor's remarks thus: "The Russian

39. Edwin O'Connor, interview with Edgar J. Allaire, *Woonsocket Call*, December 16, 1955.
40. Edwin O'Connor, "Prominent Alumnus," interview in *The Maroon and White*, June 1962, 2.

government was brutal, narrow and contrary to all principles of civilization that we hold dear, as Americans." As matters turned out, the adult O'Connor never did become a hot-blooded Cold Warrior, but he was not blind to the Soviet menace either. He also took some interest in a Little Theatre Society being formed in his junior year; he apparently had a role in the one-act *Copy* in the fall of 1934.

One last incident of his junior year is of more than passing interest. In early March 1934 the faculty moderator of the school newspaper summarily fired the entire senior-year staff for "inefficiency" and "lack of knowledge in putting a paper together," according to a sharply worded editorial by the new junior staff. Nothing like this had ever occurred at the paper. Among the names listed in the new staff is Edwin O'Connor, member of the Board of Editors. What specific problems underlay this unprecedented move remain unknown, as is the role, if any, O'Connor took in all this; indeed the fray may have been a teapot tempest. However, during his years in radio and journalism, O'Connor would have his own experiences with unexpected firings. In his writings firings or the threat thereof sometimes loom large, especially in his first novel, *The Oracle.* The act of getting fired was especially troublesome for him because according to many accounts he was a person of deep loyalty to friends and institutions. To be part of a supplanting staff on the school newspaper may not have deeply roiled his soul, but it may well have been a tiny seed that bore fruit later. At any rate he served on the staff until graduation, although none of his articles can be identified because of the absence of bylines.

Not much can be learned of O'Connor's social life during high school, or for that matter during his adult life. Such matters he felt to be strictly his own. His friend Francis Carroll remembers that he had a couple of girl-friends, but nothing "serious" or "steady," and that he took a girl from Taunton, Massachusetts, to the senior prom. Some girls thought him a bit stuffy.[41]

One off-campus appeal was vaudeville. Often after school O'Connor would spend an hour or two at the old Fay's Theatre in downtown Providence. By then obviously in decline, the old song and dance routines were relegated to warm-up acts before the movie. Worse yet, vaudeville was an even more desperately bastardized form, as xylophones jostled with monologues on the Great War.[42] O'Connor knew he was witnessing the passing of

41. Francis and Lucille Carroll, personal interview, July 15, 1998.
42. Edwin O'Connor, interview with P.C. Brooks, *Boston,* November 1964, 22–23. A tribute to the old Fay's by Robert C. Achorn in the *Providence Journal,* March 17, 2001, B7, confirms O'Connor's impressions.

a whole entertainment world, but there was something about its unembarrassed Dickensian exuberance that held the quiet boy in rapt attention.

On July 14, 1935, when he was still only sixteen, O'Connor graduated from La Salle Academy at exercises in the Metropolitan Theater in downtown Providence, where big band music and vaudeville usually held the stage. The graduates were addressed by an Assistant United States Attorney General; the band played "The Bells of St. Mary." The June issue of the school paper in its "Senior Poll" named Edwin O'Connor "Most Diplomatic Boy," a tribute to his unusual maturity and equanimity. During World War II O'Connor looked back on La Salle Academy as a "wonder-world, far removed from reality" ("CG" I, 3).[43] But this was probably a fleeting reaction and common enough in any case. Years later O'Connor was quite pleased to be inducted into the La Salle Academy Hall of Fame.

Although O'Connor was to leave Woonsocket pretty much for good in just three months, well into his late thirties he continued to call the city his "home," while his adopted Boston was merely a bachelor "residence." Often during his twenties and thirties he would come down from Boston to visit his Woonsocket family and friends, sometimes every week. He told his sister Bobby that he liked to keep close to the friends of his youth—they don't begrudge you.

---

43. Throughout the book, the abbreviation "CG," often with chapter in Roman numerals and page number, will be used for the document known as "Coast Guard," in which O'Connor describes his years in the service; each short chapter has its own pagination. The document is Number 23 in the EOCP.

CHAPTER TWO

❧ Notre Dame

(1935–1939)

Edwin O'Connor sometimes claimed that he did not really know why he applied only to the University of Notre Dame for college. Usually whenever he talked coyly liked this about his past he was providing something less than full disclosure. His sister remembers that a high school retreat conducted by a priest with Notre Dame connections made a good impression upon him.[1] Also, the pattern established in the selection of La Salle Academy as ostensibly the best Catholic high school in the state repeated itself in the selection of the best Catholic university in the country. That high ranking for Notre Dame can be disputed, especially by Jesuit educators. But the Notre Dame mystique had been established by the mid-1930s and so, like today, perception governed college selection. He probably ruled out more local Catholic colleges like Providence College as too new, or Holy Cross and Boston College as too close. No doubt there were other factors, not the least of which may have been a desire to strike out on his own, to be away from a hovering mother. In fact, his sister remembers her mother being amazed that she actually let him go.

College application then was far less arduous than today's ordeal. O'Connor did not fill out his one-page application, in longhand, until March 26 of his senior year.[2] He listed journalism as his prospective major in the College of Arts and Letters, and requested as his first choice a double room in Dillon Hall, which he got. At the bottom he lists three required references: for "clergyman," Reverend Cornelius J. Holland, his pastor; for "layman," his neighbor and family friend Samuel E. Hudson, whose occupation he lists as "Newspaper owner"; and for "N.D. Graduate, if any in vicinity," Reverend Thomas Duffy, C.S.C., "Notre Dame Missionary." This Father Duffy was most likely the retreat master who inspired O'Connor. A form accompanying his La Salle transcript notes

1. Barbara O'Connor Burrell, personal interview, summer 1998.
2. My thanks to Veronica Primrose, transcript coordinator in the Registrar's Office at Notre Dame, for help with all of O'Connor's records.

that O'Connor ranked fifth out of thirty-five students in his senior class section. A supplementary transcript noted that he ranked thirty-fifth out of 225 graduating seniors. Since students were accepted to Notre Dame primarily on the basis of class rank, these high standings most likely secured his acceptance.

As the son of a prospering doctor, O'Connor did not want for tuition, room and board, transportation, and other college expenses. In fact, it does not appear that O'Connor worked much at summer jobs at all. His sister remembers one summer job at the Woonsocket Post Office, which he thoroughly disliked and which may account in a small way for his lifelong aversion to letter writing—a major disappointment to his biographer. As the first national Catholic university, Notre Dame attracted the emerging, affluent Catholic middle class, this at a time when most Catholic colleges were "trolley car" schools for less affluent urban students.

At 3:00 one afternoon in mid-September 1935 O'Connor left for Notre Dame on the Boston and Albany train from the Worcester train station. In those years college students went with a suitcase or two, and perhaps a typewriter. The more sartorial ones had a steamer trunk sent as well. O'Connor knew no one at Notre Dame, but his good Woonsocket friend and La Salle classmate Francis Carroll was entering with him. Francis was older and at least as tall. To save money, the two tried sharing one berth, but their sizes quickly made this an impossibility. The noise of the train, especially when decoupling for the New York Central, along with understandable excitement, made sleep almost impossible. Although O'Connor and Carroll would be roommates for their first year, their interests and circles quickly diverged. Francis did not finish college, and returned to run the family hardware business in downtown Woonsocket. They remained good friends.[3]

Seventeen hours after they left, or just about as long as it would take on today's interstate, the two freshmen arrived at South Bend, Indiana. The city's taxi drivers were on strike, and so O'Connor and Carroll arrived at the gates of Notre Dame as they had at La Salle—by trolley car. Edwin O'Connor was about to begin four rewarding years.

The University of Notre Dame du Lac is located just north of the city limits of South Bend. Northern Indiana is even flatter than New England's coastal plain; gradual, almost imperceptible inclines suffice for hills. To someone from congested Rhode Island, Indiana still has an appearance of wide open prairie space. Here the Latin *campus* retains its original meaning

3. Francis Carroll, personal interview, July 15, 1998.

of a level field, and here the campus of America's most famous Catholic university was laid out.

In 1843 a French missionary priest named Father Edward F. Sorin, of the Congregation of the Holy Cross, founded Notre Dame in what was then still considered wilderness.[4] A classical liberal arts curriculum was tailored to the exigencies of the time and place. In quick order Notre Dame boasted the first Catholic law school (1869) and engineering school (1873), but the graduate school came late and slowly in 1918. The university would be governed by the Holy Cross Fathers until 1967, when governance was formally transferred to a true lay Board of Trustees. (Up until then the weak "lay" Board was always chaired by a C.S.C.) All its presidents to this day have been Holy Cross Fathers, the most famous being Father Theodore Hesburgh. In O'Connor's first year, however, in a move unusual for the era, a layman was appointed acting dean of arts and letters. The faculty of 155 had a 2:1 ratio of lay professors to clerical.

In 1935 Notre Dame was enjoying only its second decade of national repute and glory, which had less to do with academics than with athletics. The legend-in-his-own-lifetime Knute Rockne, born in Norway, had been an innovative player on Notre Dame's football squad, where he developed the forward pass. He became a chemistry instructor at the school and head football coach from 1918 to 1931. He won 105 games, lost only 12, and tied 5—an outstanding achievement—by using a creative offensive theory most famously embodied by the "Four Horsemen of Notre Dame" backfield, one of whom, Elmer Layden, was football coach during O'Connor's years. Rockne's death in a plane crash in 1931 only added to the myth. He and "the Gipper" were turned into the stuff of Hollywood through the more Hibernian reincarnations created by Pat O'Brien and Ronald Reagan respectively. When O'Connor arrived at Notre Dame, the huge new football stadium could accommodate 58,000 fans.

The incoming class of 1939 arrived several days before the upperclassmen, in hot late summer weather. Photos in the school paper and yearbook show registration being conducted on the lawn in front of the venerable Main Building, whose famous gold dome, with its crowning statue of Our Lady, was already a school logo and provided the yearbook's name, *The Dome*. By

---

4. For the history of the university, see Arthur J. Hope, C.S.C., *Notre Dame—One Hundred Years,* revised ed. (South Bend, Ind.: Icarus Press, 1978), and Robert E. Burns, *Being Catholic, Being American: The Notre Dame Story,* 2 vols. (Notre Dame, Ind.: University of Notre Dame Press, 1999 and 2000). Notre Dame's home page has a useful and thorough history at http://classic.archives.nd.edu. I am grateful to my colleagues Brian Barbour, John Hennedy, and Richard Murphy—all Notre Dame alumni—for their reminiscences.

hallowed tradition, undergraduates could not ascend the front steps of the building. At the registration tables there was the usual sorting out of classes, dorm rooms, and laundry tickets, along with information about clubs and activities, for the 800 or so new students. Because the school was committed to a Christian understanding of democratic ideals, there were no fraternities and all the spurious elitism that came with them. His records show that O'Connor formally registered on September 19. Close to the left of Main Building was the imposing gothic Church (now a Basilica) of the Sacred Heart, whose spire and carillon, along with the gold dome, are part of Notre Dame memory for the school's 90,000 graduates. The weekly campus newspaper, a magazine-format glossy called *The Notre Dame Scholastic,* announced that the university had 2,722 students, up 85 from the previous year. The dormitories were full.[5] It may have been the midst of the Depression, but Notre Dame's enrollment was rising again after dipping from a high point of 3,227 in 1930. The school was more than holding its own, as in fact did much of higher education.[6] During the 1930s Notre Dame constructed major buildings at a rate of one a year in an impressive display of hope for the future.

In the time-honored custom of Catholic education, the school year opened with a convocation and solemn Mass of the Holy Ghost (called the "Red Mass," from the vestments) in the Church of the Sacred Heart. University President Father John F. O'Hara, later to be archbishop and cardinal in Philadelphia until his death in 1960, delivered a sermon on Christian education as the only solution to communism. (There would be not a little anti-communist discourse—some intelligent, some hysterical—at Notre Dame over the next four run-up years to World War II, far more than anti-fascist discourse.) That evening the sonorous carillon bells of the same church called freshmen to their "mission," which would last almost a week. The mission consisted of 6:30 morning Mass followed by instruction, and 7:30 evening sermon and Benediction of the Blessed Sacrament. The mission was conducted by Father Eugene Burke, chairman of the English Department and moderator of the campus radio station, and someone O'Connor would get to know in both of his roles. The *Scholastic* stated that the mission was Notre Dame's "unique method of orienting her Freshmen in the ways of Our Lady's school and particularly in pointing out to them the real, true spirit of Notre Dame."[7] The educational philosophy and methodology of the Congregation of the Holy Cross infused a Catholic world view from beginning to end and would find in O'Connor an alert and eager respondent.

5. *The Notre Dame Scholastic,* October 4, 1935, 8.
6. Hope, *Notre Dame,* 458–61.
7. *The Notre Dame Scholastic,* September 27, 1935, 22.

During mission week, however, the sacred did make room for the robustly secular. On Monday September 23 there was a special freshman convocation in Washington Hall at which the frosh were taught Notre Dame songs and cheers by four male cheerleaders, all in preparation for the upcoming football game against Kansas. Coach Elmer Layden spoke. During that season, billed as a "comeback" one, Layden would have an impressive seven wins, one loss, and one tie. Notable on the team was the presence of one Bill Shakespeare, a furious running back who once scored three touchdowns in a row against Ohio State, all during the fourth quarter, to win the game.

Even though the student body, and in particular the football team, had been known as "the Fighting Irish" for at least thirty years, the school was not in fact particularly Irish American, unlike a Boston College or a Fordham.[8] Its founder had been French, there was little Hibernian display beyond a little green flag in the St. Patrick's Day dessert, and most importantly the student ethnic make-up showed significantly fewer Irish Americans than back at La Salle, this attributable to the presence of many upper Midwest students of German and eastern European origin. So whence "Fighting Irish"? It appears that, far from being an honorific appellation, "Fighting Irish" was originally a nativist slur aimed at Notre Dame by some northern Indianans for whom "Irish" was synonymous with "papists," and for whom "fighting" described that papist culture. As sometimes happens with nasty insults, the targeted group picked up the name and ran defiantly with it. In one memorable instance, however, "Fighting" became a self-fulfilling term. On May 17, 1924, during the national resurgence of the Ku Klux Klan, which was particularly strong throughout Indiana, a big Klan parade was scheduled for downtown South Bend, chosen because of the presence of Notre Dame. Although university authorities had tried to dissuade students from interfering, several hundred ignored the injunction and went downtown. Many of them waited at the bus and train stations for anyone arriving with a telltale bundle under his arm. The students would pretend to "escort" an unsuspecting Klansman and then attempt to snatch the bundle of infamous white robes. Fights broke out, and two days later the police and students mixed it up. It appears, however, that student miscreants were generally given light punishments by the school.[9] O'Connor no doubt heard of this famous incident at a school so fond of lore. This incident, along with family memories of the cross burning at 247 Gaskill Street at about the same time, may have

8. A small item in *The Notre Dame Scholastic,* March 6, 1936, 11, by Andrew Hufnagel, in fact lamented the noticeable absence of St. Patrick's Day celebration on campus. Such lapses never disturbed O'Connor.

9. Hope, *Notre Dame,* 371–78.

been the remote sources for the attribution of Klan sympathies to nasty old Amos Force in *The Last Hurrah*. Mayor Skeffington is talking with his aide John Gorman:

"Was [Amos Force] a Ku Kluxer?" Gorman said. "That I didn't know."

"Not many people do [Skeffington replied], including the people who gave him a Brotherhood award last winter. But he was, about thirty years ago. I never did know why he quit, exactly: I always suspected it was because he found out he was expected to buy his own sheet." (155)

The allusion to thirty years back would place the event squarely in the mid-1920s.

In his first year O'Connor took six courses a semester, plus the "physical training" required of freshmen. His highest grades were in biology. Although he never evinced any desire to pursue his father's profession, it would seem the son tried hard to impress him: his biology grades were 98 and 99 for fall and spring semesters. Next best was English, with 96 and 98. All his first-year grades, with the exception of one 81 in history, are the equivalent of today's B+ or better; his first year average was 92 which is considered a low A, according to Notre Dame's current conversion system. It was an impressive accomplishment. If O'Connor sometimes hinted at some adjustment problems at Notre Dame, his academic record certainly does not reveal any.

O'Connor saved one loose-leaf notebook from college, in which he kept his notes for his first-year history course, and also notes for ethics and philosophy of literature courses from his senior year.[10] For the history course he had to outline meticulously the course textbook. In spite of his neat and apparently thorough work, it seems he never could appease his professor. On April 8, the professor wrote boldly on the outline, "This poverty-stricken outline is not adequate in any sense," and grudgingly conferred a C-. The course and its curmudgeon prof have the air of a boot camp cum hazing about them.

O'Connor and Carroll lived in room 142–43 in Dillon Hall located on what was then the southwestern edge of the campus. As in most of the dormitories, rooms in Dillon were sizable enough even for the tall young men from Woonsocket. Each dormitory also had its own chapel where attendance at Mass was compulsory for a certain number of days per week. This enforced regularity started O'Connor on his lifelong habit of frequent atten-

---

10. The notebook is in the possession of Barbara O'Connor Burrell, who kindly allowed me to examine it.

dance at Mass. Some friends have speculated that for much of his life he went to Mass daily, or close to it. However, O'Connor always held that his religious exercises were strictly his own business; except to a few close Catholic friends like John Kelleher, he never talked about them.

Life in the residence halls was regimented. This was still very much an era when the norms and discipline of seminary education and clerical life in general were transposed into Catholic colleges. At Notre Dame there were strict curfews, a lights-out policy enforced by simply cutting off electricity to rooms, severe crusades against alcohol, and absolutely no question about women in the rooms. Every hall and most floors had a faculty rector, usually a priest, sometimes a bachelor layman. It all seems distant now, and yet most of this discipline was in effect well into the 1960s. O'Connor never seemed cramped by the regimen and if anything took from it habits of concentration, early rising, methodical daily planning, and lifelong total abstinence from alcohol. So disciplined and sober did he appear to some (usually not Catholics), that they thought he was bound for the priesthood. If he ever did have thoughts along these lines, O'Connor kept them tightly to himself; there is not a hint anywhere that he ever seriously considered a religious vocation.

While it may seem too obvious for commentary, it must be remembered that Notre Dame was then very much an all-male university: not just student body, but faculty as well. Even extracurricular activities had an all-male quality, like the fall play about an Antarctic expedition, *The World Waits*, by George F. Hummel. (Some plays did import women, mostly from adjacent St. Mary's College.) Commentators would often note that, except for O'Connor's last novel, his fictional world is largely a male one: radio announcers, mayors and governors, bankers, publishers, priests and bishops, old vaudevillians, family patriarchs—the list extends. His all-male eight years of high school and college, along with the strongly male tradition of Irish writing in general, would leave their influence.

Before classes had even begun, O'Connor had visitors from 247 Gaskill Street. His mother and his seven-year-old sister, Bobby, stopped to visit for two days while en route to Los Angeles to visit the relatives. One suspects that the South Bend stopover was the primary reason for the journey. O'Connor dutifully showed them around, but gave strict instructions that they were not to refer to him as "Sonny."[11] Later he would more sensibly allow the name again. For the rest of his life, outside the family he was usually called "Ed,"

11. Burrell, interview.

sometimes "Eddie," and to a small inner group "Edso," which may have been his own coinage. Some college chums would cheerily call him "Baldy" in reference to his receding hairline, a process emphasized by the dome of forehead, or "Fatso" in reference to occasional heaviness. He appears never to have been called Edwin, and there is some evidence he was not overly fond of his given name.

Notre Dame sponsored a vigorous series of speakers and famous guest lecturers. The pattern of speakers is obvious: Catholics all, they approached their respective subjects from a nuanced Catholic perspective. Taken as a group they manifest the distinct ethos of Notre Dame at this period which can be best described as an informed Catholic realism which critiqued contemporary evils while being suspicious of contemporary cures. Other symposia were especially hard on communism and pornography.

Whether O'Connor attended any of these lectures is unknown, but there was one event in December that he surely must have witnessed. In late November the school made the startling announcement that there would be a special university convocation on December 9 as part of a week of celebrations honoring the formal establishment of the Commonwealth of the Philippines, which had been a mostly Catholic U.S. territory for almost forty years. The main speaker, who would also receive an honorary degree, was to be none other than President Franklin Delano Roosevelt.

Roosevelt enjoyed immense support in 1935, but with his first reelection campaign less than a year away, he wanted to solidify his standing with Catholics, especially with the all-important Irish, who ran so many political machines, or benefitted by them. Already mayors like James Michael Curley in Boston saw the New Deal as a threat to their power of patronage, a fact noted prominently in *The Last Hurrah*. What better Catholic shrine than Notre Dame for F.D.R.'s pilgrimage: "Fighting Irish," football fans, Catholics —he could have them all, and on national radio into the bargain. And have them all he did. Five thousand people crammed the gymnasium. In attendance were the mayor of Chicago, the governor of Indiana, several congressmen, Postmaster General James A. Farley (later an acquaintance of O'Connor), one cardinal, and several bishops. Roosevelt was cheered heartily and long. Carlos P. Romulo, a journalist active in the Philippine independence movement, spoke with passion about his nation's willingness to take on any new aggressor—a veiled reference to Japan. Cardinal Mundelein of Chicago introduced his old acquaintance, the president, and took the rare step of alluding to his infirmity before extolling his social programs. The president spoke briefly. He called the world to witness the transition to a peaceful restoration of independence in the Philippines, stressed respect for human rights, and warned about the dangers of a new arms race. His day at Notre Dame was a triumph. In the 1936 election, Catholics and Irish Americans in particular gave him overwhelming support. It may be of more than passing interest that in O'Connor's work Roosevelt is the only president ever directly named, and prominently at that. The significance of that naming will become clearer when its occurrence in *The Last Hurrah* is examined.

O'Connor's most important freshman-year encounter would develop into a friendship for life. He had the good fortune to have as his instructor in English 1, College Rhetoric and Composition, the young Frank O'Malley, who was to become another Notre Dame legend.[12] O'Malley graduated from Notre Dame in 1932 at age twenty-two. After graduation, he would stay on as a bachelor don in the dormitories for his remaining forty-two years.

Frank O'Malley was slightly built and a little under average height. He had a shy, owlish demeanor accentuated by horn-rimmed glasses, a high forehead, deep blue eyes, and light reddish hair. In photographs and even more so in student cartoons, his head looks too big for his frame. All his life he dressed in a dapper fashion, combining conservative but well-tailored suits with bright sweater vests. Collar pins and an umbrella were trademarks. He spoke quietly during his lectures, which were more like talks, was utterly absent-minded, and took a genuine interest in his students during and after their college years. O'Malley inspired generations of Notre Dame students, many of whom became professors themselves. In the words of one student, Frank O'Malley "wondered whether your soul was alive or dead."[13] Notre Dame's sesquicentennial celebrations in 1991 included a symposium devoted entirely to Frank O'Malley. Two hundred former students reminisced about his eccentricities, his classroom methods, his conception of the professorate as a teaching vocation above all, and his vision of literature as the liberal arts course par excellence because of its unique penetration into the mysteries of human existence. O'Malley did not publish much, but what he did write was weighty and authoritative. Most of all, he made students appreciate the profound encounter with life that great literature affords.[14] By O'Connor's graduation year in 1939, students vied to live on O'Malley's floor in Morrissey

---

12. John W. Meaney, who was a year behind O'Connor, has written a good book on Frank O'Malley that contains dozens of reminiscences by colleagues and students. See *O'Malley of Notre Dame* (Notre Dame, Ind.: University of Notre Dame Press, 1991).

13. Quoted in Meaney, *O'Malley*, 1.

14. Kenneth L. Woodward, "The Life of a Great Teacher," *Newsweek*, October 21, 1991, 60.

Hall. Known as the "sun-gods," they were immensely taken by O'Malley's seriousness and wit. For whatever reason, O'Connor was not one of the sun-gods.

O'Connor took three courses with O'Malley: the mandatory freshman English class, Contemporary Catholic Literature (later called Modern Catholic Writers) in his junior year, and Philosophy of Literature II in senior year. In the freshman course O'Malley's goal was to make students aware of the incarnational mystery of the concrete and the spiritual as interpenetrating realities. To describe accurately a leaf or one's first kiss would open doors of perception into a world "charged with the grandeur of God," to use the famous phrase from O'Malley's beloved Gerard Manley Hopkins. Another favorite was William Blake, whose visionary poems decried "the mind-forged manacles" of the one-dimensional, soulless rationalism that pervaded the modern outlook. O'Connor's classmate William A. Donnelly remembers O'Malley's carefully detailed comments on the class's jejune first offerings. Words like "pendulous," "threadbare," "commonplace," "banal," "feckless," and "pedestrian" were freely penned in red ink, along with sardonic phrases like "your wording is often excessively usual." By the end of the year, most students caught on and were writing fresh, detailed prose.[15]

In spite of his notorious forgetfulness in most departments of life, O'Malley took patient care in getting to know his students and even offered small emergency loans for which he never accepted repayment. Although a demanding teacher and tireless commentator on student papers, it appears he was an easy grader in the end. To one class he once gave out more A's than there were students. In response to an inquiry from the dean, O'Malley, ever impatient with officialdom, told him to distribute the extra grades to students who needed them.[16] O'Connor received from O'Malley a 96 and 98 for his fall and spring terms.

O'Connor was fond of telling people, from family members to interviewers, how Frank O'Malley in a truly important way charted his course for life. One of O'Malley's customs on the first day of class was to ask his students to fill out a small questionnaire about themselves. For his choice of major, O'Connor put down "Journalism," as he had done on his college application. Before the semester was out O'Malley had convinced his young student that journalism was something you could pick up in a month; far better to sink one's teeth into literature by becoming an English major, which O'Connor promptly did. O'Connor would fondly remember O'Malley: "[He was] the

15. William A. Donnelly, letter to author, June 22, 1999.
16. Woodward, "Great Teacher," 60.

Professor Frank O'Malley in the 1930s on the campus of Notre Dame. *Photo used by permission of the University of Notre Dame Archives.*

greatest single help for me in college. There are teachers like him scattered throughout our colleges and universities, and they're worth their weight in uranium." [17] When O'Connor died, his old teacher wrote: "Ed was unusual: unusual in his candor, openness to people and existence altogether, and in his humor, that is his consciousness of the foibles of humanity. He was anxious and hopeful and bright." [18] O'Malley was too modest to add that, had he not encouraged and inspired the young man, life for O'Connor might have been Frost's other road—the one tramped by the many.

There are many other things O'Connor may have picked up from his professor, such as a tendency to airy dismissal of tiresome bureaucracy, a relative lack of concern over money and possessions and status, and a deeply religious inner life. O'Connor's friend Elliot Norton remembers O'Connor saying many times that O'Malley's greatest instruction to him was "keep it simple." [19] O'Malley was also exceptionally well read in many fields beyond literature: philosophy, theology, history, and political science. He even served as an editor of *The Review of Politics,* a philosophical and historical journal published at Notre Dame. Although he was O'Connor's intellectual superior, O'Connor owed not a little of his own voracious reading habits to his mentor.

But there was one failure in the beloved professor that would cause great sadness and concern in the student. O'Malley was an Irish bachelor all his life, and in spite of living in the midst of a bustling university, he was essentially a lonely man. Fairly early in life he developed a liking for Scotch and dry martinis, and by the 1950s he was clearly an alcoholic—a "good man's failing," according to an Irish saying at once perceptive and evasive. O'Malley's forlorn figure would be seen in mid-afternoon waiting outside the college gates for the mile-and-a-half bus ride to his favorite hotel bar in downtown South Bend, where by nightfall he would have consumed a half dozen martinis, often while conducting an informal symposium with students. For the last thirteen years of his own life, O'Connor would annually visit his old professor, who was sinking ever more deeply into the abyss. The teetotaling O'Connor abhorred public displays of inebriation, especially in the Irish, and to witness O'Malley's deterioration must have been exceedingly painful. There can be little question that *The Edge of Sadness,* the novel about the recovering alcoholic priest which O'Connor wrote during those visits to Notre Dame, was indirectly prompted by Frank O'Malley, to whom in fact the book is dedicated. In the last few years of his life O'Malley made feeble efforts to

17. Quoted by Arthur Schlesinger in the Introduction to *BL,* 4.
18. Ibid., 4–5.
19. Elliot Norton, personal interview, June 21, 1999.

overcome his problem, but he died from the ravages of heavy drinking in
1974.

Sophomore year shows a slump in O'Connor's academic record. His average was 83, nine points lower than his first year. Sophomore slumps are not
unusual, and O'Connor may simply have had a bad mix of courses and
profs. He had no Frank O'Malley to inspire him that year.

One usual suspect in such slumps is overindulgence in extracurriculars.
O'Connor did allow himself to play out one of his long-held fantasies when,
in the spring of 1937, he went out for the "yearling" baseball team. According
to his teammate Burnett C. Bauer, a catcher who became a state politician in
Indiana, O'Connor and he never amounted to much. The varsity team was
having its best season in twenty-six years, and so for the most part O'Connor and Bauer served at batting practice and played in a few inter-squad
games as well as in games with local seminarians and townies from South
Bend. Apparently O'Connor never pitched in a scheduled Notre Dame
game. He appears in no yearbook photographs, and the athletics archives reveal nothing about him. Bauer remembered O'Connor's medium fast ball
and round-house curve ball. O'Connor had such an exaggerated wind-up
that he reminded some of a Hollywood version of a praying Moslem. Opposing teams would chant "Allah, Allah" to ruffle him, but to no effect
against the unflappable O'Connor.[20] O'Connor freely admitted to many that
his baseball fantasy went nowhere. It was over in a season. As he told an interviewer in 1956, "I amounted to nothing."[21] In spite of dashed hopes, baseball would always remain his favorite spectator sport, followed distantly by
Notre Dame football, NBA basketball, and boxing.

O'Connor's grades for that spring semester are actually better than the fall
semester's; baseball cannot be blamed for the slump. A more plausible culprit
may have been campus radio. In 1934, about a decade after commercial radio's start, Notre Dame launched its radio station. The fare was mostly highbrow: news, lectures, informal talks with professors, symphony concerts.
Sometimes the station even got a national hook-up for its programs. Programming and air time were expanded in early 1936. Apparently O'Connor
had not answered the call during his first year, but he does show up as a staff
announcer in a November 27, 1936, list in the *Scholastic* of forty Radio Club
students. Competition was strong during the early years of radio's golden

20. Burnett C. Bauer, letter to Hugh Rank, March 2, 1970, Hugh Rank Papers, CRNK,
University of Notre Dame Archives.
21. Edwin O'Connor, interview with James F. Leonard, *The Boston Post*, February 13,
1956, 7.

age; a year earlier only eleven announcers were chosen out of fifty-one auditions. Radio was the newest journalistic medium and college radio stations were more prestigious than today's rock-blasting successors. O'Connor was entering the broadcast medium with which he would be associated for almost two decades as announcer, writer, and producer, eventually becoming a radio and television critic in magazines and newspapers. Along the way he would gather material for some sharp satire in the early novels, *The Oracle* and *The Last Hurrah*. There are few files and no recordings for any of O'Connor's years on campus radio. Apparently his only role in sophomore year was to be one of the ten regular announcers. His mellow voice was ideal for radio, though at first some listeners detected faint traces of a slurring that was soon overcome.

O'Connor also belonged to a newly formed Rhode Island Club. The 1937 club photo in the yearbook shows O'Connor dressed smartly in a double-breasted suit with pocket handkerchief and collar-pinned shirt. He has wavy, almost curly hair. A close-mouthed smile is pulled down at the corners in a familiar Irish tug-of-war between mirth and irony. His stance is erect and his confident stare comes directly at the camera.

During junior year, O'Connor's grades recovered. This is the first year from which O'Connor kept some course papers. He saved three. The first, "The Critical Elements in Emerson," was apparently written for the American Literature course.[22] The fifteen-page paper received an A-, though the professor did note a lack of engagement with primary sources. In his paper O'Connor notes how Emerson's perfectionist standards could only lead to a dim estimation of human nature. O'Connor's mature fiction would show a much more understanding, forgiving attitude than the sage of Concord could ever manage. O'Connor also spotted in Emerson a dislike of novelists, with the curious exception of Scott, and an antipathy toward Austen and Dickens, already two of O'Connor's favorites.

The other papers O'Connor saved were from his two semesters of Philosophy of Literature I with Professor Rufus Rauch. These two semesters, part of a two-year sequence required of English majors, combined a survey approach along with an infusion of neo-Thomistic principles—hence the "philosophy." O'Connor's first paper, dated November 2, 1937, is entitled "Humanism and Original Sin." The paper simply rehashes course material distinguishing false secular humanism from true Christian humanism; the paper received a B- and a few terse comments such as "loose terminology in

22. EOCP 11.

places."[23] The second paper, entitled "The Nature Poetry of Marvell and Wordsworth," was submitted on May 23, 1938.[24] No grade appears on it, although Rauch did say it was "a fine preliminary study of a very difficult subject." It looks fairly hefty at twenty-five pages, until one discerns the padding, a habit O'Connor could never completely shake throughout his life. Conciseness was a virtue he admired and could practice when the occasion demanded, but often lack of economy in both style and structure characterized his work. In the paper he obviously prefers Wordsworth to Marvell, but in the end O'Connor's theological and philosophical training require him to pronounce the Christian Marvell superior to the supposedly pantheist Wordsworth. Although O'Connor would always prefer fiction to poetry, he did retain an affection for Wordsworth's celebrations of pristine nature and childhood. In *The Last Hurrah* the verse-spouting Skeffington quotes approvingly from Wordsworth's "She Was a Phantom of Delight" during a radio talk aimed at the woman vote, even though Wordsworth's "perfect woman, nobly planned" is mentally canceled as Skeffington remembers less than flattering lines about women from the Irish poet Tom Moore (*LH* 251–52). For Skeffington, even in poetry Hibernia overrules Britannia.

More interesting for O'Connor's later development are thirty-two pages of typed notes he saved from his Philosophy of Literature I course.[25] These notes were apparently distributed to the class as a kind of textbook for the major. Although O'Connor had Rufus Rauch as his instructor, the document has some O'Malley influence; as young stars of the English department, Rauch and O'Malley often collaborated.[26] These thirty-two pages are a compact summary of the modern world since the Reformation and Renaissance. Today this document, heavily influenced by the ideas of the French Catholic philosopher Jacques Maritain, seems too defensive, as its unqualified statements frown on so many modern movements and tendencies. Oddly enough, it has little to say about literature. However, the coherent and comprehensive world view contained in those class notes could offer ideas and standards to a budding satirist. In this regard, however, O'Connor's underlining of one sentence from Cardinal Newman, "A gentleman is one who never inflicts pain,"[27] forecasts some of his trouble in handling satire in which pain might have to be a necessary antidote to human failings.

O'Connor's favorite course that year was surely Frank O'Malley's Contemporary Catholic Literature. Still in its formative stage, the course was matur-

23. EOCP 4
25. EOCP 2.
27. EOCP 2: 6.

24. EOCP 10.
26. Meaney, *O'Malley*, 44.

ing rapidly as it drew heavily from the ideas of Karl Adam, Romano Guardini, Christopher Dawson, Jacques Maritain, and others, in order to illuminate the works of Hopkins, Chesterton, Belloc, Claudel, Mauriac, and Bernanos. Waugh and Greene would soon be added.[28] Because one of O'Malley's special concerns was Catholic complacency, he stressed that great Catholic writers were more of a challenge than a comfort. O'Connor would continue reading from O'Malley's syllabus for the rest of his life. When he was writing *The Edge of Sadness* he must have hoped that he was taking his place on it, but there is no evidence that he ever did.

During his junior year O'Connor came into his own on the campus radio station. An article on radio in the November 19, 1937, *Notre Dame Scholastic* announced a new program called "Preview of the News with Edward [sic] O'Connor." O'Connor apparently produced, wrote, and delivered this fifteen-minute program, which aired on Thursdays at 4:45 P.M. In the following week's issue, the *Scholastic* notes that O'Connor's program would be devoted to campus news and would now be known as "Periscope on the News." O'Connor quickly put his stamp on this little program, which would be his own for the next year and half. Again, no recordings were ever made, and O'Connor preserved nothing from it. Various accounts in the *Scholastic* indicate that much of the program consisted of humorous commentary on campus events and personalities. O'Connor was trying out his satirical wings.

O'Connor did save the script for "Pontiac's Varsity Show Honoring Notre Dame" from 1937. He probably worked on the script with others. The show was on national radio and consisted mostly of facts and figures about the university, an assortment of tributes, several Pontiac commercials, and some inside jokes and undergraduate humor, such as an imitation of W.C. Fields.

When O'Connor returned to Notre Dame for his senior year, he was assigned room 234 in the somewhat more prestigious Alumni Hall at the end of the spacious green that spreads south from Main Building. One day in October as O'Connor was looking out his window he saw to his surprise a Holy Cross priest walking along in a heavy sweater his mother had knitted in Notre Dame's blue and gold colors. In June O'Connor had left the sweater, along with a radio, in someone's care until his return, but he had been unable to track them down for a month. O'Connor often referred to this incident with good humor.[29] No one seems to know how the matter was resolved, if at all.

---

28. Meaney, *O'Malley*, chap. 4.

29. James Reilly, personal interview, June 30, 1998. Mr. Reilly heard O'Connor tell the story at his induction into the La Salle Academy Hall of Fame. Apparently O'Connor

O'Connor's grades were up a notch from junior year to an 89 average. By this time O'Connor had also decided on a minor in philosophy, even though the subject was not his strong suit.

Although that year's collegiate fad was swallowing goldfish, Notre Dame kept things on a higher plane. A big event was a symposium on November 4 devoted to political and social philosophy. Jacques Maritain himself spoke, as did the Aristotelian Mortimer Adler of the University of Chicago and of Great Books fame. On February 22 seniors in caps and gowns participated in the traditional Notre Dame Washington Day. The United States flag was formally presented to the university president in Washington Hall. O'Connor saved his blue athletic ticket book from senior year—a sign of gathering "senioritis." However, except for football games, most of the tickets went unused.

Radio continued to absorb much of his energy—to the point where a small campus drama eventually unfolded. O'Connor was in the second year of his "Periscope on the News" program. The *Scholastic* had a regular radio column that covered national, local, and campus broadcasts. Another lengthier column called "The Week," written by O'Connor's classmate William ("Bill") Donnelly, was a print counterpart to O'Connor's airwaves banter. The little drama played itself out in these columns and on O'Connor's weekly "Periscope" program from February to April, 1939. Bill Donnelly speculates that the "feud" between O'Connor and himself can probably be traced to the Washington Day convocation for seniors. Bill was called upon to deliver the Birthday Ode.

My offering was less than inspired (you try manufacturing an ode to GW on demand) and my delivery was even worse. (No one could hear me, which in recollection was probably a blessing.) . . . It's quite possible—perhaps even probable—that Ed made a few comments on The Periscope, leading to my responses. . . .[30]

Bill Donnelly's quick responses over the next few weeks indicates a running feud between the two media gossips. Donnelly believes that it was all done in good fun as a way of stirring up interest in their respective efforts, and was possibly modeled to an extent on the pseudo-feud between Jack Benny and Fred Allen (a big favorite of O'Connor) on national radio.[31] His first shot appears in his March 3 *Scholastic* column and seems mild enough: "You too can be unusual! Have you ever wanted to break away from the con-

---

opened up more to his friend John Kelleher, who relates that the priest was in fact a kleptomaniac who also pilfered food from the cafeteria. *BL*, 402.

30. William A. Donnelly, E-mail to author, June 27, 1999.
31. William A. Donnelly, letter to author, June 22, 1999.

ventional and ordinary in your life? Have you ever wanted to acquire the knack of rooting out unusual news? For easy lessons apply to 'The Periscope,' c/o the university radio studio. . . ." From this it would seem that O'Connor's program was at least partly devoted to campus eccentrics whose mannerisms and peregrinations were already an O'Connor hobby. That same March 3 *Scholastic* issue profiles O'Connor, replete with photo, in the "Radio" column. Since this profile was to be the first in a series on the radio staff, it offers some indication of O'Connor's popularity on the air. Possibly Donnelly's raillery was meant to be a counterbalance.

Donnelly's next broadside appears a week later as a mock survey; it is worth reprinting as the most extended (though hardly the most accurate) item about O'Connor during his years at Notre Dame.

I. Do you listen to "The Periscope"?
  1. Yes..9
  2. No...............................499,984
  3. Occasionally.........................7
II. I listen to "The Periscope because:
  1. Ed O'Connor is an unusual man.
  2. My room mate comes from Rhode Island and he makes me listen.
  3. Kay Kyser is a southerner and you've got to listen to something ("Loyal Yankee" Answer Dep't.).
  4. His voice has such a sleep-provoking quality.
  5. Ooh geegosh, Ed O'Connor has such curly blond hair and such muscular shoulders ("St. Mary Freshman" Answer Dep't.).
  6. I always did like fiction.
  7. My radio can only get So. Bend.
  8. I thought it was a story about the navy and me brudder is a sailor (the "I Only Had To Listen Once" Dep't.).
  9. Slander cannot go unheeded (the "SCHOLASTIC's Libel Editor" Dep't.).
  10. It's a sure-fire way of persuading my room mate to go over to the caf and buy something for the two of us.
III. I don't listen to "The Periscope" because:
  1. Ed O'Connor is such an unusual man.
  2. Kay Kyser, suh, is a southerner, and ah lak 'im pow'ful well.
  3. Oh, that awful man! ("St. Mary's Senior" Answer Dept.).
  4. His voice has such a sleep-provoking quality.

5. He has been seen on the campus holding fingers with a certain beautiful girl who works in the library and I burn up with envy whenever I think upon it.
6. Never heard of the program.
7. I sold my radio the first time I heard "The Periscope."
8. Oh, *that* program.
9. I can't answer that question; it's Lent.

On St. Patrick's Day Donnelly writes that the nine who admitted to listening to "The Periscope" have been shamed into not listening, which leaves only "the wind and the waves." Around this time, in his senior year college notebook, O'Connor wrote in huge letters, "HAVE A CARE, DONNELLY!"[32]

By the following week matters had come to a head. On March 24 Donnelly begins "The Week" with this item:

> *Design for an Epitaph*
> IN MEMORIAM
> *Blessed is "The Week," for*
> *it shall possess the land.*
> Here lies Ed O'Connor, may his soul rest in peace.
> Eternal rest grant unto him, O Lord;
> He achieved great honor, but his efforts had to cease
> Because "The Week" impaled him on its sword.

And that indeed was taps for O'Connor on "Periscope on the News." The April 21 *Scholastic* "Radio" column announced that in late March the Radio Club president, Ray Kelly, had taken over the program: "Ray claims a good background for this program, having handled a scandal sheet in high school—but he hasn't been over to St. Mary's!"

What had happened? Two possibilities come to mind. One possibility is that O'Connor's programs were getting too barbed as his college days came to a close and that he was told to desist by Father Burke, faculty moderator and chair of the English department. In addition, because O'Connor was notoriously private about his romances, the reference in print to his girl could very well have caused a huffy resignation. At any rate, Bill Donnelly does not remember what happened, and O'Connor never alluded to his demise on campus radio: unless, that is, his first novel contains a clue. How strange that some twelve years later *The Oracle* would turn on an unexpected

32. Notebook courtesy of Barbara O'Connor Burrell. The date of this message is not given, but from its placement in the notes for O'Malley's Philosophy of Literature course, mid-semester seems about right. A little later, O'Connor wrote in his notebook, "I am damnably sick of school!"

crisis faced by a superficial radio commentator who frets that he may get dropped by his sponsor.

A postscript: on April 28 Donnelly noted that O'Connor's "Periscope" successor "has followed the tradition of the old one and has already made a subtle attack on us. . . ." Apparently the tradition of O'Connor's satirical wit lived on for a while. On May 26, 1939, the paper paid a brief tribute to Edwin O'Connor and Ray Kelly for doing "Periscope" in a "sporting vein."

O'Connor's first literary accomplishment of note appeared in the fall semester, when *Scrip*, the university literary quarterly, published his short story "Friends Are Made in McCabe's."[33] *Scrip* was an attractive, glossy, undergraduate journal whose art deco cover featured a simple off-center cross. The journal's title refers to the wallet or purse carried by medieval pilgrims.[34] *Scrip* published student fiction, poetry, and essays on literature. Faculty moderator Frank O'Malley, who seems to have been everywhere, would often encourage students in his classes to submit material. In O'Connor's case, however, the story was most likely written that semester in his Advanced Writing course, which was mostly devoted to short story writing; it was conducted by Professor John Frederick, who also taught at Northwestern. "Friends Are Made in McCabe's," by Edwin Greene O'Connor, was the first item in the November issue. He would never use the "Greene" again.

"Friends Are Made in McCabe's" is told by twenty-ish Peter, who is apparently an Irish American from New York. Peter appears mostly as a somewhat baffled, first-person observer of a lovers' triangle involving his old buddy Ollie Moran (possibly named after a Rhode Island beer distributor called McLaughlin and Moran), a smart young wine distributor named Phil Rotardi, and a dark *femme fatale* named Kitty who plays her role in an even darker green outfit. It is a simple story in which the hesitant lover Ollie, an undistinguished and impoverished singer at Jimmy McCabe's night club, eventually loses his girl to Phil, who had befriended him and given him a good job in his family's company. "I'm a beer baron now," Ollie tells Peter at one point, before correcting himself: "Only not exactly a beer baron. I'm in the wine business." Like O'Connor, the narrator is a self-confessed teetotaler, and it seems that Ollie is O'Connor's earliest portrait of Irish failings—in love and in liquor in this case, for the tale gets ugly as Ollie drowns his lovelorn sorrows in an angry binge. When Ollie confronts Phil in the climax, things

---

33. *Scrip*, November 1938, 2–5.

34. Many years later O'Connor may have suggested to a priest friend the title for his book: *Nor Scrip Nor Shoes;* see Chapter Nine.

get uglier as Ollie accuses him of being first a "Wop" and then a "Jew" and then finally a "Wop-Jew" before incoherently yelling, "Go on home to Hitler, you Jew!" He then knocks Phil to the floor. Peter takes Phil home and then goes home himself.

The story is mostly conversation, a preview of O'Connor's later work. A short notice in the *Scholastic* on November 18 commented favorably on the "brisk dialogue." "Brisk" in places, maybe, but for some reason O'Connor makes Phil speak in a "slow, too-exact way," as Peter himself notes. The result is an oddly lopsided, frequently stilted dialogue among the three men. Only Kitty is light with the tongue. More significant, however, is Peter's/O'Connor's bafflement at his friends' intractable triangle. The narrator repeats "I wanted to get out of there," meaning McCabe's, where all the action takes place, even though he admits, "I don't know why." It is clear that O'Connor is bothered by a broken friendship about which nothing can be done. In his late work this situation of the outsider's helplessness would resurface, most notably in *All in the Family.*

That an American story would allude to Nazi treatment of Jews in November of 1938 is noteworthy. Although the story was written before Kristallnacht, it appeared with uncanny coincidence the very week of that vandalic shattering. Of course, many previous incidents in Germany had given proof enough of Nazi intentions. O'Connor perceptively shows that just as Hitler was scapegoating Jews, so too a drunkenly violent Irish American could manufacture a Jew out of an Italian to explain the world's perfidy and thereby absolve his own failings. O'Connor would have many Jewish friends whom he admired for their tolerant humor; their view of him was reciprocal.

O'Connor was ordinarily a truthful man, but he did tend to enlarge some early achievements. Although "Friends Are Made in McCabe's" is his only appearance in *Scrip,* he would claim more than once that he was on the staff and was a frequent contributor, even if he did undercut his own imagined career quickly, as in this 1955 interview: "I wrote regular pieces for the Quarterly, but there was never any suggestion that my literary efforts inspired [the critics]."[35] In fact, he was never on the staff and had only one story published.

His senior photo in *The Dome* shows a more smiling, adult O'Connor than any previous picture. He had now reached his six-foot, two-inch height. Although O'Connor was still only twenty at graduation, Notre Dame for all

---

35. Edwin O'Connor, interview with Edgar J. Allaire, *Woonsocket Call,* December 16, 1955.

of its restrictiveness was a good match for him. He had matured socially, intellectually, and religiously: a serious young man with a good measure of charitable humor. Bill Donnelly remembers him as "friendly but reserved, full of a quiet confidence in himself."[36] At the Class of 1939's sixtieth reunion, some remembered him as a "quiet guy," although none of his close friends was among the octogenarians in attendance.[37] Judging from a spate of letters he would receive over the next few years, he had many friends by graduation, mostly from the literary set. The yearbook lists only Radio Club and interhall athletics for his activities; baseball and *Scrip* get no mention.

But who was the girl who worked in the library, mentioned so prominently in the media wars? The only bit of evidence is one letter to O'Connor dated May 2, 1940, almost a year after his graduation. It was from a "Jean" (no last name appears), who was apparently a student one year behind O'Connor at St. Mary's; more on this later. Bill Donnelly does recollect that O'Connor dated at least one girl from St. Mary's, but he cannot be more specific. The "Radio" profile on O'Connor in the March 3, 1939, *Scholastic* had slyly hinted at his extramural affairs: "He plays St. Mary's both on the air and off." A Jean who graduated from St. Mary's in 1940 died in the late 1990s. She was most likely O'Connor's Jean, but whether she was the girl in the library cannot be ascertained.

🜪

Edwin O'Connor graduated *cum laude* from Notre Dame on Saturday June 4, 1939, at late-afternoon commencement exercises in the gymnasium. The sunny day had begun with an academic procession at 8:30 into the gymnasium for a solemn pontifical Mass, where the Washington Day flag was now blessed for the day's ceremonies. Later the new Knute Rockne Memorial Fieldhouse was dedicated, the ceremony broadcast over national radio. At the commencement, William Henry Harrison, vice president of American Telephone and Telegraph, addressed the graduates in the gymnasium festooned with flags and bunting. O'Connor remembers that Harrison spoke gloomily about the Depression and war.[38] O'Connor's parents made the long trip from Woonsocket to see their son graduate.[39]

O'Connor has left one memory of that day in a 1956 newspaper article. A

---

36. William A. Donnelly, letter to author, June 22, 1999.

37. Dave Meskill, E-mail to author, June 21, 1999. Mr. Meskill was the class reunion organizer.

38. "Coast Guard Manuscript," II, 1. Found in EOCP 22, 23. The manuscript is hereafter referred to as "CG."

39. *The Dome*, 1939, and commencement program.

dotty, retired Holy Cross priest used to enjoy buttonholing hapless victims in order to discuss abstruse items like St. Anselm's ontological proofs for the existence of God. Every Catholic campus can produce a "Father Anthony McDermott," to use O'Connor's fictional name for him. "Father McDermott" also was notorious for regular visits to the library, where he would take scissors to any part of a book he found offensive. If the book as a whole was deemed unsuitable, he would check it out and throw it away. On commencement day O'Connor was taking a last tour of the campus with a friend and his fiancée. When the friend spotted "Father McDermott," he tried to introduce him to his fiancée, at which the priest waved him off and said, "No, I don't think so. I know enough people already," and tottered toward the library.[40]

O'Connor's association with Notre Dame was not quite over, however. The following months would be trying ones for him as he untypically floundered in uncertainty. A letter he received from a Notre Dame chum catches the familiar mood of jobless grads: "I hope the after-graduation gloom has not settled on you, too."[41] The only definite vocation O'Connor had, though unfocused, was to be a writer. In 1955 he told an interviewer that "even [in public school] I wanted to write. I wanted to write even more than I wanted to become a great baseball player." He added that in college he had sent out articles to several national magazines. "I got back six manuscripts with six nice rejection slips. I became convinced . . . that no one read my stuff but the office cat."[42] These manuscripts have not survived. Sometime in senior year of college he had told Father Ward of the English department that he wanted to be a writer. "You mean sit in a room and write, just that?" asked the less than encouraging professor of literature. "That's what I mean," O'Connor prophetically replied. "Then I'm afraid you'll starve to death in two months," concluded Ward, who then suggested that in the meantime he get a day job which would allow him some time to write.[43]

· Even before graduation, O'Connor had taken steps to hedge his bets. He had applied to Notre Dame for a master's program in English. On May 24, 1939, he was informed that the Committee on Awards had placed him as first

40. Edwin O'Connor, untitled article, *Boston Sunday Post,* September 16, 1956, 1 and 4.

41. Robert Heywood, letter to Edwin O'Connor, July 4, 1939, EOCP 164.

42. Edwin O'Connor, interview with Edgar J. Allaire, *Woonsocket Call,* December 16, 1955.

43. Edwin O'Connor, interview with James L. Leonard, *The Boston Post,* February 14, 1956, 1, 13.

alternate for one of the newly established apologetics scholarships for the coming academic year. However, O'Connor was simultaneously pursuing a bolder, alternative plan which seems quixotic in retrospect. For some time Notre Dame President Father John O'Hara had been trying to establish an exchange program with universities in South America, where Notre Dame had an interest going back to the nineteenth century, when it even published its catalogue in Spanish. On February 24, 1939, the *Scholastic* reported on Father O'Hara's trip to Peru, where he had represented the United States at the Pan-American Conference. While there he had used the Notre Dame network to advantage. The exchange program materialized that fall, when the son of the mayor of Buenos Aires studied graduate philosophy at Notre Dame. O'Connor must have read this item with interest and at some point before graduation he decided to act.

In mid-June O'Connor, now back in Woonsocket, received a brief letter from Father O'Hara concerning O'Connor's desire to study at the Catholic University of Santiago in Chile. He enclosed two letters of introduction to Notre Dame alumni in Santiago, and a copy of a letter to the rector of the university in which he vouches for O'Connor as a "Christian gentleman" and good student, and assures him that O'Connor has received parental permission. He admits that O'Connor's Spanish is weak, but hopes that O'Connor can enter as a special student for at least a year.[44] O'Connor proceeded with plans for this adventure by contacting a tramp steamer company. In late August Father O'Hara again wrote O'Connor, now twenty-one, enclosing his acceptance letter from the university rector in Santiago. Father O'Hara notes that O'Connor's room and board there will be 300 pesos a month—about $10! He also points out that the rector's letter is concerned that O'Connor has yet to indicate his course of study.[45]

For whatever reason, O'Connor never went to Chile. Indeed, it is not clear why he wanted to go in the first place. His nonexistent Spanish, along with his hesitancy about his field of study, suggest a lack of seriousness about the enterprise. While it was not uncommon for a young man with a literary bent to take to the roads or high seas, it seems that O'Connor's plan was a pipe dream and quite out of character. In any case he got cold feet. One big problem with his plan was the outbreak of World War II a few days after he received the acceptance letter; his decision not to go may be attributed to sensible fears about international travel. O'Connor never mentioned this

44. Rev. John F. O'Hara, C.S.C., letter to Edwin O'Connor, June 12, 1939, EOCP 227.
45. Rev. John F. O'Hara, C.S.C., letter to Edwin O'Connor, August 25, 1939, EOCP 228.

abandoned venture, but something about it stayed with him for years. One of the last works he wrote was a play entitled "The Traveler from Brazil" (1966), in which a middle-aged man, about O'Connor's age at the time, has fantasies about residing in Brazil in order to escape family entanglements and the disintegrating country. This unusual work resists easy autobiographical decoding, but it clearly involves some painful soul-searching about the difficulties in resisting overbearing parental pressures, by then a major O'Connor subject.

If O'Connor was silent about the failure that summer, so too was he about the ensuing autumn. After discarding the voyage south, O'Connor immediately fell back on his safer plan and by late September he was back at Notre Dame to pursue a master's degree in English. He quickly realized that he had made a serious mistake. First, he was now living off campus at 306 Pokagon Street in South Bend, a ten-minute walk from the university. After living agreeably in dormitories for four years, the grad student now must have seemed like an outsider at his own university, where undergraduate radio and publishing outlets were suddenly closed to him. Additionally, according to a letter from the department head, Father Ward, O'Connor did not receive one of the top scholarships; he implies that O'Connor's sudden decision to return was a bit tardy, although Ward's tone is heartily welcoming. He does go on to offer O'Connor clerical employment in the department with a stipend of $250 and a scholarship of $100.[46] Although these monies would cover most of his expenses, O'Connor must have felt a letdown, in part arising from the necessity of working on campus for the first time.

But most of all O'Connor was bored. Graduate school, as some students find out, is not a rerun of college years. Father Ward's letter had noted O'Connor's desire to study the philosophical aspects of literature, whatever O'Connor meant by that, but apparently little in his course work lived up to his expectations. There is no academic record of the two months he endured, but in his boredom and frustration he did leave an unpublished satire apparently written during or shortly after his stay. The untitled fragment centers on the exasperation of a graduate student, Peter Carew, with a Victorian seminar conducted by a fictional Professor Melton, who disregards most of that grand era in order to explicate Ruskin at tedious length. This in itself would upset O'Connor, whose favorite reading was already in lively Victorian fiction. Melton, a hidebound traditionalist, also contemptuously

46. Rev. Leo L. Ward, C.S.C., letter to Edwin O'Connor, September 8, 1939, EOCP 14.

dismisses all modern art as surrealist "rubber watches." Even more annoying is Carew's fellow student Barbacher, an obnoxiously militant Catholic: "a sinister type whose sole function [was] to patrole [sic] the universe, refuting." O'Connor's gentle tolerance shows through here as he frowns on apologetics as a bludgeon. O'Connor sums up the seminar: "A little world in which each man used as much energy as possible in doing absolutely nothing of value." At one point Carew significantly opens the window of the small, stuffy room—knowing that old Melton would soon close it.[47]

An episode that autumn provided another inducement to leave. One of O'Connor's closest friends in college had been Joseph J. McDermott, who had brought O'Connor home to Chicago several times. During these trips O'Connor had absorbed a good deal of Chicago political lore from the McDermott family. In its humor section the 1939 *Dome* has a photo of "Ed. O'Connor and Joe McDermott" seated at a round table in a campus malt shop with a pretty young woman between them, although it's difficult to say whose girl she is. The caption reads: "They wore each other's socks, used their friend's book, smoked anything, lunged convincingly for the Oliver check." The smoking refers to the straw for O'Connor's soda, which looks like an extremely long cigarette; the girl does in fact seem to be paying the check. McDermott glances darkly at the waitress from underneath bushy eyebrows. He seems to have been not at all O'Connor's typical friend at Notre Dame. Joe McDermott got into serious academic difficulty and transferred to the University of Maryland. However, a friend he was, and so when he sought readmittance to Notre Dame in the fall of 1939, O'Connor went to bat for him. One evening in late October O'Connor visited the college dean, Father Charles C. Miltner, in his rooms at Corby Hall. O'Connor must have pressed him at length because the dean wrote him a detailed letter on November 3 patiently outlining the reasons why McDermott could not be readmitted. O'Connor was already known for his strong loyalty to friends, and this rebuff may have been the final straw. His file indicates that he voluntarily withdrew from Notre Dame on November 19. He was back in Woonsocket for Thanksgiving.

O'Connor left Notre Dame with a somewhat bitter taste in his mouth; he never mentioned those wasted two months. However, he held no permanent grudge and indeed would soon recover his old affection for the school, especially for Frank O'Malley; to both he would make annual pilgrimages later in his life. Classes were a thing of the past now. He had to get that job and more importantly that time to write.

47. EOCP 13.

CHAPTER THREE

✃ *Radio Years*

(1940–1942)

Edwin O'Connor once told an interviewer that he was in radio "more or less" from June 1939 on.[1] He was being evasive, as the events of the summer and fall of 1939 have shown. Well into his forties he still needed to construct an uninterrupted line that ran from the commencement stage to a radio studio. His saving honesty allows the wobbly hedge of "more or less."

It is difficult to say for sure when O'Connor landed his first job in commercial radio, but most likely it was some weeks after his mid-November 1939 return from Notre Dame. The evidence from a few letters and family memory is scanty. Furthermore, radio was still new and few records were kept; those that were kept were almost always lost somewhere in the shuffle caused by the many changes in station ownership. The four stations where O'Connor worked over the next two and a half years have no records that cover that period.

The Depression was still very much a reality, and like anything else radio jobs were eagerly sought. O'Connor would sometimes say that he did not really know how he got his first job, a sign again of some mental reservation. In the "Coast Guard" manuscript he writes, "Just how this happened, I am unable to explain." It just did, like "measles" ("CG" II, 2). The passage fails to convince. It is quite possible that family connections in tight little Rhode Island were employed, which is to say his father's connections. A possible clue occurs in an unpublished manuscript written a few years later in which a young man significantly named Cantwell chafes helplessly while his domineering father smoothly arranges for his first job. However, O'Connor's sister remembers that her brother always was proud to have earned his way through life, and that he was grateful on many occasions that his father "never interfered."[2]

At any rate O'Connor was home at Gaskill Street for a while. At

1. Edwin O'Connor, interview with P.C. Brooks, *Boston*, November 1964, 47.
2. Barbara O'Connor Burrell, personal interviews, summer 1998.

Christmas he received a card from Frank O'Malley; the sending of these cards to favorite students past and present was an O'Malley custom. The Christmas card contained his own poem entitled "Blood of the Lamb," whose fourteen Crashaw-Hopkins lines strain imagery and theology to the snapping point. The card's printed inscription says simply, "I hope that you will be happy at Christmas and afterwards."[3] (The following June O'Malley asked O'Connor to "write again and again. Every O'Connor word pleases.")[4]

Time seems to have been heavy on O'Connor's hands for the next few months, judging from a spate of letters he received from college friends. Charles Nelson wrote "Edwin Gee! O'Connor?" a sophomoric letter full of Britishisms and chatter about mutual friends.[5] Albert Kelly wrote on stationary of Notre Dame's *Review of Politics* that the journal's editor, Frank O'Malley, is out bear hunting. Kelly went on to parody O'Malley (apparently a favorite student sport) by sighing that "we are living in a demented world, living, alas, in the shadow of tomorrow."[6] Frank Cunningham wrote self-consciously stilted gossip, possibly in parody, from Boston, where he was doing graduate work.[7] O'Connor also received a letter from Penguin Books in New York, which regretted that the company did not have automatic mailing lists for its new books: an early sign of his avid reading, but also evidence of O'Connor's leisure.[8]

O'Connor received one interesting letter in early May 1940 from the Jean he had met while at Notre Dame. This is the only love letter, or something approximating it, that O'Connor ever kept. The significance of the letter and its preservation is hard to determine, because nobody remembers anything about this Jean, and apparently O'Connor never talked about her to his family. Jean begins by apologizing for her tardiness in writing, but her mother's stroke in February has caused great worry, and impending graduation from St. Mary's College also makes her anxious. She thinks about O'Connor a lot and had started to write often. She would like to see him again: "I've missed you, Ed." She signs off, "As ever, Jean."[9] The letter hardly scorches the reader's eyes, but Jean's interest appears serious enough. No other mention of this Jean was ever kept by O'Connor, except for one intriguing letter a year and a half later from his classmate Charles Nelson. Shortly after the attack on Pearl Harbor, Nelson writes O'Connor that he is enlisting, and then asks about

3. Frank O'Malley, card to Edwin O'Connor, December 19, 1939, EOCP 230.
4. Frank O'Malley, letter to Edwin O'Connor, June 8, 1940, EOCP 231.
5. Charles Nelson, letter to Edwin O'Connor, January 14, 1940, EOCP 206.
6. Albert P. Kelly, letter to Edwin O'Connor, January 29, 1940, EOCP 175.
7. Francis E. Cunningham, letter to Edwin O'Connor, February 6, 1940, EOCP 123.
8. Ian Ballantine, letter to Edwin O'Connor, January 24, 1940, EOCP 234.
9. Jean (last name unknown), letter to Edwin O'Connor, May 2, 1940, EOCP 275.

O'Connor's plans. It is in that context that his next topic should be read: "Glad to hear the news about you and Jean. Naturally, so will she. Next to myself, I don't know anyone else I'd rather see marry her."[10] Something may have continued between O'Connor and Jean, but, given the sudden war atmosphere, it seems highly likely that O'Connor had been only kidding Nelson about marrying Jean for purposes of a draft deferment. That seems to be the only way of reading "Naturally, so will she." It's even possible that Nelson himself constructed the whole scenario; such banter is frequently found in letters from his classmates.

Right after Christmas 1939 he received a letter from Joe McDermott who asked about the "radio business."[11] Thirty years later Walter Hackett, an early radio colleague, journalist, and friend with whom O'Connor had a rare falling out, stated that O'Connor joined Providence's WPRO radio station in the autumn of 1939 as an announcer on Hackett's dramatic show, for which he was paid fifteen dollars a week.[12] The last letter O'Connor kept from Joe McDermott came in late April, and provides more evidence about the radio work. McDermott is sorry to hear that his friend is "again a gentleman of leisure," but he assures him that the "rich unexcelled resonance" of his voice will soon get him a job. He assumes that O'Connor had been working at a Woonsocket station, but there was no such station until 1946.[13] An earlier letter from O'Connor's Aunt Mary in Los Angeles also alludes to some kind of lost opportunity in radio. She enclosed a typed page of motivational wisdom culled from many sources, including Abraham Lincoln.[14] Yet by early summer of 1940 O'Connor was working again at station WPRO in Providence. O'Connor probably had some kind of apprentice-like, part-time announcing job at the station in late 1939 or early 1940 and then for some reason was dropped, only to be rehired later. In a 1956 interview he said that his summer 1940 replacement job became permanent when Ed Pearson, a veteran at the station who taught him a lot, left for a job in West Palm Beach, Florida.[15] O'Connor's radio years seem precarious at times, but apparently his career was not all that unusual.

O'Connor worked at station WPRO until early spring 1941, when he was earning eighteen dollars a week. WPRO was the newest of the three stations

10. Charles Nelson, letter to Edwin O'Connor, December. 17, 1941, EOCP 206.
11. J. Joseph McDermott, letter to Edwin O'Connor, December 27, 1939, EOCP 275.
12. Walter Hackett, "Criticism Broke Long Friendship," *Providence Journal*, December 15, 1969.
13. J. Joseph McDermott, letter to Edwin O'Connor, April 27, 1940, EOCP 275.
14. Mary C. O'Connor, letter to Edwin O'Connor, March 29, 1940, EOCP 223.
15. Edwin O'Connor, interview with George C. Hull, *Providence Journal*, February 21, 1956.

in the Providence area; now there are over twenty.[16] Like many stations of the time, WPRO was owned by a downtown department store in order to help sell the bulky RCA and Philco wooden consoles that became the first electronic parlor furniture, typically adorned with doily and photos. Some stations were even housed in the stores. WPRO was owned by the Cherry & Webb store but was located in the Metropolitan Theatre Building where O'Connor had graduated from high school. In its cramped "studios" the announcer would sit at a small desk and speak into a primitive, black, table microphone with the crescent of WPRO on top. WPRO had affiliated with the CBS network in 1937. According to his sister, O'Connor had a natural radio voice and needed no special training. She remembers that he often opened the broadcasting day, and sometimes did the evening news as well.[17] Francis Carroll remembers that North End neighbors in Woonsocket would often make a special point of tuning in the evening news just to hear Edwin O'Connor.[18] O'Connor was embarrassed when he read his first commercial, for women's hosiery, which began, "Ladies, how are your legs?" ("CG" II, 2).

About a decade later O'Connor wrote an unpublished vignette about his early days at WPRO. "The Greatest Salesman in Rhode Island" focuses on the fictionalized station manager, Irving Anstey, who is fat, wheezy, and unhappy, but who also has a streak of honesty. One day he calls in the apprentice announcer to offer a little advice: an announcer is not an actor or an artist. "An announcer is a peddler!" Anstey then launches into a wild-eyed panegyric about O'Connor's potential to become "the greatest salesman in Rhode Island," before admitting that it's "a rotten, filthy life." He then orders O'Connor back into the studio—to do it![19] This cynical journalistic figure recurs in several of O'Connor's works, most notably as Adam Flair in *The Oracle* and Edgar Burbank in *The Last Hurrah*.

Such was O'Connor's following in Woonsocket at least, that by March of 1941 he had attained enough local celebrity status to grant his first interview. Although O'Connor was now living in the Elmwood section of Providence, then a mostly blue-collar neighborhood of substantial older Victorians and rows of three-deckers, he still had a strong attachment to the North End and

16. I am indebted to a fine 1999 exhibit on radio in Rhode Island at the Rhode Island Historical Society, entitled "Live from Studio 1-A!"; to Andy Smith, "On the Air: A Century of Radio and TV in R.I.," *Providence Sunday Journal*, October 24, 1999, K1, 6-7; and to Maury Lowe, "The Golden Age of Radio," *Rhode Island Yearbook* (1971).

17. Barbara Burrell, personal interview, summer 1998.

18. Francis Carroll, personal interview, July 15, 1998.

19. EOCP 34. It is possible that O'Connor had Arthur Miller's *Death of a Salesman* in mind. The play, in which Willy Loman talks glowingly of Providence, Rhode Island, had opened a year or two earlier and was widely known.

St. Charles' parish, whose junior high school newspaper put him on page
one. This impressive little paper, *The Papyrus*, had been published for twelve
years and came out about eight times a year. Its layout and photography
were remarkably advanced for its level. The interview with "Well-Known Radio Announcer And Local Young Man," conducted by "Literary Editor"
Frank Padden, '41, apparently took place in a local drugstore "over a coffee
split generously purchased by Mr. O'Connor." (Rhode Islanders have a thirst
for cold coffee drinks, now the official state beverage.) This touching little
exercise in junior journalism does manage to catch O'Connor's typical combination of seriousness and humor. The reader learns that in an early broadcast at Notre Dame—most likely the Pontiac broadcast—O'Connor played
the part of none other than Knute Rockne. A liberal arts education gets a
plug as a good preparation for radio work. O'Connor seems to find his
WPRO work congenial enough, even though the hours are irregular. He enjoys editing and broadcasting the news, and also "writing many of the
sketches given in between the stories."[20] Here is the first mention of a frantic
on-the-job activity O'Connor would keep up for several years before and after the war. These "sketches" were important practice for his later short stories and novels. One of them would eventually provide a big career break.
However, none from his WPRO days survives.

Shortly after this interview O'Connor did a short turn at station WJNO
("The Voice of the Palm Beaches") in West Palm Beach. Ed Pearson wanted
to come back to Providence, O'Connor wanted a change, and so they simply
switched.[21] Little can be learned of his work in the spring and summer of
1941 other than that he sweltered in his little rented room, enjoyed the beach
by day, did some live interviews, and announced at night. He never found
Florida comfortable, but he did find plenty of free time to write and still
have fun at work, which mostly meant announcing a few minutes out of the
hour.[22] In an unpublished sketch he left one specific memory of a man-on-
the-spot radio interview he conducted with one Boyd Lorenzo at a nearby
army training camp. Lorenzo was a city slicker from the North who passed
himself off as a wrestling promoter; O'Connor described him as "Savonarola
in a sport coat" who detested being in the army under the nation's first
peacetime draft.[23] (O'Connor's own Woonsocket draft board had called him
up by this time, but so far he been deferred for "sub-standard vision," appar-

20. Edwin O'Connor, interview with Frank Padden, *The Papyrus* [St. Charles Junior
High School, Woonsocket], March 1941, 1.
21. Edwin O'Connor, interview with George C. Hull.
22. Edwin O'Connor, interview with P.C. Brooks.
23. Edwin O'Connor, "As It Was in the Beginning," EOCP 25.

ently nearsightedness. O'Connor claims that the draft board told him to "eat carrots while staring at distant buildings.") When his radio station came up with the idea of offering a dime to anyone willing to be interviewed live on radio, O'Connor was dispatched to the main street of West Palm Beach, where he was nearly knocked over by a stampede of people baring their souls about themselves and their families "for the tenth part of a dollar."[24]

One other item from his Florida sojourn bears mention. On June 28 O'Connor must have been immensely proud to receive a lengthy, personally typed letter from his radio hero, Fred Allen. The letter begins with Allen's typical use of the lower case: "Dear mr. o'connor." Apparently O'Connor had wired Allen an anti-Stalin joke for use on his program. Allen deadpans that the joke would never get by "the censors" at his network.[25] The American left was strenuously urging entry into the European war during that desperate summer, and any disparagement of "Uncle Joe" and the gallant Soviets was usually quashed. (Hitler had invaded the Soviet Union on June 22, so it is difficult to determine whether O'Connor's wire was sent before or after that date; no correspondence from O'Connor appears in the Fred Allen papers at the Boston Public Library. But Allen's letter was written one week into the invasion, and pro-Stalinist voices were getting fervent.)

O'Connor quit Florida and its heat before very long. Twenty-six years later he told Ralph McGill that he "departed in a one-horse shay sort of car that was ancient and ill with palsy." He got as far as Brunswick, Georgia, where he sold the contraption for thirty dollars and bought a bus ticket to Boston.[26] He apparently didn't drive again for fifteen years.

His next stint was at Buffalo radio station WBEN, from mid-summer to early September 1941. It appears that journeymen radio announcers moved around a good deal. This was his shortest stretch at a station, and little can be found about his stay there. He lived at a small downtown apartment in the University Club, then similar to a YMCA, whose records unfortunately were destroyed in a 1974 fire.

Two letters survive from this stay. One, dated September 3, is from Fred Friendly in Providence. Friendly grew up in Providence. He had been at station WEAN there since 1937 and had apparently become acquainted with O'Connor through radio work. He writes O'Connor that he is now off to join "Jimmy Stewart, Hank Greenberg and Joe Palooka in the defense of

24. Edwin O'Connor, "On Television," *Boston Post,* January 17, 1956, 12.

25. Fred Allen, letter to Edwin O'Connor, June 28, 1941, EOCP 73-81.

26. Ralph McGill, "Edwin J. [sic] O'Connor: One of the Really Great Ones," *Boston Globe,* April 14, 1968.

America," an allusion to the increasing war atmosphere.[27] Friendly was actually off to CBS in New York, where he would eventually rise to the top as its CEO and would achieve along the way a reputation as an eloquent defender of the rights and responsibilities of the electronic media. His friendship with O'Connor, however, did not develop beyond 1941.

The other letter, a few days later, is the first one from his father that O'Connor kept. Dr. O'Connor confesses that he is squeezing the letter in between patients; he has exactly fifteen minutes before a big insurance case, and is altogether "very busy" at his downtown Woonsocket office. He reports his amusement at the way O'Connor's kid sister, Bobby, now twelve, teases brother Jack, eighteen. Then he erupts about President Roosevelt. He hopes F.D.R. will be foiled in his attempt to get the country into the war, and notes that Hitler's advance into Russia has been checked anyway. Finally he could not restrain himself: "I never hated a person before but I do hate [F.D.R.] and all the fool represents." We hear in that sentence the first angry paternal voice which will be heard in so many of O'Connor's characters, and which will set up some of his sharpest conflicts. Dr. O'Connor closes by looking forward to visiting his son in a month: "anxious to get a squint at you."[28]

Dr. O'Connor's letter was addressed to the University Club, but it was returned to Woonsocket because for the third time in as many years O'Connor and radio had abruptly parted ways. One day when his boss asked him to work in effect from dawn to midnight, O'Connor simply refused the inhuman demand, whereupon he was fired immediately.[29] O'Connor was not fond of expanding on severances unless they had a redeeming touch of the comic and the absurd. We do know that while O'Connor at first enjoyed himself in radio, he later found it tedious and superficial, and in any case considered it mainly as a meal ticket with time on the job to write. His many station transfers may have been prompted by what some of his supervisors saw as a casual approach to the work. He would take humorous revenge on Buffalo in his last novel. After a happy love scene on the coast of Italy, the woman says, "Oh boy: it's even better than Buffalo!" The narrator explains this as a family joke going back to a World War I uncle who had seen Paris and said, "It's lots better than Oswego, and *maybe* it's even better than Buffalo!" (*F* 312).

O'Connor's last station before the war was WDRC in Hartford, Connecticut, which was about two hours from Woonsocket. He stayed for almost a

27. Fred Friendly, letter to Edwin O'Connor, September 3, 1941, EOCP 152.
28. John Vincent O'Connor, letter to Edwin O'Connor, September 9, 1941, EOCP 218.
29. Edwin O'Connor, interview with James F. Leonard, *Boston Post*, February 14, 1956, 13.

year, from the autumn of 1941 until early September 1942. His duties again principally involved announcing. He rented a room at 142 Kenyon Street, in a pleasant 1920s residential area of the city close to beautiful Elizabeth Park, which was famous for its rose gardens. Soon he got to know John Tehan, who was engaged to Arline Boucher on Kenyon Street. O'Connor dated Arline's sister a few times. John Tehan worked at the *Hartford Courant.* Arline wrote (and fifty-nine years later, in 2000, was still writing) book reviews for the paper, at ten cents per inch in 1941; she has since also written biographies of Henry Adams and Cardinal Gibbons. She remembers O'Connor, then twenty-three, as talkative and funny. He was also burning with ambition almost to the point of opportunistic arrogance. He showed no interest in her writing. A favorite prop was *The New Yorker,* which he carried around to advertise his good taste and possibly his literary goal, which remained unfulfilled; that famous magazine usually took a dim view of his writing. Arline also remembers that O'Connor talked little about his past but was bursting with plans for the future.[30]

His new proximity to New York City seems to have emboldened O'Connor, and so probably some time in October 1941 he got an appointment with an agency called Batchelor Enterprises. On November 11 the agency's Howard Reilly wrote that they could not accept his radio script, "Where Do You Hail From?"[31] which O'Connor intended for the Fred Allen Show. The not very funny skit, by "E.G. O'Connor," centers on one Philo Smythe who, while blindfolded, can tell his location in the country by people's accents. One day Smythe almost loses the game, and his job, when he can't recognize an obvious Brooklyn accent until the speaker pronounces the New York Giants the "Jints." This may be O'Connor's earliest extant radio script, and it shows. O'Connor also cannot resist irrelevant wordplay, that pitfall of many an "Irish" writer. For example, he pens into the manuscript margin "he don't know his ask from his answer," an emendation he knows is inadmissible and which is also highly unusual for him. Reilly concluded the letter by regretting that he has no assignments for the would-be writer because, with the Depression still on, the agency felt obligated to older and more experienced writers desperate for work. He did encourage O'Connor to write for his own radio station, advice O'Connor apparently took to heart.[32]

By February of 1942 O'Connor had landed his first agent. He stayed with the Ann Watkins Agency of New York until at least mid-1943, but after send-

30. Arline Tehan, three telephone interviews, November 1999-February 2000.
31. EOCP 16 and 17.
32. Howard Reilly, letter to Edwin O'Connor, November 11, 1941, EOCP 93.

ing the agency many fillers, sketches, radio scripts, and short stories, he had nothing to show at the end. While most of the pieces are satirical in varying degrees, the influences of vaudeville and radio contribute not a little to the silliness of most of the work, even if some of the satire is aimed at radio itself. One odd satire involves a poetaster named Oscar O'Connor who tries unsuccessfully to resign from the Book of the Month Club because it is getting too inclusive, much like a London club whose membership is getting dubious. "Something Has Died Within Me, Sirs!" has some promise, but O'Connor cannot keep its tone consistent and its targets in range.[33] Even the naming of the main character is puzzling: was O'Connor indulging in some self-parody, and if so, why? Ruth Portugal of the agency found it amusing, but realized its limitations. On February 24 she advises him to keep trying at humor, but to get away from mere farce. Most of all, she urges, he should work on developing characters and situations. Her advice is cogent, but like many beginning writers O'Connor took some time to absorb it. In an April 28 letter Ann Watkins herself writes that his spoof of advertising and women's cosmetics entitled "Oh No You Don't, George Jean!"[34] does not work and looks dated, although she does admit it has touches of *The New Yorker*, something that must have encouraged the writer. On May 25 she writes again somewhat testily that his sketch, "*My* Most Unforgettable Character,"[35] is simply not a successful parody of the familiar column in *Reader's Digest*. O'Connor's imaginary character, Bogey Smear, is a dissolute *poete maudit* cum pied piper, absentee father, and baseball player. It hardly needs saying that he does not come into focus. In late July he had sent Ann Watkins a letter of one word: "Help!" On August 4 she simply wrote back on his letter the cryptic, "You don't need [help] on this." The last letter from the agency is dated May 3, 1943; Ann Watkins is still encouraging, but O'Connor must have been losing heart by then.[36]

From February to August 1942 O'Connor was becoming anxious, if not desperate, to break into print. Since senior year of college he had been trying to establish a track record and after four years he could point to nothing. That "Help!" to his agent may have been a bit of humor, but it was poignant as well because there was a second reason for O'Connor's note of urgency. Already his agency had warned him about impending war restrictions on publishing as a result of paper shortages, but O'Connor hardly needed reminding about the war, which was getting closer to him all the time on an-

---

33. EOCP 38. 34. EOCP 18.
35. EOCP 19.
36. Letters from Ann Watkins Agency to Edwin O'Connor, EOCP 261 and 378.

other front. Shortly after Pearl Harbor, O'Connor had taken steps to stay out of the shooting as a revealing letter discloses. O'Connor actually kept a letter from a Mr. Milliken (first name unreadable), who was apparently his superior at WDRC in Hartford, to Commander Leslie Jacobs of the Navy Department in Washington. It is obvious that Milliken and Jacobs were friends. Moreover, Milliken states that he is an old friend of O'Connor's father. While the letter ostensibly asks only for advice on how young O'Connor could get into public relations in the armed forces, one need not be a cynic to see the letter as a request for special treatment. This letter moreover suggests that Dr. O'Connor may very well have interfered after all when he thought it was in his son's interest—first in helping to get his son the Hartford job, which was closer to home than Buffalo, and second in keeping him out of Roosevelt's war as much as possible. All this is speculation about Milliken and Dr. O'Connor, of course, but in the immediate aftermath of Pearl Harbor many such scenarios did in fact play themselves out. Milliken closes his letter by describing O'Connor as "rather retiring but a very fine chap . . . with a personality that commands respect."[37] A few weeks later O'Connor received another letter from someone named only Harmon who may have worked at WDRC and was now in Army public relations in Georgia. O'Connor had asked him how to get into such a job. Harmon tells him to throw around lots of loud "bull-shit" about his radio work, but also to get used to a lot of "tough shit" replies.[38]

Meanwhile radio work itself was becoming ever more war-conscious, especially after December 7, 1941. Already O'Connor had conducted daily interviews at that Florida army base for WJNO. By the time he got to Hartford, the radio networks really had "taken up the cudgels," as he notes in his "Coast Guard" manuscript. Chapter III of this document gives a lively, funny account of early war radio. Evening broadcasts often included dreadful readings of proletarian blank verse that quickly became "more oppressive than the war itself." He provides a sample:

> America,? You ask . . . What is America?
> I'll tell you what America is, mister.
> It is tall pine and scrub oak
> And birch-bark;
> Waving rows of grain: golden, flexible
> Sheaves of sunlight.

37. Letter from (first name unknown) Milliken to Commander Leslie Jacobs, U.S.N., January 22, 1942, EOCP 198.

38. (First name unknown) Harmon, letter to Edwin O'Connor, February 18, 1942, EOCP 275.

Moonlight too.
It is bath-tubs and sewerage systems
And dental hygiene.
Why, America is people, all kinds of people:
Little people, too, lots of them.
People like you, Jim Jones,
And you, Jadwigh Pryzmlski,
And you, George Washington Bonaparte Brown,
And you, and you, and you!
That's what America is, mister!
That is America!

Even if this is parody, it catches the bathetic quality of American war propaganda. O'Connor's own contribution to what he called "these defections" was a "hodge-podge" show called "On the Ball with Uncle Sam!" which public boredom quickly killed. Mostly, O'Connor's sentiments about war on the radio anticipate the short war poem in John Knowles's *A Separate Peace:* "The War / Is a bore."[39]

In early September 1942, O'Connor left WDRC, with regrets because he was still enjoying radio work. The boss gave him a big bonus, the office girls donated lots of World War II kisses, and O'Connor made a last schmaltzy broadcast ("CG" IV, 1). He was off to "war."

39. John Knowles, *A Separate Peace* (1959; New York: Macmillan, 1986), 78.

CHAPTER FOUR

❧ *Coast Guard*
(1942–1945)

"I am not, by nature, a man of military inclinations."[1] This opening sentence of O'Connor's "Coast Guard" manuscript captures the three years from September 1942 to September 1945 that he spent in the United States Coast Guard. He had been a Boy Scout, and once he was nearly inducted into the La Salle Academy marching band, simply because of his height. In grammar school he had recited lugubrious patriotic verse from the Great War, and a friend's uncle had once proudly displayed a buttocks scar from that war. But altogether he was happy his parents had sent him to schools without R.O.T.C. programs. Standing in line was not on his list of favorite things to do ("CG" I).

O'Connor said nothing about how he got into the Coast Guard, other than the fact that he simply enlisted. Whereas his memories of entering Notre Dame and radio were hazy, he simply kept mum about early September 1942. His Registration Certificate shows that on January 16 of that year the Woonsocket draft board had classified him as 1-B, then moved him up to 1-A (fit for service) on February 10, and then back to 1-B on February 26. Such are the ways of draft boards. The 1-B was for his less-than-perfect eyesight.[2]

The "Coast Guard" manuscript covers only the first of his three war years, but it is a detailed account, even though he cannot divulge some locations, and it is his best writing to date. Indeed, whenever O'Connor turned to straightforward autobiographical writing (which was not very often), his prose is refreshed and focused. At any rate, the untitled document known as the "Coast Guard" manuscript provides the best picture of his early wartime duty, and the most detailed account of any year in his life. It was written in 1943, probably during the summer, and consists of about 150 pages divided into twenty-six uniform chapters of five or six pages each. This short, unvarying chapter length most likely was a

---

1. Throughout this chapter, "CG" and/or chapter in Roman numerals and page number will be used to indicate the "Coast Guard" manuscript; EOCP 23.
2. EOCP 24.

Dr. John V. O'Connor with "Sonny" in his Coast Guard uniform during World War II. *Courtesy of Barbara O'Connor Burrell.*

habit formed from the sketches and skits of his radio days. The manuscript apparently was a completed work intended for publication, because across the top of the first page is the written message of the Coast Guard censor: "No objection to publication. H.B.T. 9/1/43." Many such "first year" accounts were published in the early years of the war in order to boost morale and enlistments. O'Connor's work was in a lighter, more skeptical vein, and its passing the censor is a tribute to the relaxed atmosphere he found in his branch of the service. Although the manuscript was never published, he evidently tried hard, because it has a shopworn appearance.

The main theme O'Connor unfolds in his manuscript is that even in wartime an unmilitary man has it pretty good in the Coast Guard. No wonder there was no trouble with the censor! He begins with a quick review of his pampered high school and college years, when isolationism and not militarism was in fashion. He also mentions his uncertainties, after college, about a career. There is no confident stance about being a writer, now that three years of rejection slips have had their chastening effect. Back in 1939 an aunt had suggested the priesthood. A college chum had urged the insurance world on him. Neither calling worked on him. His "formal introduction" to the war was through his radio war work, which he regards as suspect jingoism laced with overheated proletarian rhetoric (II, 1). He thanks the "old sulphur matches" by which he read Horatio Alger in his boyhood for his less-than-20/20 vision and the early deferment. Once he did try to enlist in the Army. When he emphasized his radio talents along with his English major and philosophy minor as good training for Army radio work, the recruiting sergeant did not comprehend. Around July of 1942 he waived the vision deferment and enlisted as a First Class Seaman (equivalent to a corporal) in the Temporary Reserve of the Coast Guard. In the Boston headquarters of the First Coast Guard District, at 2:00 P.M. on September 10, O'Connor and his Woonsocket friend Charles Carroll were formally sworn into the service "for the duration and six months" (III, 3-IV, 1).

Shortly afterward his group of thirty enlistees marched in incongruous civilian clothes through the downtown streets while kids taunted them in flat Boston accents (III, 5). The tall twenty-four-year-old O'Connor must have experienced some twinges at the turn his life was taking; on the other hand, he could have been in the jungles of Guadalcanal. Late in the afternoon they arrived at their temporary quarters in the old Brunswick Hotel, where O'Connor was to spend his first night in the city that would eventually become his own, and whose tribes and mores were to be his fictional domain.

The old Brunswick had seen better days, as had much of the city. Back in the twenties the hotel was known for its romantic soft lights and was a favorite of George Jessel, the comedian. Wartime had transformed it into a gloomy, stripped-down barracks, where the men slept twelve to a room in triple bunks. O'Connor admits to a fleeting civilian depression; his first impressions of Boston were understandably not favorable (V).

There followed the usual hours of standing in lines, but at least the uniform actually fit his "highly irregular" frame. To his surprise he and Charles Carroll got forty-eight-hour liberty on their second day, and so they dashed down to Woonsocket with their belongings in a "Millie's Lingerie" bag, which served for the duffel bag yet to be issued. He was especially glad to see his "two sisters." (By now he customarily referred to Pat Greene, age twelve, as a sibling.) Notably lacking in his account is the reaction of his parents, especially his anti-Roosevelt father. O'Connor slept late; his war was turning out not too badly (VI).

Back at the Brunswick they were subjected to a few days of training, which mostly consisted of various kinds of indoctrination. Swearing, a vice with which O'Connor seldom had problems, was particularly frowned on. To vary the fare, the men marched four blocks for drilling on the Boston Common, which traditionally had served as a parade ground, and which O'Connor was to enjoy so much in peacetime. A drill instructor once genially called him "Long John Carradine," in reference to the Hollywood actor. Such was the extent of O'Connor's first boot camp in a branch of the service he was beginning to like (VII).

After these rigors, O'Connor and Carroll got their first assignment by volunteering for it: Cape Cod Beach Patrol. They must have wondered aloud whether all wars were conducted in such a fashion. O'Connor had only been once before to "the Cape," as everyone in southern New England calls the sandy glacial deposit that loops into the dark Atlantic. That visit had been for a week with college friends back in the summer of 1938. O'Connor did not realize it yet, but in the space of a week the Coast Guard had helped to introduce him to his future winter home in Boston and his summer one at Cape Cod.

During the early months of America's entry into the war, German submarines had enjoyed good hunting off the East Coast before military authorities learned from the British experience to black out coastal lights in order to prevent ships' silhouettes from betraying themselves. A lot of oil washed up on the Cape's beaches during the summer of 1942. But the Beach Patrol was more interested in submarines landing spies and saboteurs on the long, deserted beaches during the fall and winter months. That summer German saboteurs had been put ashore on Long Island and Florida, and so the "sand-pounders" had to be alert.

O'Connor and Carroll were stationed at the newly created Brewster Coast Guard Patrol in East Brewster, on the "bay" or "cold" side, just before the Cape's arm turns abruptly north. A few days after his arrival, O'Connor wrote home. As indicated earlier, O'Connor was not much of a letter writer, and so one cannot help dwelling on his few letters that have survived. The one-page letter is written on wartime stationary provided by the USO. "IDLE GOSSIP SINKS SHIPS" is printed diagonally in bold red ink across the enve-

lope as a reminder to servicemen writing home that spies could be anywhere, along with the far-fetched implication that somehow those messages
home could be easily transmitted to submarines offshore. O'Connor always
kept a healthy sense of amusement about this paranoia. O'Connor opens his
letter by recounting his "good fortune" at abandoning "the Boston torture
chamber" of the Brunswick. On only his fifth day on the Cape he writes that
"I am already crazy about it." (O'Connor was lucky to arrive on the Cape in
early autumn, one of its most enticing seasons, when, back then at least, the
summer crowds would have left to allow the "real Cape" to reassert itself.)
He likes their quarters, a doctor's big, beautiful, heated summer house,
whose exact location he dutifully omits. Only seven live there now, but soon
they will be up to a full complement of sixteen: "a fine small unit, which is
the ideal thing." We can detect here in O'Connor's preference for a small
contingent all living in the same house an early deep-seated longing for a
sense of family wherever he went. Indeed, the whole arrangement in East
Brewster hardly seems military at all: "We live almost as civilians"; the commanding officer is "thoroughly a human being, and . . . does not believe in
observing every manual regulation that was ever formulated"; they have "a
great deal of liberty"; and so altogether they "enjoy [themselves] immensely."
The work schedule, though at present irregular, will probably be eight days
on and two days off. He says hello to "Bobby, Pat and Jack." A postscript asks
pardon for the pencil because their only pen was in use.[3]

Once the routine of duty set in, however, the Cape lost some of its charm.
As the autumn lengthened into winter, the seacoast turned bleak and cold,
and night patrols were especially uncomfortable and eerie under the new
blackout conditions ("CG," IX). Again he is careful not to divulge the routes
of these patrols, although they were obviously on beaches and dunes. In an
article written fourteen years later, O'Connor recalled a few items that probably would not have passed the Coast Guard censor. The doctor's house had
been built for only four people after all, but eventually housed thirty-two
Coast Guardsmen in "Brunswick" fashion. Beach patrol often meant twenty-
mile hikes, much of it in tiring sand. They never found a spy. However,
he did have one little adventure. One night in the strange darkness another
Coast Guardsman on patrol fired a revolver shot over his head, because
O'Connor looked so "different." After this brush with friendly fire, his closest
encounter with combat, of a sort, O'Connor took pains to look less "different." He also seems to have been mildly annoyed with a veteran of World War

3. Edwin O'Connor, letter to Dr. and Mrs. J. V. O'Connor, September 20, 1942, courtesy
of Barbara O'Connor Burrell.

I with whom he often patrolled. This much older reservist was full of tiresome war stories, his own dubious heroism, and bawdy songs. He enjoyed viciously stubbing out his cigarettes in a cottage ash tray that was made in Japan. His favorite trick was to stand sharply at attention and then salute smartly while tucking in his stomach in order to make his pants drop.[4] Such entertainment doubtless wore thin in a hurry.

What entertainment the men had was meager. By hitchhiking they could get to a movie house four miles away and take in the steady fare of B movies, which included Roy Rogers in abundance. One night when the power went out a civilian led the movie house in a rousing "God Bless America" and old favorites. That impromptu songfest was "the highlight of my night life on the Cape" ("CG," X, 7). A sympathetic mate began taking stray animals, some half-wild, into the cramped barracks. Three smelly dogs were quickly named Warren, Calvin, and Herbert after the last three Republican presidents; it would appear that the Coast Guard was mostly Democratic. O'Connor took some interest in eccentricity among the locals, especially a small group of paranoids who were convinced that a local amateur astronomer was spying for Hitler (XI). O'Connor's favorite pastime of reading was now "conducted along random and uncoordinated lines" because of the irregular hours. Besides Thoreau's *Cape Cod,* he read a little H. G. Wells, Will Durant, and P. G. Wodehouse. One day two ladies arrived at the cottage with their bookmobile and began to dispense their limited stock. When O'Connor asked for humor a la Thurber, he was presented with a book by Eleanor Roosevelt: the Cape was then a Republican bastion (XII). Mimi McConchie, now the archivist for Brewster, was sixteen at the time and remembers being a USO hostess at the house with other girls. The Coast Guard truck would even bring them to little parties at the house; she remembers the dogs barking a good deal. She also recalls that the area was then called by the Dickensian name of Bleaker Downs.[5] Nancy Carlson, also of Brewster, fondly remembers the men as "well-behaved" and well fed by townspeople, and that "Eddie" was called "the Commander" by the men, probably as a tribute to his height and bearing.[6]

In December O'Connor and some others were transferred for a little more boot camp at the Recruit Training Station in Provincetown, on the tip of the Cape. It was now cold and dark winter, inside and out. Once again

4. Edwin O'Connor, untitled article, *Boston Sunday Post,* September 23, 1956, 1–2.
5. Mimi McConchie, letter to author, March 21, 2000.
6. Nancy Abbot Carlson, letter to author, November 7, 2001. Nancy Carlson also informs me that the house was owned by a Doctor William Curtis and was close to the beach on Point of Rocks Road.

O'Connor admits that the Coast Guard version of boot camp was mild indeed; there was good conversation, and he was gaining a new appreciation of the Coast Guard tradition of weeding out petty tyrants (XIII). While at Provincetown he was promoted to "Seaman O'Connor, Squad Leader," chiefly because of his height; the promotion carried little responsibility, which was fine with him (XIV).

Shortly before Christmas O'Connor got a three-day leave. He and a friend, whom he refers to only as George, wasted no time in getting on a train at Boston for New York, where he experienced "the most famous evening in my young and untested life." The big night began with a disastrous restaurant dinner with a blind date fatally named Eloise who, while quite pretty, ate much and talked little. O'Connor reveals some insecurity about women when he tells his friend that Eloise must dislike him, at which his friend assures him that he is mistaken. After dinner, they all took in the Fred Allen Show, which O'Connor must have regarded as the high point. But quickly things began to go awry. O'Connor and his pal were in uniform, which so far had made little impression on Eloise. But during the live broadcast, Eloise became suddenly charmed by O'Connor, who, George had told her, was actually a writer for the very show they were witnessing. (George must have known of O'Connor's attempts to break into big-time radio.) O'Connor reluctantly went along with the gag, on the theory that Jack Benny could be funny because he was known to be so, a trusted recipe for success in politics as well. After the show the foursome took in a Latin-style floor show at a night club, where O'Connor notes disapprovingly how the blue jokes contrasted with the clean humor of Fred Allen. O'Connor would eventually become adept at describing people's entrances into a gathering, and thus his description of the comedian's entrance is worth quoting: "He was one big smile, and he flung himself out into the center of the floor, weaving and bobbing like a prize-fighter who has seen too many fists." Flamboyance of the flesh was something O'Connor could not easily abide. To make matters worse, the nightclub's spotlight suddenly fell on O'Connor when the comedian mistakenly called upon this naval hero of the Solomon Islands to take a bow. (Navy and Coast Guard uniforms were commonly confused.) For the second time that evening O'Connor played along reluctantly, but he ends this episode with apologies to "Mr. Allen" for the earlier imposture (XVI).

Back in Provincetown, Christmas Day 1942 began with O'Connor's being drafted into the choir at the local Catholic church during the 7:00 Mass. He freely admits to singing wildly off key, but with gusto; he was not called up for choir loft action again. He thoroughly enjoyed a big Christmas dinner (XVII).

By January O'Connor was in the Regular Reserve of the Coast Guard. He underwent his sixth physical, placed woefully low on a mechanical aptitude test, and contemptuously endured the psychiatric examination (XVIII). Then it was back to the Brewster patrol for most of January 1943. He now positively disliked the Cape's monotonous wind, cold, and ice; few places are bleaker than a summer resort in midwinter, especially to a self-confessed summer devotee. Even the conversation in the house had changed from little talk of war to futile speculation on its duration (XIX).

O'Connor left the Cape in early February, and would not return until a few years after the war, and then to a different section. He left with mixed emotions. "I am a sentimental fellow who is not easily torn from his roots," he writes, while admitting that these roots were shallow and chilly. His Coast Guard career now entered a new phase in Boston, where he underwent special training in the Chemical Warfare Branch of the Coast Guard. Curiously enough, he looked forward to this change, most likely because of its Boston venue, and he did have a good teacher for his week-long class. Each of the thirty-two students had to make an oral presentation, but O'Connor says nothing about his own (XX).

O'Connor was one of eight from the class sent to the Edgewood Arsenal in Maryland for additional course work to train promising instructors; it lasted from February 7 to March 25. He also took a few classes at the Curtis Bay Training Station nearby. Since the Arsenal was actually an Army facility where the various services could train, O'Connor admits to some apprehension at being in the Army, in a sense. But in spite of the surrounding prospect of endless Chesapeake mud flats, O'Connor again was in luck, as easy work and an early thaw lifted his spirits. He even got to take a short course in meteorology, where he quickly learned to "predict" the weather by simply consulting the *Baltimore Sun*. He easily made his customary circle of friends, and was especially taken with a Walter Dobbins from South Carolina, who was a marvelous story teller (XXI). Together they often enjoyed the culinary delights of nearby Baltimore, where H. L. Mencken, another O'Connor favorite, wrote so much. He confesses that he saw Baltimore largely through its restaurants and hotels, admitting that on one occasion he consumed three full-course dinners between noon and 6:00 P.M., and this in spite of the fact that the budding gourmand claims he customarily ate little (XXII).

O'Connor dwells on one class at the Arsenal in particular. An Army Lieutenant Grimes conducted a five-day course in educational methods for the future instructors. In the class Grimes adopted a phony casualness, offering the students cigarettes. (O'Connor says he took one, but says nothing about lighting up.) O'Connor thought he saw a chance to get light teaching duties, and in "a moment of brazen mendacity" he told Grimes that he had been a teaching assistant under Professor Rufus Rauch at Notre Dame. This is the only time O'Connor even remotely alluded to his truncated postgraduate weeks, and at least he left Frank O'Malley out of the deception, which did not succeed anyway. He goes on to mock Grimes's normal school prattle about the importance of creating bonds with students, "the process of learning," and the Dooley and Dietz efficiency system used at General Motors. Remarkably for that time in Maryland, the class was racially integrated by the presence of a "colored chap from New York." As at Boston, everyone was required to make an oral presentation, but again O'Connor fails to describe his own (XXIII). Toward the end of the week a big "academic dispute" broke out among the students about which was more humane in war—explosives or poison gas. O'Connor remained neutral on this one, as in fact he tended to be whenever discussions on big issues became heated, because he instinctively avoided situations which might impair friendships. On March 20 he graduated from the Arsenal school with a new rating of Specialist, Second Class, Chemical Warfare. At the closing ceremony he sang "Semper Paratus," badly but again with gusto (XXIV).

For the rest of the war O'Connor was stationed at the headquarters of the First Coast Guard District in Boston. In his first assignment he used his Edgewood Arsenal training to instruct Coast Guard cutter crews about gas masks and the like. Although he never put out to sea, he often had to work under bizarre conditions aboard ships at the Boston Navy Yard, where he had to compete with welders and riveters doing repair work. His first assignment was on the *Harriet Lane,* a ship with an inauspicious history obscurely connected to cannibalism in Australia. O'Connor seems to have performed reasonably well as an instructor in spite of his self-confessed klutziness. Moreover, he was now settling comfortably into Boston, albeit in unusual wartime circumstances, and was now realizing for the first time in his life that, for him, city life was indeed preferable to the country. And of all the cities he had known, Boston was the one to make his home. An indication of his love of Boston duty came in early summer when he actually became alarmed at rumors of being sent back to the Beach Patrol on the Cape in the summer (XXV).

The last chapter of the manuscript comes to a few modest conclusions. Civilians worry more than servicemen, he claims; but then his was not terribly hazardous duty. The food, he dutifully records, is not bad at all and the beef is certainly plentiful. He then curiously laments the difficulty of obtaining good domestic help during the war, noting that his own mother has gone through almost a dozen maids in a single month. Whether this last remark is an example of bland complacency or subtle irony is hard to tell. He ends by plugging the genuinely democratic life of the Coast Guard, even if it is not as democratic as the K-9 corps—this last a possible little dig at service propaganda that somehow got past the censor (XXVI).

The "Coast Guard" manuscript displays some elements of O'Connor's emerging style. Paragraphs and chapters are crafted with great deliberation. The tone is seldom introspective. There is a slightly oldish air about his style, although this tactic is often in the service of humor. Dialogue, although not used often, is well done. As to content, the work is hardly in the category of war story, because there is minimal conflict, little action, and no spectacular event. The eye and ear of the future novelist is instead attentive to the little incongruities and mishaps of life under unusual conditions. The final impression left on the reader is of a mildly amusing piece which has avoided the Big One—both in combat and in theme.

O'Connor's career as a chemical warfare instructor only lasted a few months at most. By July of 1943 he was working in the Coast Guard Public Relations Office, located during the war in the Boston Insurance Exchange Building at 40 Broad Street. O'Connor wrote little about the next two years of his war service, but at least someone had finally recognized his talents as an announcer and writer. He saved little memorabilia from this period other than a few Coast Guard concert programs and photographs; his official record discloses even less.

Desk duty at 40 Broad Street was performed by a staff that fluctuated from twelve to a peak of twenty-two when O'Connor was transferred there. Most of the work consisted of writing press releases concerning Coast Guard activities in the New England area, gathering news about Coast Guardsmen for hometown newspapers, and organizing the frequent public speeches, parades, and concerts that were such a big feature on the home front. To better handle local angle stories, Public Relations had in its ranks several newsmen and photographers from the Boston papers.[7] Soon O'Connor began to make friendships and valuable contacts in Boston press and radio circles that would serve him well for some years after the war.

O'Connor's desk work was enlivened by his endeavors at producing con-

---

7. For details about the work of this office, I am indebted to Richard W. Peuser of Old Military and Civil Records, Textual Archives Services Division of the National Archives and Records Administration, for forwarding to me *The Coast Guard at War, vol. XXIII, Public Relations* from the National Archives.

The normally reserved O'Connor had a pronounced tendency for self-dramatization, as seen in this photo, circa 1945, taken at Boston's Hatch Shell, *Courtesy of Barbara O'Connor Burrell.*

certs at the Hatch Memorial Shell on the Charles River Esplanade, at which the young Arthur Fiedler, already synonymous with "the Shell," conducted. O'Connor sometimes did the announcing also. He saved a large photograph of himself clowning during off hours in civilian garb: standing solo with arms outstretched on center stage inside the Shell, he pretends to soar to the heavens like Caruso. On the reverse he wrote, "Artiste O'Connor at Shell in Boston."[8] O'Connor reveled in playing the ham. He also saved a program for the United States Coast Guard Day festivities on Sunday, August 1, 1943, which consisted of a Fiedler concert, Coast Guard water craft demonstrations

8. Photograph courtesy of Barbara O'Connor Burrell.

on the river, and a speech by Mayor Maurice Tobin.[9] This appearance by Tobin may have been O'Connor's first glimpse of the politician whom many take as the model for Skeffington's challenger, Kevin McCluskey, in *The Last Hurrah*. O'Connor also announced at Coast Guard Port of Boston band concerts at the Parkman Bandstand, in the middle of Boston Common. A photograph shows O'Connor on the bandstand, in uniform and sunglasses, studying the program. O'Connor's family often came up from Woonsocket for both the Hatch Shell and Boston Common concerts. O'Connor also announced the weekly Coast Guard radio program on Boston's station WORL. These broadcasts usually included USO-touring radio, stage, or movie stars, many of whom made for good stories back at the office. He saved one large glossy photo of himself beaming with a radiant Alexis Smith, who was then just hitting her acting fame after appearing with Errol Flynn in *Gentleman Jim*. O'Connor had an eye for statuesque women, although this photo is not too kind to his own frame, bulging out of his Coast Guard uniform.[10]

Among the office personnel three people were especially close to O'Connor. They helped form important contacts for postwar work, and in one case also provided a fund of political lore for his novels. Louis Samaha had been a young reporter for the *Boston Record-American* back in the 1920s, but had lost the job in the Depression. In 1940 he joined the Coast Guard and worked in the Boston office until the war's end. He also used his drawing and cartooning skills for a G.I. magazine aimed for the Northeast market. "Sam" had many contacts with Boston journalists. Years after the war he remembered O'Connor fondly, especially for his set vaudevillian routine for sneaking out of the office for ice cream: O'Connor would burst into Samaha's office, do a five-second tap dance, extend an exaggerated stage arm, and ask, "Sam, do you ever have the feeling that you wanted to go?" Together they would take many unauthorized breaks at a local ice cream shop, where O'Connor would devour huge quantities; ice cream was one of his salient weaknesses.[11] That mention of O'Connor's signature vaudevillian shuffle is the first such recorded anywhere. Another good friend in Public Relations was Rudolph Elie, also from the Boston press world. Elie was a man of many talents who could never settle on one and develop it. The friendship with O'Connor would last well after the war, until Elie's early death. His sense of humor jibed with O'Connor's, as seen in this spoof of wartime censorship of letters between servicemen:

9. EOCP 24.
10. EOCP 24.
11. Louis Samaha, letter to Veniette O'Connor, March 27, 1968, EOCP 422.

My dear Greene:

It
However
                    was
inasmuch it
    to be
And that, in substance, is[12]

The most important contact for O'Connor's future development was Louis J. Brems, one-time vaudevillian, former advance man for Mayor Curley, official city greeter for Mayor Tobin, and now O'Connor's superior officer. Brems was a born raconteur who laced his stories with the accents and flamboyance of the showman. O'Connor was hooked: here was politics and showbiz wrapped into one. O'Connor did not realize it at the time, of course, but Brems was giving him almost daily installments of material that would work its way into *The Last Hurrah*.[13] Brems himself shows up briefly as a Coast Guard Public Relations officer named Hanley in an unpublished sketch entitled "The Interview," which O'Connor wrote probably in 1944 or 1945.[14] Hanley/Brems warns an interviewer from a men's adventure magazine that the Coast Guardsman to be interviewed has the "original tangential mind." The interviewer has this confirmed when the subject quickly makes him a "participant in some mysterious, revolving game, in which the principal idea was to understand nothing and arrive nowhere." The subject's name is Collio, and there is little doubt that he is modeled closely on an irrepressible Boston eccentric named Clement Norton, because they share the same physical characteristics ("big, dark, hairy, and unfairly ugly") and more importantly the same daft mentality. Clem Norton was another political raconteur in a city that made politics into entertainment. After the war O'Connor would cultivate him as his chief provider of political anecdotes, especially those of the more conspiratorial variety which always walked a fine line between veracity and fantasy. If "The Interview" can be taken as having any basis in fact, it may imply that Louis Brems had introduced O'Connor to Clem Norton. In *The Last Hurrah* Louis Brems became Skeffington's advance man, Cuke Gillen, and Clem Norton was immortalized as Charlie Hennessey. O'Connor owed Brems and Norton much.

12. Rudolph Elie, letter to Edwin O'Connor, April 25, 1945, EOCP 140.
13. Rank, *O'Connor*, 24–25.
14. EOCP 29.

O'Connor's younger brother, Jack, served in the Navy during the war. His education had been more local than his older brother's, but markedly poorer in achievement. From 1937 to 1941 he attended Mount St. Charles High School in his hometown; he also took a few summer courses at La Salle Academy. Jack then enrolled as a commuter student at Providence College in September 1941, but his four accelerated wartime semesters at the Catholic college were a washout. According to his widow, Jack was groomed by his father for the medical profession, now that his older brother was obviously not taking that route. Furthermore, Jack was more of a local type, for whom a distant education had no appeal. His fun-loving, easy-going nature somehow was more appealing to his father than the more studiously serious way of "Sonny," and so the two did a lot together, especially during summer vacations.[15] But the academic life was not for Jack, and he was dropped from Providence College in December 1942. His academic record is almost the inverse of his brother's: whereas Edwin maintained an admirably high consistency, Jack floundered at almost every subject. Clearly, he was no student. His "sister" Pat remembers him as much more interested in girls and sports.[16] Whatever he did pick up in his biology classes got him placed in the Medical Corps of the Navy. Once he came home with his service number tattooed on his arm, a common fad among sailors, and had to endure the wrath of his father.[17] Jack's little rebellion was a sign of his independence from his father. Sonny was unable to be so casual.

After working strenuously for thirty-four years, in 1944, at age sixty, Dr. O'Connor had to slow down after suffering his first heart attack. He practiced only on a part-time basis for the rest of his career, mostly at his home office. At about the same time, "Bobby" was accepted at Emmanuel College, a Catholic women's school in Boston's Fenway section, where she matriculated in September 1945.

On September 10, 1945, exactly three years after his formal swearing in, and a week after Japan's surrender on V-J Day, O'Connor received his "notice of separation from the U.S. Naval Service-Coast Guard." His honorable discharge lists him at the rank of Specialist First Class, Public Relations. He was one of the last to leave the office which by early September had only a skeleton staff.

15. Beatrice O'Connor, telephone interview, September 10, 1999.
16. Pat Greene Thibodeau, telephone interview, September 1999.
17. William Gilbert, personal interview, summer 1999.

A few times during the next couple of years O'Connor can be detected as feeling a vague uneasiness over his wartime service. Nobody had to tell him that his had been a very easy war in a branch of the armed services which in fact had provided an arduous training and hazardous ship duty for most. While he evinces no outright guilt, what surfaces is a fear that his elders, father included, might have talked about his service in a mildly deprecatory fashion. A decade later he could more casually admit in public that "my own days in the Coast Guard were notoriously untriumphant."[18] He kept a newspaper clipping about his friend Francis Carroll, who had been drafted from the family hardware business in Woonsocket and had received a battlefield promotion to Army lieutenant for heroism in North Africa.[19] The article dwells on the pride of Carroll's father, and one cannot help wondering what O'Connor thought, because no such encomium came his way. However, O'Connor's uncomfortable mood passed quickly enough. He never showed any bitterness about three years of his life unfairly spent out of circulation; after all, thousands of other young Americans his age would never circulate again. O'Connor preserved a somewhat curious distance from the war. For him World War II was never a crusade or a cause, but rather a task to be done, even if in a bewildering way and by questionable people. But outright denunciation of militarism or nationalism was not yet in the Irish-American vocabulary; that would take another twenty years, and even then O'Connor, along with so many veterans of World War II, kept aloof from the crusades of Senator Eugene McCarthy and Robert Kennedy in early 1968.

Except for the "Coast Guard" manuscript, O'Connor wrote little during those three years. It was now more than six years since his declaration to Father Ward that he was going to be a writer. Now twenty-seven, with body and spirits intact, he would have to get another day job, and along with it time again to write.

18. Edwin O'Connor, "About Television," *Boston Post,* August 24, 1954, 15.
19. EOCP 305.

CHAPTER FIVE

❧ Adopting Boston
(1945–1949)

Edwin O'Connor's discharge papers from the Coast Guard list his new address as 194 Beacon Street. Like so many who have visited or studied in New England's unofficial capital city, he had simply decided to stay in Boston. Since leaving Notre Dame he had lived and worked in half a dozen places in as many years, and so at age twenty-seven his self-confessed need for a rooted life found the traditions of Boston, from its dry wit and brick sidewalks to its unique politics and journalistic eddies, congenial enough to explore for a while. So far no other city had awakened his literary or even journalistic instincts, but Boston was to do so, even though in all his fiction he never once names the city he obviously has so much in mind.

Boston in 1945 was very different from today's prospering financial and educational city. After its moment of Revolutionary Era fame, the city was quickly eclipsed in importance by New York. Even though Boston expanded both demographically and geographically throughout the nineteenth century, it did not wholeheartedly nourish the vibrant industries that were creating the new wealth of the country, and so it never became much of a factory city. It did carry on with old callings such as shipping, including the China trade, and increasingly with banking and finance. To compound matters, the terrible famine of the 1840s in Ireland drove waves of desperate refugees into a city which the Boston historian Thomas O'Connor (no relation) described as:

[the] one city in the entire world where an Irish Catholic, under any circumstance, should never, *ever,* set foot. . . . [Boston] was an American city with an intensely homogeneous Anglo-Saxon character, an inbred hostility toward people who were Irish, a fierce and violent revulsion against all things Catholic, and an economic system that precluded most forms of unskilled labor. Boston was a city that rejected the Irish from the start and saw no way in which people of that ethnic background could ever be fully assimilated into the prevailing American culture.[1]

1. Thomas O'Connor, *The Boston Irish: A Political History* (Boston: Northeastern University Press, 1995), xv–xvi.

The stage was set for one of the most bitter and lengthy political conflicts in American urban history, and in the early twentieth century James Michael Curley, transformed by O'Connor into Frank Skeffington, was preparing his role in that struggle.

In matters cultural, Boston first attained a borrowed importance from the nearby activities of Transcendentalist writers during the mid-nineteenth century "Renaissance," which for thirty years was closely tied to the city's Abolitionist agitation. After the Civil War, however, Boston quickly fell into the inertia of cultures that preen themselves too early on their past accomplishments, meager though these may have actually been in Boston's case. The triumph of the Boston Abolitionists was so sudden and absolute in 1865 that there seemed little work to do except to become genial and genteel. Thoreau was dead, Emerson was passing into his dotage, and the generation of "schoolroom poets" and social novelists offered thin fare. To be sure, the city's elite promoted culture as it saw it during the rest of the century, founding the Museum of Fine Arts, the Boston Public Library, and the renowned Boston Symphony in its splendid home at Symphony Hall. Boston adopted a sense of culture that adulated Europe in general and England in particular. The calls for an original American culture preached by Emerson and practiced by Thoreau and Whitman were forgotten in the rush to become the "Athens of America." In their haste to endow the past and sing their paeans in temples of a borrowed order, they left the home fires to die out. Boston's Gilded Age culture was becoming Anglophile in political outlook and nostalgically Romantic in cultural affairs. To take an example: when Boston's red brick, neoclassical Symphony Hall opened in 1900 the single name of "Beethoven" was enscrolled high above the proscenium. The building had a stolid London look, and while its praise of the world's greatest composer may have been accurate enough, the singular honor accorded him seems curious at best in the city that had fought more than one American revolution.

Writers then and since have not been kind to the overlords of what Oliver Wendell Holmes wryly called "hub of the solar system." William Dean Howells depicted the city's intra-Yankee tensions in *The Rise of Silas Lapham* (1885). In 1917 T. S. Eliot's nine-line "The *Boston Evening Transcript*" used the old Brahmin newspaper to symbolize its effete readership. J. P. Marquand's wonderfully ironic Pulitzer-winning 1936 novel, *The Late George Apley,* is practically the last word on the subject and was something of an influence on O'Connor, particularly the conflict between Yankee and Irishman, and even more so the conflict between father and son. Apley's own son knows that by 1920 "Boston has become a backwater in which the greatest activity is the conserving of wealth and the raking of literary ash heaps."[2] In his new city O'Connor's first literary efforts indicated that he too would join in this critique of Beacon Hill and Back Bay, but as it turned out he had a different angle on the city and a wider terrain to map. His early efforts to insert himself into Boston's literary culture by creating himself as an outsider critic of Brahmin Boston would eventually be superceded by his selection of the Boston Irish as his natural subject. Still, he did not abandon his earlier interests, and in any case did not wish to sever his lifelines to Boston's literary set. Consequently, he eventually realized that the story of the Boston Irish lay precisely in their conflict with the Boston Yankees. This long adaptation to Boston even as he probed its various surfaces would be a ten-year effort and will be the substance of the next four chapters.

The modest rent for O'Connor's first boarding house room at 194 Beacon Street would surprise anyone seeking to live in the area today, when most of Beacon Hill and the Back Bay are Boston's premier upscale districts, as indeed they once were intended to be. But Boston by mid-twentieth century had reached the bottom of a long financial decline that had converted whole blocks of grandly planned Back Bay townhouses into cheap lodging for transients and students. The fact that Mayor James Michael Curley's fiscal policies in no small way contributed to this decline was probably not lost on O'Connor, but those policies did afford him the opportunity to take up his first civilian residence in a once-proud "red brick."

He was settling into what would be "Edwin O'Connor's neighborhood" of addresses clustered within a mile of each other, most within a few blocks— and close to Boston's literary world as well. For his remaining twenty-three years he lived in eight different locations. Most of his addresses form a roll call of prominent Boston locations: twice in a row on Beacon Street in the Back Bay (1945–46); Brimmer Street on the bottom of Beacon Hill (1946– 49); Marlborough Street in the Back Bay (1949–55); Beacon Street again, but now on Beacon Hill (1955–62); Chestnut Street on Beacon Hill (1962–65); Back Bay again on Marlborough Street (1965–67); and Commonwealth Avenue (1967–68). This pattern of addresses closely corresponds to O'Connor's years of obscurity, eventual triumph, and incipient decline. But to live in this neighborhood was extremely important to O'Connor because it provided practical living arrangements at all stages of his career, helped to foster important contacts in his own inimitable way, and established an agreeable mi-

2. John P. Marquand, *The Late George Apley* (1936; New York: Random House, 1940), 280.

lieu in which to write. And always in the background was the fact that these addresses, especially the highly fashionable later ones, meant that he had "arrived."

Tourists who are taken on the mandatory route around this charming old Boston are usually surprised that such an extensive urban area could be so well preserved. There is nothing in America quite like this homogenous district, on average about a third of a mile wide, that runs southwest from the State House atop Beacon Hill to Kenmore Square two miles away. Handsome three- and four-story townhouses and apartments blend gracefully their eighteenth-century Georgian and nineteenth-century Parisian styles. Red bricks, black shutters, stone steps, boot scrapers, brass nameplates, iron railings, and gas lamps are the icons of this Boston. A few restaurants, hotels, and business establishments maintain low profiles; they hardly need to advertise anyway. Venerable points of interest like the gold-domed State House, Boston Common with the adjacent Public Gardens, and the broad Mall on Commonwealth Avenue are all proud features of this gentle, though slightly dowdy cityscape. It was also the neighborhood where Irish urban myth, so beloved by Irish American politicians even in the late twentieth century, holds that many a front window prominently displayed the infamous "NO IRISH" sign. However, no photographic evidence of this supposedly ubiquitous sign exists.

To pay the rent at 194 Beacon Street, O'Connor used contacts from his Coast Guard years and got back into radio. For about a year he worked as a producer for Boston's old Yankee Network radio station WNAC, which was then one of the city's prominent stations, but which is now long gone. WNAC had an unusually high number of Rhode Islanders, like Walter Hackett, on its staff and this connection too no doubt helped. This first postwar year is the most obscure of his adult life, and thirteen years later O'Connor himself admitted to only a hazy memory of his work at the station. Technically he was a writer-producer at WNAC, but in fact everything he did was ultimately controlled by the station's salesmen.[3] Two observations about his memory here. First, we note again that haziness about transitions in his life which he does not want to dwell on; and second, it is clear that whatever attractions radio once had for him were not recaptured in the more commercialized broadcasting industry which the war had enhanced so much. Around this time he told Walter Hackett, "Writing for radio is like writing

3. Edwin O'Connor, interview with Frank Falacci, *Boston Sunday Globe*, August 9, 1959, 37.

on ice. We should both get out of it."[4] At his first opportunity O'Connor was prepared to jump for good.

In early 1946 he moved to another boarding house, a few blocks down at 426 Beacon Street. This address of only a few months was his most distant from the inner O'Connor orbit. Over the mansard roofs O'Connor might have seen the steel skeleton of the first John Hancock Building rising over the Back Bay. This postwar harbinger of a renewing Boston, a stubby twenty-six-story building of prewar design, would remain the city's only real skyscraper until the mid-1960s, when Boston sprang upwards.

Some time right after the end of the war O'Connor began work on his first novel, or at least the first we know about. Unfinished and untitled, the ninety-nine pages of the "Anthony Cantwell" manuscript consist of seven chapters and two mostly irrelevant prologues.[5] Hugh Rank dates the manuscript to O'Connor's Coast Guard days, citing the fact that some chapters are typed on the blank side of Coast Guard-printed material.[6] But this dating can be challenged on several counts. As one of the few personnel left in the Coast Guard office at war's end, O'Connor probably had simply hauled off some of the plentiful stacks of paper waiting to be thrown out. Secondly, the story explicitly takes place two years after the war's end, in 1947, although in this regard O'Connor may have uncharacteristically projected his story a year or so ahead. More importantly, the story has a definite postwar feel to it; indeed, the whole plot concerns a young demobilized soldier who now must get his first real job. Thus, the best date for the story's composition seems to be from late 1945 to some time in 1946.

The unhappily named Anthony Cantwell is the first of O'Connor's several semi-autobiographical characters, with the possible exception of the narrator in "Friends Are Made in McCabe's." If the truism that first novels are invariably autobiographical holds, then this story provides some illuminating material for O'Connor's transition to Boston's culture. First of all, the story has touches of Evelyn Waugh's early black humor. A big favorite of O'Connor, Waugh was riding high after *Brideshead Revisited* in 1945. Waugh was also a hit with his American publisher, Little, Brown and Company, Boston's premier publisher, to which O'Connor may already have been aspiring. More to the point, the protagonist of the story has some rough similarities to its author, as will many of O'Connor's later protagonists, narra-

---

4. Walter Hackett, "Criticism Broke Long Friendship," *Providence Journal*, December 15, 1969.

5. EOCP 32.   6. Rank, *O'Connor*, 25.

tors, or important secondary characters. Both O'Connor and Cantwell are in their mid-twenties and are temporarily uncertain about a direction in life, like so many vets right after any war. Significantly, however, in one of the prologues O'Connor has Cantwell hail from Massachusetts, not the distant province of Rhode Island, and furthermore confers on him an Anglo name along with a degree from Harvard, though with an English major. Thus far, a partial self-portrait, but with a proper Bostonian upgrading.

As the novel gets under way, Cantwell is dozing on the family couch one month after his return from war. O'Connor abruptly brings on the father who firmly takes charge of his son's future employment. Chapter I marks the first of O'Connor's many portrayals of a determined, authoritarian father under whom the son chafes, usually ineffectually. Jonathan Cantwell is a successful lawyer full of a "grim benevolence" and an "exhausting embrace of . . . altruism." For years he has employed a courtroom manner ("a torturing question-and-answer process") to badger his son into this or that activity and work. In the South Pacific, Anthony had dreaded the inevitable confrontation with his father upon his return home, and had fantasized about subduing his small-sized father: "Breathing bitterness and defiance, his voice hard with a subdued fury, he had forced Jonathan to give way." But as always, Anthony's fantasy quickly crumbles when the father asserts himself, and chapter I ends thus: "For one great and blinding moment, Anthony thought of striking out against his father and revolting. The moment, however, quickly passed, and Anthony Cantwell compromised by feeling extremely sorry for himself." Seldom has the oedipus complex been so plainly rendered. While it is tempting to read a straight autobiographical situation here (the self-made hectoring patriarch of relatively small stature and the veteran son who needs direction), the relationship between fiction and fact is seldom so easy. There is no evidence that any such scene actually transpired between Edwin and John O'Connor. As O'Connor often said, his father never interfered in his chosen careers. But since this pairing of fathers and sons will become such a recurrent pattern, and since it usually shows up with an emotional pressure unlike anything else in the author's output, one cannot help speculate that in some more undetectable region of his mind O'Connor, like many sons with successful self-made fathers, harbored unresolved feelings about his father's dominance. Furthermore, because "Cantwell" comes at the moment of O'Connor's transition to a new life in Boston, which he probably suspected was not wholeheartedly endorsed by his father, we notice from this point in O'Connor's career a tendency to find in older men the favoring paternal figure he needed.

The rest of Anthony Cantwell's story can be quickly summed up. Through his father's political influences Anthony gets a teaching position at St. Mansard College in Fender, Indiana. A curious institution with a checkered past and some odd resemblances to Notre Dame, it seems to be conducting some hush-hush postwar government research on a large scale. Thus begins what promises to combine a satire of academia with a spy novel, while the father-son conflict is left behind. Anthony's career at St. Mansard is as episodic and bewildering as the institution itself, and the novel quickly spins out of control. It is painfully obvious by chapter V that O'Connor does not know where he is taking his story. At one place he crossed out some dialogue and wrote in the margin, "unnecessary crap," an atypical message to himself in both content and diction. His satirical targets are too many and altogether uncoordinated, from the Marine-style physical education class conducted by Beak Burnside (a veteran of both world wars whose name is an inside Rhode Island allusion to that state's bungling General Burnside of Civil War fame), to a group of Y.M.C.A. germ fanatics, to the author of a skeptical philosophical study, *Reluctances,* whom the college president confuses with Cantwell. The manuscript mercifully ends in the middle of chapter VII. O'Connor often said that he seldom wrote with a clear outline in mind, preferring to let the narrative take its course. This method can be fruitful for writing fiction, of course, but satire makes special demands on clarity and control. O'Connor obviously lurches from topic to topic and has no real story to tell, none at least that has much to do with its putative hero. At least O'Connor knew when to stop, and he never referred to this early attempt at a novel again.

In 1981, when he was in his eighties, Edward Weeks, the editor of *Atlantic Monthly* from 1938 to 1966, published his reminiscences, in which he proffered the following memory:

> At a luncheon postwar three close friends, New Englanders of Irish descent, were contemplating their future. "I'm going to run for Congress," said Torbert McDonald [*sic*], former football captain and star halfback at Harvard College, then studying for Law School. . . . "How about you, Eddie?" Edwin O'Connor . . . was equally positive. "As soon as I can get the time," he said, "I'm going to write a novel about Boston." They turned to the third. "I'm going into politics," said John F. Kennedy; "what else can I do?"[7]

---

7. Edward Weeks, *Writers and Friends* (Boston: Atlantic Monthly Press/Little, Brown, 1981), 193.

The confusions here are curious, from that "luncheon postwar" to the misspelling of MacDonald's name. Although all three did realize their dreams, O'Connor was not "close friends" with either man. Kennedy and MacDonald had been Harvard classmates and P.T. boat commanders; O'Connor probably got to know them through his Coast Guard work. Weeks was in his dotage when he wrote this, and must have assigned himself an inept copy editor, or none at all. The most likely scenario behind Weeks's anecdote is that O'Connor probably told Weeks about a real-enough lunch, but that both he and Weeks worked it up, saving Kennedy's line for the closer. If the words attributed to O'Connor are correct, this would be the first known announcement of his intentions about a Boston novel. Since Kennedy entered politics in the 1946 Congressional campaign, the meeting of the three men can be dated to late 1945 or very early 1946. The Anthony Cantwell story, which was not ostensibly about Boston, was probably sputtering out by then, and the shape of a Boston novel was yet to come. Meanwhile, he aimed small pieces at *Atlantic Monthly.* Edwin O'Connor began his campaign by aiming at the top.[8]

O'Connor's entree to print was radio. His first *Atlantic Monthly* articles were about radio, and his first novel portrayed a radio commentator. In one way or another, since sophomore year at Notre Dame in 1936, O'Connor had been doing radio work, from which he had only a couple of breaks, the longest of which was his first year in the Coast Guard. Employing the time-tested maxim that one writes best from experience, especially when young, he put his decade of experience to use.

During his two wartime years in Boston he had made several contacts beyond newspaper and radio journalism. A man he had met only once briefly, *Atlantic Monthly* associate editor Charles Morton, invited him one day to lunch. (A rumor has it that Morton had heard some of O'Connor's impromptu sketches on WNAC and was impressed.) At lunch Morton talked mostly of his new expensively tailored sport coat.[9] Thus began O'Connor's friendship with the crotchety, eccentric editor of the extensive "Accent on Living" section of the *Atlantic.* Morton was always on the lookout for good writing with an idiosyncratic slant. In the June 1946 issue O'Connor broke into print with his article "The Fairly Merry Widow" in the "Radio" column.[10] Throughout his life O'Connor rarely marked up a book or maga-

8. The magazine goes under two titles, *Atlantic Monthly* and *The Atlantic,* sometimes even in the same issue. The two titles will be used interchangeably here.

9. Edwin O'Connor, eulogy for Charles Morton, October 1967, Hugh Rank Papers, University of Notre Dame Archives.

10. *Atlantic,* June 1946, 134–35.

zine, but he did neatly underline his name in the contents of his own copy of the magazine. The beginning of O'Connor's professional writing career coincides with a rich and unusual association with one of the country's most respected magazines. Throughout his life O'Connor maintained deep loyalties and special affection for people and institutions that had helped him. His fealty to the *Atlantic* for this humble start would be unique. He had an especially strong fondness for Charlie Morton, who had accepted that first article.

Issues of the *Atlantic* were bigger then; O'Connor's inaugural column ran in a 200-page issue. The single-issue price was thirty-five cents. *Atlantic* was a technically a "slick," but about half of each issue was in fact a "pulp" insert because of postwar paper shortages. Covers were plain unillustrated announcements of the main contents, and the full Table of Contents was unaccountably buried in the middle of the issue. Another oddity was the absence of a masthead. Advertising was plentiful enough, and even had bold dashes of early color. But the magazine still had a restrained Boston air about it. It did allow itself the small pagan luxury of placing its logo of Neptune reining in a sea horse at several places in each issue. The writing was uniformly excellent.[11]

O'Connor was in good company in his debut issue. James B. Conant, president of Harvard University, called for a new dedication to academic scholarship now that the war's demands were over. Also from Harvard, John V. Kelleher, then a Junior Fellow and soon to be a pioneer in Irish studies and a close friend of O'Connor, wrote on Finley Peter Dunne's turn-of-the-century Irish American bartender/sage, Mr. Dooley. There was fiction from John Hersey and the third installment of excerpts from Thomas Heggen's *Mister Roberts*. Cyril Connolly sent over from England an article on the death of an American expatriate man of letters, Logan Pearsall Smith. By coincidence, a large ad in the back promoted Rhode Islander Edward McSorley's *Our Own Kind,* a novel about the Irish of South Providence which just may have whetted O'Connor's ambitions to do likewise for Boston.

O'Connor's "The Fairly Merry Widow" is a witty review of weekday soap operas with titles like "Valiant Lady," "Young Dr. Malone," "Portia Faces Life," "A Woman of America," and "Just Plain Bill." O'Connor perceptively notes that not much had changed since the prewar variety, except that now widows are more prominent and thus the level of the histrionic has risen. Taken together, the programs constitute an unreal world of hardly credible carica-

11. For a concise review of the magazine's covers, logos, and layout, see the untitled piece by the magazine's editor, Michael Kelly, in the February 2001 issue, p. 6.

ture. He closes by giving thanks that at least the weekends are free of them: "The American people . . . do like a little time off for good behavior."

Now that he had broken in, O'Connor became something like a regular contributor to *Atlantic*. Over his lifetime O'Connor published eighteen items in the magazine, mostly media critiques or fiction. Most of these were published between 1946 and 1955; one was published posthumously. Although he did occasionally publish in other magazines and even in one academic journal, the *Atlantic* always had first claim on his loyalty because it inaugurated his professional writing career and drew him into literary Boston.

"The Fairly Merry Widow" was followed by five more *Atlantic* radio columns. "No Laughing Matter" laments the deadliness of so much recycled radio humor, the worst of which (Rudy Vallee's) reminds him of a dental surgeon who has talked for years to the "partially anesthetized" and is altogether "minor league Abbott and Costello, if there is such a thing."[12] "Here in the Studio . . ." holds forth on the new phenomenon of live audience shows "which have as their goal the human laugh." The most baffling of these are shows with a preponderance of sight gags which must be described to the listeners, as if radio were the still-unavailable medium of television.[13] His most caustic column was "Prove You're Human!" in early 1947. Here he castigates radio quiz shows as proof of "reverse evolution" for their positive rewarding of ignorance. In O'Connor's imaginary show, the contestant wins simply by evincing proof—any proof—that he or she is human. Presided over by that "magnificent funster," bald Curly Cornwallis, the program showers one contestant with a veritable cornucopia of prizes for mumbling her own name after several unsuccessful tries at articulation.[14]

When television became widely available in 1948, an event not hailed by the lingering radiophile, O'Connor's radio columns stopped for a while. However, three years later he did write another radio piece, which had a new hometown interest. Although O'Connor never calls the station WWON, or identifies its point of origin as Woonsocket, "It's Spontaneous" clearly has these two entities in mind.[15] He begins the column by relating how in the "living room" at "my home" recently he caught a new radio show by accident. O'Connor had been living in Boston since 1943, but in 1951 he still considered 247 Gaskill Street as "home." The article lampoons a transparently phony quiz show in which the contestants, all of whom just happen to be

12. *Atlantic*, September 1946, 130–32.
13. *Atlantic*, October 1946, 137–38.
14. *Atlantic*, February 1947, 113–14.
15. I am indebted to my colleague Mario DiNunzio, who worked for WWON in the 1950s, for confirming some details and even spotting some station employees.

station staff, display an unerring ability to match specific British monarchs with their dynasties with an authority only an historian could muster.[16] As a sendup of blatant corruption of a sort, the column could very well be an indirect commentary on the notorious political shenanigans of his home town and state.

These radio columns in *Atlantic* were well written, especially the early ones. O'Connor could turn a trenchant phrase, roast a deserving target worthily, and all the while keep a consistent tone and irony. So much promise did this writing have, in fact, that one could speculate on where O'Connor's career might have gone had he decided to continue as a columnist. "Prove You're Human!" is especially notable as a sardonic exposure worthy of Mencken or Waugh. At least two columns show that O'Connor obviously took a general's care in planning his assault. While to be sure he had something to say, he also wanted to be noticed, especially by editors at the magazine. After all, he had more ambitious endeavors in mind than back-page "Accent on Living" columns, especially as a satirist who wanted to write fiction. But he also displays a certain superciliousness as he plays to the upper-middlebrow galleries. Peering down was part of his adopting certain Boston manners, in which conveying the impression of inherited good taste counted for so much.

In October 1946 O'Connor, emboldened by his early successes with the *Atlantic,* finally cut his ties with radio for good when he resigned from WNAC after one year with the station. He was going to try out the world of free-lance writing. This audacious step for someone with such a slender publishing record was probably taken with deliberation enough; he seldom sought fresh woods and pastures new on a whim. Besides, writing had been a long-term goal, and he must have sensed that the omens were auspicious: a baptism by *Atlantic*'s Neptune was bracing. But he knew he could not go it alone, and so on the advice of Charlie Morton he contacted Helen Strauss at the William Morris Agency in New York in early October. The two hit it off well at a lunch in New York for which the impoverished young writer insisted on paying, as he almost always did. Thus began a fruitful relationship between writer and agent that lasted until her departure from the Morris Agency in 1967. O'Connor felt deep gratitude for Charlie Morton's advice.

In her memoirs Helen Strauss reveals that at this time Dr. O'Connor "strongly disapproved" of his son's postwar work, first in broadcasting and now in the even more precarious calling of free-lance writing: "[He] felt that his son would be wasting his life. The lengthy hand-to-mouth existence that

16. *Atlantic,* January 1951, 88–90.

accompanied his earliest writings only aggravated his father's sense of betrayal."[17] It seems that Helen Strauss, fourteen years O'Connor's senior, was something of a confidante, of whom O'Connor had only a select few. Her words shed light on the father-son conflict in "Anthony Cantwell," but they need not imply any sort of open antagonism. (Strauss did not always understand her client; for example, in the same passage she thought that his devout Catholicism was a sign of his desire to be a priest.) In fact, at this time Dr. O'Connor wrote his son a brief friendly note and enclosed a newspaper clipping on the way different authors write—a tacit encouragement, even if he thoughtlessly wrote the note on his prescription pad.[18] But Strauss did realize her new client's potential, and O'Connor was indeed fortunate to land such a good agent, who had been instrumental in turning an agency for vaudevillians into a first rate literary agency. She would also represent James Michener, Robert Penn Warren, Herman Wouk, Leon Edel, Edith Sitwell, James Baldwin, Archibald MacLeish, and Ralph Ellison.

O'Connor's career move was accompanied by another change of address. Some time before November 1946 he had moved into a single room at a boarding house at 5 Brimmer Street, located at the western base of Beacon Hill called "the Flat," close to the Charles River Basin. Brimmer Street now is a strictly high-rent district, but like his Beacon Street addresses, it had its share of shabby genteel housing in 1946. The naval historian and Harvard professor Samuel Eliot Morison lived a few doors down; he and O'Connor got to know each other, but Morison was the crusty sort that O'Connor generally avoided. O'Connor's Brimmer Street address was the first of three for him on Beacon Hill.

On election night in 1946 Mrs. O'Connor wrote her son.[19] Most of the family was listening to the results of the off-year congressional races. Dr. O'Connor was cheering Republican gains as the G.O.P. made its first post-New Deal comeback. Edwin O'Connor's politics, while never bound to party or ideology, were mostly Democratic and another source of some mild tension between father and son. His mother strikes a note of concern about the pace of his new writing career, but then typically offers the encouragement that seldom came from his father. She hopes that he and his sister, Bobby, now a junior at Emmanuel College, can get together for dinner in Boston: "I mean Dutch—because she has her allowance," she adds, obviously con-

17. Helen Strauss, *A Talent for Luck* (New York: Random House, 1979), 167.

18. John Vincent O'Connor, letter to Edwin O'Connor, January 6, 1947, EOCP 218.

19. Mary Greene O'Connor, letter to Edwin O'Connor, November 7, 1946, courtesy of Barbara O'Connor Burrell.

cerned for his threadbare finances. She also hopes to see him during upcoming long weekends. Her sign-off has lots of customary kisses.

Radio columns were one thing, but O'Connor's more important break came with the publication of his first short story as "An *Atlantic* 'First'" in the September 1947 issue.[20] By age twenty-nine he had written scores of radio scripts; some of these had aired, at least locally, but there is no way of retrieving them now. All that remain are a few scripts in his papers, and if they are representative, his others are no big loss. He had written several dozen short stories and sketches, but with the lone exception of the story in Notre Dame's *Scrip*, nothing had been published. He had completed one book-length manuscript about his Coast Guard experiences, and had done the unfinished Anthony Cantwell novel, but still had nothing to show. Sheer determination and perseverance kept O'Connor at his typewriter, and so when "The Gentle, Perfect Knight" came out, he felt an ecstatic moment on seeing his name prominently in print at last, and in an issue which also published Wallace Stegner, Sir Osbert Sitwell, Peter Viereck, Harry Levin, and John Ciardi. His gratitude and joy can be sensed in his letter to Edward Weeks on learning of the story's acceptance:

Dear Mr. Weeks:

The present relationship between yourself and my story—"The Gentle, Perfect Knight"—, pleases me immensely. You have liked it, you have bought it, you will publish it—this is a threefold pleasure that is all the more delightful to me because it is so unaccustomed. Your letter was one of the first that I have received from an editorial office that was not a cheerful mimeograph reminding me of the historical example of Robert Bruce and his silly spider.[21]

He alludes here to a legend about the Scots patriot who, while hiding from the British on a remote island in 1307, watched a spider try to fasten its web to a ceiling beam, only to fail repeatedly before succeeding at last. Inspired by the spider's eventual success, Bruce left the island and began driving the English from his native land. Weeks must have enjoyed the letter as much as he enjoyed the short story, and to this day O'Connor's framed letter is displayed prominently in the magazine's offices.

In Weeks's own acceptance letter to O'Connor he recounts how he laughed aloud over the story.[22] Although he found it economical, he did sug-

20. *Atlantic*, September 1947, 59–63.

21. Edwin O'Connor, letter to Edward Weeks, June 24, 1947, courtesy of Peter Davison and the staff at *Atlantic Monthly*.

22. Edward Weeks, letter to Edwin O'Connor, June 20, 1947, EOCP 91.

gest some cutting at the end, which O'Connor dutifully performed. Weeks had detected a nagging problem in O'Connor's work—his inability to know when to stop. Often editors and readers would point out the exact spot for an effective and memorable ending which O'Connor had glided past with a strange unawareness of dramatic closure. Along with the contract, Weeks also included, no doubt much to O'Connor's surprise and delight, a form for the story's entry in the *Atlantic Monthly* and Metro-Goldwyn-Mayer "Awards for *Atlantic* Firsts" competition. (Apparently all "Firsts" were entered in this competition, a way of getting new talent for MGM.) O'Connor was signing his first movie rights contract, and although nothing ever came of this one, he must have had an understandably heady moment. His mother wrote from Woonsocket that the "good news" of the story's acceptance "topped the day" for the family.[23]

In retrospect, it is hard to see what a movie studio could have done with "The Gentle, Perfect Knight." It is a slight piece with neither cinematic promise nor enduring literary merit, but it does mark a stage in O'Connor's adoption of Boston. The story in brief: Iris Munro, a wallflower at twenty-seven, gets invited to a friend's dinner party to meet yet another prospect, this time an Arctic explorer named Avery Winton. Avery at first seems like a refreshingly different and appealing prospect, until at dinner he insists on eating only his own food, which he has brought along, an Indian preparation called pemmican, consisting mostly of meat and fat. To make matters worse, Avery then boorishly holds forth in great detail on the nutritional virtues of this and many other Indian and Eskimo delights as well. Squeamish Iris is overcome and suddenly leaves Avery, pemmican, and romance for home around the corner.

As with most of his fiction, O'Connor does not designate a particular setting for his story. However, the characters' names—Iris Munro, Camilla and Douglas Chase, Avery Winton—could easily be from Boston's society pages. Then too, one tiny detail reveals a lot. When Iris is leaving, O'Connor writes: "[T]he door closed after her, and she was on the brick step." O'Connor was never much of a visual writer; Weeks himself said that "he wrote with his ears," referring to his knack for dialogue.[24] But sometimes O'Connor's visual images imply a lot, and here that brick step could be taken as a marker for Beacon Hill, a veritable hill of red bricks for its houses, sidewalks, alleys, walls, and even some streets. In fact, in April of the very year O'Connor published the story, there occurred on Beacon Hill an incident known as "The

23. Mary Greene O'Connor, letter to Edwin O'Connor, June 25, 1947, EOCP 219.
24. *Book-of-the-Month Club Bulletin*, January 1956, 6.

Battle of the Bricks." Infuriated that the city was going to "improve" some sidewalks by replacing bricks with cement, some Beacon Hill ladies staged a sit-down on West Cedar Street and defied the construction crews. Since Curley was mayor at the time, the battle lines took on a special class and ethnic intensity. The bricks were saved, and in fact this blue-blood uprising was an important formation moment in Boston preservation history.[25]

Another Boston touch occurs in the description of the actual meal served by the hostess: "It aimed at nourishment, little else: there was a steady, boiled potato touch to all the food. . . . Tonight there was a heavy soup, not unlike oatmeal. . . . Next came the meat, each plate high with a pair of tan croquettes drowned in a sauce of chalk." When describing food, O'Connor is often at his best; what he lacked in visual sensibility, he made up with auditory and gustatory ones. When he could, O'Connor took a gourmand's interest in food, and he never failed to be amazed that Boston's upper crust ate so meagerly. That "boiled potato touch" would be memorably recycled in *The Last Hurrah*, when the skinflint publisher Amos Force plays host:

There . . . was the piece of codfish: it was dry, it was tasteless, it was inedible. There were the watery canned tomatoes. There was the small, dull boiled potato. There was the bread but, as before, there was no butter. There was not even margarine. It was a meal fit for the workhouse and the dining companions of Mr. Force (78–79).

Next to this Avery's pemmican begins to appeal. To be sure, Irish American culinary traditions hardly could be called haute cuisine. But at least the Irish served food generously, in a fresh state, with plenty of potatoes and always with butter—no "workhouse" fare for them, with all the horrific associations of that famine-era word. Even stingy old Charlie Carmody throws a grand birthday feast in *The Edge of Sadness*. Puritan/WASP/Victorian Boston had developed (or retarded) its palate in a way that represented for O'Connor a stunting of the soul.

Finally, the characters in the story are Boston types. Iris's finicky reaction to pemmican hints at sexual priggishness; whether O'Connor realized this is another question. Camilla, the hostess, is too hearty by half, with a "voice ringing like a good ship's bell." Her dullard husband Douglas is notable for just sitting there, rousing himself as he "wiggled a greeting." Avery Winton, at first so attractive, reverts with the pemmican business to a Boston type: the monomaniacal explorer away from human society too long, who now has an alarming nutritional obsession. The dinner party is a portrait of a group gone lifeless at the center, with only eccentricity left at the edges. O'Connor's

---

25. Barbara W. Moore and Gail Weesner, *Beacon Hill: A Living Portrait* (Boston: Centry Hill Press, 1992), 22.

touch is light, and his censure sympathetic. However, O'Connor needed to engage the characters with each other more: as with "Friends Are Made in McCabe's" nine years earlier, the only response to life's challenges by the character from whose point of view the story is told is to simply go home. In fact, O'Connor dwells on going home for a long stretch at the end, in spite of the cuts suggested by Weeks. Iris will not even let Avery escort her: "'No!' said Iris. She almost shouted the word. 'That is,' she added hastily, 'I just live around the corner.'"

There then occurs an odd image in which a reader's hastily formed Beacon Hill impression dissolves with one misstep. When Iris finally departs, O'Connor writes that she steps "down on the grass." Suddenly the locale is tony suburbia; Beacon Hill does not grow front lawns. The reader looks again: there was no mention of brick sidewalks after all, only brick front steps. Beacon Hill's front steps are invariably granite slabs. As in some of O'Connor's work, the actual locale is quite hazy—are we in city or suburb, town house or detached colonial, Beacon Hill or Wellesley? One thing is clear, though: there is as yet no Irish American in sight amidst this Yankee menagerie. O'Connor is getting to know the Establishment first. But as a short story, "The Gentle, Perfect Knight" has too much of the shaggy dog.

A more explicitly Boston piece is "The Coward," an unpublished short story written some time in the late 1940s.[26] Again, Boston is never named, but the landmarks are unmistakable: the "broad avenue" where "they have the Easter Parade" is Commonwealth Avenue; a large downtown green is Boston Common; a river with boat rides down to the university suggests the Charles River and Harvard. Stephen Farnum, the title character, comes from genteel stock: "Grandfather Farnum used to lead the Easter Parade." Now that stock is literally shabby, to wit, Stephen's discreetly invisible patch sewn into his crotch—a symbol of masculine inadequacy. At forty-one he has few illusions about his failure as a lawyer and husband. In early spring he takes a Boston stroll with his son Stevie, aged eleven.[27] A flashback takes us to a baseball game the previous summer at which they had met the father's old college teammate, Sam Felton, now a star player. Stephen had exaggerated his college baseball career to his son; Felton plays along with the "thin plank of fact" and consequently the father is a hero to his son. But when their springtime stroll takes father and son to the river boat for a ride down to the university, ominous clouds literally and figuratively gather. When a woman

26. EOCP 26.

27. A remarkable coincidence: years later O'Connor would gain a stepson, also a Stevie and also aged eleven.

falls accidentally, she blames Stephen and her beery beau makes him apologize cravenly. The story ends as the father tries to persuade his disillusioned son that "one can't brawl in a public place."

"The Coward" has potential for a good short story about disillusionment, that subject which the genre can handle so well. But the story needed work, especially in character development, and it seems the ending gave O'Connor some problems, because the last half page is written in with pencil in a tentative fashion. This would not be the only time a story's resolution involving a particularly painful father-son motif would give O'Connor trouble. "The Coward" was his most pointed portrait of Brahmin Boston to date. Backsliding in finances, resting on imaginary laurels, and underperforming in sex, that class had had its noontime in Boston's weak sun. But O'Connor had not yet recognized that he was admonishing a moribund equine.

Brahmin-baiting was not O'Connor's only exercise during the late 1940s. He wrote a piece on vaudeville intended for the magazine market entitled "Here She Is, In Person!"[28] It was handled by the Morris Agency, but was never published. In it he marvels that radio had not yet quite killed vaudeville. The old art "prospers like a tough, unlovely weed in cities . . . in vast and drafty theaters." It would appear that O'Connor still took in a show once in a while, although he was careful to patronize Boston's notorious burlesque house, The Old Howard, only when it had the more innocent variety of vaudeville acts: the pudgy "ballerina" doing boogie-woogie, the mandatory harmonica player, and the main event in the person of Miss Sherry Carewe, a fading buxom B-film ex-goddess and now a dreadful singer. Over the whole enterprise floats "a vast hovering cloud of moths." O'Connor's fascination with a waning entertainment he once enjoyed is palpably nostalgic. He also wrote a short story about a semi-reformed Irish-Italian Chicago mobster who now seeks to make up for his apparent sterility by adopting a half dozen upper-class castoffs in a eugenic bid to get perfect kids. "Family Man" again partakes of the shaggy dog syndrome, and was never published.[29]

By early 1948 O'Connor was also helping Ted Weeks with his ABC radio program "Writers of Today." The *Atlantic* editor realized that O'Connor knew the medium well, having worked as an announcer, writer, producer, and now as critic. For a year and a half Weeks employed O'Connor to edit the script and coach him on his delivery, at fifty dollars a week, money which

28. EOCP 28.   29. EOCP 27.

the struggling writer desperately needed.[30] O'Connor saved only one letter, written in the early days of their radio work, from the many he received from Ted Weeks. Weeks thanked "Eddie" for his considerable help, especially for his "imaginative ear." He enclosed the first small check and regretted that it was not bigger.[31] One letter from O'Connor to Weeks during this period survives. After some banter about the Red Sox ingloriously losing their third game in a row to the lowly St. Louis Browns, O'Connor quite confidently advises "Ted" in detail about his last program for the 1948–49 season.[32] It would appear from this letter that O'Connor was much more than a mere voice coach or script proofreader. In his memoirs, *Writers and Friends,* Weeks devotes several pages to O'Connor but never mentions his help on the radio program, although he had told Hugh Rank about it during an interview.

Weeks had been with *Atlantic Monthly* since 1924, and had been its editor for ten years. In the mid-1920s he was one of Hemingway's discoverers. Like George Apley, Ted Weeks was a member of those Boston clubs which Marquand had satirized so deftly. According to Peter Davison, who inherited Weeks's battered writing desk, Ted was a very sociable and charming man with a large measure of what used to be called "dash." A painfully slow reader, Weeks tended to overedit, especially with writers he felt were only average. He could also be patronizing toward younger authors, and so for his part O'Connor remained guarded in their relationship.[33]

In the summer of 1948 O'Connor took another indirect passage to inner Boston, this time via Wellfleet on Cape Cod. It had been more than five years since he had been "down," or "out," to the Cape, which he had left with no particularly fond memories during his early Coast Guard days. But he had left in the dead of winter, and now sunny postwar summers beckoned. Wellfleet is three towns further out from Brewster on the "lower" or more remote Cape, where the arm is so skinny the towns easily straddle what is by that point little more than a large elevated sandbar. To some out there this is the "real" Cape, in contradistinction to the much more developed "Irish Riviera" of the "upper" Cape, whose Tara/Camelot is Hyannisport. The lower Cape's string of five towns from the elbow out to the tip still has a noticeably WASP culture that was preserved with the establishment of the Cape Cod National Seashore under President Kennedy. It is far less commercialized and a haven for those who prefer a quieter place. Wellfleet in particular was a colony for

---

30. Rank, *O'Connor,* 35–36.
31. Edward Weeks, letter to Edwin O'Connor, February 19, 1948, EOCP 262.
32. Edwin O'Connor, letter to Edward Weeks, June 11, 1949, courtesy of Peter Davison.
33. Peter Davison, personal interview, March 11, 1999.

many Boston professors and writers, and notoriously so for psychiatrists, although the latter camp did not ordinarily mix with the others. An old seaport that had peaked during the whaling decades of the nineteenth century, its town center is on the sheltered Cape Cod Bay side, while its great bluffs and beaches are on the other. Between the two is a large area known as Wellfleet Woods, which consists of small sandy hills covered with scrub pine and oak, along with a series of freshwater glacial ponds. The unique mixture of salt air, ocean surf, warm sands, pine woods, berry bushes, and jewel-like ponds is both invigorating and relaxing, and casts a spell not easily broken. "In town" there were many old boarding houses from whaling days, and there O'Connor rented a room for several years running. Once or twice he rented a cottage on one of the ponds. From 1948 on, his summers were spent in Wellfleet, where he did much of his writing.

O'Connor was now thirty and already a man of regular habits. His early Wellfleet routine, remembered by many, consisted of some writing in the morning until about noon, then a bicycle ride three miles east from town to the great outer beach. He always brought at least two books. The afternoons were spent reading, swimming, and socializing. O'Connor devoured books, especially novels, and was already systematically rereading favorite authors like Dickens. Swimming was his only vigorous exercise as an adult. He was a powerful swimmer who enjoyed a swift plunge into the great rollers. Socializing always came easily to him, in spite of his reserve. He made friends on the beach easily and was warmly included in several cliques. By the early 1950s he was an accepted junior member of Wellfleet's literary set. Wellfleet was becoming a happy combination of glorious Cape summers and the business of making important literary contacts.

Meanwhile his brother's college career was floundering again. Jack had been readmitted to Providence College in September 1946, but it was clear that any kind of medical career was becoming problematic, especially after he was dropped by the college again in May 1948. His mother's letters to his older brother comment wryly on Jack's endless round of girls, parties, and sports. Jack had his brother's friendly personality, but little of his discipline.

On January 9, 1942, during a blind date in snowy Times Square, Jack had met Beatrice Musalo from Brooklyn's Bay Ridge section. In the late summer of 1948 Jack left Woonsocket and enrolled as a special student at Columbia, still pursuing some kind of medical career. But Beatrice was more on his mind, and he married her on June 26, 1949. He never made any headway at Columbia and after one last attempt at optometry, he went into business.

The couple settled in Massapequa, Long Island, to raise their family of four boys and two girls. Jack's abstemious older brother was a marked contrast in so many ways.

In June 1949 Barbara graduated from Emmanuel College. At her commencement ceremony Congressman John F. Kennedy, then serving his second term, was the main speaker. As he filed in, he caught O'Connor's eye and stopped to chat and catch up. Barbara began applying for teaching positions.[34]

O'Connor's father was ill in March, although in a short note to his son he brushed it off as a "false alarm." He also thanks his son for what appears to be a repayment of a small loan, and insists that Sonny actually overpaid, which is highly likely. O'Connor in general did not approach his father for monetary help during these financially trying years, but there must have been times when he had to swallow pride and write. Dr. O'Connor makes no fuss over the matter.[35] A letter from his mother in May pleads with him not to bring a present for Mother's Day because he cannot afford it. Her son's poverty could not be disguised.[36]

When he left Brimmer Street for his second Wellfleet summer, he instructed that mail sent to Wellfleet after September 1 be forwarded to 247 Gaskill Street in Woonsocket. Apparently O'Connor had decided not to return to Brimmer Street, but he had no new place lined up. However, he did come up occasionally to Boston from Wellfleet to tend to affairs, and on one of these trips he found new lodgings, on the fourth floor of 11 Marlborough Street, a rooming house which faced the side of the *Atlantic Monthly* building. He was practically living above the shop. The quarters were cramped for a big man, and Marlborough Street was not as fashionable as Beacon Street or Commonwealth Avenue, even though it runs between them. In 1949 O'Connor's end of the street housed a lot of students and 11 Marlborough Street had a neglected look in spite of the ivy-covered bricks. But he must have liked it well enough because he lived there for the next six years. He was just around the corner from Beacon Hill, next door to *Atlantic Monthly*, and an easy walk to the Public Gardens and downtown: he must have felt at the center of the Hub.

---

34. Barbara O'Connor Burrell, personal interview, summer 1998.

35. John Vincent O'Connor, letter to Edwin O'Connor, March 11, 1949, courtesy of Barbara O'Connor Burrell.

36. Mary Greene O'Connor, letter to Edwin O'Connor, EOCP 219.

CHAPTER SIX

♌ *From First Novel to "Roger Swift"*
(1950–1952)

By 1950 Edwin O'Connor still had little to show for a decade of nearly continuous efforts at getting published. A handful of 1,500-word columns on the endangered medium of radio, and one short story—all of these in the same magazine. Since the fall of 1946 he had eked out a precarious living, styling himself as a free-lance writer but in fact getting most of his income as a poorly paid consultant to Ted Weeks, whose radio program ceased in May of 1949 and along with it O'Connor's only semblance of a steady income. But according to his sister, who had been teaching since September 1949 at the Andrews Street School in Woonsocket, even in his most frustrating times he maintained a cheery outward demeanor.[1] Many who worked at *Atlantic Monthly* offices in those days attest to his unvaryingly sunny disposition when he paid the noontime call that was now almost a daily ritual. To family and magazine staff he put on the best face he could, but close friends like Arthur Schlesinger and John Kelleher remembered that he always had a streak of melancholy. While gloom never mastered him, it was certainly understandable if it showed itself once in a while as he contemplated a discouraging stream of those mimeographed rejection form letters he had described back in 1947. To his great credit, he kept working hard at his craft and never lost hope that he would have real success.

A big part of O'Connor's problem was lack of focus. In the postwar years he was feeling his way as a writer, touching on a small number of subjects from soap operas to wallflowers, and still had not hit a distinctive stride or discovered his great theme. It can be safely said that O'Connor had not yet written a truly serious piece of work, with the possible exception, strangely enough, of his lone college story. In looking over hundreds of pages of his unpublished radio scripts, sketches, articles, short stories, memoirs, and novels from 1940 to early 1950, one wonders

1. Barbara O'Connor Burrell, personal interview, summer 1998.

when at last he would take some serious risks. Not that O'Connor had to be a ponderous Thomas Mann. He knew his best talents ran to comedy, and he never lost his admiration for Dickens and Waugh, who could fuse serious critiques with illuminating humor. But by now he must have felt the chilly drafts from Marvell's winged chariot of time: he was thirty-two, all his friends from Woonsocket and Notre Dame were working in the postwar boom, and his own kid sister, ten years his junior, had a full-time teaching position. He needed to rid himself of too much superficial radio experience, and what better way to exorcize that past than to write about it.

In late September 1949, after his second long Wellfleet summer and the realization that there would be no more fifty dollars a week as Weeks's right hand on radio, O'Connor began work on the manuscript that would become his first published novel. The September 1949 dating can be arrived at from the many topical allusions that were so unusual for O'Connor before this book, and afterwards as well. In order to catch the feel of contemporary radio broadcasting, O'Connor alluded to events even as they were happening. Thus, the writing probably began shortly after President Truman's September 23 announcement of the first Soviet atomic tests, mentioned in the first chapter. O'Connor wrote the book in just five months. First entitled *On Top of the World* (taken from a description of the main character as "sitting on top of the world"), it was published as *The Oracle* in April 1951.[2] The cover depicted three ovals: a radio microphone, a huge blabber's mouth (which also formed the "O" of the title), and a halo over the blabber's head. The dust jacket blurb begins: "This book is dedicated to all those who have ever wanted to silence their radios with a shotgun and wondered how the proprietors of certain soothing voices can take themselves seriously." O'Connor was firing one last big salvo at his former career.

There had been a run-up to *The Oracle,* as well as one false start. Some of the radio columns in *Atlantic,* especially "Prove You're Human!" were on the verge of breaking out into satirical narrative. Then sometime between 1947 and 1949 O'Connor had started his second novel which, like the Anthony Cantwell story, was also unfinished. The "Luther Sudworth" story, in brief, concerns a famous radio figure of only twenty-five, who grew up as a yokel in McCarthy, Maine. When he was a boy his mother took him on a strange pilgrimage to Rudy Vallee's abandoned house. This ritual is followed by a bizarre game called "Find Your Way Home," in which Luther's father deliberately gets him lost in the snowy woods and gives him false directions in a

---

2. *The Oracle* (New York: Harper & Brothers, 1951).

game that can only be renamed "Oedipus meets Isaac." At eighteen Luther consults the town oracle, a former high school principal named Mr. Osgood, who lives alone "like Thoreau" in a house literally made of nuts, which aptly describes his mental condition. When the young bumpkin announces to family and townsfolk that he is off to New York City and radio, all are delighted to see Luther off. In the big city Luther becomes Vice President in Charge of Practical Research, whose duties consist in being an unsuspecting barometer of the appalling taste of Mencken's "booboisie." His office is an actual broom closet, which doubles as his home. O'Connor took Luther Sudworth's adventures no further.

Although more focused than the Anthony Cantwell story, "Luther Sudworth" is too thin and its premise too difficult to sustain. Oddly for O'Connor, who was already becoming noted as a gifted mimic in social circles, there is little attempt to make Luther sound like a hick. One possible explanation is that, like Anthony Cantwell, Luther Sudworth has a tangential relationship to his author. Most striking in this regard is the following passage from the first chapter: "I preferred being in the company of older people, such as the grizzled old men who held in their knobby heads the secrets of a bygone age" (3). Hardly the speech of a hayseed, that sentence nevertheless can easily stand as a significant gloss on O'Connor's life.

O'Connor abandoned the dead-end tale of Luther Sudworth for the much more promising material of Christopher Usher, protagonist of *The Oracle*. The novel takes Usher through a month of his life when his world comes crashing down. Usher is a nationally syndicated radio commentator whom we first see broadcasting while buck naked because the studio's air conditioning has broken down. This emperor of the air waves may have no clothes, but that does not stop his orations on global issues from an utterly parochial, sentimentally optimistic, exclusively American angle. He is forty-five and has been married to his good wife, Meredith, for twenty-one years. For some months, this apostle of the wholesome American way has also been seeing a voluptuous former Hollywood starlet named Lura Andriescu, who had been born more humbly as Irish American Etta Pendergast. Meredith's father, the stern and acerbic Dr. Edmund Wrenn, has always disapproved of her marriage and never misses an opportunity of reminding the couple of Usher's beginnings as a lowly sportswriter. Usher's old friend, General "Beak" Blackburn—now recycled, promoted, and aged from "Beak" Burnside in "Anthony Cantwell"—comes to visit and offer his usual disastrous advice to the vaguely right-wing broadcaster. A Mr. Churchill Chan from the Kuomintang embassy politely but fruitlessly urges Usher to advocate military intervention in behalf of the nearly hopeless Nationalist cause. (Mao in fact proclaimed the People's Republic of China on October 1, 1949, while O'Connor was working on the first chapters; it is clear by the book's end that Mao is in power.) Against the advice of network executive Adam Flair, a dourly cynical realist, Usher demands a big pay raise from his sponsor, Bernie Udolpho, whose colorful family hails from the killing streets of Chicago. But Udolpho had decided to go straight with a product line of salves and nose sprays. This shrewd millionaire puts off Usher's demand for a few weeks, and the resulting delay forms the bulk of the book, as the once confident Usher becomes increasingly worried that Udolpho will refuse his demand. A lecture tour fails to buoy Usher's spirits and he feels betrayed by Flair's lack of support. He wallows in self-pity, first with his wife, with whom he quarrels, and then with his mistress, who now appears to be taking up with another. General Blackburn, ever the bumbler, tries to arrange for a reconciliation between husband and wife at the Club Ga-Ga, whose profusion of tropical vines and vegetation suggests a jungle. Because of his arrogance and foolish pride, and unaware of the arranged peace meeting, Usher arrives at the club drunk and with Lura. There he literally falls with Lura at his wife's feet. As a result of all this, Usher loses both women. Lura leaves for Hollywood with her ex-husband in a tentative Magdalenean move toward reform; in a hint of things to come, earlier she had been called an "inverse Magdalen." At the end, Udolpho agrees to meet Usher's demands after all, and so Usher's triumph is one of greed only, whose irony he fails to appreciate.

At 216 pages, *The Oracle* is the shortest of O'Connor's five published novels. At its deepest level, it is a satirical parable on the seven deadly sins. From avarice to sloth, they are parceled among the various characters, with Christopher Usher getting the lion's share. Pride especially goes before a fall for this cheap version of Emerson's self-reliant man. Usher had closed his eyes and ears to the wisdom of books and the past after a period of "shameful . . . self-mistrust" (38) when he was younger, and is now impervious to all creeds but his own. "Christopher was far too self-sufficient to believe in God. . . ." (12). In this respect O'Connor learned much from his reading of Evelyn Waugh's novels, in which a monstrous modern pride, utterly unrecognized by most of his sinners, hurtles the world into a great gulf. Flannery O'Connor was about to launch her own career in which shallow American self-sufficiency came under her gimlet stare. Pride is a special target for these Catholic writers. The modern version of this most deadly sin, which preens itself with such unctuousness especially among the quasi-educated, gets a whole sheaf of satirical barbs. Christopher is a parody of a Christ-bearer, in spite of his canned "spiritual twist" speech on "Gandhi and Christ." His real identity is found in his last name's allusion to Poe's Roderick Usher, whose house literally does fall down. In some ways direct and indirect, O'Connor's education at Notre Dame was bearing fruit in *The Oracle*, as his satire finally had a worthy goal.

For the first time, O'Connor sprinkled a work with some specifically Roman Catholic material. Lura has a luminous "ivory" crucifix above her matching television set, and when she flings a shoe at Usher in rage, she hits the crucifix and then bewails her bad luck in a foreshadowing of her reformation. A poison-pen office memo is called a "memento mori," because it hints at Usher's demise in radio. Usher would not recognize the significance of a genuine memento mori if a real skull were grinning right at him. At another point he is found uncharacteristically reading an historian who sounds like Christopher Dawson, the English convert to Catholicism who stressed the cultural unity of the Middle Ages and whose insights were important to Frank O'Malley. Needless to say, that book fails to hold Usher's attention. In the penultimate chapter of the novel the distraught Usher does briefly "investigate the consolations of religion" in a rare moment of "humbling himself" (165). The episode takes Usher to, of all places, a Jesuit church a block from home. This church may be modeled on Loyola House, a Jesuit center on Newbury Street in Boston. More likely, O'Connor simply borrowed a situation from Waugh's *Brideshead Revisited* in which the spiritually illiterate Rex Mottram takes instruction at a Jesuit center in London so that he can marry into the Marchmain wealth. Like Mottram, Usher is blithely at sea throughout his hilarious instruction. To top it off, Usher finds out that all the books which the old Jesuit has lent him are in Latin! For Usher, Catholicism is a closed book because he cannot and will not understand the wise old priest, who reminds the obtuse Usher, "I speak only in the light of ultimate concerns" (169). As his story ends, Usher revels in cheap spiritual theatrics as he rejoices on coming up from a "darkness of soul" and from the "purgatory of his experience," all of which have made him a better man (215–16).

As a satire on radio, *The Oracle* exposes the medium's crass commercialism through Udolpho's snake oil products, through the jaded cynicism of executives like Adam Flair, and most of all through the overblown rhetoric and pseudo-messianic reputation of news commentators. At the time O'Connor wrote, the likes of Gabriel Heatter and Walter Winchell still aired their distinctive if eccentric versions of the news in a style pregnant with alternating breathy and dead-air implications. Radio was a "hot" medium, to use the old

McLuhan term, in which commentators created flamboyant personas. But by the time *The Oracle* was actually published, the "cool" medium of television was already putting them to pasture. O'Connor saw their ilk as a creation of World War II, when radio news and commentary became an almost hourly obsession for millions. Usher's nine years in radio in fact began at the outbreak of that war, and he frequently fantasizes that his efforts on the airwaves were mightily instrumental in the fall of Mussolini and Hitler, and could again do the same to Stalin and Mao.

As in all O'Connor's subsequent novels, the family gets special attention. To be sure, from *The Odyssey* and Genesis to *Finnegans Wake* and family sitcoms there is no more enduring arena for an exploration of human conflict than the family, however defined. O'Connor viewed the subject through Catholic teaching that stressed the family, not the individual, as the basic unit of society. Individual rights and desires should not trump the legitimate concerns of the best social preserver of fundamental human dignity. In this respect, there is an inevitable tension in America between the new culture's pursuit of atomistic fulfillment in so many different ways and the older wisdom which reminds us of limits and responsibilities for the common good. As a parable, *The Oracle* unambiguously delineates the fall of the house of this Usher as a result of his mindless "philosophy" of the self-centered American way and his corresponding behavior with the siren Lura, whose allegorical name suggests "lure." Usher's "ideas" have consequence, O'Connor reminds us. While Usher may seem more like a hypocrite in preaching a sentimental wholesomeness while practicing lasciviousness, O'Connor shrewdly sees the connection between self-preoccupation and submission to the flesh. Early in the book O'Connor wrote of Usher: "Whenever possible, he preferred the simple solution; here was the common sense out for the inheritors of Dante and Racine" (4). Usher's "common sense" is individualistic American drivel blandly unaware of more serious ways of interpreting history and constructing a just society.

Although the parable may not have a full-blown normative character who stands as some kind of center of insight and rectitude, Dr. Edmund Wrenn is a move in that direction. He had heard the hollowness of his son-in-law from the outset, as he seldom fails to remind those concerned, and he plays Chestertonian sleuth at the end when he nabs Usher. The fact that he is the strongest father character in the novel (indeed, practically the only one) cannot be overlooked. In fact, he is the strongest and wisest of all the characters. He is also a medical doctor, as was O'Connor's father, and his role here suggests a physician to the soul as well, albeit in the acerbic tones of Dr.

John O'Connor. His fictional ancestor in O'Connor's works is Anthony Cantwell's father; there were to be many more, most not as admirable. His first name, however, resonates more with "Edwin," and "Edmund Wrenn" may be an expanded anagram, consciously done or not, of "Edwin." If so, we have a clue that Dr. Wrenn's words and actions are O'Connor's own, even if they have the sound of his father. It is worth noting that O'Connor dedicated this first book "to my mother and my father." Finally, both Wrenn and Usher have similar eyes. Usher's are "pale-blue" (3) and Wrenn's are "faded blue" (17). O'Connor usually does not provide detailed physical descriptions of his characters; we hear them more than we see them. Therefore, any visual tag stands out, and indeed blue eyes will become memorable signatures in so many later father figures. But here, both father and son-in-law have strikingly similar light blue eyes. One way to account for all this is to assume that for O'Connor an ideal family should have a unity. Another more plausible explanation is that Wrenn and Usher represented for O'Connor the quintessential father/son conflict as he saw it, and the visual bridge established it. The interesting O'Connor family trait here is that both Dr. O'Connor and his son had light blue eyes, by most accounts.

In fact, Usher bears an odd physical resemblance to O'Connor himself, as if the author were having some fun at his own expense. Early on he is described as "a big man, a solid man" with a "slight tendency to fat" (3). This is close to a self-portrait. And later when Lura tempts her downcast lover with a "drinkie-winkie," O'Connor writes:

"No, no, I never touch it." It was true; when he had first gone on the air, prudence had dictated the way of total abstention. He knew that it was but a short step from the friendly drink to the fuddled reason, the thick speech, the incautious remark; along such a road had broadcasters perished (192).

O'Connor was already a confirmed teetotaler (and nonsmoker). The reasons were probably many: a physical aversion or intolerance, some early signs of stomach trouble, embarrassment over the stereotype of the drunken Irishman, the sad example of Frank O'Malley, and finally simple economy—he could barely afford to dine, let alone to wine. This passage from his first novel hints at yet another reason: dedication to his work. O'Connor was an early morning writer who needed a clear head. Furthermore, like Usher he had undoubtedly known some in the radio business who had in fact "perished" through the bottle. But in the novel Usher does get quite drunk, another sign of his moral fall now made literal by his physical collapse at Club Ga-Ga. As a big-framed toiler in radio studios, Usher is part of O'Connor's past, but the similarities end there. He was putting that part of his career to rest.

Lura shows at least an ambiguous move back toward family. She is to re-marry her husband Bubu Andriescu, who has come back from Rumania. Bubu nervously totes a gun and is prepared to use it against Usher: some things are worth fighting for. He blurts out somewhat incoherently, "Marriage is sacred: I know the American laws!" (209). The couple is headed back to Hollywood, a dubious move to be sure, but this will not be O'Connor's last novel in which there is a touch of family reconciliation.

Another distinctive O'Connor trait in *The Oracle* is the anonymity of the city where the story takes place. It seems fairly large, yet compact enough for Usher to consider walking from home to studio—not unlike Boston. The opening paragraph places it somewhere on the Northeast coast, where the "normally temperate city . . . sweltered . . . [in] a sullen, humid blanket of air, so unfairly blown north from subtropic muck" (1). Later, "a sudden shift of wind . . . brought the smell of the sea across the city" (7). Those who know Boston's summer weather and its natural air conditioning from the east wind will instantly recognize this weather pattern. Finally, one of the four newspapers Usher customarily reads, the *Journal-American,* is made up by O'Connor for his unnamed Northeast city. There had been a *Boston Journal* in the early part of the twentieth century, and in 1950 there was a Boston tabloid known as the *Record-American.* O'Connor disguised his concoction in order to reveal his city to the journalistic cognoscenti. Although there are only a few Boston markers, it seems probable that this was the city O'Connor had in mind. "Boston" is never used for any of his cities, and he would often coyly deny that books like *The Last Hurrah* and *All in the Family* were set in Boston. Few ever believed him. Unlike its thinly disguised presence in the later novels, Boston as such is of no real consequence in *The Oracle;* still, Boston was on his mind as he made the transition from adopting Boston to developing his great subject.

O'Connor offered his book to the Atlantic Monthly Press in early 1950. Two of the three readers' reports were not encouraging. They found the novel's characterization too weak and its plot too disjointed. These critiques are fair enough. But a third report was more willing to take a gamble that O'Connor was better than this first book, saying he "writes smoothly with an undercurrent of irony and humor."[3] Also, Charles W. Morton, long with the *Atlantic,* wrote to the director of the press: "I am impressed by O'Connor's determination to make a full-time independent writing man out of himself in the field of fiction. . . . He worked with Ted on Ted's radio series and we all got to know him rather well. I should consider him an extremely good

3. EOCP 366.

risk."[4] Charlie Morton, as is evident, was already one of O'Connor's friends on the staff. He was quite the eccentric, and therefore almost sure to be cultivated by the younger O'Connor. But in the end Atlantic Monthly Press turned the book down.

Helen Strauss, O'Connor's hardworking agent, then sent the book to Harper & Brothers in New York. On May 9, 1950, she wrote to O'Connor that Harper was interested. She quotes at length from a letter by Dick Sheehan at Harper, who found the plot entertaining and the details sharp. He did suggest that alterations were needed to make Usher less loathsome; he sensed that O'Connor risked losing his reader by creating a thoroughly unlikeable protagonist. Strauss concluded her letter by urging her author to work with Sheehan. She was sure they could get a good contract—$500 up front, and more later.[5] On May 31 Harper's Frank S. MacGregor wrote Helen Strauss that the publisher would offer $500 now as an option, 10 percent royalties on sales up to 5,000 books, 12.5 percent from 5,000 to 7,500, and 15 percent above 7,500.[6] Strauss wrote O'Connor the next day about the good news, and that the money would come the following week.[7] O'Connor must have been elated that something big might finally be coming his way.

Late in his life, when O'Connor wrote a short article for *The Writer* on first lunches with publishers, he was writing from personal experience, although *The Oracle* and Harper are never identified. O'Connor presents the whole ritual as a typical but misleading rite of passage for aspiring authors. During lunch the publisher's hearty optimism pleases the neophyte author, who is led to imagine that great things will happen with this first book.[8] O'Connor may have projected his own hopes onto this memory, but his advice to new authors was sound: don't get too excited by the prospects for your first book.

It took Harper almost a year to exercise its option. In the spring of 1951 things finally began to move, though uncertainly. Harper's lawyers first wanted to ensure that there would be no legal problems with O'Connor's satire on radio. Specifically, they were concerned about a lawsuit from Gabriel Heatter who, more than any other radio commentator, resembled Christopher Usher.[9] Heatter entered radio in the 1930s. His World War II

---

4. Quoted by Arthur Schlesinger in the Introduction to *BL*, 6.
5. Helen Strauss, letter to Edwin O'Connor, May 9, 1950, EOCP 376.
6. Frank S. MacGregor, letter to Helen Strauss, May 31, 1950, EOCP 372.
7. Helen Strauss, letter to Edwin O'Connor, June 1, 1950, EOCP 376.
8. "The Publisher and the Pep Talk," *The Writer* (April 1967): 31–32.
9. O'Connor's friend Robert Taylor thinks that Usher may also have been partly modeled on O'Connor's colleague, the local print and radio journalist Walter Hackett. Personal interview, April 5, 1999.

broadcasts rallying American support for the Allied cause made him famous. Before America's entry into the war, the British Embassy actually fed him tips. When reporting the news of the Fuhrer's death, Heatter thrilled, "Ah, Hitler is in Hell tonight!" This was a take on his own famous nightly opening, "There's good news tonight," delivered no matter how dire the events of the day were. Heatter frequently personalized the news by turning all sorts of horrific events into stories of personal courage and hope. In this respect, this extremely shy man, who did most of his broadcasting from his Long Island house instead of a New York studio, was enacting out his many phobias in order to distance them, as he confessed in his autobiography. He particularly rejoiced in stories of dogs rescuing people. At the height of his fame in the later 1940s, he was reputed to reach an audience of twenty million.[10]

In *The Oracle* some specific Heatter-Usher parallels are the World War II broadcasts and a kitten that saved its mistress (an all-too-noticeable switch from Heatter's dog). More generally, O'Connor gives large play to the bright optimism of Usher's broadcasts. Gabriel Heatter is not co-extensive with Christopher Usher, however, but rather is only the most obvious inspiration for the fictional character. Usher's slimy personal life is all O'Connor's invention.

Harper's law firm of Greenbaum, Wolff & Ernst had queried O'Connor about the Heatter-Usher problem, and on February 15 they found his replies satisfactory. They concluded that from a legal point of view Usher was not Heatter but a "composite" figure, and that O'Connor's device of actually naming Heatter in the book as one of the few great ones still working was a good protective manoeuver. They also noted that O'Connor would make some changes to tone down a "lady commentator" in the novel who sounded too much like the gossip columnist Louella Parsons.[11] O'Connor simply expunged the lady. When *The Oracle* was published, Marion Young of the Martha Dean radio program liked the book, but wrote O'Connor that she did not dare to use it on the program because "you-know-who" is on the same network.[12] It seems, then, that in spite of his almost paralyzing shyness, Heatter was a man to be reckoned with. In the end nothing came of the matter, although it would not be O'Connor's last brush with libel law.

Helen Strauss had tried to interest the usual book clubs, but to no avail.[13]

10. Irving Fang, "Gabriel Heatter," *American National Biography* (New York: Oxford University Press, 1999).
11. Frank S. MacGregor, letter to Edwin O'Connor, February 19, 1951, EOCP 372.
12. Ramona Herdman, letter to Edwin O'Connor, April 12, 1951, EOCP 372.
13. Helen Strauss, letter to Edwin O'Connor, April 3, 1951, EOCP 376.

The Oracle was published by Harper on April 25, 1951. It sold for $2.75. As they waited for the reviews, Strauss wrote O'Connor, "This is a period of great tension for you".[14] Ten years later O'Connor claimed in a newspaper article that when his first novel was published there was a deafening critical silence.[15] His memory was faulty, because in fact *The Oracle* was reviewed widely enough for a skimpy first novel. And certainly Harper's publicity department cannot be faulted, because it ran good-sized ads in the usual book review pages. O'Connor seems to be confusing reviews with sales, which he does readily admit were embarrassing. In the same article he tells of meeting a friend, many weeks after publication, who waved his arms excitedly (this sounds like Clem Norton) and asked, "Hey, about your book! When is it coming out?"

Certainly Woonsocket was not silent. On April 25 *The Woonsocket Call*'s Edgar J. Allaire gave *The Oracle* a glowing report, complete with a picture of the whole dust cover. (This dust cover has an unflattering, menacing photograph of the author.) The new but short-lived *Woonsocket Sunday Star* gave author and book front page headline treatment: "Literary Fame Comes Early To Young Woonsocket Author." The article, actually more of an interview than a review, bursts with excusable hometown pride, even if its headline proved to be woefully premature in conferring laurels. O'Connor told the anonymous reviewer that he saw his novel as an indictment of radio commentators who have too much unaccountable power. The article ends: "Naturally his family is proud of the success he had achieved through his talent and hard work, just as the whole of Woonsocket is pleased that he has risen so high in such a demanding field."[16]

O'Connor went on the road to Providence to do some publicity. One day in early April, "W. T. S.," as the book review editor Winfield Townley Scott signed himself, was in his *Providence Journal* office writing about O'Connor for his weekly book column, "Bookman's Galley." As he was writing the words, "[Edwin O'Connor was] once of this region, but I knew little about him," coincidence appeared:

[B]elieve it or not . . . in the door came a tall, handsome, lightish-haired, youngish (you begin to put 'ishes' on as you poke through the thirties) fellow who was, of course, O'Connor himself. And I've just had, contrary to some occasions, a really pleasant half-hour's interruption. We talked publishers, publishing dates and the

14. Helen Strauss, letter to Edwin O'Connor, April 12, 1951, EOCP 376.
15. Edwin O'Connor, "Author Tells All About Curley and Skeffington," *Boston Globe*, June 5, 1961, 1 and 5.
16. *Woonsocket Sunday Star*, April 22, 1951, 1.

problem of meeting them in reviews, book pages, editors, writers and friends it turned out we had in common, Cape Cod, the provincialism of New York, and seven or eight other things. . . . I liked his evident high regard for good writing.[17]

This little episode nicely catches O'Connor's quiet aggressiveness on behalf of his career, an aggressiveness easily and naturally blended with sociability and serious literary interests. At his best, he could charm the gruffest cigar chewer in any city newsroom. He may have been soft-spoken and reserved, but one often hears that "there was nothing shy about Ed O'Connor."

The *Providence Journal's* actual review of *The Oracle* was written by its veteran reviewer, Maurice Doblier, who gave the novel high marks, although he admitted that this was not *the* great novel about radio. He especially liked the characterization of Usher and also the many deft minor portraits and cameo appearances. He concluded by hinting at more good things to come from the new author.[18]

In Boston Rudolph Elie gave his friend's book a glowing review in the *Herald,* for which O'Connor was then working. The review is too gushy to take seriously; it is clearly the response of an old pal and colleague.[19] A more measured review appeared in the *Boston Globe.* Joseph Dineen liked the book but did not place it on supernal literary heights. He also notes that O'Connor's short stories and articles were "attracting considerable attention" in Boston.[20] As if to make amends for the rejection of the manuscript, Ted Weeks gave the book a brief plug in his monthly *Atlantic* column, and while not fulsome in his praise, Weeks did think that "[l]ike Saki, Mr. O'Connor has produced a caricature which comes outrageously close to reality."[21] Boston's literary set was small at midcentury, a fallow time for its literature as well as its commerce, and anyone could get to know everyone. O'Connor's coziness with people in radio, newspapers, magazines, and book publishing was noticeable, but not unusual.

Distant New York was not so complimentary. John K. Hutchins did give some sensible praise. He liked O'Connor's "fierce drollery that remains just this side of farce." He concluded by predicting good things: "If one book means anything, Mr. O'Connor is going to be a bright and valuable man to have around."[22] But Robert Phelps gave the novel short notice in the *New*

---

17. W. T. S., "Bookman's Galley," *Providence Sunday Journal,* April 8, 1951.

18. "'The Oracle,' a Radio Phony," *The Providence Sunday Journal,* April 29, 1951.

19. "Edwin O'Connor's First Novel Excellent Comic Narrative," *Boston Sunday Herald,* April 29, 1951, B4.

20. "A Radio 'Gabber,'" *The Boston Sunday Globe,* May 13, 1951, A59.

21. "The Peripatetic Reviewer," *Atlantic Monthly,* May 1951, 79.

22. Unidentified New York newspaper clipping, June 2, 1951.

York Times, dismissing Usher as a mere "cardboard specimen" of the real thing.[23] In the "Briefly Noted" section of *The New Yorker* of May 12, a forty-five-word review found *The Oracle* very funny at points, but "not funny enough to keep a whole book going." Although it may be true that in Boston O'Connor had the help of friends, nevertheless it seems that the rivalry between New York and Boston was not confined to baseball. Throughout O'Connor's career, there would be a marked contrast between favorable Boston reviews and generally less-than-enthusiastic New York reviews.

There was one New York review which O'Connor may have appreciated more than many others. Writing in *Commonweal,* Robert Wichert had generally fine words for the book, noting that O'Connor had injected a sincere strain in Usher, thus making him almost but not quite a tragic figure. Wichert did note, however, some contrivance and windiness in the book.[24] *Commonweal,* a journal of opinion edited by lay Catholics, was a quarter of a century old and had attained a respectability among the intelligentsia that few Catholic publications ever did. O'Connor liked its refreshingly different and independent stance in an era when the majority of Catholic periodicals were theologically adolescent, politically right-wing, or both.

An oddity about *The Oracle* was its greater success in England, where it was published that same year by Reinhardt & Evans. Dust jacket blurbs by none other than Noel Coward and Bertrand Russell helped to boost sales. Coward wrote: "I enjoyed it immensely. It is a brilliant and fascinating story of a modern social phenomenon." Russell, then seventy-nine, wrote with uncharacteristic blandness: "The Oracle gave me much pleasure and I thought the satire excellent and not overdone. The book is entertaining as well as true to life." A third blurb by Val Gielgud smugly gave thanks that "we [British] are mercifully preserved" from the "horrifying" radio antics in the American's novel. Unspoken postwar anti-Americanism may have led some of these reviewers to take O'Connor as a young man angrier at his culture than he actually was.

If Boston's literary community was small, Rhode Island's was practically nonexistent. Nevertheless, Providence had an annual book fair back then, and O'Connor was invited to speak. He shared the platform with Jessica Dragonette, a singer whose success-story autobiography entitled *Faith Is a Song* had just been published, and with an unidentified syndicated monsignor whose suave arrogance in rebuking contemporary literature carried him half an hour beyond his allotted speaking time and nearly caused an au-

---

23. "Radio Rogue," *New York Times,* June 10, 1951, 22.
24. *Commonweal,* July 27, 1951, 386–87.

dience uprising. Afterwards, many women surrounded O'Connor, but not as fans: they wanted to know what he talked about with Jessica Dragonette.[25] When the Rhode Island Library Association held its annual meeting on May 22, the program proudly announced that Edwin O'Connor, "Author of the newly published novel," would be a featured speaker. O'Connor's talk was entitled "Certain Aspects of the Modern Novel." It appears that his was a last-minute invitation, and that when he accepted he did not really have a specific subject in mind. No copy of his address survives, but the recording secretary at the meeting summarized it thus: "Mr. O'Connor . . . made comparisons between some well known stories & classics for boys and girls and radio programs for children."[26] This hardly sounds like a disquisition on Joyce and Faulkner. No account of the reaction to O'Connor's first known public talk as a man of letters was recorded. But it is worth noting that he never lost his fascination with stories remembered from his Rhode Island boyhood, and that when invited to his native state to give a talk, he apparently discarded his first topic and indulged in some youthful nostalgia. O'Connor would not give many more public talks because he felt uncomfortable with the formality required; he also thought he was wasting precious time in preparation and travel.

On publication day his sister sent a congratulatory telegram while visiting New York. Bobby was excited to see *The Oracle* in Manhattan bookstores, and she even saw someone carrying a copy on Fifth Avenue.[27] His mother wrote, bursting with pride. She talks excitedly of the Woonsocket newspaper interviews and the many phone calls to 247 Gaskill Street. However, she frowns on the ugly photo of her son on the dust jacket.[28] Rosalind Wilson, daughter of the eminent Edmund Wilson whom O'Connor recently met at Wellfleet, announced the "beginning of a brilliant literary career."[29] And O'Connor got more than one speaking invitation that May. After talking with "your mother," the Altar and Rosary Society at St. Charles' Church asked O'Connor to speak at the next meeting.[30] There is no record of O'Connor's response, but it is unlikely that he accepted. After all, the Lura Andriescu material was "hot

25. Edwin O'Connor, "The Book Fair," *Atlantic Monthly*, July 1966, 124–25.

26. Ida M. Anderson, "Minutes of Annual Meeting of the Rhode Island Library Association," May 22, 1951.

27. Barbara O'Connor, telegram to Edwin O'Connor, April 25, 1951, courtesy of Barbara O'Connor Burrell.

28. Mary Greene O'Connor, letter to Edwin O'Connor, April 23, 1951, courtesy of Barbara O'Connor Burrell.

29. Rosalind Wilson, letter to Edwin O'Connor, April 23, 1951, EOCP 266.

30. Kathryn M. Conklin, letter to Edwin O'Connor, May 7, 1951, EOCP 122.

stuff" for 1951, especially coming from an Irish Catholic young man, and even if none of it was pornographic. One wonders whether anyone in the Society had read the book.

Sales of *The Oracle* were dismal. Some two years later he had earned a total of $720 in American royalties, enough to set aside for his first trip to Ireland. Just how unsuccessful the book was can be seen in a letter from the William Morris Agency in 1954. It seems the accounting office needed to know whether he had ripped up or cashed the check from the British royalties they had sent him recently. It was for thirty-nine cents—and this from the country where it sold better![31] At a "final melancholy lunch" in New York his hospitable publisher could only say that these things happened. "'Nobody knows why,' he said. '*Nobody knows why.*'"[32] O'Connor was immensely disappointed in his sales, but he eventually shrugged it off and in later life looked back on the whole affair with humor. He had a soft spot for his first book, and he sometimes told people that *The Oracle* was really much better than its sales indicated. He did not refuse an opportunity for paperback editions; there were several after he became famous, one of which, by Lion Library, had a lurid cover. At the same time there was a hardcover reissue, ironically enough by Atlantic Monthly Press. The BBC did a radio adaptation, and it also showed interest in a television adaptation, apparently never done, shortly before O'Connor died.

There is also a question of O'Connor's intentions concerning a theatrical version of the novel. In a twenty-two-page undated manuscript, O'Connor roughed out an outline of a three-act, eight-scene stage version, accompanied by equally rough stage sketches. He only completed the first scene.[33] Hugh Rank thinks this manuscript was O'Connor's first go at the story and that O'Connor abandoned it to write it up as a novel. If so, this would not be a customary route for an author to take, although it should be said that something like this did transpire more than a decade later with another of his works. It seems just as likely that O'Connor started a stage version only after the novel came out, hoping perhaps for a success in the theater which had been denied him in the bookshops. The matter of which came first cannot be settled for certain.

One problem with *The Oracle* was bad timing. When the novel appeared in 1951, radio and its windbags were becoming rapidly superannuated. National television may have been only three years old, but it had caught on

31. Jane Wilson, letter to Edwin O'Connor, October 12, 1954, EOCP 376.
32. Quoted in Schlesinger, *BL*, 6.
33. EOCP 37.

with a swiftness amazing even to its promoters. To read a novel about an overheated radio jerk would be like wanting to read about a silent film star in 1930, three years after the talkies had changed the medium forever. Few would have been interested. And here we see the embryo of an O'Connor problem. So strong was his sense of people and customs passing away that he frequently ran the risk of indulging his own nostalgia and relying on an *ubi sunt* formula to carry him. Sometimes this worked well; sometimes not. The odd thing is that in the middle of writing his novel about radio, O'Connor got a job as a television critic. He should have understood the significance of the abrupt change of technology in America. (Significantly, the luxury television set in Lura's apartment is never turned on.) When studying O'Connor's life and work, one senses that he sometimes saw the world through a lens several years old.

When O'Connor heard that Harper was interested in *The Oracle* in early May 1950, he could be excused for thinking that his ship had come in. *Atlantic* had published a short story in March, and a new magazine called *Flair* had accepted another for its July issue. Later in the year *The Yale Review* accepted a fourth story. To crown things financially, an article on baseball was published in *Atlantic* and then in *Reader's Digest*. No other year would ever see such success in acceptances, nor such a variety of work—novel, short stories, magazine articles, and then at the very end of the year, television reviewing. This success came just at the right time and gave O'Connor the impetus to keep going for the next stretch of lean years. And like so many struggling writers, he had to juggle the demands of workaday journalism with his literary aspirations.

The *Atlantic* story, his second in that magazine, was entitled "The Inner Self."[34] An uncharacteristically psychological title for O'Connor, it turns out to be something of a set-up for a spoof of self-preoccupation. A withdrawn thirty-one-year-old widow named Anne Stephens, who prefers observing people from alcoves, meets Dr. Bernard Brady at a post-theater party. Once she gets over his bizarre moustache, which he wears "in memoriam" for his deceased father, she begins to fantasize about him as a noble man of medicine, until her sister-in-law punctures this illusion with the revelation that Brady is merely a dentist. Anne retreats into her shell. The story contains clear similarities with "The Gentle, Perfect Knight" of three years earlier. In each case a youngish, unattached woman has a few minutes of illusions about a prospective man, only to be sadly let back down into her world. This

---

34. *Atlantic Monthly,* March 1950, 64–68.

second story is not as satisfactory as the earlier one, which had problems of its own. "The Inner Self" has about it the feel of a reprise, which in turn rais-es the question of why this situation in the two stories had such a draw for O'Connor. Although he was not shy in social situations, he was a private man in many ways. The central characters in his first two published short stories could be versions of his own private world and unmarried situation. In fact, his sister's congratulatory letter to him notes that the whole family could hear his voice in much of the story.[35] Finally, it might appear that the story moves toward criticism of social snobbery when Anne dismisses Dr. Brady as a mere dentist, but the story does not operate that way. O'Connor seems more interested in the absurdity of the situation, from Brady's mous-tache to Anne's mistake. A shaggy dog was once again a party guest.

A very real dog does inhabit "Animal Life," published a few months later in *Flair*.[36] This short-lived monthly first appeared in February 1950 and sus-pended publication the following January; it brought out one annual issue in 1953 before expiring. *Flair* is the most curious magazine O'Connor published in; no doubt it was more Helen Strauss's doing than his own. Published by Cowles Magazines, which owned *Look,* among others, *Flair* was a large, glossy monthly with a self-consciously arty appearance. In fact, the July is-sue's yellow cover is a clear throwback to the notorious *Yellow Book* of the 1890s. The cover was also racy: a cut-out of voyeuristic binoculars looks into the first page where a girl cavorts in a swimsuit. The tame pages of the issue, however, turn out to be far less salacious than those in *Esquire* of that time. The contents featured mostly fashion for men and women, along with fic-tion and light verse.

The write-up quotes the author on his decision to give up radio: "[it] sud-denly seemed a little silly—and certainly presumptuous—for a grown man to be constantly reminding his fellows to wash up and smell nice." O'Connor also claims that Boston is the most congenial American city. A photo of the author was taken by twenty-two-year-old Stanley Kubrick of the Cowles staff, some years before his movie making debut. "Animal Life" was accom-panied by a full-page silhouette caricature of a menacing great Dane by staff artist "Shum." No other short story by O'Connor got such splashy treatment.

The main character of the grim tale is Colonel Charles Sinclair whose surname was Christopher Usher's alias for his visits to Lura. Both "Sin-clairs" sin clearly. Colonel Sinclair is a fiftyish boor who entertains guests in his rural stone cottage. He is full of an eccentric but animalistic vitality, as

35. Barbara O'Connor, letter to Edwin O'Connor, March 21, 1950, courtesy of Barbara O'Connor Burrell.
36. July 1950, 34–35; 96–97.

when for example he talks at length of the male bittern's habit of regurgitation after mating. For his finale, he summons with his flute a great Dane named Rupert for a series of tricks, before chaining and enraging the beast and then calming it in a crude display of mastership. Mrs. Sinclair—tall, drab, and somber—is not amused, and the guests soon leave. Then we see the Colonel in his even truer colors as a thoroughly obnoxious wife-baiter who enjoys inflicting a nightly browbeating. But on this night after her husband goes to bed, Mrs. Sinclair summons Rupert, and with one blast of the flute dispatches the foaming dog to her husband's bed.

"Animal Life" was O'Connor's best short story to date, and the most unusual one he ever published. It reveals a side of the author seldom seen. The story is also unusual in its violence, although the ultimate violence perpetrated by Rupert on his master is mercifully left to the imagination. Finally, the Colonel combines the savagery of ex-Marine "Beak" Burnside in "Anthony Cantwell" with the sharp tongue of Anthony Cantwell's father and Christopher Usher's father-in-law. But this latest incarnation of male authority has no redeeming qualities, and his fictional fate seems richly deserved.

In July Helen Strauss's assistant wrote that *The Yale Review* had accepted a story and would pay seventy-five dollars.[37] "Parish Reunion" marks O'Connor's only appearance in an academic journal. *The Yale Review* was then a general magazine of history, politics, and the arts. It also published poetry and short fiction. O'Connor's story was published in the September issue.[38] The fact that "Parish Reunion" is as different from "Animal Life" as that story was from "The Inner Self" indicates something of O'Connor's intensifying creative life at this time. Curiously enough, however, it turned out to be practically his last short story. The form was not congenial to O'Connor, who seemed to need a bigger canvas at this point; also, he was worldly enough to realize that short stories seldom made an author rich or famous. Nevertheless, in turning away from the form just as he was improving his talents, O'Connor may have been closing the door on a genre he might easily have excelled in some day. (He was to publish only one more short story; although it appeared in 1957, it was in fact written at this time.)

"Parish Reunion" is O'Connor's first story with Catholic characters and situations, making its appearance in *The Yale Review* all the more remarkable. The story centers on Dublin-born Father Desmond Sugrue, the elderly pastor of the mostly Irish American Saint Brendan's parish, which is holding

---

37. Esther Mrus, letter to Edwin O'Connor, July 25, 1950, EOCP 376.
38. *The Yale Review*, September 1950, 59–69.

its annual reunion. Father Sugrue, "remote and rather severe," endures this dubious American ritual of "good-fellowship," which to him is a pale substitute for genuine parish life. This year the reunion is not even in the parish hall, but in a hotel ballroom where the Order of the Red Men had cavorted the night before. His curate, Father Karski, is everything the pastor disdains: "He was hearty, he was muscular, he was convivial, he was modern." This embodiment of muscular Catholicism promotes "lawn parties, barbecues, smokers, bridges, beanoes, and monster outdoor rallies." He is also an avid golfer, which to the pastor suggests "profane ambitions." After enduring the usual parish bores and politicians, Father Sugrue is surprised to see Looney Noonan take the stage. Looney is the church janitor, who in his less than sane moments likes to dress up in priestly vestments in the sacristy; the pastor knows that a "large proportion of the servants of the clergy were apt to be a bit dotty." But on this night Looney has more serious business in mind: a defrocking. In an astonishing pantomime, Looney delivers to the assembled parish a brilliant "parody of good-fellowship" followed by a grotesque imitation of a golfer. Father Karski's humiliation is complete when the ballroom erupts into laughter. Father Sugrue secretly sides with Looney, who must be punished, but not too severely.

For the first time O'Connor has brought together the father figure and the vaudevillian, paternalistic authority and satirical entertainer. They may coexist somewhat awkwardly here, but this story reveals two strong impulses in O'Connor's work: to teach with authority and to entertain by comic exposure. The teaching office is significantly held by the much older of the two men, while the clown's role is reserved for someone closer to O'Connor's own age. Both men are tacit allies against an American vulgarization which could ultimately lead to a secularization of the Church. The Father Karskis are to be guarded against more than a whole convention of Red Men. And yet, this is probably too harsh a judgment, because the pastor knows his curate is at bottom a good priest, just a misguided one. Like Dickens, O'Connor often finds it difficult to condemn out of hand.

"Parish Reunion" is also O'Connor's first "Irish" fiction. Father Sugrue heads the cast, an austere de Valera-period type from Ireland's capital city. His other curate is Father Devaney, and so the Polish American Karski is outnumbered. Other characters—Noonan, Meagher, Darcy, Kilgallen—round out the Irish parish roster. Most are eccentrics, some are bores, all have a story to tell, even if done through mime. O'Connor clearly favors the older, the traditional, the more austere. The Karski way is too new and smacks of everything that would make Catholicism less distinctive—in short, everything that would make it like suburban Anglo-Protestantism, where "good-fellowship" could easily replace faith, hope, and charity. "Parish Reunion" can be read as the inaugural story in O'Connor's turn to Irish material, and thus marks a significant stage on the road to *The Last Hurrah* and subsequent works. There are no Beacon Hill blue bloods to roast here: the Irish can just as easily spit their own, with a Polish American tossed in for flavor.

In August, the *Atlantic Monthly* published O'Connor's only writing about his favorite sport. "What Night Does to Baseball" was republished the next month in *Reader's Digest*, at half the original length but with an illustration.[39] The unabridged *Atlantic* article is one of O'Connor's longest published essays. As in "Parish Reunion," O'Connor takes the traditionalist side, arguing that the quality of the game suffers under the lights, and that its new night-time popularity is driven mostly by front office demand for profits. He quotes a few unnamed players who agree, and also Tom Yawkey and Joe Cronin, the owner and the general manager respectively of the Boston Red Sox. O'Connor implies that Yawkey and Cronin are among the shrewdest men in baseball—a debatable point, especially with regard to Yawkey—and that therefore they ought to know. That is pretty much how O'Connor leaves the matter, by arguing from authority. The piece disappoints because there is little first-hand reporting from Fenway Park, which was in fact much visited by the author. However, O'Connor had spent his past three summers at Wellfleet and had not recently enjoyed the nighttime spectacle at Fenway during warm weather. Thus it is no accident that the closest he comes to fresh eye-witness reporting is a brief mention of a dismally chilly night game in Boston during April, which is hardly a representative example for the country as a whole. His family was delighted at the appearance of one of his articles in two magazines. His mother wrote, "I thought Bobbie would be heard all over Woonsocket—she yelled so with delight." Woonsocket may not have widely subscribed to *Atlantic Monthly*, but everyone knew *Reader's Digest*.

During the summer of 1950, probably on expectations of sales from *The Oracle*, which Harper had just accepted, O'Connor spent his third summer at Wellfleet in the unaccustomed luxury of a small rented cottage in the Wellfleet Woods. After this Thoreauvian summer it was back to boarding houses in town for several ensuing summers. In material he excised from a book review he wrote fifteen years later, O'Connor recalls that his rented cottage was three miles from the nearest restaurant, and that his only trans-

---

39. *Atlantic Monthly,* August 1950, 48–50; *Reader's Digest,* September 1950, 123–25.

From left to right: Mrs. Mary O'Connor, Dr. John V. O'Connor, Barbara ("Bobby"), and "Sonny" on Cape Cod, 1952. The occasion was a surprise party for the parents' thirty-fifth wedding anniversary. *Photo courtesy of Barbara O'Connor Burrell.*

portation was a bicycle. For the first time in his life he was forced to cook with some regularity, and on a kerosene camp stove with only a haughty French cookbook as a useless guide.[40] Letters from his mother that summer display a mixture of amusement and concern. Summer was the one season when his Woonsocket family did not see much of Sonny. While it was easy to hop on a train in Boston and be in Woonsocket within the hour, as O'Connor so often did, there was no reliable transport from the outer Cape. Sometimes O'Connor hitchhiked to Boston or Woonsocket. Occasionally the family visited him. A photo taken in 1952 shows father, mother, Bobby, and Sonny on the beach. All are in swimsuits, except for Dr. O'Connor, who is wearing street shoes, a long-sleeve shirt, and a necktie with gold tie pin. Dr. and Mrs. O'Connor had been lured to the Cape, where they were given a surprise thirty-fifth anniversary party by the family. A letter from father to

40. EOCP 71.

son in the late summer of 1950 expresses relief that his own Rhode Island beach vacation in Point Judith is nearly over and that "[w]e'll all be back on regular duty very soon."[41]

A little earlier Dr. O'Connor had written somewhat awkwardly to his son. He apologizes for his neglect in writing, but his wife finally made him do it. The reason soon becomes clear. He had been hesitant to write because it might appear he was calling in some little loans, which had now been repaid anyway. These loans were apparently small and infrequent, but since O'Connor was now thirty-two, they probably caused their share of unspoken tension. A bigger worry for Dr. O'Connor was Jack, now twenty-six and seeking admission to Columbia to study optometry. He calls this Jack's "last stand," and asks that Sonny write and encourage him.[42] Jack did get accepted a month later, to everyone's relief and even amazement, including his own, but he never completed his studies.

As 1950 drew to a close O'Connor realized that free-lance articles for magazines and a contract for a novel were not enough to pay the rent—even during his best year to date. Accordingly, he sought more regular employment by contacting old friends in the Boston newspaper world. Rudolph Elie, his office mate and friend from his Coast Guard years, had been working at the *Boston Herald* for three years and now became the key player in helping O'Connor land a part-time job as that paper's television critic.[43]

Edwin O'Connor wrote these columns under the pseudonym of "Roger Swift." His two year stint as Roger Swift is the only known instance when O'Connor wrote under a pen name. But why now? The most obvious answers are that he felt his new job to be something of a comedown from the empyrean of the *Atlantic,* and also that he did not want his budding career as a novelist to be tainted by any perceived association with hack journalism. However, the identity of Roger Swift was no secret in Boston, at least among the literati. O'Connor never would say why he chose the pen name he did, but one could speculate that "Roger" sat well with Anglophile readers of the staunchly Protestant and Republican *Herald,* whereas "Swift" evoked the great Anglo-Irish master of anonymity, disguise, and satire.

O'Connor's columns, usually called "On Television," appeared for two years, from early December 1950 to shortly after Thanksgiving of 1952. They usually ran three times a week on weekdays only, but sometimes they ran

---

41. John Vincent O'Connor, letter to Edwin O'Connor, August 29, 1950, courtesy of Barbara O'Connor Burrell.

42. John Vincent O'Connor, letter to Edwin O'Connor, August 21, 1950, EOCP 218.

43. Robert Taylor, personal interview, April 5, 1999.

only twice or even once a week. In all, he wrote about 150 Roger Swift columns. He was paid fifteen dollars a column by the *Herald,* which was notorious for its frugal use of part-timers. His approach to the work mixed professional seriousness with a redeeming casualness; after all, how seriously could anyone really take television, even during its "golden age"? When summer rerun season came, he took an extended holiday and headed for Wellfleet where, he says in one column, television was little known.[44]

O'Connor took his column seriously enough. While some of his reviews had a hurried, last-minute quality, and although a few were simply fillers, O'Connor was too proud to waste his talents and too shrewd to endanger his rent check. Most of the columns had something to say, and they said it well. He could be by turns witty, caustic, gentle, kiddish, scolding, and laudatory, but he was rarely solemn or nasty and never smarmy. At his best, O'Connor could excoriate American culture for the crass lies and greed perpetrated by the television industry and swallowed so eagerly by the public. Indeed, as his column went through its second year, he began to complain that the sheer silliness and fakery of most television programs was actually increasing. A few times he took time out from a critique to act as mock interviewer in order to expose the plain dumbness of it all.

O'Connor had to buy his own television set—another *Herald* economy— which he bought with the help and advice of Rudolph Elie and Bob Taylor after a fortifying German lunch at Jake Wirth's.[45] There were only two television stations in Boston at the time, NBC affiliate WBZ-TV and CBS affiliate WNAC-TV. The fare was thus limited and in a few weeks a television critic could get to review just about everything from amateur hours (Roger Swift found them unwittingly hilarious) to zoo programs (usually dull). Sometimes in Woonsocket he would watch Providence's two stations because their program lineups differed from Boston's somewhat, and many *Herald* readers in Boston's southern suburbs could pull in Providence. Once when visiting his old friend Francis Carroll, he wanted to see how Carroll's young daughter responded to a program for kids, but she simply took no interest of any kind.[46] This incident probably shaped O'Connor's own dim view of most programs with or for children.

The "On Television" columns in the *Herald* spread blame and praise in roughly equal proportions. The first column, on December 6, 1950, is a negative review of a game show, a genre he seldom enjoyed, that took the young medium to an early low. *What's My Name?* actually used a ventriloquist's

---

44. Edwin O'Connor, "On Television," *Boston Herald,* September 8, 1953, 14.
45. Taylor, interview.
46. Francis Carroll, personal interview, July 15, 1998.

dummy as the program's emcee (Paul Winchell and Jerry Mahoney), and so O'Connor dryly noted: "It is possible, I suppose, to regard this as one of the most extreme gestures of self-criticism ever indulged in by an American industry." This put-down nicely set the tone for his negative reviews. He took special delight in tweaking a gaggle of people: Gary Moore was garrulous; Faye Emerson was famous mostly for her hairdo; Kate Smith's show was a "masterpiece of carelessness"; Abbott and Costello were already outdated in the movies, let alone on television, and he found their unabridged "Who's on First" routine interminable. Bert Parks was silliness personified, Sam Levenson was not really good with kids, and Fred Allen was a big disappointment at first. (O'Connor observed with care the mostly unhappy attempts of radio stars to cross over into television.) Bob Hope was and always had been lackluster, Arthur Godfrey had no talent whatsoever, sleepy Mel Torme was lazy, Sinatra's new incarnation as a worldly guy was singularly unfunny, Dennis Day was dull on his own program, and ditto for Red Skelton. Walter Winchell had been laughable as a radio commentator, and was even more so on television. Margaret Truman's pathetic appearance as a pianist and singer reminded Roger Swift of Dr. Johnson on women preachers.

One of these columns almost put O'Connor in harm's way. On February 14, 1951, Roger Swift took issue with the cartoonist Al Capp's ad hominem television attacks on people with whom he politically disagreed. Capp used his guest appearances on a television show called *Who Said That?* as a bully pulpit. Although Capp lived just two blocks from O'Connor, he knew neither O'Connor nor the identity of Roger Swift. When he read the attack on him, he said he hoped to "give [Roger Swift] something swift." He later wrote a favorable review of *The Oracle* for the New York *Herald Tribune*, not realizing that Edwin O'Connor and Roger Swift were the same person. A few days after the review appeared, when Capp was working in his studio, he was surprised to find the Edwin O'Connor he had just reviewed at his door. O'Connor thanked him for the review, and pumped him for a little information on comic strips, to aid him in the portrayal of Adam Caulfield in *The Last Hurrah*, by then under way. Only as he was leaving did O'Connor reveal that he was Roger Swift. Capp's anger dissipated and he got a chuckle out of the incident.[47]

O'Connor also frowned on televison wrestling as incomprehensibly spurious and shabby, and considered its audience to be utterly baffling. Ted Mack's amateur show always hit a "dead level of mediocrity." A show where

47. Al Capp, "When Al Capp Met O'Connor," *Boston Sunday Globe*, May 27, 1962, A3.

couples actually wed and were then showered with sponsors' gifts was an appalling lapse of values. (Any show which demeaned marriage and the family was sure to incur his displeasure.) He scolded *Juvenile Jury*, in which kids sat in judgment of adults; it was not only unfunny, it was one of those unwitting American acts of self-destruction. At the other end of the life span, he thought the risque humor of octogenarians on *Life Begins at Eighty* creepy in the extreme. The snooping premise of *Candid Camera* was hardly a noble one. During *You Asked For It* he wore ear plugs, as he did during several other programs. Early talk shows were pretentious, like the *Mike and Buff* show starring a young Mike Wallace and his real life spouse. He actually forced himself to watch six installments of a vapid program live from the Stork Club in New York, which starred the Stork Club itself; O'Connor never failed to be amazed that such a program could exist. He found female impersonators in poor taste, and indeed frowns on any kind of off-color humor. Baseball he found ill-suited to the medium. Unlike other baseball parks, Fenway Park in parsimonious Boston only used two or three cameras. Seldom did one get a sense of the field as a whole. On April 17, 1952, O'Connor also made an interesting and perhaps revealing comment: "To watch baseball on television is suddenly to become aware of one's loneliness." A rare slip by the reviewer.

On his good list Roger Swift placed Ed Wynn's good-hearted goofiness very high, although he predicted correctly that Wynn would not last long in television. Jimmy Durante was also near the top, along with Jack Benny, Burns and Allen, Victor Borge's piano routines, Beatrice Lillie as television's funniest woman, Groucho Marx for his sharp command of English, Jerry Lewis, *Amos n' Andy* with nary a reference to their "race," Sid Caesar and Imogene Coca, the young Steve Allen, and Wally Cox as Mr. Peepers. Some Bostonians got high marks. He predicted great things for young Frank Fontaine, whose career never did soar. With Bob and Ray he was on surer ground. Bob Elliot and Ray Goulding got their start in the late 1940s on Boston's WHDH radio station where they mastered deadpan New England comedy. O'Connor thought that on radio they had no rival for their uncanny put-downs, but that their initial attempts on television were somewhat awkward.

He enjoyed the early Walt Disney shows, even though they were largely excerpts from Disney classics. *I Love Lucy* grew on him. He always wrote affectionately about Ed Sullivan's variety shows, containing as they did a memory of vaudeville. Although he disliked parades, he confessed to delighting in the Macy's Thanksgiving parade, especially when he watched it with little children around. World Series baseball was an improvement over coverage at Fenway Park. He delighted in Dizzy Dean's mangled commentary, but Red Barber's folkisms wore thin.

Roger Swift took less pleasure in "serious" television, such as it was. He did enjoy early efforts at drama like Pulitzer Prize Playhouse, which did Wilder's *The Skin of Our Teeth;* Studio One for productions like Graham Greene's *England Made Me,* even if it drained off Greene's spiritual depth; and the Somerset Maugham Theater, while dissenting from the program's claims for Maugham's superlativeness. But too many attempts at serious drama were either dull, pretentious, or watered down.

For someone who would be hailed as a political novelist, O'Connor seldom reviewed political coverage on television. Perhaps he was heeding restraints from higher up in the *Herald.* Nevertheless, he did like broadcasts of Senate crime investigations. He thanked CBS for its unusual public service in reading aloud until 4:00 A.M. the first POW lists from the Korean War. He thoroughly enjoyed the coverage of General MacArthur's big day in Washington, when he gave his memorable "old soldier" address to Congress after being fired by Truman. One senses here O'Connor's customary sentiment for the noble has-been, although he carefully sidesteps the political issues involved. A live atomic bomb blast curiously fails to move him, as he concentrates solely on the technical details of televising such a bright light. He enjoyed President Truman's live tour of the White House, as well as Eleanor Roosevelt's appearance on a news panel. He welcomes the rare academic who turns up, like his new Wellfleet friend Arthur Schlesinger Jr. from Harvard University, although he hints that Schlesinger's weekly show is a tad dull. Finally, in one of the last Roger Swift columns, he commended Bishop Fulton Sheen for bringing ultimate seriousness to television, though in an excessively theatrical manner.

Roger Swift rarely lets us get a direct peek at Ed O'Connor; the mask fitted tightly. He did once indulge in a bit of nostalgia when watching a spring training interview with Boston Braves manager Tommy Holmes in Florida: he claims he donned his old West Palm Beach Invincibles uniform, a memory (genuine or fictional) of his WJNO months in 1942. And in another place he mentions cycling around Boston a lot. Otherwise, the personality behind Roger Swift comes across through his judgments. He clearly likes watching comedy best, drama next, and politics third. In these can be seen O'Connor's approach in his next and most famous novel: politics is above all drama and at its highest pitch, great comedy.

Shortly after Thanksgiving 1952 O'Connor was unceremoniously fired from the *Herald*. As with similar painful moments from his past, he was reluctant to talk about the incident. What caused the firing? Was it his increasingly carping tone? Or was it the friendliness shown toward some Democrats, and this in a staunchly Republican newspaper? Or the high praise of Bishop Sheen at the very end, in what even *Herald* staffers jokingly called a strictly "A.P.A." (American Protestant Association) paper? O'Connor's friend Robert Taylor indicates that the *Herald* was just acting like Scrooge, firing the non-union O'Connor and making do with an in-house substitute on the cheap.[48]

A story that O'Connor was fired on Christmas Eve has circulated but is not strictly true. The *Herald* conducted a staff review around Thanksgiving and simply let people go in early December, to be sure still in time to spoil the Christmas season. It must have been a bitter pill for O'Connor. He stored up many *Herald* memories and unleashed them in some of the most vitriolic pages of *The Last Hurrah*, especially in scenes of firing or quitting involving newspaper personages. The very intensity of those scenes testifies to the wrench O'Connor must have felt at getting dropped after two years of good work.

During his *Herald* years, O'Connor renewed his friendship with Rudolph Elie and struck up one with Robert Taylor. The three *Herald* writers became inseparable. Elie was seven years older than O'Connor, who was in turn seven years older than Taylor. All three had served in the war, and all had ambitions as novelists. They styled themselves "the amuses" because of their appearances in various sections of the amusement pages. Of the three "amuses," the outgoing Elie was perhaps the most versatile but also the least fulfilled. He covered a wide spectrum of the arts as a reviewer for the *Herald*, and became especially known for his music reviews. His problems as a writer stemmed from lack of focus and lack of that single-minded dedication so important for the long-haul task of writing a novel. Even the title of his regular column, "The Roving Reporter," indicates something of his restless spirit. Inspired by O'Connor's later success, Elie did finish a novel called *The Girl in the Golden Slipper*, but it was never published, even though O'Connor went to bat for it. O'Connor felt sorry about the unrealized hopes of the talented Elie, who died young at forty-seven.[49]

Robert Taylor had served in the Navy during the war, graduated from Colgate in 1947, and did postgraduate work in English at Brown University.

48. Robert Taylor, *Fred Allen: His Life and Wit* (Boston: Little, Brown, 1989), 305.
49. Taylor, interview.

Like Elie he became knowledgeable in many areas as a reviewer of art, music, film, and theater for the *Herald* from 1948 until 1967, when he switched to the Boston *Globe,* where he served as an art critic and book columnist. For several years he was editor of the *Globe's* Sunday book review section. Over the course of his productive life he has interviewed hundreds of people in many fields. He published one novel, *In Red Weather* (1961), and an interesting study of the famous upstate New York tuberculosis sanitarium in *Saranac* (1986). His *Fred Allen: His Life and Wit* (1989) shares with O'Connor a great admiration for the radio comedian. Bob Taylor still writes book reviews for the *Globe.*

In those early *Herald* years, O'Connor, Elie, and Taylor would hand in their columns at the old *Herald* building downtown and then talk endlessly over frugal meals at the Hayes-Bickford cafeteria on Tremont Street, or at Thompson's Spa or The Laboratory Kitchen. For a payday treat they would walk further afield to Kneeland Street near the theater district for the turn-of-the century sawdust atmosphere of Jacob Wirth's German American restaurant. As the youngest of the trio, Bob Taylor would marvel at his older friends' range and wit as they covered literature, art, and music. He referred to them as "my Harvard and Yale." Bob Taylor credits O'Connor especially for opening him up to the deeper possibilities of literature.[50] In one of their nightly sessions the talk turned to writers who died young, like Robert Louis Stevenson: a strange forecast for two of the three "amuses."[51]

In the fall of 1951, O'Connor succumbed to the temptation to earn a little more money by teaching. He had never taught in an academic setting, and the experience proved to be short-lived. For all of his natural affability, verbal dexterity, and broadcasting experience, he was uncomfortable in classrooms or at any kind of lectern. From mid-September to mid-January O'Connor taught one class in English composition in the evening division of Boston College's Intown College at 126 Newbury Street. In the early twentieth century Boston College had moved out from its cramped Civil War-era buildings in the South End to suburban Chestnut Hill, but the one-time "trolley car" school still made provision for young adults who worked full time in the city. The facility on Newbury Street near Copley Square was ideally placed for Boston's clerical workforce, which could get a college degree there in six

---

50. Robert Taylor, "The Way I'll Always Remember Ed O'Connor," *Boston Globe,* March 25, 1968.
51. Taylor, interview.

years. The peripatetic O'Connor could easily walk the four blocks from Marlborough Street.

The Intown College catalogue for 1951–52 lists Edwin O'Connor, A.B., under "Officers of Instruction." Five names before his own is that of Elliot Norton, who taught drama. Norton was already well known as a drama critic at the *Boston Post*. He and O'Connor would soon become friends. One other name catches the eye. An accounting instructor named Stanley Dmohowski very likely lent his name, slightly altered, to one of O'Connor's best comic creations, Father Stanley Danowski in *The Edge of Sadness*. O'Connor had kept the college catalogue, and like many another writer before him, may have scanned a list of names for one that somehow fit a character he had in mind.

O'Connor's teaching experience quickly turned sour through no fault of the school. A few years later, in a talk given at Notre Dame, he recalled the time:

> I once taught a course in writing at an eastern college. I taught it for one semester and I nearly went mad, simply because I bitterly resented the time I had to take out of my own work for it. The plain truth was that the students I had were not getting much of a break, because I wasn't really interested in them. I was interested, passionately, in one thing: getting on with my work, and I regarded their work as an unfortunate, if financially necessary, obstacle in my path. Now, when a teacher starts to regard his students as obstacles, it seems to me that the danger flag is up and waving wildly. So I quit; it was the only honest thing to do.[52]

The context of this passage is O'Connor's insistence on the writer's dedication to his work, a theme he develops at considerable length.

O'Connor gave this talk after the great success of *The Last Hurrah*, but he was looking back to the very year he started on that book. We can catch something of his early excitement as his first truly great story got under way, and of the unexpected "obstacle" that his teaching presented. Something too of his own laborious writing habits, noted by several who knew him best, comes through. Even during his most excited and productive periods of creative endeavor, his deliberate but inefficient writing habits made him resent any unnecessary intrusions on his time and attention. He did not come back to teach for the spring semester, and for the next few years he somehow got along with television reviewing, some free-lancing, and little else. His teaching days, such as they had been, were over.

52. Untitled lecture delivered at University of Notre Dame, 1956?, EOCP 46, 11–12.

CHAPTER SEVEN

ॐ *Persevering*
(1953–1955)

One morning in mid-January 1953 O'Connor's landlady at 11 Marlborough Street heard cries from above. Mrs. Stevens rushed up and found that her fourth-story lodger had collapsed and was bleeding profusely from the mouth. O'Connor was rushed by ambulance to Boston City Hospital, where he was given blood and the sacrament of Extreme Unction simultaneously. ("When I was a boy," says the dying Skeffington in *The Last Hurrah,* "we called it Extreme Unction. The penny catechism didn't go in much for euphemisms.") O'Connor had nearly died from a massive sudden hemorrhage caused by a bleeding ulcer. Roderick MacLeish, a journalist and broadcaster who was also working at *Atlantic Monthly,* rallied the staff for blood donations. Peggy Yntema, who would soon become O'Connor's editor at Atlantic Monthly Press, and Phoebe-Lou Adams, who wrote *Atlantic* book reviews for decades, lined up with others.[1] The *Atlantic* was now literally Edwin O'Connor's lifeblood.

The suddenness of the hemorrhage was alarming and portentous. To the extent that stomach ulcers can be attributed to stress, O'Connor's attack is understandable. He had just been fired from his steadiest source of income, such as it was, and although Ted Weeks was again calling on his services—this time for help in editing Fred Allen's memoirs—O'Connor's long-term financial outlook was not promising. The commercial failure of *The Oracle* cast its shadow; better sales of the book in England did not compensate. He had passed Aquinas's perfect age of thirty-three, and would reach Dante's midway point of thirty-five in six months. He ate precariously for a big man, could barely afford his garret-like digs, and, given his slender prospects, could hardly get serious about the few women he dated. Some of his friends knew that O'Connor's private life and inner feelings were carefully concealed behind his buoyant demeanor. Although he was a person of great integrity and con-

1. Peter Davison, E-mail to author, March 23, 1999.

sistency at bottom, and although he was certainly not a divided personality, his outward cheer and humor did not readily disclose the complexity and tensions within. In this respect he resembled a certain kind of recognizable Irish American male: assimilated, still a bachelor, decorous but somewhat immature at the margins, devoted to family back home, full of wit and charm, protective of his inner life. Although the Depression and World War II had hardly traumatized him, the long stretch of these consecutive national struggles left their marks on his generation, which had learned to postpone gratification for so long that the habit finally became an outlook. This was the generation that bumped up hard against the sixties counterculture.

Recovery in the hospital took several weeks. Years later Ted Weeks wrote with his customary haziness that O'Connor "was permitted no cigarettes or alcohol in the future."[2] Remarks like this have prolonged the notion that the utterly sober Edwin O'Connor was either an alcoholic or a recovered one. O'Connor no doubt was aware that he was convalescing in the hospital that Mayor Curley built, or so went the Boston Irish myth—a compound of much truth which stood, however, on the conveniently forgotten historical fact that Boston Yankee philanthropy had founded the institution during the 1860s cholera outbreak among the poor.[3] For almost two years, off and on, O'Connor had been at work on a novel inspired by Curley's last and permanent defeat in Boston politics in 1949. O'Connor's stay in the hospital which Curley had so enlarged as to become identified with it may have given O'Connor a fresh appreciation of the rogue's public works.

O'Connor was visited every day by Father John Ryan, S.J., a hospital chaplain. They shared an interest in theater and had a mutual friend in the drama critic Elliot Norton. Over the years O'Connor frequently enjoyed dining and talking with Father Ryan and other Jesuits at Loyola House on Newbury Street.[4] During his hospital stay he also became friendly with Monsignor Francis J. Lally, who was editor of the respected diocesan paper, *The Pilot*. Monsignor Lally eventually became O'Connor's confessor. A cosmopolitan man with a liberal outlook, he was a traditionalist at heart. Although O'Connor did not know many priests, these contacts formed during his illness, along with his friendship with Father Holland in Rhode Island, would become valuable for the long gestation years of *The Edge of Sadness*. He came

2. Weeks, *Writers and Friends*, 207–8.
3. Jack Beatty, *The Rascal King: The Life and Times of James Michael Curley 1874–1958* (Reading, Mass.: Addison-Wesley, 1992), 38–39. Beatty's book is indispensable for understanding Curley and his Boston.
4. Rev. John Ryan, S.J., letter to Veniette O'Connor, March 25, 1968, EOCP 421.

to know them as friends who had their share of troubles and foibles, even as they endeavored to be faithful to their calling.

Before his hospitalization, Helen Strauss had landed O'Connor an overseas assignment for *Life* magazine, which wanted a report on BBC television. She wrote him at the hospital to express her concern and to tell him that *Life* was now worried about O'Connor's delay in getting to England. The upcoming coronation of Elizabeth in June would crowd out any other reports on England for some time, and O'Connor might lose the assignment. She also said that *Vogue* would be interested in an article on Ireland.[5] As it turned out, O'Connor did the *Life* article, but nothing for *Vogue*. Thus plans had already been forming for O'Connor's first European trip when his doctor encouraged an extended stay in Ireland during recuperation.[6] No doubt the blandness of the cuisine was a factor in his prescription. Also, O'Connor had wanted to see Ireland for some time, especially now that he was writing about Irish American politics. He told one interviewer, "I worked on [*The Last Hurrah*] for about four years. As I got into the story, I decided I'd better take a trip to Ireland, to see whether they had the same type of politician. I thought I'd better get at the roots of this thing, if I could."[7] Professional journalism and medical advice coincided nicely with personal and creative interests.

With the $750 in royalties from *The Oracle* that he had saved, O'Connor was off to Ireland and England. O'Connor left Boston on Saturday March 7, ten days before St. Patrick's Day. He would leave for Ireland or other destinations on or near St. Patrick's Day many times in subsequent years, so his selection of this date cannot be coincidental. It appears he was anxious not to be in Boston during the hooley. March 17 had been a holiday in Boston since the Revolution, but hardly out of homage to Ireland's patron saint. By a remarkable coincidence, the British naval blockade of Boston was lifted on March 17, 1776, and the day the British fleet sailed away has been officially known ever after as Evacuation Day, a name that annually pumps out a flow of Boston Irish bathroom humor at the expense of the Brits. When the Irish began to run the city, the holiday festivities, especially the big parade in Irish South Boston, became more firmly associated with St. Patrick, as an American victory over England dovetailed wonderfully with ethnic pride. But the shamrock and shillelagh claptrap annoyed O'Connor. As an assimilated

5. Helen Strauss, letter to Edwin O'Connor, February 2, 1953, EOCP 376.
6. Barbara O'Connor Burrell, personal interview, summer 1998.
7. Edwin O'Connor, interview with Lewis Nichols, *New York Times Book Review*, February 5, 1956, 19.

American he took a dim view of any kind of organized public display of ethnicity, especially parades. In particular he found the St. Patrick's Day antics of his fellow Irish Americans, and the spectacles of public daytime drunkenness, deeply embarrassing. It appears he did not want to hear derision of three-decker "Southie" from his friends and associates in red brick Back Bay. A consequence of O'Connor's absence from Boston on March 17, and all that this absence implied, would be a neglect of important segments of Irish America in his work. For example, while O'Connor deals effectively with the nature of political wakes in *The Last Hurrah*, when it comes to depicting the lower-middle class at Knocko Minihan's wake, O'Connor is less convincing.

O'Connor took with him several letters of introduction from a new friend, Professor John V. Kelleher at Harvard University, perhaps the most respected pioneer of Irish studies in the United States. Kelleher is widely admired for his medieval scholarship and for his translations from Irish. For years he was acting chair of the Celtic Studies Department, until his retirement in 1986. O'Connor had looked him up at Harvard during the early stages of writing *The Last Hurrah*, and the two hit it off well, although they had many friendly arguments too. John Kelleher became one of O'Connor's closest friends. At the Harvard Faculty Club or at Kelleher's home in suburban Westwood they would talk at length about literature, politics, religion—and always about the Irish. A modest man who never overcame a stammer, John Kelleher takes no credit for helping O'Connor on background for *The Last Hurrah*. But surely O'Connor learned much from him, if only to sharpen his own developing insights about Irish Americans. And there is more than one place in *The Last Hurrah* where in fact something close to a professorial tone can be heard. O'Connor wrote in Kelleher's copy of the novel, "Out of the memory that his advice, while this book was being written, was the only useful advice I received."[8]

John Kelleher was among the first of several Harvard professors O'Connor befriended, usually in Boston, sometimes at Wellfleet. The first had been the historian Arthur Schlesinger Jr., who summered in Wellfleet. Kelleher and Schlesinger became his closest friends among the professorate. Also in Wellfleet he got to know Harry Levin, an early Joyce critic and author of *The Power of Blackness*, a study of the pessimists during the American literary renaissance. Another professor friend from Harvard's English department was Daniel Aaron, who specialized in American literature. He wrote a good study of the American writers' infatuation with communism in the 1930s.

8. John Kelleher, personal interview, May 29, 1999.

O'Connor got to know the economist John Kenneth Galbraith, the historian Oscar Handlin, and the architect Walter Gropius, all at Harvard. O'Connor knew few professors from the many other colleges and universities in the Boston area. A common denominator in most of these Harvard professors was their allegiance to a variety of left-leaning causes, an allegiance often defiant during the paranoid years of the early 1950s, when Harvard was denounced as "red, not crimson" by the cruder Cold Warriors. O'Connor shared some of the liberalism of his professor friends, and put it on show now and then in his books, though he came by his brand in a less academic and more experiential way. But he paused before the more questionable claims and claimants of American liberalism. Thus, in *The Last Hurrah, All in the Family,* and elsewhere, O'Connor indicates the need for intelligent reform of the political process, while remaining skeptical about the reformers' motives and methods.

O'Connor became good friends with another Harvard professor with an interest in Irish literature. Although he was not a member of the regular faculty, Jack Sweeney was a popular figure at Harvard. He taught several courses in the General Studies program. In the early 1950s Jack Sweeney met and married Maire MacNeill, daughter of Eoin MacNeill, who as a Celtic scholar had cofounded the Gaelic League in the 1890s. Maire worked in the Irish Folklore Commission and in 1962 published a highly regarded book, *The Festival of Lughnasa*. In the late 1960s Jack and Maire retired to Ireland where they lived until their deaths twenty years later. In Boston the Sweeneys lived only a few doors away from O'Connor's 48 Beacon Street address. O'Connor got to know them through John Kelleher and was a frequent guest at their apartment.[9]

O'Connor started a travel journal on his Irish trip, but like his 1929 diary for the California trip, it stops abruptly after several days. He used only five pages of a small blue exam booklet. Nevertheless, the diary is valuable for the first week, March 8–15, of his two and a half months in Ireland. After landing at Shannon, where all North American flights landed in an effort to develop the tourist trade in the desperately poor "West," O'Connor set out for Dublin. He took a bus to Limerick, where he went to Sunday Mass and ate breakfast at a shop that felt colder than outside. Another bus took him to Limerick Junction, where he caught the train to Dublin. Service was notoriously slow and unpredictable. O'Connor makes no comment, however. He was seldom in much of a rush.

9. John Kelleher, letter to author, July 3, 2000.

In Dublin he went to the Shelbourne Hotel, where he stayed for most of his time in the country and where he spent many mornings working on *The Last Hurrah*. The Shelbourne Meridien, as it is called today, is one of the most expensive hotels in the booming new Dublin, but in 1953 O'Connor could stay for twenty-two shillings and six pence, or less than ten dollars a night, breakfast included. Dublin was a bargain for Americans. O'Connor came to cherish the old place for its friendly staff, its bygone ambiance, and for its St. Stephen's Green location, which must have reminded him of the Ritz-Carlton across from the Boston Public Gardens. It became his home in the city that became his favorite after Boston. The Shelbourne's origins go back to 1824, but its present six-story brick and limestone appearance dates from 1863. A charmingly creaky old place replete with wrought iron lift, tea rooms, and a well-trained staff, it was a grand hotel in the continental style and its appearance and location have made it a Dublin fashion spot for most if its history. Among those who have stayed there are Princess Grace, John and Jacqueline Kennedy, Harold Wilson, Peter O'Toole, Stan Laurel, James Cagney, John McCormack, Elizabeth Bowen (who wrote a memoir of the hotel in 1951), Maureen O'Hara, Graham Greene (who wrote much of *The End of the Affair* there), John Hurt, and hundreds more of the glitterati. During the 1916 Easter Rebellion, the hotel was a garrison for the British Army. The Irish Free State Constitution was drafted there in 1922. On Friday the 13th, in May 1976, a huge I.R.A. bomb did considerable damage to this allegedly British establishment; fortunately only one staff member was injured. In the late 1990s the hotel was a secret venue for ancillary meetings associated with the peace process for Northern Ireland.[10]

O'Connor's first night was spent in a small, depressing room with a tiny window. The only amenity for the tall "Yank" was a deep and generous seven-foot bathtub in which he could actually float back and forth. He did enjoy a good filet mignon dinner for under two dollars. The next day's fine weather lifted his spirits, and he changed his room for the better. He then took a leisurely walk down O'Connell Street, Dublin's exceptionally wide main boulevard. He browsed in Duffy's bookstore and had another good steak at the Dolphin Restaurant.

On Tuesday he met Conor Cruise O'Brien, then head of information for the Department of External Affairs and already an intellectual young Turk for his iconoclastic political views in a country still bound to a shopworn na-

---

10. For a fascinating account of the hotel, see Michael O'Sullivan and Bernardine O'Neill, *The Shelbourne and its People* (Dublin: Blackwater Press: 1999). I am further indebted to Michael O'Sullivan for conversation during my stay at the Shelbourne on May 3, 2000.

tionalism. Under the name Donat O'Donnell he had just published a fascinating and challenging book, *Maria Cross,* on the difficulties inherent in the Catholic imagination of modern writers like Mauriac, Greene, and O'Faolain. O'Connor was impressed by him, and possibly took away from him some of the skeptical views about Irish nationalism which Skeffington harbors in *The Last Hurrah.*

That same day O'Connor pronounced *The Irish Times* the only good newspaper in the city; apparently he sampled the other half dozen. He especially liked the *Times'* satiric "Cruiskeen Lawn" column by Myles na gCopaleen, one of the several pen names of Brian O'Nolan. He also met Peadar O'Curry, editor of the Catholic weekly newspaper, *The Standard.*

That night he took in his first play in Dublin, Jean Anouilh's *Ring Around the Moon,* at the Gate Theatre, for only 5/6, or about $2.50. Judging by the playbills he saved from his trip, O'Connor took frequent advantage of the inexpensive ticket prices for good theater in both Dublin and London. At the Gate he also saw Jules Romains's *An Apple a Day,* Fry's *A Sleep of Prisoners,* and Yeats's *The Countess Cathleen,* a famine play that was controversial at its premier in 1899. Dublin's more famous Abbey Theatre had lost its original small building to fire in 1951, and so during the lengthy rebuilding the once ardently nationalist Abbey Players had to use the Queen's Theatre—a not uncommon Dublin irony. Abbey playbills still carried the brown and black stylized logo of Maeve with her Irish wolfhound. O'Connor also saw Abbey productions of Paul Vincent Carroll's *Shadow and Substance* and Denis Johnston's *The Moon in the Yellow River.* He took in a student production at University College Dublin, then located on St. Stephen's Green. Dublin is of course one of the great literary cities of the world, although this was a secret well kept from Dubliners themselves in the 1950s. O'Connor must have perceived in this unconscious philistinism another similarity with Boston.

On Wednesday he had lunch at the Unicorn with Professor Roger McHugh and his wife. McHugh was the first professor of Anglo-Irish literature at University College Dublin. O'Connor liked the McHughs and became fairly close to them. Later in the day he met Sean O'Faolain for a long talk. O'Faolain at fifty-two was one of Ireland's few independent voices in the depressing conformity of the time. As a member of the loyal literary opposition, O'Faolain chose to remain the critic within-the-walls in his fiction and especially during his six years as editor of the literary monthly *The Bell.* In this journal he courageously denounced the exasperating censorship laws which often denied the country its own best literature. He told O'Connor that what Ireland needed to shake up the complacencies of Church and State was its version of America's *Commonweal* magazine. According to John Kelleher, O'Connor liked O'Faolain and his work. Later in his stay O'Connor publicly defended O'Faolain when some petty Dublin infighters were sniping at him. O'Connor called one of O'Faolain's detractors a fifth-rate journalist to his face. He was getting to know the field and the way the game was played. For the most part, though, O'Connor disliked the Dublin literary and journalist set.[11] No doubt their habit of resorting early to any number of watering holes was to him a sad waste of time and talent. At some point he also got to know that other master of the Irish short story, Frank O'Connor. An interviewer later found that Edwin O'Connor could superbly parody Frank O'Connor's "rich, wild and basso tongue . . . in all his guile and wit and lyricism."[12]

On Thursday O'Connor records his first writing in Ireland. He refers to a play he was working on, but none of this work survives. Was he temporarily inspired by his surroundings, or just taking one of his several breaks from *The Last Hurrah?* That evening he saw his first film in Ireland, a mediocre British production; a real Irish film industry was thirty years in the future.

Friday March 13 turned out to be a lucky day. After lunch at The Bailey, where he observed an arrogant American Information Service officer make a boorish scene, he went for dinner to the home of Niall and Hop Montgomery, friends of John Kelleher. O'Connor's first impression of Niall Montgomery was "fine fellow with nice wife and handsome children." Thus began O'Connor's most cherished friendship in Ireland.

Niall Montgomery was an architect by profession, a scholar and writer by inclination, and a noted Dublin wit, as his father had been. Wiry and intense, he was by turns brilliant, nervous, and opinionated, and always a man of great integrity. As architects had time to spare in the stagnant Ireland of the time, Niall threw himself into a number of cultural efforts. He published a few modernist poems and wrote some Joyce criticism, as well as technical papers on architecture. His abundant energy also was directed toward historical and cultural preservation. For example, he was instrumental in saving the Martello Tower at Sandycove that *Ulysses* had made famous. Later, more important building commissions came his way. A few years before he died, he gave a one-man show at the Peacock Theatre that encompassed drawing, painting, and sculpture. Around the same time he gave a series of lectures at the Sorbonne, and at his death in 1987 he was working on a book about Joyce and Proust. He also knew practically everyone of importance in Dublin's

11. Kelleher, interview.
12. Harvey Breit, "In and Out of Books," *New York Times Book Review,* March 18, 1956, 8.

cultural circles, including Jack Yeats, Samuel Beckett, and Patrick Kavanagh. Early explorers of Irish literature from America, like Richard Ellmann, John Kelleher, and Jack Sweeney, were frequent guests. When Myles na gCopaleen was too drunk to write "Cruicksheen Lawn," Niall sometimes penned them in for him.[13] Niall's son James carries on the architectural firm today at the same location on Merrion Square.

Hop was the antithesis of her husband. ("Hop" came from her maiden name, Hopkins; her first name was Roseanna.) She was earnest, prosaic, practical, and maternal. While Niall's letters to O'Connor over the years that followed scintillate with high-spirited repartee and an endless delight in the follies of his countrymen as well as his own, Hop's letters by contrast straightforwardly deliver family news and holiday greetings.

Although utterly dissimilar, husband and wife worked well together and made O'Connor feel like one of the family during his many visits to their home, especially for Sunday lunches of homemade scones, brown bread, cheddar cheese, jams, "gye" (Guinness yeast extract), and tea. Often O'Connor would arrive at the Montgomery home, not far from Merrion Square, before Niall. He would then hide with the four children in order to surprise Niall, who invariably would spot O'Connor's large cap and dryly announce to the house, "Hello, Ed." O'Connor and Niall got on famously because their humor ran on the same track; they were often heard laughing uproariously. Niall had a prickly side, but with O'Connor he was totally at ease. The surviving three children—James, Ruth, and Rose Mary—remember O'Connor as a giant with a huge head and "brownish" skin from summer tanning. He often brought or sent "fiercely exotic" American presents, especially at Christmas. He was, according to Ruth, "definitely the most important and special character of our childhood." O'Connor often told stories to the children in "that wonderful low voice," and could wiggle his ears and make odd sounds. He liked to make a display of reading the death notices in the *Irish Times,* where he hoped to spot the entry for Frank Sinatra, whom he detested. For a time he was "soft" on a distant cousin of the Montgomerys, but because of her much younger age nothing happened. Montgomery family life was conducted along Victorian lines, as O'Connor's own had been. In one of those paradoxes Americans find hard to understand, it was the very formality of such family life that could often generate high spirits and comedy. A few years later the Montgomerys were astonished to learn that *The Last Hur-*

13. Kelleher, interview. For this portrait I am also indebted to communications from Bruce Stewart and John Graby, and to an obituary by Padraig Murray in the 1987 Royal Institute of the Architects of Ireland *Yearbook.*

rah would be dedicated to them. O'Connor was deeply grateful for the hospitality and friendship shown him, and may have associated a renewal of energies for his novel with their kindness. In their copy of the novel he wrote, "To Hop and Niall who remain my favorite people north of the Equator. Come to think of it, south too. Ed."[14]

On Saturday O'Connor took his first short trip outside the city, by bus to Dalkey, a few miles down the coast. He found the seascape lonely, as he often did anywhere, but he found plenty of amusement in the locals' gab. That night he went to the Abbey, where an undistinguished play was followed by a one-act play, entirely in Irish. Naturally O'Connor found it "incomprehensible," but compared to its predecessor it at least showed some life during this fallow period for the Abbey. On Sunday his last diary entry records a walk along the Liffey to the huge Phoenix Park. Back at the hotel, he finds that Niall Montgomery had dropped off for O'Connor's perusal an article in progress on Joyce. O'Connor's journal abruptly stops at this point.

Of O'Connor's three abrupt cessations of the extant travel journals, this one is the most frustrating. One would like more impressions of his first trip abroad, and especially of the country and city where he felt most at home when outside the States. From what can be constructed from some scattered notes elsewhere in his diary, and from letters, friends, his own interviews with American journalists, and from some extended passages in *All in the Family*, it seems that O'Connor's first trip to Ireland lasted almost three months, most of it in residence at the Shelbourne. He typically wrote in his room in the morning, walked around and socialized from noon on, and took in a play or movie in the evening if he did not have a dinner invitation. He had not greatly altered his Boston habits.

Dublin was a small, quiet, provincial city, even if it was the new Republic's capital. It possessed neither wealth nor style, and that was fine by O'Connor. These were the end years of the "de Valera era," a distinct time in modern Ireland when its rural identity was privileged over urban and industrial development. O'Connor felt comfortable in this Ireland because its quiet Catholic way of life appealed, at least for a time. Oddly enough, he says hardly anything about those Irish politicians he was supposedly researching. As usual, he was observing people instead.

Additional scattered notes in his travel journal record humorous observa-

14. For details of the Montgomery family life and the family's friendship with O'Connor, I thank the surviving children—James Montgomery, Rose Mary O'Brien, and Ruth Bourke—who granted me a spirited group interview on May 4, 2000, in the Shelbourne Hotel.

tions or stories he heard. (He had not yet learned to be skeptical of Irish anecdotage.) One brief entry involved an Irish lad too shy to go home to his wife on their wedding night. Another told of a man who, finding a long queue at the confessional, went to the head of the line with the excuse, "I have a mortal sin on my soul." O'Connor notes the Irish propensity for odd nicknames like "the Bird" or "the Pope." He briefly records a trip with Niall Montgomery to witness a Tostal bonfire on Slane Hill; but such was the Irish negligence about time that the flames were out when they arrived. ("An Tostal" was an annual festival of the arts newly sponsored by the government; it was an immediate flop and is long since gone.) Once during a trip to the west he noticed two Anglo-Irish types disdainfully surveying the "native" Irish in the hotel dining room; the two began murmuring, "Mau Mau." Their allusion to the Kenyan terrorists who were much in the news reveals the postcolonial arrogance of a ruling caste "staying on" with a fixed sneer. O'Connor knew their counterparts in Boston.

Another side trip took him to Northern Ireland. He later told a *New York Times* interviewer that in Londonderry some I.R.A. people asked him what Irish Americans would do if "we fought England." O'Connor replied, "I had to tell them that all my life I had been associated with Irish Catholics and hadn't heard it mentioned. I had to tell them we wouldn't do anything."[15] This says a good deal about just how assimilated O'Connor's Irish Catholics were, or at least how assimilated he was. To be sure in 1953 the Irish Republican Army was only a shadow of its legendary past in the 1920s, even in Northern Ireland. But not all Irish Catholics in the Republic or the States were as unaware or as unsympathetic as O'Connor seems to have been. Some of this encounter in Londonderry works its way into *The Last Hurrah,* when Skeffington explains his own "foreign policy that meets local requirements." One of his two major points always pounded out at Irish American rallies is: *"All Ireland must be free"* (Skeffington's emphasis). But privately Skeffington believes that "in twenty years the Irish issue will be about as burning as that of Unhappy Ethiopia" (254–55). Twenty years later Londonderry and the "Irish issue" were burning in more senses than one; O'Connor did not always play the political prophet well.

Out of his first Irish visit three other pieces of writing survive. The first is a single manuscript page most likely written shortly after his arrival. In it young Kilgore had just spent his first day walking in Dublin. "He had been alone all day; he knew no one in the city." At midnight in his hotel room he

15. Interview with Lewis Nichols, 19.

finds that Radio Eireann has already signed off, but he finds an Armed Forces Network disc jockey playing Sinatra.[16] Loneliness in a strange land comes through in this author who needed daily social contacts. The following year O'Connor published "The Meet at Cabinteely," a lively account of being driven, probably by Niall Montgomery, to a point-to-point horse race: "no stands, no stables, no railings, no paddocks; only the horses and their jockeys." Anyone who has ever been driven along country roads in Ireland will recognize this passage: "My host ... maneuvered his small car in a strange pattern of diagonals, as if he were a yachtsman trying to catch a favoring breeze."[17]

O'Connor's longest writing about Ireland, however, was done over a decade later, and remains the only depiction of Ireland in his fiction. Perhaps he needed time for certain Irish experiences to sink in. In any case, 88 out of the 434 pages of his 1966 novel, *All in the Family,* capture the country in vivid writing. To intensify the experience of discovering a new country, he first presents Ireland through the narrator's memories of a summer when he was only eleven years old. This first passage of 79 pages (Chapters Two and Three) is the longer of two sections on Ireland; the second one takes place some thirty years later, when the same first-person narrator visits Ireland with his wife.

Young Jackie Kinsella goes to Ireland with his father in the mid-1930s, shortly after the drowning deaths of his mother and younger brother. His father had inherited a good deal of money, and so for their first two weeks they stay in fine style at the Shelbourne Hotel, never named as such but unquestionably the very place. While Jackie's father at first mopes about in Dublin as he relives honeymoon memories of the city, Jackie is on his own at the hotel for hours on end, and so, like O'Connor himself, he easily strikes up a friendship with the staff, including the manager, Mr. Daniel Guilfoyle. This Dickensian, benevolent father figure gives Jackie a veritable tour of the establishment: "We spent several hours together and he showed me all the parts of the hotel" (*F* 36). Michael O'Sullivan, who has written a history of the Shelbourne, believes Guilfoyle to be modeled on Bernard Molloy, who had been manager since 1937.[18] From the tiny rooms under the roof where many of the help lived, down through "secret back stairways" to storage rooms in the basement, to the main office with its walk-in safe, to the laundry with its washerwomen reminiscent of Joyce's "Clay," to the carpenter

16. EOCP 68.
17. *Atlantic,* July 1954, 94–96.
18. Michael O'Sullivan, personal interview, May 4, 2000.

shop and the huge kitchen—it all is accurately rendered and clearly repre-sents tours of the hotel given to O'Connor himself at his "home away from home" (34). And this indeed is the essence of O'Connor's presentation of the Shelbourne: not just a hotel but a home with a large extended family of sorts, to all of which he developed a typically deep and affectionate loyalty. Just as a mournful Jackie responded to Mr. Guilfoyle's kind attention, so too did a lonely O'Connor come to regard the old hotel as his home, and its staff as part of his family ideal. Jackie's father realizes that the old hotel was "get-ting a little shabby around the edges" (35), and Dublin as a whole was "small and . . . dingy and . . . down at the heels" (40), but this was how he—and O'Connor—liked this poorer version of Boston. Michael O'Sullivan also notes that the Shelbourne was then still a prominent center of the "chipped and faded" world of dying Anglo-Ireland, where the chips and fading were perversely favored as markers distinguishing this displaced class from the upstarts in the new nation.[19] Just as O'Connor had gravitated toward Beacon Hill and the Back Bay of Boston, so too the passing gentility of Dublin's old-er world drew him.

Chapter Two of *All in the Family* was all about Dublin, but the much longer Chapter Three takes father and son to County Kerry, where Jackie lives for a summer with his American cousins at their father's "castle." In spite of its length, however, this chapter has much less to say about Ireland than Chapter Two. With its celebrated lakes, mountains, and peninsulas, County Kerry may be the most beautiful part of the island, but O'Connor largely ig-nores this touristscape. The trips O'Connor made through the Irish country-side failed to inspire him as much as dear, dirty Dublin.

The car trip to Kerry begins on a sunny April day. In his new English car Jackie's father "drove quickly through the light Dublin traffic and in no time at all we were all out in the country" (45). After a brief description of the mountains of Kerry in the distance, Jackie speaks: "It was all very beautiful; I said to my father, 'But didn't you even know you had lots of money?'" (48–49). Jackie's abrupt switch from landscape to family history nicely traces O'Connor's own delving into the fortunes of the assimilated Irish American family. The contours of successful but stressed Irish American life were more important to him than the Ring of Kerry.

The property owned by Jackie's rich American uncle is a vacation retreat. The "castle" on the estate is a big disappointment to Jackie, whose imagina-tion had conjured up medieval citadels from his childhood reading.

---

19. O'Sullivan, interview.

"[I]nstead all I saw was this very old building that looked like a tall stone box. It was thick and square and ugly with no towers or anything . . . everything looked silent and deserted" (54). This small ruin is a rich foreshadowing symbol of the fate of his uncle's family. His uncle's actual residence is a large white house with an impressive circular drive and well-tended landscaping. There is even a private chapel for Sunday Mass at the house—a glance back at Waugh's Brideshead, whose chapel and sanctuary lamp Charles Ryder remembers so well. O'Connor may have modeled castle and house on actual places, but he left no indications. More likely, they were both composites of various buildings he saw.

Jackie stays here until boarding school in the fall. "Our tour of Ireland ended right here at the castle" (66). This would be Jackie's last Edenic summer, a summer which soon becomes much more American than Irish. He has a great time with his three cousins, all boys, as they enjoy American pastimes from board games to baseball:

Ireland made no difference to us. I mean the fact that we were *in* Ireland, because what we did there was not a bit different from what we would have done at home. We didn't play any Irish games, and we didn't play with any Irish boys—we didn't even meet any. . . . Once, I remember, I thought it would be good if we could have a regular [base]ball game, with a full team of players on each side, so I suggested that we could ask [some Irish boys], but James said no. He said that they didn't know the game (69).

This is a good picture of his uncle's fully assimilated Irish American family, so assimilated that it cannot connect with its roots. It has traded hurling for baseball. But the boys at least did form close bonds in Ireland as that summer drew its enclosed neighborhood feeling from O'Connor's boyhood at Hoyle's Field in Woonsocket.

Thirty years later, circa 1965, the narrator of *All in the Family* returns to Dublin with his wife; now O'Connor draws on a recent trip with his own wife. The couple stays at the same Dublin hotel, which has changed little save for a new "American" wing of charmless utilitarian design. Again, it is obviously the Shelbourne. Mr. Guilfoyle, now in his eighties, still cheers with his "Ah ha ha ho!" trademark laugh. By then he has seen hundreds of the powerful and glamorous at the old place—famous writers, American senators, Hollywood tramps, stingy Cardinals—and of course he has a story for each of them. Then the couple moves to a rented house in Kerry for five months. A great peace comes upon the once-estranged couple as they find love again. The narrator, a writer himself, is renewed in his work, and his wife becomes pregnant with their first child. Thus fulfilled by touching the Holy Ground once more, Jack Kinsella can return to America and "to a family of my own" (434), the novel's closing words. "A family of my own": this above all was Ireland's significance for O'Connor. It was a country that placed the family at the center of its Christian society. The problem for Ireland's American offspring, the novel strongly implies, lay precisely in maintaining that traditional valuation. O'Connor's depiction of Ireland and the Irish in *All in the Family* was his most extensive, and his last. Significantly, most of that Ireland was thirty years in the past, just as Skeffington's best years as an old-style Irish American politician were far behind him.

O'Connor spent the last few weeks of his trip doing research on BBC-TV for the *Life* article. Apparently he had to make his visit coincide with the coronation of Queen Elizabeth on June 2. As a result, he had to miss his sister's wedding back in Woonsocket. Barbara had met William Burrell during a Rhode Island summer vacation. Bill was from Providence and became a teacher like Barbara. While teaching at Providence's Classical High School, he began work on his doctorate in education at Harvard. Eventually he joined the faculty of Salve Regina College in Newport, Rhode Island, where he later held administrative positions for many years until his retirement in the mid-1990s.[20]

Little can be found about O'Connor's stay in England; apparently it was a time of work mostly. The famous city gets treated in his fiction for only two pages, again in *All in the Family*, and so that novel may contain some hints about his stay there. The narrator finds that he and his wife "found ourselves sticking very close to London" (301) with few trips to the country, just as O'Connor had done in Dublin; and as in Dublin, there was much theater-going. But work on fiction writing had stalled, and so the narrator comes to regard his London stay as "a penitential experience" (303). This last may be a clue that in June of 1953 O'Connor was anxious to get back to Boston and *The Last Hurrah*.

The fruit of O'Connor's weeks in London was "Do They Want it Dull?" which appeared in *Life* later that year.[21] This article, replete with six photographs, remains his splashiest magazine piece ever, back when *Life* was still a national institution. O'Connor adopts a breezy tone. He does admit that BBC-TV productions like the coronation, newsreels, and drama—"high-minded stuff"—make the American television critic envious. He is gratified

20. Barbara and William Burrell, personal interview, summer 1998.
21. *Atlantic,* November 2, 1953, 109–16.

to see that the American World War II series, *Victory at Sea,* is popular. And he seems relieved that children's programming is blessedly far less violent than the American counterpart. But in the main he finds BBC-TV as numbing as "Auntie," its radio counterpart. There "life is never funny," especially marriage, which is treated in a grimly sociological manner—a sharp insight into one of the many malaises of dreary postwar Britain. BBC-TV even makes sports programs boring, witness a lengthy interview with a ping-pong player. Political debates he finds surprisingly limp. Saturday night lets up as a kind of "fun night," but the music hall fare from provincial cities is lamentably unfunny slapstick. O'Connor was hardly the first to note the marked difference between American and British humor, but he was probably the first to see that television did not change British humor very much. He saw a curious reluctance to exploit the medium's potential for spontaneity: *Monty Python* was far in the future. He ends his article by suggesting that the national game of cricket may help to explain the inconceivable dullness of BBC-TV.

Just in case the *Life* article fell through, O'Connor also wrote a more serious twelve-page article, "Television in Britain: Monopoly Style," intended for *Atlantic Monthly.*[22] It is more researched and sober and has the familiar *Atlantic* hallmarks of historical context and balanced presentation. Here he has much more praise for items like the famous Sunday night dramas, which were not only presented live but presented live all over again on Thursday nights! He also admires the lack of commercialization in a quasi-state company determined to keep standards high. Clearly O'Connor is aiming his article at the magazine's readership, and a comparison of his *Life* and *Atlantic* pieces on the same subject shows two distinctive sides of O'Connor: the comic lampooner of the dull, and the sober admirer of high quality. Indeed, O'Connor's whole literary career was one long effort to get these two sides synchronized. *Atlantic* did not publish his article, which must have disappointed O'Connor, because he had obviously worked hard on it.

By early July he was back in the States. He returned to Ireland several times and invariably stayed at the Shelbourne. He would always visit the Montgomerys, who remained his closest Irish friends for the rest of his life. His next four novels explore Irish American life: politics, religion, class structure, customs and entertainment, and above all family life. While he found the Irish to be quite different from Irish Americans, especially in their politics, he nevertheless enjoyed the quieter and slower pace of life and

22. Courtesy of Peter Davison of *Atlantic Monthly.*

above all the sparkling conversation and humor. Dublin was his transatlantic version of Boston, complete with its parks, river, and musty airs, and just foreign enough to make Boston stand out in slight relief. It was also a good place to write a novel.

⁊

Shortly after O'Connor was dropped from his *Herald* job in December 1952, Ted Weeks again helped out the struggling *Atlantic* family member by giving him work he knew would not be refused because it offered him a chance to meet and work with none other than his old radio hero, Fred Allen.[23] Weeks needed help in editing a book of Allen's radio scripts. Just before O'Connor's hospitalization in January 1953, Ted Weeks and O'Connor had driven to New York to meet with Fred Allen and his wife, Portland Hoffa, in their small apartment. Allen probably would not have remembered any of his brief correspondence with O'Connor from the early 1940s, and so when they met O'Connor decided that a bit of mimicry was in order. Accordingly, when he found that Allen had been typing a letter concerning his tax problems with the state, O'Connor launched into the rolling oratory of Boston's Curley: "Surely, my dear man, you would not begrudge our fair state a small return for the schooling and inspiration which have led to your triumphant career." Allen's stony face lit up with laughter and a friendship began.

Robert Taylor closes the acknowledgments section of his 1989 book on Fred Allen by noting that his own friendship with O'Connor curiously formed one of "life's symmetries":

. . . those distant evenings in the early fifties when I had the privilege of dining every night—in cafeterias—with the wittiest man in Boston, Edwin O'Connor. He often brought along a Fred Allen script, and Ed, then editing *Treadmill to Oblivion,* would read aloud sketches, "doing" (as T.S. Eliot and Dickens put it) the police in different voices. It never occurred to me then that thirty years later I too would study what I then thought of as the sacred texts.

Treadmill to Oblivion was the first of Allen's two memoirs; the other was published posthumously. The book was illustrated with wonderful Hirschfeld caricatures that emphasized Allen's sagging eye pouches, even though these appeared only late in life as a result of illnesses. Half the book consists of edited radio scripts, and the other half running commentary by Allen. O'Connor worked closely with Ted Weeks and Allen, but O'Connor

23. Robert Taylor, O'Connor's friend, wrote an excellent book to which I am indebted for the facts of Allen's life and especially for Allen's friendship with O'Connor: *Fred Allen: His Life and Wit* (Boston: Little, Brown, 1989), especially 188–89 and 303–7.

always insisted that Allen was a good writer and that his own role should only be advisory and editorial. Something of O'Connor's own bristling against editorial direction comes through here. After dedicating the book to Portland, Allen has a kind of second dedication-cum-acknowledgment:

> Ed O'Connor, who has the memory
> of an elephant, helped me with this tome.
> Ted Weeks, who has the energy
> of a beaver, also helped.
> It proves that with an elephant's memory,
> a beaver's energy and two friends
> a radio actor can write a book.[24]

The clear implication is that O'Connor did the bulk of the editing, which was no doubt a labor of love. When *Treadmill to Oblivion* was published in 1954, it became the bestselling radio memoir of its kind.

Fred Allen was born John Sullivan in Cambridge, Massachusetts, in 1894. His ethnicity and devout Catholicism were bonds with O'Connor. During high school he worked as a runner for twenty cents an hour at the new Boston Public Library which now houses his papers as well as O'Connor's. It was there that a chance peek at a book on juggling inspired his first act in vaudeville, when he styled himself the world's worst juggler. Later vaudeville wanderings took him as far as Australia. Like many vaudevillians, he entered radio and from 1934 to 1949 reigned as one of the undisputed masters of the medium. His wife, Portland, a Jewish convert to Catholicism, was one of the principal players in the cast of characters called "Allen's Alley," which included Falstaff Openshaw, Titus Moody, and blowhard Senator Claghorn, who has entered American popular mythology. Allen's show was a hit with both the masses and the highbrows because he had the rare gift of intelligent, sympathetic humor which kept its subtle skepticism from becoming corrosive. Like Mark Twain and Will Rogers before him, he spoke as an American to Americans by combining a large dose of common sense, a stubborn inability to be awed by the high and mighty, and a non-ideological comic outlook. He perfected a dry New England humor delivered in a Yankee deadpan manner. Allen worked extremely hard at his craft—writing his own scripts, answering fan letters, rarely taking vacations, which turned out be working

24. Fred Allen, *Treadmill to Oblivion* (Boston: Atlantic Monthly Press/Little, Brown, 1954).

holidays anyway. When television came along, Allen's half-hearted attempts to make the transition were embarrassing, and when he died suddenly on St. Patrick's Day in 1956 he was already becoming a forgotten figure. Nevertheless, many later comedians from Steve Allen to David Letterman owed him much. Although O'Connor only knew the Allens for three and a half years, so close was their friendship that O'Connor traveled with them on their only trip to Ireland (O'Connor's third) in the fall of 1955.

Fred Allen was almost a quarter of a century older than O'Connor, one of the writer's many older friends from a fading generation. This Irish American Catholic from the Boston area who had successful careers in vaudeville and radio but who stumbled in television was in some indirect and general way a source for the portrayal of Skeffington in *The Last Hurrah*. The mayor's entertaining running commentary in particular owes not a little to Allen, and the "Allen's Alley" crew has a kinship with the mayor's entourage. Traces of Allen the vaudevillian also show up in *I Was Dancing*, although O'Connor's manipulative Daniel Considine has none of Allen's charitable spirit.

During the impoverished years when *The Last Hurrah* was a work in progress, some income continued through occasional articles on the media, primarily television now, for the "Accent on Living" section in *Atlantic Monthly*. "Halls of Ivy" in late 1952 was O'Connor's last column purely about radio. This article was prompted by a newspaper ad for a disc jockey school. O'Connor imagines student Artie Pumple readying himself for final exams by rehearsing his "Conrad Mountbatten" disc jockey persona, a blend of arrogant male sexuality and smarmy anti-communist patriotism. O'Connor's canny take on the annoying drivel of "Mountbatten Chattin'" has not lost its freshness decades later.[25] "The Case of the Sober Shamus" compared the new television detectives to their radio ancestors and found them lacking. He notes how television detectives like Boston Blackie and Martin Kane may smoke heavily in order to advertise sponsors' products, but since hard booze ads were banned the detectives were duds precisely because of their diligence in *not* drinking on the job—an odd jab by the abstemious O'Connor. A Carl Rose illustration depicts a chain-smoking hard-boiled dick virtuously pushing away a whiskey bottle.[26] In "Gold Among the Boo-Hoos," O'Connor is at his devastatingly best satiric form as he excoriates the sham compassion of

25. *Atlantic*, November 1952, 118–19.
26. *Atlantic*, June 1953, 88–89.

programs like *Strike It Rich,* which offer up loads of tears and advertising for their downtrodden guests and viewers. He closes:

There remain disaffected only those malcontents and irreconcilables who for some unfathomable reason feel that assistance predicated upon the compulsory exposure of private grief to public view is both tasteless and degrading, and that the whole chop-licking business is, from beginning to end, enough to make the blood run cold.[27]

His last "Accent on Living" article appeared in June 1955; an accompanying note says that "Edwin O'Connor . . . has just completed his second [novel], which deals with an Irish American political theme." Indeed, it would be the success of that second novel that would end the necessity of writing "Accent on Living" squibs. In "The Indirect Approach" O'Connor wryly presents the fruits of two weeks of research into watching nothing on television except the commercials, this after years of mistakenly watching the programs—a distant allusion to his role as newspaper television critic. While programs were now "weary, predictable repetitions of each other," the commercial remained lively because it was really a "whatisit," as distinct from a "whodunit." Thus, the successful commercial keeps viewer interest because for much of the time the viewer is kept in the dark about the product actually being advertised. For example, a twirling ballerina turns out to be a pitch for a watch.[28] O'Connor anticipated by two years some of Vance Packard's findings in *The Hidden Persuaders,* but without the paranoid undertone of that book and so many like it. O'Connor's sensible spoofing alleges no dark Madison Avenue conspiracies. Nevertheless, his caveat emptor implication is clear: open your eyes, use your mind, and watch your wallet. This "Accent on Living" column hints at weariness with television, and is one of several clues in print that he was about to retire from it all.

A more regular employment for O'Connor had resumed in October 1953 when, after a ten-month hiatus, he became a television critic again, now for the *Boston Post* thanks to some friends there who got him on board. O'Connor felt deep gratitude for their efforts. The *Post* was a blue-collar newspaper that was deeply in trouble but easier to work for than the *Herald* had been. Boston newspapers in the 1950s were an undistinguished lot. The *Globe* was more or less Democratic, in tune with the area's political demographics. The *Herald* and *Traveler*—morning and evening papers of the same company—

27. *Atlantic,* February 1954, 86.
28. *Atlantic,* June 1955, 87–88.

were definitely Republican and ran the hardest-hitting editorials in a state with many targets to hit. Oddly enough, these papers still had a slightly larger circulation than the *Globe* did. The tabloid *Record-American* was merely sensationalist, famous for the argot of its clipped headlines, memorialized by John Updike's essay on Ted Williams's last day at Fenway Park: "Hub Bids Kid Adieu." The *Post* was harder to pin down; it usually played things safe by remaining uncontroversial. The venerable *Christian Science Monitor* was also published in Boston, but this respected national newspaper was ironically little known in the city of the religion's Mother Church.[29]

O'Connor's column was called "About Television" at first, and was later changed to "On Television," although the bungling *Post* often got the two titles mixed up. It ran usually three times a week, but sometimes only twice or even once a week, from October 13, 1953, to January 19, 1956. O'Connor wrote about 300 columns for the *Post*, and so his 150 columns from the *Herald* brings his total output of television columns to 450. But once again the fifteen dollars for each column helped pay the rent at 11 Marlborough Street. Unable to transfer his "Roger Swift" pseudonym from the *Herald*, he now wrote under his own name, and was occasionally touted on page one as a *Post* columnist. He even got a front-page story on August 3, 1954. "Post TV Man Combs Cape in Vain Hunt for Liberace" recounts an assignment in which he conducted a half-hearted search for the bizarre pianist, who was rumored to be vacationing on Cape Cod. O'Connor had someone drive him around the outer Cape, because he still did not drive. The only famous person he spotted was Boston attorney Joseph Welch, famous as Senator McCarthy's antagonist, studying the prices on a Wellfleet supermarket window. O'Connor's column usually alternated with a syndicated television column by Faye Emerson (famous for hairdos), which state of affairs undoubtedly evoked ambivalent feelings in the Boston reviewer.

High on O'Connor's good list once again were comedians. Jimmy Durante topped the list, but O'Connor also liked newcomers like George Gobel for his subtlety, Ernie Kovacs and Jonathan Winters for their originality and promise, and Senor Wences. He admired the English understatement of *Alfred Hitchcock Presents*, in which the best parts of the program were the famous host's openings and closings. O'Connor had less to say about more serious productions, but he did like Rod Serling's *Patterns* and Clare Booth

---

29. A personal note: as a newspaper boy in the Boston suburbs of the mid-1950s, I came to know the religious and political bents of my customers: Irish Catholic Democrats took the *Globe*, Yankee Protestant Republicans the *Herald-Traveler*. Fewer and fewer took the ailing pro-Democratic *Post*. A couple of subway commuters took the *Record-American* for its convenient size. The one subscriber to the *Christian Science Monitor* was the village atheist.

Luce's *The Women*, which he found to be a remarkably negative picture of her sex. One column begins on a Johnsonian note: "There is nothing which so quickly summons up the force of inertia as the prospect of visiting a museum."[30] The "museum" in question was actually the Rare Books Department at the Boston Public Library. O'Connor admits to liking a tour on local television given by the keeper, Zoltan Haraszti, a colorful womanizing Hungarian whom O'Connor later got to know as a neighbor on Beacon Hill. O'Connor could not realize at the time that he was viewing and reviewing the repository for his own papers.

Negative reviews now outran favorable ones by a greater margin than they had in the Roger Swift columns. His very first column easily put down *Bonino*, starring Ezio Pinza. Jackie Gleason was too repetitive, although his sidekick, Art Carney, was okay. Even Fred Allen disappointed as host of a silly game show. On more serious efforts, he found *Omnibus*'s seventy-three minute production of *King Lear* patently ludicrous. Cronkite's *You Are There* historical recreations were "preposterous." *The Millionaire* was odious. The formulaic father-bashing in *The Life of Riley*, with goofy William Bendrix, got his hackles up. He also frowned on the short-lived *Duffy's Tavern*. O'Connor may have been subconsciously reacting to Irish stereotyping in these last two shows, although it should be noted that he had liked *Duffy's Tavern* as a radio show written by a team headed by Abe Burrows, whom he later knew as a good friend at Wellfleet. O'Connor saw right through *The $64,00 Question*: some transparent fakes, even if they are Ivy League professors, do not require a congressional investigation. He shrewdly noted that advertisers cleverly placed their props in shows, like all those modern kitchen scenes that dominated family sitcoms sponsored by appliance makers. As always, he was baffled that shows like Art Linkletter's *People are Funny* actually encouraged people to make willing fools of themselves. Sometimes O'Connor struck a George Apley note, as in this huffy June 1, 1954, put-down of the British comedian Richard Hearne: "[His act] was merely hectic, knockabout stuff, rather in the Red Skelton vein, and I found it distinctly disappointing." Once, when bemoaning the staleness of television jokes recycled from radio, O'Connor actually waxed philosophical in what probably remains the only piece of Thomistic television reviewing: "Saint Thomas Aquinas defines the beautiful object as that which gives pleasure upon being seen. A television joke does not fit within this category."[31] Such tongue-in-cheekery was appreciated by colleagues, but probably not by the *Post*'s readership. On July 26,

---

30. *Boston Post*, December 12, 1953, 5.
31. *Boston Post*, July 15, 1954, 9.

1955, in a tired mood after finishing *The Last Hurrah,* he admits that he's not always up on things like youth fads and dances—an imprudent slip for a reviewer of the newest medium; O'Connor could sometimes sound old before his time. As in his Roger Swift incarnation, he took a casual approach to his employment. On March 27, 1954, barely five months into the job, he announced to his readers that he was taking a "modified sabbatical," which turned out to be almost two months in Ireland. (After a month there he had to write Charlie Morton at the *Atlantic* for a $100 cash advance because the "dizzy pay department" of the *Post* had almost lost track of him. His second trip to Ireland was "marvelous if expensive.")[32] He spent much of the summers of 1954 and 1955 at Wellfleet and mailed in his irregular columns.

In 1954 an unfortunate episode at 247 Gaskill Street exposed some of the strains of upper-middle-class Irish American family life. Orphaned in 1935, Pat Greene had lived for nineteen years as a member of the family. Pat remembers her aunt, Mary O'Connor, as "stern," and Dr. O'Connor as even more so. She graduated from Rhode Island College in 1952 and taught in the Woonsocket schools for two years, thus following in the steps of Mrs. O'Connor. But when she announced her intention of marrying an Army serviceman, both Dr. and Mrs. O'Connor firmly disapproved and eventually disowned her. She saw little of the family after that, and never saw Sonny again. Her marriage lasted, and today she does correspond with O'Connor's sister.[33] This sundering of a close family tie highlights the class tensions in O'Connor's social stratum. O'Connor never publicly mentioned this incident during his life. However, his fictional portraits of unbending paternal figures do intensify from this time on.

An earlier unbending paternal figure had appeared in O'Connor's unpublished novel "A Young Man of Promise."[34] The dating of this second completed novel is a problem. The catalogue of his papers lists its date uncertainly as "1953?" In his study of O'Connor, Hugh Rank dates it from 1950–51 in one place, and from 1952 in another.[35] The work is much less topical than *The Oracle,* so historical allusions other than an early Cold War backdrop are of little help. O'Connor did tell several interviewers that he had written the novel during one or two fallow periods during the writing of *The Last Hurrah,* which could conceivably place it anywhere from 1950 to 1955. He also

32. Edwin O'Connor, letter to Charles Morton, April 27, 1954, courtesy of Peter Davison.
33. Pat Greene Thibodeau, telephone interview, August 2, 1999.
34. EOCP 41.
35. Rank, *Edwin O'Connor,* 51 and 15, respectively.

The Shelbourne Hotel in Dublin, circa 1953. O'Connor always stayed at this "chipped and faded" center of Anglo-Ireland. *Courtesy of Shelbourne Meridien Hotel.*

said several times that he began both novels at about the same time, which would place its inception in late 1950 and early 1951. The best guess for sustained work on "Promise" appears to be 1952—after *The Oracle,* but before the final push on *The Last Hurrah,* with which it has some important ties. One further point: O'Connor said in several interviews that when he read over the completed manuscript it did not sound right and so was never sent out.[36] However, the manuscript at the Boston Public Library is contained in a large folder from the London publishing firm of Pearn, Pollinger, & Higham, who had apparently rejected it. Evidently O'Connor had hoped for some success in England, where *The Oracle* was then selling better than in the States.

"Promise" looks back to "Anthony Cantwell" and forward to *The Last Hurrah* as it circulated a few items from the earlier work and injected many more into the later one. The St. Mansard College of "Cantwell" becomes Mount Mansard College in "Promise"; however, little of the silly mysteriousness of the place survived the name change, for "Promise" was to be more serious. More importantly, the narrator and protagonist, Kevin Rowan, writes

36. For example, his interview with James F. Leonard, *Boston Post,* February 15, 1956, 7.

the "Little Simp" comic strip for a newspaper owned by one Amos Force. This Kevin Rowan becomes Adam Caulfield in *The Last Hurrah,* via an awkward transmigration, where he still writes "Little Simp." In "Promise" Amos Force is Kevin's patron of sorts because Kevin works as "a publisher's whim" (11). Amos Force appears as a nutrition-obsessed preacher of brotherly love who wants to annihilate the Reds with atomic bombs; Kevin describes him as a "proprietary homunculus" (Chapter Seven). When Amos Force reappears so memorably in *The Last Hurrah,* he is the embodiment of cold and cracked Yankee parsimony. This second Amos Force is even more crabbed and unbalanced, and looms large in *The Last Hurrah,* when O'Connor took his full revenge on the *Herald* for firing him in late 1952. Furthermore, he extended Amos's thin bloodlines to his father, Caleb, who had publicly fired and humiliated Adam Caulfield's grandmother from her post as a domestic over petty theft of needed food. Skeffington sums up the Forces, son and father, in a devastating simile: "like getting a rat out of a mouse" (*LH* 66). Also transferred from "Promise" to *The Last Hurrah* is Ralph, the managing editor and a minor character in both novels, and Edgar Burbank who is of some importance in both works. The newspaper world of *The Last Hurrah,* a world O'Connor knew fairly well by 1952, was first created in "Promise" and then adapted to the later novel with varying degrees of success.

Thirtyish Kevin Rowan is his father's only child; his mother had died some years back. This is the first significant instance of a striking pattern in O'Connor's novels, wherein the mother dies so that a father-son conflict can emerge more starkly. Many subsequent main characters will be motherless or widowers, because O'Connor needed to clear the ground in order to concentrate on the all-important subject of fathers and sons. If we except *Benjy,* only at the end of his career in his unfinished play "The Traveler from Brazil" is a mother-son scenario given significant attention.

The first chapter introduces Kevin's father as the "kindly but remote" president of Mount Mansard College. He shares a few traits with Anthony Cantwell's father. Father and son live together in the president's house, even though for years Kevin had been away from home at school and in the service. Although they have become somewhat closer since the mother's death, the father looks on Kevin's comic strip with "polite distaste." Little Simp is a small orphaned boy whose pet chipmunk, "Daddy," is always perched on his shoulder. Simp often says, "I guess it's just . . . the only Daddy I ever did know." (Freudians, take note!) Together boy and chipmunk, like Orphan Annie and Sandy, do battle in which "the twelve-year-old American child [is] successfully pitted against the powers of international evil" (17), an easy comic strip task during the Cold War. O'Connor's sendup of such silliness does not obscure the doubling of the father-son relationship.

In Chapter Two the main conflict gets under way when Kevin meets Mrs. Anna Archibald at his Uncle Timothy's house. Timothy is a tiresome amateur theologian. He is another paternal figure, but much more distasteful than his brother. (O'Connor sometimes splits his father figures into ideal and odious types.) Anna is O'Connor's idealized woman: tall, leggy, graceful, with long dark hair. A German by birth, she had married an Englishman who was later killed as a spy by Hungarian Reds. She thus comes in a shade of Graham Greene, as his father notes to Kevin who, like O'Connor, was an avid reader of the newly famous novelist: "A beautiful woman, a spy, a bit of practical theology" (32). And in fact the novel does begin to develop in a Greene-like fashion, although it will hardly end as such. The title of the novel that had made Greene a bestselling author in 1948 is even alluded to at a critical moment which Kevin calls "the heart of the matter" (179). As is frequently the case in dealing with Irish American males, Anna takes the initiative in befriending Kevin. She had tired of New York and its intellectuals, who were full of Trotsky, Freud, and homosexual British poets (an allusion to *Partisan Review*), and she now prefers Kevin's city. As usual, this city is unnamed, but Kevin confides to her that, having published some short stories, he is now working on a novel about a city very different from New York. The autobiographical placards could not be more obvious.

Subsequent scenes needle the pretensions of the city's arty set; at one particularly phony party Dylan Thomas, then on one of his notorious American tours, fails to show up. O'Connor gets back on track when a more resolute Kevin proposes marriage to Anna, who accepts. But trouble, in the form of carping Uncle Timothy, appears. Anna is not Catholic, and so the wedding ceremony will not take place at the customary nuptial Mass but only as a short, private ceremony in the rectory—a remarkable foreshadowing of O'Connor's own wedding a decade later. More Catholic than the pope, childless but rich Uncle Timothy objects strenuously and threatens to disown his nephew. He even berates Kevin for not entering the priesthood. But a much bigger problem arises when it turns out that Anna's husband is alive after all. Hopelessly in love, Kevin and Anna apparently consummate their love, in a rare moment for O'Connor, when "clasped together . . . we sealed . . . our promise" (Chapter Eight). This is as explicit as O'Connor ever gets on sex.

The stage is now set for the showdown between Kevin and his father. Determined to marry a divorced Anna and brave excommunication (then an automatic penalty) from the Church that Kevin now conveniently sees as uncompromising, and supported by the Greeneian Anna who sees herself as "a conspirator," Kevin appeals to "the one person by whom I wanted so desperately to be understood" (150). His father is moved by Kevin's plight, but he is unimpressed by Kevin's slippery logic and terminology. He scorns Kevin's notion of getting things "fixed" with Anna as he reminds his son of the state of his soul. Kevin convinces himself that in this showdown between desire and religious dictates, his father will surely lose. Suddenly, however, O'Connor pulls the rug from under Kevin when Anna finds that she loves her restored husband after all. In the important penultimate chapter, a second long confrontation ensues between son and father, who now plays confessor. He begins by assessing Kevin's life in the third person: "On the agreeable waters of indolence this young man assiduously practices the deadman's float." In his peroration he challenges Kevin: "Do you think a Faith, born and bred in the bones, believed in, however tremulously, for a lifetime, can be so easily shelved?" This rolling, figurative rhetoric with its Victorian Hibernicisms has Skeffington's signature and thus derives from Curley. But only partly so. From someone in his life O'Connor had picked up the tone of a slightly frumpy disparager. Sometimes O'Connor spoke this way himself, though to be sure parodistically; certainly he gave the voice to many of his characters. Given the unmistakable autobiographical elements in "Promise," along with its sharp conflict of son with father, a plausible case can be made that at least some elements of Kevin's father, curiously never named, derive from the author's own father. This is the first of at least three novels—"Promise," *The Edge of Sadness,* and *I Was Dancing*—which position toward the end an extended conflict between father and son. The matter is not resolved satisfactorily in any of the three cases.

O'Connor now softens the picture of the father, who admits that he feels like "Pascal among the Jesuits" (205) in countering Kevin's rationalizations. Moreover, he admits to being a failed eighteenth-century literary scholar; like Kevin, he has not published anything significant. He thus feels compromised in his position as president of a college he dislikes anyway. In the novel's most unexpected scene, father asks son: "Do you perhaps see a faintly familiar pattern?" (207). He urges Kevin to leave the newspaper and his arty friends. He also asks Kevin to leave home itself, as he sets a mild deadline of a week for this last request. Furthermore, for his own good, Kevin should take his book-writing seriously. But O'Connor ends Kevin's story unconvincingly. When the week is up, Kevin decides that his father's humble confession gives credence and urgency to his vocational advice, and so he will indeed work hard at finishing his book; however, he will also remain in his father's house if only to show the father his new resolution. O'Connor wants it both ways: independent success by a Kevin still bound to his father. "Promise" tried to resolve a Graham Greene triangle, but he let his own personal and filial concerns muddy the outcome.

Whether there was an Anna in O'Connor's life remains a question mark for this most private of people when it came to romantic attachments. However, for several years in the mid-1950s O'Connor was interested in at least three different women on the Cape, all of them of German origin like Anna, and two of them beyond reach as married women. These women were stunning and much sought after. Sometimes O'Connor's romantic yearnings for these women, which were never fulfilled, overlapped.[37] They certainly help to explain his long leisurely sojourns in Wellfleet. Was there a German woman who preceded Anna, or were O'Connor's romantic longings a matter of life copying his own art, or at least his fantasy? Apart from the subplot of *All in the Family,* "A Young Man of Promise" is O'Connor's only novel with a love interest.

As O'Connor stood poised on the biblical midway point of thirty-five, he was groping for the resolve to finish his magnum opus—that urban novel which Kevin had described to Anna. "Promise" can be read as self-laceration for O'Connor's postwar years of dawdling, as it may have seemed to his father at least. It was also a transition to *The Last Hurrah.* There an inside allusion employs a much more interesting protagonist to act as gravedigger for Kevin Rowan, when Frank Skeffington derides his political opponent as a jejune "young man of promise" (*LH* 311).

The roots of *The Last Hurrah* are many. As O'Connor worked on the book with renewed energy from mid-1953 to early 1955, he gathered up many strands as far back as boyhood memories and as recent as yesterday's headlines. Fred Allen was not alone in noting that O'Connor had "the memory of an elephant," and the normally self-effacing O'Connor himself often credited his own powers of listening and remembering as his best assets. The book was to be about the political Irish, and to do justice to his characters O'Connor knew that a writer had to record above all their tones, diction, and oratory. Like a latter-day bardic *fili* who preserved Celtic mores, lore, traditions, laws, and history by stupendous feats of memory, O'Connor set himself the task of organizing his vivid memories of speech and transforming them into a twentieth-century urban epic with a tribal chieftain at its center. From the

37. Ati Johansen, telephone interviews, March 7 and 10, 2001.

most local of Rhode Island political memories some twenty years old, to the larger post-Roosevelt national scene, he wove his story slowly and deliberately. He also incorporated material from his Notre Dame years, his broadcasting work, Coast Guard duty, and newspaper stints as television reviewer. Finally, intertwined in the many elements of the novel was his continuing concern with the nature of family.

The work of organizing and synthesizing all this material was laborious, given O'Connor's writing habits, which were by now unchangeable. He told an interviewer at the time:

I never have outlined. When I start I have no idea how to carry through. I write—I form the story, as I go along. The first draft of the book is final, although I correct as I go along. I rewrite a great deal as I go. I may rewrite a page a dozen times, but then it is final; I don't go back. I don't write easily; the work is painstaking; but I write consecutively.[38]

Rhode Island politics, with its intense local flavor, was O'Connor's first schooling. His memories of Congressman Ambrose Kennedy, along with the involvement of an O'Connor family elder in Woonsocket politics, have already been noted. From these first sources O'Connor saw Irish American politicians as colorful, humorous rascals with endless yarns to spin. The miniaturized politics of his home city and of the smallest state taught him that indeed "all politics is local," as Congressman Tip O'Neill, who inherited Curley's congressional seat, so famously put it. Also, in *The Last Hurrah* O'Connor for the first time alludes briefly to a town called Derrford (*LH* 29), which he would use again briefly as Deerford in *The Edge of Sadness* and *All in the Family*. The details culled about this Derrford/Deerford, especially its large French-Canadian population, point to a small city much like Woonsocket and may hint at other submerged Rhode Island lore. How much detail from Rhode Island O'Connor eventually used may never be known; one suspects it may be considerable.

He did draw on one widely circulated incident during Rhode Island's Irish-Italian clashes from early in the century. It seems that a gruff Irish American pastor had installed a statue of St. Rocco in the church to appease newly arrived Italian immigrants. But when promised funding for the statue was not forthcoming from the Italians, the pastor delivered an ultimatum from the pulpit. If money did not come in, he thundered, then "Rocco, me bucko, out you go!" *The Last Hurrah* changes the circumstances to a falling out among Italians during the election. Old John Gorman ponders the fate

---

38. Edwin O'Connor, interview with George C. Hull, *Providence Journal*, February 21, 1956.

of the betrayed party and thinks, *"Enrico, me bucko, out you go!"* (*LH* 89; O'Connor's italics).[39]

Also from Rhode Island came the name for O'Connor's most famous character. At La Salle Academy O'Connor probably knew at least two students named Skeffington, one of them from Woonsocket, the other a Francis Skeffington who was killed in World War II. More important than these, however, is the J. F. Skeffington Funeral Home in Providence. According to the current owner, John M. Skeffington, O'Connor took the name Frank Skeffington from this establishment's colorful history. When he was a teenager in the late 1950s, John M. Skeffington was with his father at the Lafayette House restaurant in Foxboro, Massachusetts. His father spotted O'Connor and went over to talk to the man who had written *The Last Hurrah*. When his father asked O'Connor if he got "Frank Skeffington" from his family, O'Connor replied that he had. O'Connor explained that he borrowed the "Frank" from an uncle, J. Frank, so as not to cause any embarrassment to the business. The father of this J. Frank Skeffington was a James Skeffington from Ireland, a Providence ward heeler from earlier in the century, and founder of the Skeffington funeral business. As ward heeler he helped Irish immigrants get on the police and fire departments.[40] As funeral director he provided that curious center for Irish gatherings which O'Connor would use so effectively in Knocko Minihan's wake in Chapter Eight. Incidentally, although that wake has become part of Irish American folklore, many people now have a faulty memory of the scene: it was not at all the boozy affair of inaccurate recollection, but instead was a sober political wake at which Skeffington shone.[41] Politics and funeral homes had a close relationship for the Irish. Finally, while Skeffington is actually an English name, it is occasionally found in Ireland. During his travel in the west of Ireland, O'Connor may have seen the old Skeffington Arms Hotel on Eyre Square in Galway. Francis Sheehy-Skeffington, an idealistic pacifist, was murdered while under arrest by a crazed army officer during the Easter Rebellion of 1916.

O'Connor's ear for political folklore was further trained during those Chicago visits to Notre Dame classmates' homes, which were alive with Irish American political talk. O'Connor often cited these Windy City visits as stir-

39. My thanks to my colleague Professor Paul O'Malley of the Providence College history department for spotting this item. Many years later, an Italian pastor retrieved the banished statue from storage and announced to the parish, "Rocco, me bucko, in ye go!" Rhode Island parish politics can be as amusing as the other kind.

40. John M. Skeffington, telephone interview, June 11, 1999.

41. John Kelleher and O'Connor had long talks about Irish wakes, but neither could ever remember witnessing a wild Irish American wake, which leads one to conclude that it may have been the rare exception and hardly the rule.

ring his first unformed desire to write a great political novel. Something in the smoky political air of Chicago that had inspired Finley Peter Dunne to create the famous barroom pundit Mr. Dooley at the turn of the twentieth century also intrigued the East Coast visitor. O'Connor told a Boston interviewer that at parties he would seek out older political types among the Irish: "I'd open an avenue for them to discuss politics and then sit back and listen. I'd take careful note of everything they said. I'd put it down in a notebook later."[42] Chicago's mayor during those late Depression years was boss Edward J. Kelly, who fulfilled the city's requirement that its mayors look beefy and jowly. His high-handed rule from 1933 to 1947 worked successfully with Roosevelt's policies, thus providing an exception to the tacked-on thesis in *The Last Hurrah* that the New Deal spelled the demise of the old-time bosses.[43] Chicago was unique among big American cities, because fiscally conservative rural Republicans in the state legislature had unusual oversight powers with respect to the Democratically controlled machines in the city and Cook County. This inevitable clash of an older, prudent ethos with urban immigrant demands is a major topic in *The Last Hurrah*.

During his prewar radio years, O'Connor also tasted the political flavors of four cities, three of them in the Northeast and in the hands of Irish American political machines. Little in his work of that time shows a movement toward specifically political themes, but he took a keen interest in blowy rhetoric like the radio war hype that amused and dismayed him. His Skeffington would be a colorful orator, if nothing else, though cut from the cloth of an earlier era.

Perhaps the first person who piqued O'Connor's interest in Boston's redoubtable James Michael Curley was Louis Brems. O'Connor got to know this trouper from the old Keith Circuit vaudevillians during his two Coast Guard years in Boston, when Brems was a Naval Reserve Lieutenant Commander and O'Connor's commanding officer. In *The Rascal King*, Curley's biographer Jack Beatty describes his subject's liberal employment of show business talents, Louis Brems chief among them. Brems's specialty was warming up political rallies before Curley arrived, by calculation, quite late. Brems was known for his "Uncle Dinny" stories, which appealed to the Irish love of mockery of their own. In one such story, Dinny has drowned while drunk, and his widow is surprised that Dinny's union has collected $5,000 for her. "Glory be to God," said the widow. "He couldn't hold a job. Couldn't

42. Edwin O'Connor, interview with James F. Leonard, *Boston Post*, February 14, 1956.
43. See Michael F. Funchion, "The Political and Nationalist Dimension," in *The Irish in Chicago*, ed. Lawrence J. McCaffrey (Urbana, Ill.: University of Illinois Press, 1987), 83–87.

write. Couldn't read." To which a friend replied, "Thank God he couldn't swim."[44] Brems also did a stint as an official city greeter for Mayor Maurice Tobin, who had defeated Curley in 1937. From this born raconteur, who had worked with both Curley and his opponent, O'Connor heard hundreds of stories and anecdotes, mostly humorous as required by the irrepressible politics of the city, and many of which enlivened *The Last Hurrah*. O'Connor kept a large glossy photo of the dapper Brems in uniform and always gave him credit, as he did in a 1964 interview when he thanked Brems in particular for introducing him to a "hilarious group" of Boston political zanies.[45] O'Connor paid Brems the compliment of putting him into the novel as Cuke Gillen, an ex-vaudevillian, now city greeter for Skeffington. While Gillen's role is not a major one, he is one of the few characters in *The Last Hurrah* with a clearly recognizable source. His appearance is memorable:

He was a small, spruce, agile man with a spike of grey moustache and thinning hair parted exactly in the middle; somehow there hovered over him, like a coat of invisible dust, the aura of a bygone age of entertainment: the Keystone Cop, the solitary banjoist, the Old Soft Shoe, and the man in the boater and the blazer. . . . He had a high, penetrating nasal voice, and told stories in a variety of dialects (*LH* 118).

From all accounts, this replicates Louis Brems. However, O'Connor hints that Brems may have incurred Curley's displeasure with his tendency to go overboard with the ethnic jokes. Skeffington sternly warns his advance man that "[w]e're in a sensitive age, Cuke" (121). Nevertheless, Brems's tales satisfied two of O'Connor's requirements for a good story: that it be about politics, and that it be conducted in vaudevillian style.

Another major source for material about Curley was one Clement Norton, a Boston original. By the time O'Connor got to know him, Clem Norton had served on the Boston City Council and the Boston School Committee, and for some years had been superintendent of Commonwealth Pier. As a perennial candidate for mayor, he had run poorly against Curley several times. Toward the end, he campaigned as a one-man operation from his own blaring sound truck. Once he had saved Curley from serious injury or even death when he restrained a frightened parade horse Curley was riding; the horse fell over seconds after Curley dismounted.[46] By the time O'Connor knew him, Norton was a political fringe figure, but according to Arthur Schlesinger middlemen and has-beens were O'Connor's favorites because

44. Beatty, *Rascal King*, 410–11.
45. "Edwin O'Connor: Bostonian on Broadway," interview with P. C. Brooks, *Boston*, November 1964, 49.
46. Beatty, *Rascal King*, 286.

they divulged more than sitting politicians. Schlesinger also notes that John F. Kennedy was fascinated by Norton and invited him to Hyannisport once.[47] Well read and informed, Norton was nevertheless not quite *compos mentis*— although with Clem Norton one could never quite tell whether his fantastical anecdotage was serious or for show. O'Connor had met him during his Coast Guard service, and had drawn him not too favorably in "The Interview." A year after O'Connor died, Norton said that when deep into writing *The Last Hurrah* O'Connor would actively seek him out for Curley lore, sometimes lying in wait on Boston street corners frequented by the talkative quack. Norton also claimed that when he realized O'Connor was writing a novel based on Curley, O'Connor promised him that he too would be in the book. O'Connor could not get enough Curley from Norton, but this source alone should dispel any simplistic Curley-Skeffington parallel: Norton was hardly a balanced witness. Norton always did admire Skeffington's faithfulness to Curley's oratorical fog; it was Norton's way of taking some credit.[48] Curley died poor, and years later Clem Norton ended his own days in a pauper's hospital, where he would bang his spoon and shout, "I'll tell Jim Curley about this!"[49]

Clem Norton is immortalized in *The Last Hurrah* as Charlie Hennessey; like Brems-Gillen, this is another bona fide borrowing from life.

He was almost always alone these nights, but he was never lonesome, for he was excellent company for himself. . . . He was a sallow, happy tub of a man in his fifties with bulging excited eyes; every night he roamed about his house at a joyous half-trot, whistling loudly and tunelessly. He fed the horsemeat to the hounds, and if he thought of it he fed himself. Sometimes he hurled himself into a chair to read anything that was handy—this was part of his "keeping up": he subscribed to twenty widely various magazines. . . . He would talk into [his tape recorder] without hesitation for a half-hour or more and then . . . would listen with appreciation . . . (*LH* 96).

O'Connor had written an earlier eighteen-page sketch of Clem Norton entitled "C.B." and had sent it to Helen Strauss; nothing came of it.[50] C.B. is Cornelius Bernard Cullinan, a middle-aged Irish bachelor and political loser. His passion for political ranting on behalf of dubious causes such as big-eared children makes him a social boor. One night after a particularly embarrassing outing, he retires to his lonely bed with the knowledge that his "racial

47. Arthur Schlesinger Jr., personal interview, April 3, 1999. Professor Schlesinger also has a memorable portrait of Norton in *BL*, 10.
48. Robert L. Hassett, "Clem Norton Speaks, and Jim Curley Comes Alive," *Boston Herald-Traveler*, April 18, 1969: 3.
49. Beatty, *Rascal King*, 286.
50. EOCP 42. O'Connor had also written an early unpublished version of the Knocko Minihan wake scene entitled "De Mortuis." EOCP 43.

weakness" for the gab makes him a misfit. This version of Clem Norton is more poignant than the Charlie Hennessey one, but for *The Last Hurrah* O'Connor could not have any tragic figures other than Skeffington.

O'Connor saved two letters from Clem Norton, from 1956 and 1966.[51] Each is typed even closer than single-spacing, on a tiny 3-by-5-inch piece of paper, front and back, without any margins. Norton leaps from topic to topic with breathtaking alacrity, but seldom says anything about himself or O'Connor. He lived in a multiform world of his own.

When O'Connor recorded three passages from *The Last Hurrah* in 1962, he made sure that one of them included Charlie Hennessey, even though the album description pointedly omits him.[52] To spare Clem Norton any embarrassment, perhaps O'Connor did not wish to call unnecessary attention to Hennessey's source. O'Connor chose the scene in chapter five (*LH* 95–99) in which Festus "Mother" Garvey fruitlessly implores the eccentric Hennessey to join the alliance against Skeffington. O'Connor gives Hennessey a snappy voice full of verbal ticks like "my dear man" and his all-purpose "Marvelous, marvelous!" (Norton retained "marvelous" to the end of his life.) Garvey's hoarse dimness is a nice counterpoint. In listening to the recording one becomes keenly aware how real these characters and voices were to the author.

Beyond Brems/Gillen and Norton/Hennessey, the identification of characters in *The Last Hurrah* becomes a guessing game—with the obvious exception of Curley/Skeffington. O'Connor himself sometimes hinted that he modeled only a few characters directly from life. For the most part he usually created composites or, as in the case of Amos Force, an allegorical figure—in that case one of doddering New England Yankee stinginess and anti-Irish vituperation gathered from O'Connor's experiences at the *Herald*. Still, some people close to O'Connor insist that they have spotted some suspects. A friend wrote him that he recognized the original of Caleb Force: "the little man down by the Esplanade that had to be walked on a leash."[53] Arthur Schlesinger believes that the Nathaniel Gardiner who appraises Skeffington so judiciously was lifted from the career of Henry Lee Shattuck, who was one of the last Yankees in Boston politics. He was an uncle of McGeorge Bundy, an important adviser to Presidents Kennedy and Johnson: at twenty-two he ran for his uncle's retired seat on the Boston City Council and lost.[54] O'Connor was careful to create a wise Yankee like Gardiner; otherwise he ran the

51. EOCP 207.

52. *The Last Hurrah: Selections Read by Edwin O'Connor* (New York: CMS Records, 1969).

53. Kenneth D. Clapp, letter to Edwin O'Connor, March 7, 1956, EOCP 111.

54. Arthur Schlesinger Jr., personal interview, April 3, 1999.

risk of loading the dice. Peggy Yntema, O'Connor's editor at Atlantic Monthly Press, believes that the nincompoop son of banker Norman Cass was inspired by Boston Fire Commissioner Russell Codman, a Yankee whose bedroom was fitted out with fire alarm communications equipment.[55]

There is more general recognition that the character of Skeffington's opponent, Kevin McCluskey, owed something to Maurice Tobin, who defeated Curley for mayor in 1937 and 1941, and who served as Secretary of Labor under President Truman. But Schlesinger notes that Tobin was more solid and independent than his fictional counterpart.[56] As Curley's reformist antagonist, Tobin made alliances with moderate Republicans and those Irish who were finally embarrassed by Curley. Tobin's reforms were modest, but they at least pointed the way to a more sensible and tolerant governance. In transforming him into the easily manipulated mannequin of McCluskey— Skeffington thinks of him as a "six-foot hunk of talking putty" (*LH* 156)— O'Connor knew he was creating a caricature only remotely connected to Tobin.

One of the funniest McCluskey episodes can be pinned not on Maurice Tobin but on the veteran diplomat Averell Harriman in his 1954 campaign for governor of New York. In one of his television columns O'Connor unmasked the absurdity of candidate Harriman's live appearance at home on NBC's new *Today* program. While Harriman is talking about the housing issues, his wife enters with a tray of coffee, apologizes to the camera and says, "He works so hard ... that he forgets all about food!"[57] O'Connor found such antics unintentionally hilarious. He quickly arranged a similar fate for McCluskey, whose squeaky-clean wife bears him a tray of milk and cookies during a televised interview: "I have to remind my husband that a candidate is supposed to eat as well as work," she informs the interviewer (*LH* 280).

The chief source for *The Last Hurrah* is the man himself: James Michael Curley (1874–1958). O'Connor never admitted to the obvious source for Frank Skeffington, and would even protest mildly to those who insisted on the parallel. Most people winked back. While to be sure O'Connor's Skeffington is not Boston's Curley in all respects, and while Skeffington may be something of a composite figure, nevertheless Curley was, far more than any other source, O'Connor's inspiration. Put another way, without a Curley *The Last Hurrah* would have been impossible. One reason O'Connor had to walk

55. Peggy Yntema, personal interview, April 10, 1999.
56. Schlesinger, Introduction to *BL*, 14.
57. *Boston Post,* October 16, 1954, 5.

a careful line with Skeffington's pedigree was His Honor's well-known Hibernian fondness for intimidation by lawsuit. As it turned out, O'Connor did have cause to be concerned.

James Curley was born in the slums of Roxbury in conditions little removed from the notorious Irish shantytowns of a few decades earlier.[58] His father died when James was only ten; later James added his father's name "Michael" to his own. Throughout his career he made considerable political hay out of his boyhood deprivations, which were real enough but whose rehearsal wore thin during post-World War II prosperity. Intelligent, diligent, and always shrewd, Curley advanced without a high school diploma but with plenty of lines from Shakespeare, a prominent trait in Skeffington as well. He entered politics in his twenties, in 1900, when he served on the old Boston Common Council. Then it was higher up to the state legislature in 1902. After serving as a city alderman, he was elected to Congress, where he served from 1911 to 1914. He then began the first of many terms as mayor of Boston, for which he is most famous. He was mayor from 1914 to 1918, 1922 to 1926, 1930 to 1934, and 1946 to 1950. He ran for mayor ten times altogether. He was governor of Massachusetts once, 1935 to 1937, and ran unsuccessfully two more times. He was in Congress again from 1943 to 1946; he ran four times in all for that office. During his whole adult life Curley was a campaigner, and this is the man *The Last Hurrah* depicts. For the first half of the twentieth century Curley dominated Boston politics. It is a measure of the road traveled by the Irish in politics that for the second half of that century Massachusetts Democrats became enthralled with the very different political and personal styles of the Kennedy family.

Curley was a tough, determined politician. Like the newcomer to a game whose rules favored the cup-holders, he threw the rule book away and had great fun in doing so. He made ethnic politics a thing of symbolic antics, where resentment marinated in grandiloquence. He accomplished a great deal for the forgotten of Boston, especially of course for the Irish, but his unscrupulous methods nearly bankrupted the city and incurred the wrath of the Yankee establishment, which still had financial power. Toward the end of his long career Curley began replaying himself badly, and in his reelection bid for City Hall in 1949, he suffered his last defeat as an incumbent, even though he ran pathetically two more times. The 1949 defeat by John B. Hynes was the immediate catalyst for O'Connor's novel. Hynes, now regarded as an

58. The reader is again referred to Jack Beatty's excellent biography of Curley, *The Rascal King*, from which much of this information is derived. An earlier 1949 biography, *The Purple Shamrock*, by Boston newspaperman Joseph F. Dineen, is less reliable.

important early architect of the new Boston, had been appointed temporary mayor in 1947, when Curley was in a federal prison for mail fraud. But in 1949 the prosaic Hynes won City Hall by his own efforts.[59] (After five months, Curley was released from prison in November 1947 by President Truman, who needed Irish American votes for the upcoming election; Truman gave Curley a full pardon in 1950. None of this got into O'Connor's novel.) O'Connor blended Curley's 1949 defeat with his defeats by Tobin in 1937 and 1941. O'Connor also made a few attempts to bring his novel into the mid-1950s, as when Charlie Hennessey bemoans the soldier-president from Kansas in an obvious allusion to Eisenhower. But the patina of the novel belongs to an older era of colorful rogues like Curley who made up the rules as they went.

Ever since Louis Brems had regaled O'Connor with tales of Curley in 1943, O'Connor's attention had been drawn toward this living legend. But for a long time, probably up to Curley's defeat in 1949, O'Connor failed to see that in Curley's life, especially his last defeat, lay the stuff of the novel about Irish Americans and Boston he had wanted to write. Urban politics was the story of the Irish immigrant experience. O'Connor was drawn especially to the later, over-confident phase. The book could look back to a fading time, and glimpse the future as well.

So fascinated did O'Connor become with Curley that he would listen rapturously to recordings of Curley's speeches.[60] He also kept a Curley campaign comic book, probably from 1949. It is full of laughable, bloated accounts of Curley's feats.[61] He also knew several of Curley's campaign songs. In the late stages of writing his novel O'Connor had become a noted adept at "doing" Curley and his assorted henchmen. Peggy Yntema remembers O'Connor at a dinner party actually phoning Curley at his famous Jamaic-away mansion with the shamrock shutters. Curley was then out of public office for some years, but he listened avidly to the mysteriously confidential voice delivering fresh dispatches of gossip about City Hall. The party guests had to stifle their guffaws as O'Connor held the old rogue spellbound.[62] For years O'Connor had been intrigued and amused by florid rhetoric, especially the Hiberno-American style. After the clipped Kennedy diction, Americans forgot how prevalent the older rhetoric had been in American public dis-

59. For a good account of the Curley problem in this bizarre but transitional era, see Thomas H. O'Connor, "A Hopeless Backwater," in *Building a New Boston: Politics and Urban Renewal 1950–1970* (Boston: Northeastern University Press, 1993).

60. Barbara O'Connor Burrell, personal interview, summer 1998.

61. EOCP 305.

62. Yntema, interview.

course, F.D.R. being perhaps its last notable practitioner. It is possible that O'Connor read in the 1932 La Salle Academy yearbook the rolling stiltedness of a eulogy to a recently deceased student. Sonorous phrases and romantic allusions such as "the youthful Galahad" sound eerily like Skeffington's soaring memorial to a "little drunken maniac . . . dripping spittle on his lapels" named Eddie McLaughlin, one of the three selections O'Connor recorded. Here rhetoric and reality barely touch as Skeffington virtually canonizes the shabby miscreant and anticipates God himself: "Well done, Eddie McLaughlin! Well done, thou good and faithful servant!" (*LH* 124–28)

But platform buffoonery was not the only side to Skeffington, or even to Curley. In the June 1946 *Atlantic,* where O'Connor made his first appearance, he surely read an article on Finley Peter Dunne and his Mr. Dooley by his future friend John Kelleher. Kelleher writes of Dooley's "natural kindliness, combined with a bitter hatred of hypocrisy." Dooley's strong sense of evil underscored his belief that utopian dreams are impossible; hence his suspicion of reformers. Some of these qualities found their way into Skeffington's dismissal of the "Goo-goo ladies" (an allusion to the Good Government Association, an anti-Irish Yankee front), though to be sure kindliness is more pronounced in Skeffington than it was in his model.

John Kelleher of course talked with O'Connor about Curley. He particularly remembers Curley's wildly inaccurate blarney about Ireland. Unaccountably, Curley antagonized Prime Minister Eamon de Valera by taking a swipe at the Irish Civil War of 1922–23, which "Dev" had instigated. During a 1947 visit to Boston, de Valera refused to meet Curley, who nevertheless always made it a point to invite himself to any fete for "Dev."[63]

Curley's undeniable corruption did not escape O'Connor's notice, but he took pains to put it into the context of long-denied Irish grievances exacting their revenge. Also, O'Connor disputes the contention of Mother Garvey and a host of Republican opponents that Skeffington fed at the public trough for his own gain. O'Connor lets Charlie Hennessey come closer to the truth when he disabuses Garvey of this obsession:

"Frank Skeffington a rich man: oh, marvelous! . . . The man's not rich. He has no money at all. It's all legend. He's stolen millions, but it's gone, all gone . . . like slush down a manhole in March! Frank doesn't even want to be rich; he *has* to get rid of the money. . . . Oh, good-hearted! You have to say that for him. A crook and no culture . . . but a grand heart" (*LH* 99–100).

O'Connor's friend Professor John Kenneth Galbraith remembers O'Connor as a self-styled expert on sniffing out political corruption.[64] O'Connor's in-

---

63. Kelleher, interview.
64. John Kenneth Galbraith, personal interview, November 11, 1999.

terest in the subject was seldom partisan and never ideological. He was more interested in personalities and tactics as good subject matter.

Today Curley's monuments are many, even as living memory of the man fades. Many hospitals, schools, roads, parks, and playgrounds owe their existence to him. The Kennedy people spurned him as old hat, but a newer generation of revisionists is more willing to accord Curley a place in American political history as the spokesman for the downtrodden who had no social safety nets. Three sculpted likenesses of Curley can be easily found in Boston. One was done in 1930 on a historical relief commissioned for the tercentenary of the city's founding. But one must look closely at the figures of the arriving English settlers. Jack Beatty accepts the Boston urban myth that Curley, who was mayor at the time, commanded the sculptor, John Francis Paramino, to place his own visage on one of the English faces.[65] And indeed there is one notable likeness that captures something of Curley's boldness and arrogance, though not on the figure Beatty sees. This sculpture resides on Beacon Street as it ascends Beacon Hill at the Common, across the street from one of O'Connor's later addresses. In 1980 Lloyd Lillie did two statues of Curley which are grouped near the new City Hall. The standing Curley is an aggressive, barrel-chested orator. The Curley seated on the park bench is the helping friend, and the pats of well-wishers have polished the knee of this Curley to a bright shine.

There were other, more personal factors which drew O'Connor to Curley. It helps to remember that a large chunk of *The Last Hurrah* came over, not always happily, from "A Young Man of Promise," which had worked itself into an unresolved father-son conflict. Adam Caulfield is Kevin Rowan with a new name, but he is still the creator of the "Little Simp" comic strip. In *The Last Hurrah* both of Adam's parents had died in a car accident: O'Connor clears the ground early (*LH* 64). Adam's mother, Skeffington's sister, was named Mary, as was O'Connor's own mother (*LH* 173–74). In Adam's boyhood his father had been "notably cool" toward his notorious brother-in-law on political grounds, even though he could not help choking in laughter when Skeffington paid social visits and entertained everyone with tales from City Hall. As an adult back East from the Middle West, where he lived for years, Adam now "wondered about this man of magic who could make his father laugh out loud" (*LH* 64). Adam is barely noticed in the commentary on *The Last Hurrah*, which is understandably devoted to the presentation of Skeffington. Furthermore, Adam is admittedly little more than a colorless device in some ways. But as in much of O'Connor's work we feel a family en-

65. Beatty, *Rascal King*, 272.

ergy at work somewhere. Adam Caulfield is drawn to his famous uncle because during the three years since his parents' deaths he has come to see Skeffington increasingly as "both an extraordinary and a complex person"; Adam has "a curiosity to know him further" (*LH* 65).

In *The Last Hurrah* fathers who disapprove of Skeffington come off badly. Caleb Force had inaugurated the bitter antagonism between the Forces and Skeffington. Norman Cass Sr. is a cold fish and betrayer of colleagues; at least Norman Cass Jr. liked the excitement of a fire siren. Most intriguing, however, is Adam's tiresome father-in-law, Roger Sugrue, a "preposterous parent," amateur theologian, and parish snoop full of monologues devoted to *"The Irish in America; The Church; Himself (A Poor Boy Succeeds)"* and *"Frank Skeffington's Crime"* (*LH* 21; O'Connor's italics). His pedigree in O'Connor's work consists of Anthony Cantwell's father, Mr. Kilgallen in "Parish Reunion" (where "Sugrue" was used for the old pastor, oddly enough), and Kevin Rowan's Uncle Timothy. Early in his courtship of Sugrue's daughter, Maeve, Adam had adopted prudence:

No Frontal Assaults on Daddy. At least, he thought, not yet. Still the temptation was often hard to resist; it was really extraordinary, he reflected, how perpetually provocative his father-in-law could be. Even the mildest of his dicta, delivered in that nasal, all-knowing voice, could be relied to stir Adam from inertia into belligerent if unspoken opposition. Indeed, looking back on it, Adam was sure that . . . it had been Roger's smug, unflagging attacks upon Skeffington that had left him determined to know and to like this uncle . . . to whom he was literally almost a stranger. (*LH* 23; O'Connor's italics).

It could not be plainer that Adam is in search of a father figure to replace his dead father, who had frowned on Skeffington, and also in order to defy his father-in-law, who condemns Skeffington. For O'Connor it was a search for an ideal father: generous benefactor, raconteur, entertainer above all. Nathaniel Gardiner, lawyer and philanthropist and "almost the last of a remarkable species that had once flourished in the city," is the only father who speaks sensibly about Skeffington—and this to his own son (*LH* 103–10). Gardiner comes close to an ideal, but, ensconced as he is in his stuffy club, he has no fun in him.

For his part, Skeffington is saddled with an empty-headed, pleasure-seeking son who puts in a few hours a week at his City Hall sinecure. Francis Jr. is partly modeled on Curley's ne'er-do-well son, Paul.[66] Well into his thirties,

---

66. Francis Curley, another Curley son and a former Jesuit, once claimed that "[O'Connor] might have done some of his writing at the Ritz-Carlton bar, but he did his research in all the barrooms around town, especially Southie, because he would go in and buy drinks for old codgers there, and get them started telling stories." Quoted in Shaun O'Connell, *Imagining Boston: A Literary Landscape* (Boston: Beacon Press, 1990), 124–25. The allegation

Francis still lives at home and is only dimly aware that his father has a difficult campaign under way. At several points Adam almost dresses down his
cousin like a scolding brother, and Adam does take over as dutiful son by de-
fault when his uncle is dying. Failed by his playboy son, Skeffington had earlier sought out Adam to be an observer during the campaign. Ostensibly
Skeffington wants his nephew to have a box seat at "the greatest spectator
sport in the country," as he calls the old-time political campaign full of entertainment, personalities, and historical importance in that "grand freak" of
a city, never named but obviously Boston (*LH* 70–75). But later Skeffington
muses on the reason "which really mattered" to him:

"the growing desire to have someone of his own family observe him in the conduct
of his last campaign. . . . And it had to be [Adam]; apart from him there was no one
left. Except of course, Francis, Jr. At the thought of his son, Skeffington's lips tight-
ened into an unpaternal grimace" (*LH* 77).

Just as Adam wanted to see in his uncle the ideal father, Skeffington virtually
adopts Adam as the serious, intelligent son he never had.

The parallels to O'Connor's own family situation are pressing. As O'Connor felt that his own father was too remote, he sought the company of older
men whose wisdom and humor he cherished. From them he constructed his
paternal ideal. But he still wanted to be admired by his father, who seldom
encouraged his work. Accordingly, his Skeffington took Adam seriously (he
even reads "Little Simp") by bringing him into the inner sanctum of City
Hall.

One further crucial point ties much of this together. O'Connor usually
wrote his novels, by his own admission, with little planning or outlining—
much as Dickens did. Although there are several hints in *The Last Hurrah*
that the campaign will be not only Skeffington's last one but his death as
well, O'Connor probably inserted these hints only after he decided that
Skeffington's death would make a fitting end to the story. That death comes
when the defeated mayor comes home to an empty house on election night
and suffers a massive heart attack. He lingers for a few days, then is waked
and buried. As O'Connor wrote these last chapters of his book in late 1954
and early 1955, his own father was declining from at least two serious heart
attacks of his own that finally forced him to terminate his part-time medical
practice on November 14, 1955. As O'Connor added this material to his book
he was rehearsing his father's imminent death (Dr. O'Connor held on until
September 1956), while mourning the loss of a paternal ideal.

---

is preposterous. O'Connor was a teetotaler who always wrote in the seclusion of his room;
the "Southie" story is about as factual as Mayor Curley's oratory. Such legends about
O'Connor and his book were bound to arise in a city that thrives on rumor.

CHAPTER EIGHT

❧ *Success At Last*
(1955–1956)

The Atlantic Monthly Press ran an annual contest to encourage submissions to its fiction list. The top selections would be automatically published. First prize was $5,000, which is about $50,000 today; the winning submission would be known as the Atlantic Prize Novel. As a member of the *Atlantic* family who was by now a daily visitor to its offices across the street from his rooms, O'Connor of course knew about the contest and was even encouraged to enter it by several staffers, most especially by Seymour ("Sam") Lawrence, who was the press's director. After demurring for a decent interval (he said he felt uncomfortable doing such business with friends), he entered the barely finished novel.[1] He had pushed himself to finish the book to his satisfaction. Working laboriously and inefficiently on this longest and most complex work to date, he nevertheless submitted it just under the deadline in March 1955.

In her memoirs Helen Strauss says that she had earlier submitted a small portion of the novel to Harper, who, remembering sales of *The Oracle*, brusquely rejected it. Doubleday followed suit. Her memory of the next move seems faulty. She claims that O'Connor then suggested that "I take the snippet of the new book to Little, Brown. It seemed poetic justice to return to the Atlantic Monthly-Little, Brown family where he and we had begun." She claims that Little, Brown accepted it but would offer no advance until the book was finished, and that it was Atlantic Monthly Press who gave O'Connor money to finish the book after the contest was over.[2] But O'Connor had submitted a finished manuscript to Atlantic Monthly Press, as the contest rules stipulated, although to be sure there was much trimming to be done. What probably happened was that Little, Brown became interested only after Atlantic

---

1. Edwin O'Connor, interview with George C. Hull, *Providence Journal*, February 21, 1956.
2. Strauss, *Talent for Luck*, 168.

Monthly Press became interested, as was the customary procedure between these two establishments.

Since 1917, Atlantic Monthly Press had acquired and edited about twenty high-quality books a year for the much bigger Little, Brown to print and market. Atlantic Monthly Press published no books of its own. By 1971 it could count winners of two Nobel Prizes, ten Pulitzers, and three National Book Awards among its authors. The close, not to say intimate, relationship between these venerable institutions encapsulates the tight little world of highbrow publishing in Boston during that time. The relationship, however, has long since dissolved as a result of corporate takeovers and mergers for both. The once-proud Atlantic Monthly Press is a nameplate at Grove Press. Little, Brown—an icon of literary Boston going far back into the nineteenth century—now exists in New York as a subsidiary imprint of Time-Warner. O'Connor would have been devastated to see this diminishment at the hands of New Yorkers. Certainly many staffers were.

The title of the manuscript O'Connor submitted to the Atlantic Fiction contest was *Not Moisten an Eye*. This ungainly title was only changed when several people convinced O'Connor that the name, supposedly from the sentimental nineteenth-century Irish poet Thomas Moore, just would not do. However, no one has discovered the exact source, if any, of the original title. Perhaps for O'Connor to "not moisten an eye" implied a disinterested anatomy of his subject, a Bostonian version of Yeats's famous epitaph, "Cast a cold eye / On life, on death." It may also reflect his upper-middle-class, dry-eyed response to death. At any rate, O'Connor himself came up with the better title in May and announced it at a little celebration with Bob Taylor and Rudolph Elie at Boston's famous Locke-Ober Café.[3]

If O'Connor enjoyed an insider's advantage in the contest, the first two out of three readers were not informed of it. Peggy Yntema relates that the first reader, Dudley Cloud, was dubious about the book. O'Connor's friend Charlie Morton came down on it as well.[4] Shortly after O'Connor's death, Yntema dryly told Arthur Schlesinger that these first two readers "have since found happiness outside the publishing profession."[5] But in fact Morton continued to work happily at *Atlantic Monthly* until his death in 1967. The

3. Robert Taylor, personal interview, April 5, 1999. Al Capp claimed that in their 1951 meeting O'Connor told him that his provisional title for his new book was *The Last Hurrah*, and so it is possible that O'Connor had earlier toyed with this alternate title. See *Boston Sunday Globe*, May 27, 1962: A3. Then again, Capp was not always reliable.

4. Peggy Yntema, personal interview, April 10, 1999; I am deeply indebted to Mrs. Yntema for many of the ensuing details about O'Connor and her role as his editor.

5. *BL*, 11.

confusion here mirrors some of the considerable controversy that O'Connor's entry aroused: Boston politics were not restricted to City Hall or the State House. Just in case O'Connor was hearing ominous rumors, Helen Strauss wrote in mid-March that her "espionage agent" (obviously a mole at the Atlantic) had just informed her that O'Connor still had a shot at the prize.[6]

Peggy Yntema herself was the third and decisive reader. She knew O'Connor early on and became his long-time editor in 1955. The fact that she was nine years his junior may have caused some strain, especially since he, with his perfectionist writing habits, resisted editing in the first place. But this astute reader was in a very real sense his discoverer at a crucial moment and O'Connor always remembered he owed her everything. She found O'Connor very likeable and engaging but not particularly handsome, although she realized that many other women did—especially after he became successful. In those hard-pressed years he dressed out of necessity informally, even shabbily, but was careful about his favorite colors of grey, blue, and green. She thought him a little shy and lonely, but with a strong need to be liked. His patented daily entrance routine at the *Atlantic* offices—the vaudeville shuffle, the jokes, a toss of a coin out the window as if money was no concern—were ways of overcoming some of his inhibition as "an Irish mother's son." The flip side of that well-known Irish pattern was his need to be tribal chieftain, or at least a center of attention. Loyalty to him from friends and associates was crucial, as it was to Irish politicians generally. In turn he showed intense loyalty to others. Some years into their editor-writer relationship, around 1964, O'Connor campaigned hard to get Peggy a genuine promotion that recognized her talents. But just when he achieved his goal, she had to turn the promotion down, reluctantly, to devote time to family and her work on the Board of Higher Education.

Yntema's report on O'Connor's novel came immediately to the point. She "read it in one big gulp" and found the novel to be "profoundly moving . . . its scope is very great."[7] She recognized a Dickensian quality in O'Connor's portrayals and emotions, and did not mind some "hammy" scenes and even "shameless tear-jerking," because the book was "vastly readable . . . and the talk—the endless, various, garrulous, vituperative, sentimental, funny, bombastic Irish talk—is the reason." The story covered Irish politics in a comprehensive way, and raised the saga of Skeffington to near tragic heights as the

6. Helen Strauss, letter to Edwin O'Connor, March 18, 1955, EOCP 376.
7. Trade Editorial Report, Atlantic Monthly Press, on *The Last Hurrah*, April 1, 1955, courtesy of Barbara O'Connor Burrell.

new order supplanted the old. In one of the more imaginative descriptions of Skeffington's position in the book, she saw him as a king in an Egyptian painting, "twice the size of his attendants." Interestingly, this Bostonian reader says not a word about Curley. She predicts that it will be a "memorable book."

She would accept the book even if unrevised, but she did nevertheless offer some suggestions. She spotted a persistent problem: the author's garrulity too often made explicit what was already clearly implied. Adam and his wife Maeve were weak. Yntema could not fathom why Maeve's "obvious ass" of a father (Roger Sugrue) was still such an influence over her after a year of marriage; here she came close to detecting one of O'Connor's hidden emotional undercurrents. She found Adam's comic strip "a bit too much" and badly in need of trimming. She also wished for "more physical detail" and she wished the author would put a few identifying objects in rooms. (O'Connor lived in almost monastic quarters before and even for some years after the book's success; his characters speak in rooms that are almost never furnished with detail.)

After considerable office wrangling, Yntema's "thunderous report," as she calls it, won the day. She recalls an occasion a few years earlier when O'Connor realized that everything had fallen into place for him, even though the novel was then only in its embryonic phase. He had come into the office and after the usual antics said, "I've got it!" He knew then he was onto something far greater than anything he had done. In early 1953, she had helped to save O'Connor's life with her own blood. Now in 1955 she rescued his flagging career with a vigorous critique that won him the Atlantic Prize. Her reader's report marks the beginning of the end of O'Connor's fifteen years of toiling in obscurity. Coincidentally, her report was issued on April Fool's Day, but she remains convinced that her judgment on the manuscript that became *The Last Hurrah* was sound.

The prize winners, out of hundreds of submissions, were announced in early June. From Woonsocket he received a congratulatory telegram: "CONGRATULATIONS SON, DAD AND I ARE WITH YOU IN SPIRIT ON THIS HAPPY OCCASION AND WISH YOU EVERY POSSIBLE HAPPINESS AND SUCCESS WHICH YOU SO RICHLY DESERVE. DAD AND MOTHER"[8] From Ireland Conor Cruise O'Brien sent congratulations on an auspicious day in Irish literature, June 16—a date widely celebrated as "Bloomsday" in honor of Joyce's protagonist in *Ulysses*. By custom a joint committee of staffers

8. Telegram from Dr. and Mrs. John V. O'Connor to Edwin O'Connor, June 8, 1955, EOCP 218.

from Atlantic Monthly Press and Little, Brown selected which winners would be published through their special arrangement.

During this period Peggy Yntema worked closely with O'Connor to edit his manuscript. She remembers his secretiveness during this phase of the book's development; he did not want it generally known that he was taking direction from others. Nevertheless, he submitted to her discernment and they began trimming what she now concedes was a wordiness that bordered on the "frumpy."

The "Printer's Copy" of *The Last Hurrah*, dated June 22, 1955, is the most edited of his extant manuscripts and reveals his weaknesses at this stage of his career. Most of the cuts consist of a sentence here and there, sometimes half a paragraph, rarely anything more than a page. In all they amount to about twenty manuscript pages. These cuts often consisted of unnecessarily explicit passages that sometimes made dialogue, characters, and scenes trail off unmemorably. For example, when Ralph, Amos Force's managing editor, leaves his boss's appalling boiled dinner, O'Connor writes in the published version: "Before he reached his taxi, he was very wet indeed" (*LH* 83). This nicely follows through on Force's soggy fare. But the original manuscript had added another sentence: "Taken all in all, the evening had not been success-ful."[9] O'Connor sometimes grievously neglected the old dictum, "Show, don't tell." A little earlier when Force was haranguing Ralph, O'Connor orig-inally had provided a running commentary on Force's mind by means of Ralph's ruminations. These get crossed out. O'Connor only had to open Force's mouth to ventilate his crazed hatreds.

O'Connor also was persuaded to cut back on his characters' garrulity. Thus, the trimming of Nathaniel Gardiner's long discourse on Skeffington in Chapter Five gives him more concision as a Yankee lawyer. Even Skeffington himself gets pared back by half a page when he holds forth too long on poli-tics and wakes in Chapter Eight. "Little Simp" material amounting to several pages mercifully met the axe. Adam's colleague Burbank gets reduced in im-portance at several places. Burbank's makeover also renders this man with the "small, faded, effeminate face" (*LH* 26) less overtly a homosexual esthete. The newly sensitive age that Skeffington spoke to Cuke Cullen about (*LH* 121) also made O'Connor cut material that might be construed as ethnically offensive. In Chapter Ten, when Skeffington rebukes philandering Johnnie Byrne before firing him, O'Connor heavily crossed out a sentence that is now barely readable: "A Chinese laundryman would beat you in your own

9. Printer's copy of *The Last Hurrah*, EOCP 44:97. References to this manuscript will be: (Printer's 97).

ward" (Printer's 266). Similarly, a few innocuous passages on Italians were dropped, although the unnecessary Camaratta subplot stayed in.

In the original Chapter Eleven Jack Mangan tells Adam, "There's nothing like a family tie-up to knock the hell out of principles" (Printer's 331). O'Connor excised the sentence. A "family tie-up" of a more indirect nature than that of Skeffington and his nephew Adam is highlighted by two deleted passages concerning Skeffington and his son. Chapter Twelve now ends with Skeffington collapsing on his stairs. The original version ended with Francis Jr. coming home from a night club to fetch a present he had forgotten for some girl. He finds his father on the stairs, but his reaction is not recorded. In the next chapter, cut also at the end is the son's arrival home a half hour after his father dies. Francis had been out with friends, and later simply drove around town alone. Five of the book's fourteen chapters originally ended with some reference to Francis Jr., who is altogether a minor player; it is almost as if O'Connor felt compelled to sew in something about father and son, even if this thread dangles. Clearly the encroachment of the son was recognized as awkward by Peggy or O'Connor or both, and some of it just had to go.

By August Charlie Morton was reading galley pages while vacationing in Nova Scotia. Whatever his earlier thoughts about the novel had been, Morton now was lavish in his praise. He found Skeffington to be "a first-rate human being," and the book "a lovely piece of work." He concludes by noting rapidly, "no baloney, no tricks, much meat, authority, effective writing, subtlety."[10]

As Little, Brown and Company began to take over the fate of *The Last Hurrah*, O'Connor came to know Arthur H. Thornhill (1895–1970), the company's third president and chairman of the board.[11] Thornhill was the same age as Ted Weeks but was not at all "literary" like the editor of the *Atlantic*. A warm, extroverted man, he had no airs and presented himself to proper Bostonians simply as a good book salesman. With Thornhill, O'Connor developed a much closer bond than with Weeks, one that has been described variously as paternal and avuncular. O'Connor loved and trusted him completely. They lunched once a week at Locke-Ober's, where Thornhill would tipple and report on O'Connor's sales and prospects. O'Connor dedicated his last novel to him and at the end of his life was contemplating a novel

10. Charles W. Morton, letter to Edwin O'Connor, August (date unreadable), 1955, EOCP 202.

11. My thanks to Peter Davison, Peggy Yntema, and Robert Manning—all of the *Atlantic*—for their reminiscences of Arthur Thornhill.

about a publisher based on his friend. Arthur Thornhill was such a Boston fixture that when he died at his table in Locke-Ober's, that table was retired and removed. Thornhill's only child, Arthur Jr., once recalled that his own non-Catholic father and the very Catholic O'Connor once lit candles in the Paulist Center chapel for him when he had a serious operation.[12]

Little, Brown's office at 34 Beacon Street soon became a frequent stop during O'Connor's midday rounds. Located across the Common and almost on the crest of Beacon Hill, the modest four-story red brick building with a wrought iron verandah commanded one of Boston's best prospects. It was only a stone's throw from Bullfinch's gold-domed State House; for a political novelist it was a center of considerable gossip as well. Still, when *The Last Hurrah* was published, O'Connor would claim that he had never been inside either the State House or City Hall.

Thornhill began to realize that Little, Brown just might have a huge best-seller on its hands. The time was ripe for such a political and Irish novel. And with Curley now more a legendary folk hero than a political power to reckon with, it seemed safe for a novel loosely based on his exploits. Accordingly, as O'Connor told an early interviewer, the author received a $175,000 guarantee from Little, Brown.[13] This figure, whopping for the time, especially for a still unknown author, was more money many times over than O'Connor had earned to date; by comparison the Atlantic Prize money was merely a tip. Helen Strauss was driving a hard bargain with Yankee horse traders. In divulging this big figure O'Connor was understandably excited and proud, but also terribly naive. He learned to be more prudent quickly enough.

Fast on the heels of this good news came a highly lucrative deal with the Book-of-the-Month Club. The editorial board of the Book-of-the-Month Club in 1955 was chaired by Clifton Fadiman and included O'Connor's fellow Bostonian John P. Marquand, who must have been wondering if he had met his heir as Boston's interpreter. Late in 1955 the club prepared seven pages of its January bulletin to feature *The Last Hurrah* as the main offering for February, to coincide with the book's publication. A big drawing of Skeffington's campaign headquarters was followed by three pages of Fadiman's report to the readers, in which he puffed the novel's "exuberance," Skeffington's "craggy integrity," and the many minor portraits worthy of Hogarth and Daumier. A typical sentence: "Skeffington is a broth of a boy and this is a broth of a book." The tint of condescension there was probably

12. Arthur Thornhill Jr., letter to Anne Ford, January 20, 1970, EOCP 276.
13. Edwin O'Connor, interview with James F. Leonard, *Boston Post,* February 14, 1956, 13.

not lost on O'Connor. Two pages of excerpts from Skeffington's speeches follow. Finally, Ted Weeks wrote a biographical sketch which begins accurately enough, "The Eddie O'Connor story is a success story in quiet dimensions." But then Weeks develops the story with his customary casualness about the facts, implying for example that O'Connor was driven out of economic necessity to find a job within days of college graduation, a statement wrong on two counts. Weeks seemed determined to turn his young friend into Horatio Alger as he recounts O'Connor's frugal life over so many years. O'Connor was being presented as the familiar American myth of hard work and economy leading to financial gain, a myth that grew longer legs in the postwar boom of the 1950s. Weeks also notes that O'Connor was now "good and tired" after his hard four years on the novel, and indeed his photographs from this time do show the first signs of an aging that would accelerate rapidly. Perhaps there was even a note of concern on Weeks's part. But he catches himself and ends by coyly informing the women, presumably, that the suddenly rich O'Connor is still a bachelor![14] The Club offered the book to its members for $3.95, only a nickel below the regular price.

O'Connor was also offered an $80,000 contract with the Reader's Digest Book Club. While he pondered the literary ethics of an abridgement of his work, he phoned his friend Edmund Wilson for advice. "Take the money, my boy, take the money," said Wilson.[15] O'Connor, like many others, regarded Wilson as the greatest living American critic. O'Connor may have had a twinge or two that he was suddenly rich while Wilson, who had no regular academic employment, earned little from his pen.

When *The Last Hurrah* was still in galley proofs in July, Helen Strauss contacted Harry Cohn, the tough head of Columbia Pictures. She believes that he snapped up the story unread, trusting instead her instincts. "He wasn't the sort to let paper work interfere," she wryly notes in her memoir. Cohn phoned her immediately and offered $150,000, "take it or leave it." She countered that it was worth a quarter of a million dollars, but he held fast and gave her a weekend's deadline. When she phoned O'Connor, he thought Cohn's offer was wonderful. She tried to convince him to go for more, but he played it safe and they accepted. Columbia was then much sought after by authors following its success with James Jones's *From Here To Eternity* in 1953.[16] The film version had to wait until 1958.

14. *Book-of-the-Month Club News Bulletin,* January 1956.
15. Charles E. Claffey, "Life & Times of a Political Chronicler," *Boston Sunday Globe,* May 22, 1983, A19.
16. Strauss, *Talent for Luck,* 168–69.

꽃

Twice in 1955 O'Connor was eager to take some time away from Massachusetts and visit old friends. His first trip was in May. For the first time since leaving in November 1939 he journeyed back to South Bend, primarily to visit his mentor and early inspiration, Professor Frank O'Malley. Little survives from this ten-day trip, except O'Connor's claim that the new title for his novel came to him as he was sitting in the lobby of the Morris Inn on campus.[17] The problem with O'Connor's account is that the Trade Editorial Report, dated April 1, clearly indicates that *The Last Hurrah* was already the book's title. The trip to South Bend was a pilgrimage of thanksgiving for all that Notre Dame and O'Malley had done for him. Nevertheless, the days he spent at his alma mater must have had their painful moments, because O'Malley's alcoholism was no secret on campus and must have been obvious to O'Connor. Nevertheless, this 1955 trip began a tradition of annual visits, usually in October, that he missed only once or twice. He told a Providence interviewer that on the way home from Notre Dame, he learned that he had won the Atlantic contest by a unanimous vote of the judges.[18]

In late September he took a one-week trip to Ireland, his third in as many years, with Fred and Portland Allen, their first and only. At the time Allen was working on a second book, more of a real autobiography than *Treadmill to Oblivion* had been, and again with O'Connor as quiet editor over a two-year period. *Much Ado About Me* takes Allen up to 1928, just before he left vaudeville for the radio career which his earlier book had covered. Once again O'Connor provided brief suggestions, but he let the gifted Allen speak for himself. *Much Ado About Me* was published after Allen's sudden death the following year and sold well. O'Connor provided a brief epilogue, where he notes that Allen had much more fun doing precarious vaudeville than he did in his rich and famous radio years. He commends Allen's skills as a writer who only used his "collaborator" as a sounding board and little more: "[I]t is a pleasure to report that the touch of the ghost is not upon these pages." The O'Connor who so disliked being edited himself allowed the "rare and wonderful book by a rare and wonderful man" to stand on its own.[19]

Unfortunately, nothing about the Ireland trip survives in the archives of either O'Connor or Allen. According to second- and third-hand accounts, it

17. Edward Fischer, "Edwin O'Connor, Raconteur," *Notre Dame Magazine*, winter 1988–89, 49–50.

18. Interview with George C. Hull.

19. Edwin O'Connor, epilogue, *Much Ado About Me*, by Fred Allen (Boston: Atlantic Monthly Press/Little, Brown: 1956), 363–65.

was an uproarious jaunt. In Dublin they visited the Montgomerys, who apparently did not fully grasp Allen's great fame. The children do, however, remember Allen's wizened face as the most wrinkled they had ever seen.[20]

O'Connor had written Hop and Niall Montgomery in late July to inform them of his dedication of *The Last Hurrah* to them. A "dazed" and profusely grateful Niall wrote back with nonstop wit full of what he called his "Niallogisms." He predicts that the wild rumor mills of Dublin will be shortly conferring upon the Montgomerys the Nobel Prize.[21] Niall was one of the few people O'Connor had consulted when the novel was a work in progress, and so O'Connor sent him galleys in September. In early August Niall wrote to congratulate O'Connor on the movie contract. Somewhat ruefully, but with no hint of envy, he fantasizes what sudden wealth would do for himself: "The hobnailed liver and the words TANQUERAY, GORDON, LTD. written on my heart." He is amazed that his friend still stays so absolutely sober and that he can do without a Mercedes. When Niall learned of Fred Allen's death in 1956, he immediately wrote O'Connor to offer condolences. He comments on the "merciless and unrelenting" nature of American success.[22]

During the summer of 1955, spent at Wellfleet as usual, O'Connor began disengaging from the journalistic odd jobs that had kept the wolf from the door of apartment No. 4 at 11 Marlborough Street. He handed in an "Accent on Living" column, "The Indirect Approach," which would be his last for a long while; it appeared in the June *Atlantic*. For nine years these columns, plus two short stories and two short articles, had earned him a few badly needed dollars and more importantly had kept him in circulation at 8 Arlington Street. Now his days as an amiable but very part-time employee were to be remarkably transformed. Earlier in the year he had a short article on boxing published in a television magazine, where he accused television commentators of serious ignorance of the sport.[23] Such negligible journalism was now quickly becoming a thing of the past, as seen in his half-hearted attempts at a *Life* story on Don Sharpe, who had been by turns an actor, writer, and radio personality, and who was now at forty-three a high-powered Hollywood agent and producer for shows like *I Love Lucy*. Helen Strauss had landed O'Connor the assignment and by the summer he had amassed about a hundred pages of notes and clippings in preparation.[24] *Life* had even sent a

20. Personal interviews, May 4, 2000.
21. Niall Montgomery, letter to Edwin O'Connor, August 2, 1955, EOCP 199.
22. Niall Montgomery, letter to Edwin O'Connor, March 18, 1956, EOCP 199.
23. "Fighting Words," *TV Program Week*, February 26–March 4, 1955, 27.
24. EOCP 45.

$900 advance. But the article O'Connor eventually submitted in September was too flimsy even for *Life*. Judging from a letter Strauss received from Jay Gold, the article focused too much on personal detail and not enough on an evaluation of Sharpe's power. Helen wanted O'Connor to advise her on whether he would undertake a revision. He never did, most likely because he just did not have his heart in the man and his story. Don Sharpe was not a James Michael Curley or a Fred Allen.

Excitement, anticipation, and travel during 1955 cut into his television reviewing for the *Boston Post*, and he began dropping hints in his column that the end was near. For example, on December 8 he wrote a wistful tongue-in-cheek column about the early heroic days of television—all of six years back—and mourns that "the hour of glory has passed."[25] For its part the *Post* belatedly recognized the talents of its television reviewer, as rumors about O'Connor's impending success spread. Accordingly, on September 20, 1955, the newspaper ran a half-page promotion touting O'Connor's "About Television" as a "column for those who enjoy a sharp, penetrating style, witty and revealing." The name "Edwin O'Connor" was approaching headline status, but he was still paid fifteen dollars a column. O'Connor's last column appeared on January 19, 1956. Although his leave-taking is never explicitly announced as such, it is memorable. He relates a story, probably picked up during his BBC-TV researches, of the Cambridge University don who moonlighted as emcee of a television quiz show. One day he "gloweringly" told viewers that television was making him violently deranged, and then abruptly announced his departure. O'Connor admired the don's refreshing honesty: the subtitle of O'Connor's own last column was "Sometimes the Truth Hurts."[26] So ended his four on-and-off years as television critic for two Boston newspapers. The radio veteran's discomfort with the newer medium had been showing for some time. It comes as no surprise that *The Last Hurrah* takes special delight in skewering McCluskey's bumbling television campaigning, which nevertheless is the stuff of contemporary victory, as the delighted Festus Garvey knows: "Oh by God that's good! . . . The cute little baby bottom shootin' right up into the camera so's every woman in the audience feels she can reach right out and give it a lovin' pat! . . . By God, the little behind is worth a thousand votes in the pocket" (*LH* 281).

An important event during this transitional season was O'Connor's move from 11 Marlborough Street to 48 Beacon Street, about a quarter of a mile

---

25. *Boston Post*, December 8, 1955, 4.
26. *Boston Post*, January 19, 1956, 10.

away on Beacon Hill, in December 1955. As if to symbolize his new relationship to both Atlantic Monthly Press and Little, Brown and Company, he now
lived between them and could walk to either one in a few minutes. No. 48
Beacon is a singular building which O'Connor seems to have chosen with
some deliberation. Its tall and narrow twelve stories stick up obtrusively like
a mini-skyscraper over the section of Beacon Street that Oliver Wendell
Holmes once called "the sunny side that holds the sifted few." It is almost as
if O'Connor wanted his move to Beacon Hill to parallel the upstart career of
Curley, who entered Boston politics just about the time the building went up
and who was just as upsetting to the hill's denizens.

More important, though, is the apartment he chose to rent: a unit on the
top floor which is remembered vividly by John Tosi, O'Connor's friend and
real-estate agent. The building, he remembers, had a tiny elevator which
could barely hold O'Connor. Furniture had to be carried up flights of stairs
that wrapped around the elevator shaft. The view from O'Connor's aerie was
stunning: to the west he had an unobstructed view of the Back Bay and the
Charles River, and to the north he could look out over most of Beacon Hill
and even catch a bit of the dome on the State House. Other visitors remember O'Connor's tidy two-room apartment with kitchenette as spacious
enough, with neatly stacked books as the most abundant furniture in both
rooms. Arthur Schlesinger remembers the "almost monastic air" of the
apartment, "especially in the bedroom where a simple crucifix hung above
what can only be described as a pallet."[27] O'Connor may have lived on upper
floors since 1945 out of economy, but in late 1955 he was seizing a view of the
city that would accord well with his imminent meteoric fame. His residence
at 48 Beacon Street turned out to be the longest of his eight civilian addresses in Boston.

Preceded by considerable hype and lavish advertising, *The Last Hurrah*
was published on Saturday, February 4, 1956, when Edwin O'Connor was
thirty-seven. (November had been the original publication date, but the
publishers delayed to let suspense build through advance reviews and personal interest stories.) Miriam Woods's drab dust jacket rendered the title in
yellow script against a dark green background. At the bottom appeared "The
Atlantic Prize Novel." On the back O'Connor's formal photograph, by
Boston's high-end Fabian Bachrach Studios, had him in suit and vest with
hands in his pockets and looking pensive in a staid Bostonian way. It was not
the O'Connor most people knew. The 427-page novel cost $4.

27. Schlesinger, Introduction to *BL,* 16.

His family, of course, was delighted. Whatever misgivings they had harbored about Sonny's years of self-denial mixed with long stretches on Cape Cod and in Dublin were forgotten. The eldest son had finally come through by sheer diligence and good luck. But as in most joyous Irish family celebrations there were edges of sadness, to borrow from O'Connor's other famous novel. Dr. O'Connor had taken to his last bed, and so the family brought to his upstairs room a large cake in the shape and colors of the book.[28] Like most sons with strong-willed fathers, O'Connor must have had conflicting emotions coursing through him. Hugh Rank believes there is reason to doubt that Dr. O'Connor, who was slowly declining, ever fully appreciated his son's accomplishment.[29] However, both Barbara and Bill Burrell are sure that Dr. O'Connor was fully aware of his son's achievement. In any event it must have been a bittersweet occasion for O'Connor, who had not yet won his father's full approval. From J. M. Synge and James Joyce to Hugh Leonard and Frank McCourt, modern Irish literature is full of sons presiding at the deaths of fathers, real or surrogate. As Sonny stood in his dying father's bedroom with the confectionary simulacrum of a literary accomplishment that awakened Irish American possibilities in literature, he was reenacting generations of Irish literary history in a new key.

Advance news stories and reviews had already appeared in the New England press, but no city celebrated O'Connor and his book as much as Woonsocket did. "Native Son Hits Literary Jackpot" crowed the *Woonsocket Call* in December as it gushed about "the first Woonsocket product to become a genuine literary celebrity," this two months before publication.[30] On publication day the *Call* published what amounted to a special Edwin O'Connor issue, which consisted of a huge special interest piece, an editorial, a book review, and two smaller items about O'Connor's burgeoning national recognition. Accompanying all this were eight photographs of O'Connor in his new apartment, at Atlantic Monthly Press with Ted Weeks and Charlie Morton, and in front of the Massachusetts State House. (Surely Boston City Hall would have been more appropriate.) The big lead story by the paper's gifted Edgar J. Allaire gives a rare glimpse inside Atlantic Monthly Press's offices.[31] Allaire and a photographer recorded the easy office banter and the friendly atmosphere. At one point O'Connor picked up a manuscript lying

28. Barbara O'Connor Burrell, personal interview, summer 1998.

29. Rank, *Edwin O'Connor*, 6.

30. Edwin O'Connor, interview with Edgar J. Allaire, *Woonsocket Call*, December 10, 1955.

31. Edgar J. Allaire, "A Day with a Woonsocket Author Who Has 'Arrived,'" *Woonsocket Call*, February 4, 1956, 5.

on a desk and said, "Get a picture of Charlie throwing this manuscript into his waste basket—it'll be a typical shot." Was this a not-too-subtle jab at his novel's second reader for the Atlantic Prize? Allaire and his photographer were amazed at O'Connor's patient geniality during their several hours with him. O'Connor often showed considerable courtesy to journalists because he remembered his own newspaper years; besides, he was careful not to be condescending to Woonsocket and its paper. Allaire also wrote a glowing review that finds nary a flaw in the novel. The newspaper's editorial, "A Son of Woonsocket Writes a Hit Novel," strikes a note of personal friendship with a neighborhood boy, and was thus probably written by Buell Hudson, the publisher and old family friend whose father had been one of O'Connor's references on his college application.

Other Rhode Island reviews glowed. The diocesan paper gave the novel a big plug.[32] *The Providence Sunday Journal's* chief book reviewer was full of praise, an irony in a newspaper once notorious for its anti-Irish stances. The review was followed by several excerpts of "Skeffingtoniana." O'Connor's mayor was becoming as legendary as Curley himself.[33] A few weeks later George C. Hull of the same paper had a follow-up interview with O'Connor, one of the best from this period. Hull's interview may be the first indication of O'Connor's concerns with the public's intrusions into his cherished privacy and also with the long reach of the Internal Revenue Service. He scotched rumors that his next novel would be about Yankee Boston. An accompanying cartoon showed the author's high-domed head in front of a funereally draped portrait of a grinning Skeffington.[34]

If Rhode Island was understandably generous in its praise, Boston's papers were a bit more restrained. The *Globe* ran a subdued but favorable review which found Skeffington's death and funeral one of the two best scenes; few would agree today.[35] More amusing to O'Connor must have been the acclaim from his old nemesis, the *Herald,* in a review which found Skeffington to be a wonderfully sympathetic character. The reviewer, however, was careful only to glance at newspaper publisher Amos Force.[36]

The first item in *The New York Times Book Review* for February 5 was

32. Fred J. Donovan, "Skill, Insight, Laughs Insure Long Life for 'Last Hurrah,'" *Providence Sunday Visitor,* February 23, 1956, 5.

33. Maurice Dolbier, "Skeffington Re-Election Bid; O'Connor Sure Victor," *Providence Sunday Journal,* February 5, 1956, VI–10.

34. Edwin O'Connor, interview with George C. Hull, *Providence Journal-Bulletin,* February 21, 1956.

35. Daniel J. O'Brien, "Our 'Irish' Politicians," *Boston Sunday Globe,* February 5, 1956.

36. Alice Dixon Bond, review of *The Last Hurrah, Boston Sunday Herald,* February 5, 1956.

penned by none other than John V. Kelleher, identified as "Associate Professor of Modern Irish History and Literature at Harvard University." Kelleher begins authoritatively: "Here, after a century of trying, is the first successful Irish-American novel." Later he says, "He has the whole essential Irish-American story here, every shade and facet of it." O'Connor avoids the Scylla of misty-eyed nostalgia and the Charybdis of self-hating novels "usually dominated by a gloomy sensitive young narrator whom we may call Studs Dedalus," a swipe at the James T. Farrell ashcan school and third-rate imitators of Joyce. Kelleher sees the book as a lament for the "wild vigor" of an earlier Irish American generation now being supplanted by a "newer generation as by a glacier of unflavored gelatin." But he also sees Skeffington's political tragedy as a peculiarly Irish one—the failure to use considerable political gifts in a statesmanlike way.[37] Kelleher's review is valuable because it may reflect ideas that he and O'Connor swapped during their many long talks.

Accompanying the review was an interview with the author by Lewis Nichols, in which O'Connor contradicts his own remarks in the Hull interview about his next book: it may indeed be about "the other side, the Yankee side." (O'Connor never wrote it; he was probably only toying with the notion.) A section where O'Connor holds forth on the old bosses is worth quoting:

> The young people nowadays lose sight of the fact that those old boys held people by personal loyalty alone. Now they are dying out, will not come back and belong to history.
>
> All the old boys hate Roosevelt, thinking of him as a master of perfidy. He finished them. The old boys needed the environment of a highly localized society. Roosevelt took that away.[38]

This thesis about F.D.R. is inserted abruptly into *The Last Hurrah* through Adam's friend Jack Mangan (*LH* 374–75). It is true that by Roosevelt's second term Curley and the president were cool to each other, but the novel itself makes no preparation for Mangan's interpretation of Skeffington's defeat, and it certainly comes as a surprise to Adam and many readers as well. Historians and political scientists have questioned its merit.[39] When it is remembered that O'Connor's self-made father was by his own admission a vehement Roosevelt-hater, the plot thickens here with family interest. Given that the scene with Mangan occurs late in the book and was therefore written

37. "The Hero as an Irish-American," *New York Times Book Review,* February 5, 1956, 1.

38. Edwin O'Connor, interview with Lewis Nichols, *New York Times Book Review,* February 5, 1956, 18.

39. See, for example, Charles H. Trout, *Boston, the Great Depression, and the New Deal* (New York: Oxford University Press, 1977), 276ff.

during Dr. O'Connor's declining years, and given the odd circumstance that Mangan, a McCluskey backer, had come to the mayor's mansion to expound to Adam, who was attending to the dying Skeffington upstairs, it seems that personal emotional pressures may have dictated Mangan's thesis. It was as if O'Connor in some strange fashion had found in Roosevelt a Skeffington nemesis that would appease his own dying father, even if it had little to do with any developments in his novel.

John O'Donnell's column "Capitol Stuff" in New York's *Daily News* heaped the accolades high on February 7. He also could not resist expanding O'Connor's Roosevelt thesis into a diatribe on the "New Deal socialist state." The contrast between Kelleher's more skeptical view of Curley in the *Times* and O'Donnell's tub-thumping for him in the *Daily News* is a striking indication of the political spread already formed in Irish American life. None other than James T. Farrell wrote a warm review in the New York *Post* on February 5.

Not all New York reviews were so laudatory as these. In a stunningly wrong-headed review in *The New Yorker,* the novelist Anthony West, son of Rebecca West and H. G. Wells and a *New Yorker* staffer since coming to America from England in 1950, wrote probably the most vile notice of *The Last Hurrah.* He slams O'Connor for muddled thinking about Skeffington's public thievery: "[T]he line of thinking he advances is at once extremely simple and extremely confused." West concludes: "Mr. O'Connor's sentimental presentation of that barbaric figure . . . is more than hard to take. It persuasively pretends that mean vices are virtues, and it is that rare thing, a genuinely subversive book."[40] West appears to have Curley in mind more than Skeffington, and in any case his pen drips with postwar British vitriol about American politics. That last phrase about the book's alleged subversion no doubt is West's coded declaration of his mid-1950s anti-McCarthyism as he imputes real subversiveness to an Irish Catholic mayor. The irony is rich here: as O'Connor presents him, Skeffington practices far more works of mercy than the aggregate of his enemies, of whom West has little to say.

Not all British reviewers followed West, however. In England *The Listener,* BBC's prestigious magazine, called *The Last Hurrah* one of the best American novels ever. "I have never read anything so American," said the reviewer, by which he meant that O'Connor got the American vulgarity down well, even if Skeffington is presented sympathetically.[41]

The major American middle-to-highbrow magazines were highly favor-

40. Anthony West, "When in Rome . . . ," *The New Yorker,* February 11, 1956, 113–16.
41. Anthony Rhodes, review of *The Last Hurrah, The Listener,* July 5, 1956, 29.

able, *The New Yorker* excepted. *The Saturday Review* put a large drawing of O'Connor on its cover for author of the week. Inside, Howard Mumford Jones wrote warmly of his humor and tolerance. He slyly alluded to Curley's propensity for seeing actionable material everywhere when he calls him "J-m-s C-r-y." He considered O'Connor's presentation of political complexities worthy of Browning, which is saying a lot. Jones was one of the first to call the novel a "male book" for a male world, a description that might seem plausible but for the fact that O'Connor received voluminous fan mail from women. A brief accompanying bio quotes O'Connor on Skeffington's superiority over his assumed model, Curley: "My man is far different. He has extensive capacities."[42] *The Reporter's* Gouverneur Paulding gave the novel one of its most thoughtful reviews. Paulding saw that the protagonist of the "rich and healthy" novel was not idealized; O'Connor had carefully let Skeffington's critics, especially the cardinal, make their points. Paulding reminds readers of the plight of the immigrant Irish, who had little choice but to fight roughly.[43] A curiously tepid review ran in *Atlantic Monthly*, of all places. Charles J. Rolo liked the book, but thought that, in whitewashing Skeffington, it lacked depth. Rolo ended limply by saying that the book's good qualities compensated.[44] Rolo was something of a dandy—unlike O'Connor, who still dressed often in postwar GI garb—and was an eternal chatterbox during his infrequent visits to Boston. He was often caught in the awkward position of reviewing Atlantic Monthly Press books in *Atlantic*; hence, the fumbling review of *The Last Hurrah*. (He also knew little about Boston's ethnic warfare.) Thereafter, O'Connor was never heard to say anything complimentary about Charles Rolo.[45]

The national news magazines came through for O'Connor and Skeffington. *Time* thought that while Skeffington should have been gauged better, O'Connor nevertheless accomplished a rarity in American fiction—he brought his man "alive, with love." The magazine ran a photo of Curley seated in front of his own portrait.[46] *Newsweek* likewise stressed O'Connor's sympathetic portrayal of Skeffington, and called Knocko Minihan's wake a wonderful "set piece."[47]

42. Howard Mumford Jones, review of *The Last Hurrah, Saturday Review,* February 4, 1956, 12; biographical sketch by John Haverstick.

43. Gouverneur Paulding, "—And He Was Always Good to the Poor," *The Reporter,* February 23, 1956.

44. Charles J. Rolo, "The Great Skeffington," *Atlantic,* February 1956, 80–81.

45. Peter Davison, E-mail to author, June 27, 2000.

46. "'Outrageous Old Crook,'" *Time,* February 13, 1956, 94.

47. "A Vote for O'Connor," *Newsweek,* February 6, 1956, 88–89.

Book reviews were one thing. Quite another occurred when sales of the book soared that winter and spring, and the phenomena of Edwin O'Connor and *The Last Hurrah* as a Boston roman à clef grew apace. A man who was little known became a celebrity in a matter of a few weeks, especially in the Hub. He told Conor Cruise O'Brien that one Boston bookstore reported to him that "we keep big stocks of your book, ready wrapped up. Every now and again, someone will push open that door from the street and just stand there waiting to be served. So we just hand that person the book we know he wants and collect the money. He goes away happy."[48] Interviews, book signings, photo sessions, publicity trips to New York, author's luncheons, and invitations of all sorts—much of this was new to O'Connor and not altogether to his liking, although he endured them cheerfully enough for a while. All the attention was even pleasant at first. Although hardly antisocial and certainly not a morose introvert, O'Connor nevertheless soon began to guard his privacy even more. He always insisted that a writer's job was to write, and that most other activities were distractions. His own pleasant diversions were few and modest. Reading headed his list, followed in rough order by daily socializing, Red Sox baseball, plays and movies, amateur magic, and swimming in summer. Already quite settled into a bachelor routine, he would learn over the following months and years to keep distractions to a minimum.

His recent employer, the *Boston Post*, ran a lengthy three-part interview on February 13–15. O'Connor opened up more to this paper than any other. He obviously felt affection for the newspaper that had kept his soul and body together for over two years. In most of the interviews O'Connor gave during this time he tells the same basic story of boyhood in Woonsocket, education at La Salle and Notre Dame, radio work, Coast Guard, radio again, and then years of free-lancing and the failure of *The Oracle* before talking of *The Last Hurrah*. Curiously enough for a writer so engrossed with the Irish American family, he hardly ever mentions his own.

The guessing game of who's really who in *The Last Hurrah* was played with gusto. A *Boston Globe* story in May rounded up the current suspects. Curley of course dominated this rogues' gallery, but many other mayors from Newark's Frank Hague to New York's Jimmy Walker to Kansas City's Tom Pendergast were offered as stand-in candidates for Skeffington. Bostonians knew better. Louis Brems of course became Cuke Gillen. John Gorman is alleged to be modeled on West End ward boss Martin Lomasney. But O'Con-

---

48. Quoted by Conor Cruise O'Brien in letter to author, August 4, 1999.

nor himself usually said that all such speculation was simply wrongheaded. He told the *Globe* that at a restaurant he had overheard some politicians identifying the book's characters: "They were 100 percent wrong."[49] Clem Norton had been boasting for months, correctly enough, that he was a character too. At the time Norton was writing a this-and-that column for nearby Lynn's *Telegram-News*. The final entry for his April 23 column catches some of the quidnunc's stylistic quirks:

Edwin O'Connor, author of "The Last Hurrah!" [sic], comes from Rhode Island. Lives on Marlborough street, Boston. Bachelor. Summers in Wellfleet, Cape Cod. Dad a doctor. O'Connor is typically Irish. Shrewd, Warm, kind, understanding, knows politics, understands human behavior, is a top writer. . . . Tickled he hit the "jack-pot". Gifted with Celtic imagination, plus the genius to write. He told me I was in "The Last Hurrah!" May be the "Charlie Hennessey."

Awards of various sorts came quickly. The Associated Press wasted no time choosing O'Connor as "Author of the Week" when the book was published: "Edwin O'Connor, the name that politicos as well as the general public are going to be talking about . . ." (The current bestsellers in fiction that week were MacKinlay Kantor's *Andersonville*, Herman Wouk's *Marjorie Morningstar*, Cameron Hawkley's *Cash McCall*, John O'Hara's *Ten North Frederick*, and Patrick Dennis's *Auntie Mame*. Irish American authors were well represented, but they usually were not writing about the Irish American experience.)[50] On April 16 he received an award from the Notre Dame Club of Chicago "for his conformity to high standards of literature."[51] The next day he was guest speaker at the Book and Author Luncheon at Boston's Sheraton-Astor Hotel, where he confessed to being mildly upset, though also amused, that so many people claimed to recognize themselves in his novel.[52] In 1957 the Catholic Writers Guild of America presented O'Connor with its Golden Book Award, given "to the American Catholic author who has written the book judged the best of the preceding year's literary output."[53] On September 25, 1956, O'Connor was one of five Bostonians who received the Greater Boston Annual Achievement Awards[54] On February 20, 1957, he was one of twenty-five honored by the National Conference of Christians and Jews.[55] O'Connor probably got the award because of the presence of Sam

49. Joseph M. Harvey, "Hurrah for Whom?" *Boston Sunday Globe*, May 13, 1956.
50. *Woonsocket Call*, February 4, 1956, 5.
51. Unidentified newspaper clipping, April 16, 1956.
52. Unidentified newspaper clipping, April 18, 1956.
53. Items courtesy of Barbara O'Connor Burrell.
54. *Woonsocket Call*, September 20, 1956.
55. *Boston Herald*, February 21, 1957, 32.

Weinberg as one of Skeffington's loyal lieutenants, although today O'Connor's description of Weinberg's "unmistakably Jewish face" (*LH* 42) would surely disqualify him.

O'Connor turned down some invitations. One of the earliest came from the dean of the New York School of Social Work, which was affiliated with Columbia University. O'Connor was invited in March to take part in a panel discussion of his novel, surely one of the fastest recognitions in American literary history and an indication of the book's rapid and wide appeal. O'Connor sent his regrets, although he was probably amused that after the panel discussion on April 6 coffee was to be served in the school's library, which had once been the personal library of Andrew Carnegie.[56] Later, O'Connor received one of the panelists' papers, the first known academic paper on O'Connor's work. Violet M. Sieder, a professor of social work and a specialist in urban planning and community welfare, commented on the sociological aspects of *The Last Hurrah*. Sieder's brief paper praises the book's "penetrating analysis" of urban politics when the old political bosses worked for people, not with them—surely a debatable point. She is disturbed that Skeffington contemptuously dismisses political reformers. From this point the paper quickly develops into a screed for social planning. In fact, at the paper's end she unashamedly plugs her school, whose graduates, "indoctrinated with a sense of social cause," will further citizen participation.[57] Had he been there, Skeffington would have been reaching for his oratorical gun. O'Connor was asked by the dean to comment on her paper. Apparently he had better things to do because his copy remains unmarked.

On April 3 O'Connor received a clubby letter with an oddly cool tone inviting him to be guest of honor and speaker at the annual meeting of the Brokers Institute of the Boston Real Estate Board. O'Connor was selected because of "your recent book with its local flavor which is so interesting and familiar to all of us."[58] Later that month the Ford Hall Forum, a venerable speaker's series that met in Boston's Jordan Hall but which was losing audiences to television, hoped that O'Connor would speak before the November elections. Suggested topic: "America's Changing Political Scene," or whatever he would prefer.[59] In early May the Citizens' Charter Committee of Hartford

56. Kenneth D. Johnson, letter and enclosures to Edwin O'Connor, March 26, 1956, EOCP 119.

57. Violet Sieder, untitled paper on *The Last Hurrah* presented to meeting of the Library Associates of the New York School of Social Work, Columbia University, April 9, 1956, EOCP 120.

58. Richard B. Fowler, letter to Edwin O'Connor, April 3, 1956, EOCP 101.

59. Louis P. Smith, letter to Edwin O'Connor, April 26, 1956, EOCP 149.

hoped that O'Connor would speak to them on "Good Government Through Literature" or "It Can Happen Here."[60] Did O'Connor laugh or cringe? *This Week Magazine*, a Sunday newspaper insert which boasted the largest magazine audience in the country, hoped he would write a short "relaxed and friendly" piece for them, with no heavy preaching. (It was, after all, a *Sunday* magazine.) It would pay $250.[61] In June the Boston Public Library Professional Staff Association invited him to speak at their fall meeting.[62] In the following January NBC's Public Service Program wanted O'Connor to do a segment on the political novel for educational television, in return for $100.[63] To all these earnest requests O'Connor evidently sent polite regrets.

Cartoonists had a field day with O'Connor's distinctive appearance. Someone sent him a poster which featured the huge, thick, tweed coat he had bought in Ireland. The caption reads: "Will Success Spoil Ed O'Connor?" A newspaper cartoon in the sports pages showed O'Connor in Fenway Park's VIP skyview seats along with the boxer Rocky Marciano. Another Boston newspaper cartoon emphasized O'Connor's big head, curly but receding hair, big smile, and twinkling eyes.[64]

By September the novel had been high on the bestseller charts for twenty weeks, sometimes occupying the top slot from March to May, and had sold two million copies. *Life* reported that the "the last hurrah" had already entered the language.[65] Those three words of the title constitute Edwin O'Connor's only entry in Bartlett's *Familiar Quotations*. As might be expected, the phrase most frequently occurs in political journalism. Evans and Novak's *Inside Report* column used it on July 22, 1970, at the retirement of John McCormack of Massachusetts, longtime Speaker of the House. In turn, when a later speaker died, *Newsweek* ran a story entitled "The Last Hurrah for Tip O'Neill, 1912–1994."[66] The phrase gravitates easily to Bay State politicos. The phrase still regularly occurs in the political and editorial pages from the *Times* to the hometown weekly. Sportswriting, an art devoted to that other American contest, also has found the phrase evocative, especially for the retirement of Boston greats like Carl Yastrzemski and Larry Bird. Even bullfighting attracted the phrase, as in a *New York Times* article on May 10, 1970:

60. Catherine G. Cox, letter to Edwin O'Connor, May 7, 1956, EOCP 159.

61. William I. Nichols, letter to Edwin O'Connor, May 22, 1956, EOCP 377.

62. Linda M. Pagliuca, letter to Edwin O'Connor, June 13, 1956, EOCP 98. (Pagliuca's "Teen About Town" column in the *Boston Post* may have influenced his decision to decline.)

63. William W. Parish, letter to Helen Strauss, January 29, 1957, EOCP 254.

64. Unidentified poster and cartoons, EOCP 358–60.

65. Introduction to "A Hurrah for Curley by Curley," *Life*, September 10, 1956, 120.

66. Article by Eleanor Clift, January 17, 1994, 22.

"The Apartado: Last Hurrah Before the Ole!" When Boston's ailing Cardinal Cushing announced his retirement in 1970, *Commonweal* ran a story on October 2 entitled "Another Last Hurrah." Finally, no survey of the phrase would be complete without mention of an eponymous Boston restaurant and bar. In 1969 Dunfey's Last Hurrah opened off the lower lobby of Boston's old Parker House Hotel. It was almost adjacent to old City Hall; Curley got his haircuts there. Midway between the State House and the new City Hall, Dunfey's Last Hurrah quickly became a favorite trough for politicians. Closed in 1997 while the Parker House underwent extensive renovations, it reopened upstairs two years later as the Last Hurrah Bar and Grill. The mahogany walls have dozens of Curley photographs, but not one of the author who lent his phrase to the establishment.

James Michael Curley soon got in on the fun. Out of office for six years, he was now an anachronistic icon in Boston's cult of nostalgia. But there was still some fight in the eighty-one-year-old lion, and when *The Last Hurrah* went on sale, the lion growled. Jack Beatty begins his account of the amusing interaction of Curley, Skeffington, and O'Connor thus: "Edwin O'Connor was about to come to rescue [Curley] from the politician's hell—the realm of the forgotten."[67] Curley quickly took, or pretended to take, the novel as a biography of himself. He was especially upset that "my mother" was portrayed as stealing food. The thinness of Curley's skin is a well-known Irish trait and a tiresome one at that. When he threatened legal action, his sons dissuaded him. What happened next is a mixture of Curley's political savvy, his customary truth-stretching for laughs, and the fantasizing of the elderly. Surprised to hear that the country was swinging toward Skeffington as a downright likeable rascal, Curley did an about-face and embraced O'Connor's hero as his alter ego.

An early sign of this transformation took place only a month after the book's appearance, when O'Connor had his only personal encounter with Curley.[68] One day as O'Connor was making his downtown rounds he noticed Curley getting into a cab in front of the Parker House. Emboldened, O'Connor stuck his head inside the cab's window and introduced himself. This is O'Connor's account in the *Atlantic:*

67. Beatty, *Rascal King,* 513. Unless otherwise noted, the following Skeffington-Curley material is from Beatty, 513–20.

68. O'Connor wrote about the meeting twice: "Author Tells All about Curley and Skeffington," *Boston Evening Globe,* June 5, 1961, 1 and 5; "James Michael Curley and *The Last Hurrah,*" *Atlantic,* September 1961, 48–50. Also see Introduction to *BL,* 15, where Arthur Schlesinger recounts the meeting the way O'Connor told him. The three accounts agree substantially. Curley left no account of the meeting.

There was a long pause while he looked at me; then suddenly he laughed. "Well, well," he said, putting out a hand. "Nice to see you. You've written quite a book. I like that book."

I said I was pleased to hear this; rumors to the contrary had been reaching me with some persistence.

"No, no," he said, waving all rumors to one side. "That's a fine book. I enjoyed it. Do you know what part I enjoyed most?"

"No," I said. "No, I don't."

He said, almost dreamily, "The part where I die."

I thought I had better nail this down quickly; I said, "Isn't it strange, Governor, that so many people confuse fact with fiction? Skeffington with yourself, for instance. I know, and you know, the difference between the two, that the one isn't like the other—"

"Yes," he said, nodding gravely. "Yes, there I am in my bedroom, dying. Breathing my last. I'm lying flat on my back with my eyes closed, when suddenly into the room comes. . . ."

And then he went on to give me the complete scene from *The Last Hurrah,* more or less as I had written it, except for the insertion of himself whenever Skeffington had appeared in the original. It was quite a performance, completely engrossing and not a little eerie.

Curley may have been putting on his best "Irish bull" manner for O'Connor, and a lot more besides. They parted with vague talk of having lunch some day, but to O'Connor's regret they never did. However, for some reason Curley, through his middlemen, continued to threaten legal action, especially during the book's filming.[69]

Curley had been working on his own memoirs for some time, and now *The Last Hurrah* prompted him to secure a ghost writer and rush into print in order to capitalize on Skeffington's celebrity. *I'd Do It Again: A Record of All My Uproarious Years* appeared in early 1957.[70] Arthur Schlesinger makes the wry observation that Curley reinvented himself in his book to be like the more loveable Skeffington, thus transforming "art into nature."[71] The book's title is a tale in itself. In public Curley had fallen into the habit of blithely assuming that he and Skeffington were one and the same; his fawning listeners went along. Since "his" death in *The Last Hurrah* was his favorite scene, he es-

69. Curley was not the only one to threaten litigation. In 1958, a New Jersey author, Frank J. Rochna, claimed *The Last Hurrah* had too many similarities to a recent book of his own. But Atlantic Monthly Press's law firm found "no actionable similarity between the two books." The matter never went forward. EOCP 180, 181.

70. (Englewood Cliffs, N.J.: Prentice-Hall, 1957). The unnamed ghost writer was John Henry Cutler, a former Dartmouth professor and later a newspaper editor in Duxbury, Massachusetts; Beatty, *Rascal King,* 518. Curley mentions Skeffington only once, and O'Connor not at all.

71. Review of *I'd Do It Again, Saturday Review.* May 27, 1957.

pecially enjoyed reliving, so to speak, "his" dying. Accordingly, he would describe at length Skeffington's penultimate words. But he altered those words significantly. In the novel when those around the sickbed think Skeffington has died, the smug Roger Sugrue tells everyone that Skeffington, having met his judgment, now would do it all differently. Like Tim Finnegan, however, Skeffington is not quite dead, and he rouses himself to shout in a hoarse whisper, *"The hell I would!"* (*LH* 401; O'Connor's italics). Curley, sensitive to lace-curtain disapproval of vulgarity, would routinely bowdlerize Skeffington and make him say, "I'd do it again." Hence, the title of his memoirs.

The confusions besetting life, art, and politics grew even stranger during the Massachusetts presidential primary election in the spring of 1956. As he so often did, Curley ran that May as a delegate to the Democratic national convention. In the polling he came in third, just 79 votes behind Senator John F. Kennedy. However, 160 votes were cast for Frank Skeffington. No love had ever been lost between the old Curley and the new Kennedy camps, and so Curley took some solace that in a sense he had topped Kennedy with Skeffington's help. *Time* magazine even reported the incident on May 21.

A near-meeting between O'Connor and Curley took place in early August when Curley spoke at the University of New Hampshire. A reporter for the *Woonsocket Call* covered the talk as well as the reaction of O'Connor, who was in the audience. Curley's talk was mostly of his own accomplishments. When asked about O'Connor and his novel he said, "I rather like the man who wrote that book." Afterwards O'Connor told reporters, "Governor Curley says he is Frank Skeffington. We are in some disagreement on that point." He admitted, however, that he enjoyed Curley's vintage performance at the podium.[72] Curley's talk was later the substance of the lengthy article in *Life* mentioned above.

One interesting "what if" occurred just before publication of *The Last Hurrah*, when Ted Weeks alerted O'Connor's friend Professor P. Albert Duhamel of Boston College that it would be fascinating to get O'Connor and Curley together on Duhamel's new book program on Boston's WGBH-TV. According to Duhamel, when rumors of the threatened lawsuit circulated, Boston College's president called Duhamel to his office and told him to back off on that program. The fact that one of Curley's sons was a Jesuit who apparently disliked O'Connor may also have been instrumental in the Jesuit president's decision. Duhamel threw together a hastily arranged substitute program featuring a political scientist and the chief book buyer for the

---

72. "O'Connor Denies Curley 'Hero' in Novel, Tells Ex-Mayor So," *Woonsocket Call*, August 7, 1956. The title is misleading; the two did not meet then.

Boston Public Library. It was a "wet skyrocket," according to Duhamel. When O'Connor found out through another Jesuit about the president's intrusion, he was miffed. He also blamed WGBH, into whose studios he promised never to enter again. For years he pestered Duhamel for details about the collapse of the televised summit with Curley; their friendship was also strained. When Curley's *I'd Do It Again* came out, O'Connor refused Duhamel's invitation in January 1957 to appear on the program.[73]

O'Connor received more fan mail for *The Last Hurrah* than for his other novels combined. Its popularity exceeded its literary merit, and O'Connor often humbly implied as much. It was the kind of novel that appealed for all kinds of extra-literary reasons—civic, ethnic, political, nostalgic, personal, and even religious. O'Connor ascribed its runaway success to election-year interest, to the fact that no novel like it had appeared recently, and to the Curley connection, which he disingenuously hastens to add was unintended.[74] O'Connor saved about sixty glowing letters and only two rebuking ones. A sampling follows.[75]

His old pastor, now a monsignor, wrote from Rhode Island with praise for the book; Holland was so proud to call O'Connor his friend (165). Clem Norton sent a postcard from Miami where all copies of the novel were sold out. "I've been stirring them up," he said. (207). A lady in North Dakota wrote that Bismark's only bookstore informed her that the book was out of print. John Kelleher sent his parody of early Celtic verse in which he kidded O'Connor about his silence on his characters' origins. An excerpt:

> Sad be that man! The saints of Ireland to be cursing him.
> The wisdom of Ireland to be fasting on his doorstep.
> The poets satirizing his niggardliness always.

He enclosed a copy of his article on Joyce's "The Dead" that became a classic in Joyce studies (174). Daniel Aaron, at the time a professor at Smith College, implicitly complimented O'Connor by describing a fatuous 1931 letter by a Boston Brahmin which claimed that the Irish (and the Jews) had no literary talent (72). The wife of a famous refugee Bauhaus architect then living in Massachusetts wrote "Dear Ed" that the novel was a good exposé of the wretched state of Boston politics. In her utterly humorless way she devel-

---

73. P. Albert Duhamel, letter to author, March 25, 1999; P. Albert Duhamel, letter to Edwin O'Connor, January 28, 1957, EOCP 135.

74. O'Connor, "Curley and *The Last Hurrah*," 49.

75. For convenience these letters will be simply designated by their number in the Edwin O'Connor Papers.

oped at length a Germanic analysis of all that was wrong with Boston in particular and American culture as a whole (155). One wonders if she smiled even once when reading the book.

From Notre Dame Frank O'Malley wrote that the book was "just plain great" and that "in all my life I have never been so happy as a teacher, never so proud" (232). Father John J. Cavanaugh, C.S.C., wrote that "you have done much to boost our spirits here and the prestige of Notre Dame everywhere." On a recent visit to the Palm Beach home of Joseph Kennedy, "who knows Boston politics well," he found the Kennedy patriarch "enthusiastic" about the book. Father Cavanaugh, who was director of the University of Notre Dame Foundation, concludes with a not-too-veiled appeal for a contribution to the author's alma mater (110). In March University President Father Theodore Hesburgh, C.S.C., wrote to tell O'Connor that West's *New Yorker* review was completely unfair. A month later he wrote that it was nice to talk with O'Connor and Notre Dame alumni in Boston, that a copy of *The Last Hurrah* was prominently displayed in the university library, and that he was praying for O'Connor's ailing father (163).

Many readers commented on O'Connor's presentation of Irish Americans. From Ireland Christine Cruise O'Brien was surprised that O'Connor's Irish Americans spoke a "peculiar form of Anglo-Irish" much like the Irish themselves (212); not all would agree with her. Jack Sweeney's wife, Maire, used her best Dublin adjectives in bold script: "Grand" and "Gorgeous" (275). Americans tended to like the spirited roughness of the Skeffington generation, like the Wells College professor who liked its older romantic courage (128). A Maryland newspaperman thought O'Connor had captured the "puzzle" of the Irish in America who are so different from their counterparts in Ireland (195). A Philadelphian opened his letter, "May you write while the blood warms your arm. We've waited 50 years for this!" He said that his own city has plenty of Irish eccentrics: "Six men, all claiming to have killed Michael Collins. The wake of Parnell continues and Cuchulain can be seen daily in a Cadillac" (112). From the Viking Books Publicity Department a fan wrote that the novel is the first depiction of the "curious Yankee-bred breed of Gaels" who wax nostalgic over "Just an Irish Lullaby" but who know little of genuine Irish culture (193). Even a few certified blue bloods sent their congratulations, like the gentleman who sent two pages of doggerel on the hypocrisy of his own kind who began as enslavers and now engage in "lectures, endowment, bird lore, and hospitals." He liked the Irish for their unabashed vivacity (160).

The novel reminded an elderly grammarian of the 1890s when she first started to teach. She was amazed to find no "errors of grammar" whatsoever in the book (156). But one reader did spot a confusion about the seasons in a novel which begins, "It was early in August," then has a Spring Dance that night, before resuming the campaign in autumn (186). These confusions resulted from O'Connor's lapses in coordinating some changes he made during revision.

Several people, all women, detected O'Connor's fundamental decency. A writer friend who was working on a study of the talented but controversial Father Leonard Feeney, a Boston Jesuit who had recently been excommunicated for his rigorously exclusionary ideas on salvation, wrote that O'Connor's success "couldn't happen to a nicer guy—or a better writer" (124). An Alabaman woman gushed vaguely how deeply the novel had made her *"feel."* She does make one interesting observation: "I'm sure you love others in order to write such a story . . . how happy you must be!" (109). A delightful fan letter came from a resident of Jewish nursing home in New York. She had read the novel aloud to other seniors who loved it so much that they declared O'Connor their new "pin-up boy" (201).

Inevitably some people tried to cash in on O'Connor's success. Two people wrote with projects for a stage version. One wrote on letterhead of the United States Information Agency (244). The other would-be adapter, who was only half way through the book, promised that his stage version would be less local and definitely less Catholic. He went on, with no trace of irony, to decry Hollywood remakes that do violence to the originals (136). (A few people recall that O'Connor did speak vaguely about the possibility for a musical version of his novel.)

All sorts of others wrote. A One World advocate running for president sent two of his tracts promoting an ideology called "equitism" and called for a world radio university (126). A prisoner in Connecticut thanked O'Connor for the nostalgia of the book; he would be released in three years and would take to the "highroad" (137). A mother in Michigan named her daughter Maeve after Adam's wife. Perhaps the most unintentionally comical letter came from a woman from Boston's Mission Church parish. It begins, "This is an appeal for money. I might as well tell you the truth right off the bat without beating around the bush," and concludes, "You must be considering giving some of [your] loot to charity of some kind" (106).

O'Connor kept two negative letters which appealed to his sense of the ludicrous. An industrial engineer who claimed to have written twenty-eight stories, three of which became successes on Broadway, frowned on O'Connor's alleged dim view of the Irish (153). A paranoid lady in San Francisco tore into O'Connor for trashing his "race" and religion. Since the world was always waiting to ridicule the Irish, why was he making it so easy? She then unaccountably signs off by saying that it was a good, enjoyable book (139).

The novel even received praise from a world leader. In 1961 when he was President Kennedy's ambassador to India, John Kenneth Galbraith was asked by Prime Minister Nehru about a good book for vacation reading. Figuring a political tale might appeal, Galbraith recommended *The Last Hurrah*. Nehru reported back that O'Connor's novel was "the best political novel he had ever read." Galbraith believes that Nehru, half a world away in a very different culture, responded to the book's universality.[76]

By 1961 *The Last Hurrah* had been translated into twelve languages. O'Connor sent John Kelleher a copy of the Swedish version, *Sista Hurraropet*, with his inscription in "Swedish," which he then "translated" as if he were Knute Rockne: "The only thing dumber than a dumb Swede is a smart Irishman," a reversal of an old ethnic joke.[77]

The Last Hurrah is the only Edwin O'Connor novel still in print. Little, Brown, now a subsidiary of Time-Warner, still publishes the paperback version. For a while in the 1980s the paperback's cover got the "classic" look: a plain silver background with a simple script for the green title. More recently, the cover appears with a picture of men speaking on a Boston street. The book is sometimes used in college literature and political science courses.[78] In 2000 a generous portion from Knocko Minihan's wake was included in the impressive *Irish Writing in the Twentieth Century* anthology, where *The Last Hurrah* was listed as one of the twenty-eight recommended Irish novels of the century.[79] In 2001 a shorter passage, also from the wake, was included in Harvard University Press's *Writing New England*.[80] It has been filmed twice (1958 and 1977). In 1999 it was given a decent stage adaptation by Eric Simonson at Boston's Huntington Theatre, where many elderly in the audience were heard reminiscing about Curley. In fact, for its publicity the Huntington used a famous photograph of a jubilant Curley arriving in Boston's South Station after his release from prison. The play received mixed reviews.

76. John Kenneth Galbraith, personal interview, November 12, 1999.

77. John Kelleher, personal interview, May 29, 1999.

78. In a recent informal survey of my own students, I was gratified that so many enjoyed the novel. However, some did admit that its pace was too slow.

79. David Pierce, ed., *Irish Writing in the Twentieth Century: A Reader* (Cork: Cork University Press, 2000), 673–80; 1321.

80. Andrew Delbanco, ed., *Writing New England: An Anthology from the Puritans to the Present* (Cambridge, Mass.: Belknap Press of Harvard University Press, 2001), 181–83.

꧞

The Last Hurrah made O'Connor an affluent man and, for several months, the most famous novelist in the country.[81] His book was much talked about in offices and bars, at dinner tables, and especially in the corridor of power that runs from Boston to Washington. He eventually got so pestered with telephone calls from lushes and cranks that he secured an unlisted number.[82] But within a year his fame began slowly to wane, to be briefly revived with his next novel in the early 1960s. By almost all accounts the money and fame did not change O'Connor substantially, and for the next six years he lived a simple but comfortable bachelor's life while maintaining the sunny disposition and friendly wit that readily emerges during his friends' reminiscences. A widely reported quip by O'Connor on his newfound affluence captures his knack for Bostonian self-deprecation: he said that he was surprised to discover that Filene's Basement, Boston's chaotic bargain basement, actually had an upstairs.

In the early summer of 1956 O'Connor threw a celebration party for Wellfleet friends that reveals much about the man. He bought fifty steaks to barbeque before realizing that his tiny rented cottage was entirely inadequate for so many guests. When he told his neighbors Gustav and Vita Petersen about his difficulty, they generously offered their cottage on Slough Pond for the party. Although the Petersens' cottage was not much larger than his own, the outdoor party was a great success. O'Connor was delighted to be able to repay the many friends he had made at Wellfleet.[83]

The Last Hurrah depicted a dying breed of politics, and therefore it necessarily entailed the demise of a man who was tribal chieftain to his loyalists and a father figure to nephew Adam Caulfield. *Adam* (whose wife is Ma*eve*) is the obvious American innocent who gets a political and ethnic education from his notorious uncle. In a sense Adam at thirty-three is a version of the assimilated O'Connor, who came to Boston knowing little about urban Irish American mores. Skeffington, in turn, in an odd way represents O'Connor's father's generation: harboring resentments long endured, determined and hardworking as it became assimilated (Skeffington's house and neighbor-

---

81. His friend Francis Carroll recalls O'Connor dropping into the Carroll hardware store in Woonsocket sometime in 1956; O'Connor said, without boasting, that he would never have to work for anyone again—a cherished Irish dream. Francis Carroll, personal interview, July 15, 1998.

82. Joe Harrington, "A Success Year," *Boston Sunday Globe*, January 13, 1957, A24. When O'Connor forgot his new number and called to get it, it took all his powers to convince the telephone company that he was indeed the author Edwin O'Connor.

83. Vita and Gustav Petersen, personal interview, June 10, 2001.

hood are not unlike 247 Gaskill Street), outspoken to the point of self-paro-dy, snappish and witty all at once. Whatever ambivalent feeling O'Connor may have had toward his dying father, he would seldom again visit death on his fictional fathers. In fact, henceforth his fathers show a remarkable ability to evade death and endure.

Perhaps John Kelleher best captured the appeal of *The Last Hurrah* when he wrote of it thirteen years later:

[U]nnoticed till then by anybody, the public humorlessness that settled down over the American Irish about the turn of the century when the Irish societies drove the Irish comedians off the stage had silently lifted. The Irish could laugh at themselves again. Unfortunately there was not a hell of a lot left to laugh at.[84]

We can now see that in helping to part the lace curtains O'Connor had inaugurated the rediscovery of Irish America that continues unabated into the twenty-first century.

84. John V. Kelleher, "Edwin O'Connor and the Irish-American Process," *Atlantic,* July 1968, 48–52.

CHAPTER NINE

ஜ் *Interlude*
(1956–1957)

Thoreau opens the second chapter of *Walden* thus: "At a certain season of our life we are accustomed to consider every spot as the possible site of a house." After six months of unaccustomed fame and fortune, O'Connor was ready to build his own house in a spot Thoreau had written about in *Cape Cod;* there is even a Thoreau Way close by. In the spring of 1956 O'Connor bought twelve prime acres in an area known as Wellfleet Woods. For almost a decade of summers he had bicycled through the outer Cape's most extensive forest on his way to the beach. This enchanted spot, the first he ever owned, was deep in one of the last undeveloped parcels of its size on the outer Cape. O'Connor bought his land just before the creation of the Cape Cod National Seashore brought development to a halt. He chose his site for an elevation which promised striking panoramas, for the seclusion offered by the woods in a tangle of one-lane sandy roads, and for its proximity to the majestic oceanside beach, half a mile distant. It was an ideal location for a writer's retreat, especially for a writer who responded to the subtle austerities of the humble woods and the immense, bare beach.

O'Connor had known Heyward Cutting of the Cambridge architectural firm of Chermayeff & Cutting ever since 1953, when Cutting began summering on one of the small glacial ponds close by.[1] In his typically easy manner O'Connor would often stop by at the freshwater pond to rinse off the salt from his swim. He would chat with Cutting and his wife, and tell stories and do magic tricks for their sons. One day in the summer of 1956 O'Connor took Cutting and his ladder to the top of his new land and there among the bearberry ground cover, wild blueberry bushes, twisty scrub pines, and larger oak trees they "sat right down and worked on the problem," as Cutting describes the day. Then Cutting put his twelve-foot ladder to a tree and had O'Connor climb to the top and

---

1. I am most grateful to Heyward Cutting for his detailed letter of April 29, 1999, and for the blueprints and drawings of the house.

face east. "I told him he was looking out of his future kitchen window." Later when O'Connor had difficulty reading the first blueprints, Cutting built a small basswood model of the house, which O'Connor treasured during the dreary Boston winters.

O'Connor was impatient for the house to be built at once. Cutting was at pains to point out that a substantial house could not be built in a summer and that O'Connor would have to be on hand to go over details as construction proceeded. Also, senior partner Serge Chermayeff would have to give final approval, after his return from a European trip. O'Connor anxiously waited for the authoritarian Chermayeff's return. In the end both O'Connor and Cutting were relieved at Chermayeff's approval and were delighted at his suggestions.

The site on the low hill was more advantageous in 1956 than today. In the nineteenth century much of that part of the Cape was denuded as its few large trees went for shipbuilding and houses, and in the mid-twentieth century a second growth forest of scrub oak and pine was taking over. Most of the trees were quite small because the great hurricanes of 1938 and 1954 had kept the forest low, and winter nor'easters also regularly pruned and leveled. Today the pine trees have grown higher than the house, and only with difficulty can one see the jewel-like ponds to the west, the distant high dunes in Truro to the north, and the ocean to the east.

From the outside the house is simple, boxy, and homely. Like much Bauhaus-inspired architecture it arrests the eye, though few but an architect and his mother could like it. Seen today, it has a dated look. The basic plan is a large central upthrusting cube with smaller cubes jutting from the sides. Abrupt flat roofs and rectangular window slits complete the hard-edge symmetry. To be sure the house avoids Cape Cod cuteness, but at a price. One wonders why O'Connor, who was usually so traditional, admired his first house. Likely explanations could include deference to an authority, especially since friendship was involved, and the redeeming features of the interior.

The interior indeed comes as a surprising relief.[2] In order to provide a large entertaining area that could enjoy the surrounding views, the house was built, in a sense, upside down. The ground-level floor has two bedrooms, a study, and a bath. Warm woods and bricks lend a coziness, although this level seems a bit cramped for a large man. Upstairs is a stroke of

2. Some of the interior details were described in a large feature article by Virginia Bohlin, accompanied by four photos, in the *Boston Traveler,* August 25, 1959, B42. O'Connor must have been amused at this treatment by the newspaper company that had fired him unceremoniously seven year earlier.

O'Connor's summer house at Wellfleet, built in 1957. *Photo taken by author, 1999.*

planning genius. Essentially it is one large room with a ten-foot ceiling and a wide central fireplace. One half includes the kitchen and dining area. Here all the built-in appliances are ranged compactly on one wall. This linear arrangement might appeal to a bachelor who was beginning to take a serious interest in cooking, but most women would find the layout too regimented. Little use was made of cabinets or closets; cookery and utensils were arranged on shelves in plain view and thus easy to snatch. The living area has informal birch furniture from Design Research of Cambridge, some of it consisting of built-in benches. Again bricks and dark woods predominate. Wooden shutters and a few bamboo curtains keep it uncluttered; no ordinary curtains or drapes interfere with the views. The effect is quietly handsome and simple in this unmistakable bachelor's house that required only a brief weekly cleaning. Much of the interior—furniture, appliances, even some of the art work and crockery, including the large Corningware coffee pot—is exactly as it was in O'Connor's time. Surprisingly little has been changed by the current owners.[3]

Two small patios adjoin the house. Above, two screened porches project over the bedrooms below, and a precarious ship's ladder goes to the roof over the main part of the house, where O'Connor sometimes would sunbathe on the few days he did not go to the beach. From this roof today one can still catch glimpses of the panorama once enjoyed below. Hans Namuth took a series of photographs of O'Connor and the house, apparently for a *New York Times Sunday Magazine* story which was never done. One photo shows a delighted O'Connor scampering on the roof of his new house.

When the house was completed in April 1957, O'Connor finally was more than a summer boarder in Wellfleet. He now had a writer's retreat in his favorite vacation spot and a place to do some real entertaining. Over the years many of his Boston and Cambridge friends stayed at the house. Typically he would come early in the season, before Memorial Day, and stay well after Labor Day, that golden time for the Cape lover. Limited heating allowed for later weekend trips well into the Cape's mild autumn.

Just as O'Connor had chosen a high perch at 48 Beacon Street from which to view the Boston he wrote about, so now he owned a hilltop view of Wellfleet, the other end of his Massachusetts axis. He had come up in the world and was enjoying it. But with fame came those sunburned gawkers that the Cape grows as easily as its cranberries. O'Connor was downright wintry to those unfortunate enough to find his retreat in the maze of woods and winding tracks. Although he suppressed anger far better than his father, he nonetheless was upset at any disturbances to his routine, especially during mornings devoted to writing. John Kelleher eventually made a sign for him in Gaelic. One side has his name, Edwin O Concobair, followed impishly by "Esq." The other side says (freely translated from the original), "Beat it, nosey." O'Connor never did display the wooden sign outside. How many American Irish could read it anyway? Instead, he kept it on the brick mantle of his fireplace.[4]

With fame and new possessions also came a trace of exclusiveness. Just months after taking possession of his Wellfleet house, he complains in a letter to another summer resident that new real estate developments in Wellfleet really upset him. There is no trace of irony in this letter that evinces the

3. I wish to thank co-owner Aileen Ward for the kind hospitality, cooperation, and information she gave to me during a visit on June 28, 1999.

4. My thanks to O'Connor's stepson, Stephen Weil, who still has the sign; and also to John Kelleher for verifying details and translating.

familiar "close the gates" stance of the newly arrived. He thinks the proposed national park for the Cape might help, but he is unsure.[5]

O'Connor's other indulgence was his Porsche. For years he had turned his abstemiousness into a clipped self-deprecation: "Doesn't smoke, doesn't drink, doesn't drive."[6] This remarkable feat of self-denial for a mid-twentieth-century American male was compromised in 1956 when O'Connor at last succumbed to the allure of German engineering. German cars were catching on and O'Connor wanted the best. The time was past for ferries, buses, and the occasional hitchhiking to and from the Cape, and for dusty trains to Woonsocket. Accordingly, after taking some refresher driving lessons in Boston from a white-knuckled Rudolph Elie, O'Connor bought a yellow Volkswagen Karmann Ghia, which was soon replaced by a red Porsche. Those who knew him best understood that this expensive car was not a status symbol or a pathetic attempt at sex appeal. O'Connor simply enjoyed anything well made, and in any case the car was more of a toy than a statement. He kept the Porsche for a few years until, he claimed, he was nearly blown off the highway by a stiff crosswind. He next bought a more sedate Mercedes sedan. It would appear O'Connor never became a really good driver, as a few fender benders attest. The story of the aerodynamic, road-hugging Porsche being blown sideways just does not ring true.[7]

After years of failing health and several months in a near comatose state, Dr. John Vincent O'Connor died at home late on Friday night, September 14, 1956. He was seventy-one. His first heart attack had occurred in 1944, and since 1946 he had conducted a limited practice from his home office only. The front-page obituary in the *Woonsocket Call* said that he was known for a "psychological approach to illnesses, and for the fatherly interest he took in his patients." The funeral at St. Charles' was a big Irish send-off in a state that still estimated one's importance by the number and rank of ecclesiastical dignitaries on the altar. Bishop Russell J. McVinney, the crusty bishop of Providence, headed the list of ten priests, which included O'Connor's confessor, Monsignor Lally. Dozens of physicians, nurses, and pharmacists were present, as were Buell Hudson of the *Woonsocket Call*, former Congressman

---

5. Edwin O'Connor, letter to Margaret Marsh, November 19, 1957, EOCP 282.

6. Barbara O'Connor Burrell, personal interview, summer 1998.

7. For information on O'Connor's adventures with cars, I thank Robert Taylor, Peter Davison, and Stephen Weil. When O'Connor worked in Miami in 1942, he may have used a radio station car, but when exactly he first learned to drive is not known.

Ambrose Kennedy, and Arthur Thornhill from Little, Brown. Interment was in St. Charles Cemetery in nearby Blackstone, Massachusetts.[8]

O'Connor talked only a little of his father's death, and showed even less emotion. One explanation lies in the determination of assimilated, affluent Irish Americans to distance themselves from the wailing at "ethnic" wakes and funerals, or even from their own early ancestors at the notorious Irish wakes which traditionally commemorated and defied death with ritualized "keening," along with smoking, drinking, and even dancing. But in O'Connor's case the ethnic explanation serves only up to a point.

Peter Davison, who had joined the *Atlantic* staff shortly after the death of O'Connor's father, records in his 1973 autobiography the mysterious beginning of his own long career as a poet. In August of 1957, while in therapy and full of grief over the loss of his mother and still in turmoil over his own father, the poet and academic Edward Davison, Peter happened to be reading a manuscript of Stanley Kunitz's poems for the Atlantic Monthly Press.

The austere cadences of Kunitz's work began to generate a strange mood in me. I stood up and walked unsteadily to my desk. The poem I wrote had, I thought, to do with a friend of mine, the novelist Edwin O'Connor, whose incapacity to express openly the warmth of his feelings made him and me uneasy, as two who could not confess their capacity to feel pain.

This is the poem, ostensibly about O'Connor, that Davison wrote:

> *The Winner*
>
> I hear a child inside,
> Crying to be let out.
> "No," shouts the swaggering Self,
> "Mind shall destroy all doubt.
> Out with all doubt, I say!
> Stifle that treacherous word!
> I have high deeds to do
> Twirling my deathly sword."
>
> Mind's on his mettle now,
> Deft at his surgical art,
> Stunning my pain with pain,
> Drowning the infant heart.

Of course, as Davison himself later realized, the poem was more about him-

---

8. Details from two items in the *Woonsocket Call*, September 15 and 17, 1956. On September 18 the paper printed a letter from Clem Norton, who thanked the Woonsocket police for providing details about the funeral over the phone.

self than his new friend, and was in any case an example of "sentimental discharge" which he had to get beyond.[9] Neither he nor O'Connor were able to express grief over their losses, he now realizes, and in O'Connor's case this emotional impasse led indirectly to the strangest piece O'Connor ever wrote, his 1957 "children's story," *Benjy*.[10]

In contrast to his understandable reticence about *The Last Hurrah*, O'Connor was more forthright about the genesis of *Benjy*. In fact, in nailing up his source for all to see he was more open about this book's specific origin than any other, and this in itself might put us on guard. Authorial coyness about sources and inspirations is well known, and there is certainly enough feel of the shaggy dog in this story (a nearly literal one, as it turns out) to make caution warranted.

The facts as O'Connor freely told them are curious. Shortly after his father died O'Connor, along with his sister and brother-in-law, brought his mother to Atlantic City for a short stay. O'Connor thought a change of scene would be good for everyone, so off they went to the scene of his parents' 1917 honeymoon trip. This is the account as O'Connor told *Newsweek*:

> Last year I was in Atlantic City with my mother, and there was a horrible child in the hotel dining room. Of course, awful children can sometimes be so winning. But you realized that this child has been spoiled by his mother since conception. The father was a weedy little man who was clearly just paying the bills.
>
> I also remember an English family of three that I once saw in the Shelbourne Hotel in Dublin. The father's teeth stuck out and he made obscure English noises. There was a great deal of discussion about the little boy's porridge. It was plain that the Irish cook was going to have to make a great many concessions for this little boy. Faced with such scenes, I suffer from premature crotchetiness. That accounts for *Benjy*.[11]

If Atlantic City was fashionable in 1917, the four subsequent decades had not been kind to the boardwalk resort, as its nineteenth-century notions of leisure activity became increasingly dated. For O'Connor the tatty New Jersey resort was definitely not the secluded quiet of unspoiled Wellfleet. Those two little brats, whatever they were doing, were an embodiment of everything spoiled, and they released something in O'Connor that had to come

9. Peter Davison, *Half Remembered: A Personal History* (New York: Harper & Row, 1973), 184.

10. Peter Davison, personal interview, March 11, 1999.

11. "The Bachelor Explains It," *Newsweek*, October 21, 1957, 118. The accompanying photograph by Hans Namuth shows O'Connor looking upwards impishly. O'Connor's sister corroborates the Atlantic City incident.

out fast and hot. But a problem remains: O'Connor's account of origins does not quite square with the story he actually wrote.

Benjy: A Ferocious Fairy Tale was written in a few weeks that autumn.[12] The following summary blends O'Connor's story with the thirty-one large illustrations by Ati Forberg, with whom O'Connor worked closely. Any inaccurate illustrations by Forberg would surely have been overruled by the author, who was particularly fussy about this book.

Benjamin Thurlow Ballou lives in Smiles, Pennsylvania, with Mummy, Daddy, and an Airedale named Sid, the semi-shaggy dog of the tale. Benjy's domineering, smothering Mummy is a massively corpulent college grad who proudly reads books ("texts" to her) under a framed diploma, while remote Daddy, a swaybacked and chinless nebbish without diploma, often hides inside the big television consoles he repairs for a living—a striking literalization of having no life beyond television. He is clearly the "little weedy" father in Atlantic City. Benjy was a superhumanly good little baby who even avoids wetting the bed. Now he is an excruciatingly model first grader. His syrupy goodness, manifested in nearly continuous hugging and kissing of Mummy, is unmasked in an early incident with his building blocks. When only three years of age, Benjy spells out "MUMMY DEAR" with his blocks. What next follows is noteworthy:

> But that wasn't all of the game. Oh no! There was more to come. After all the hugging and kissing was over—and this sometimes took a very long time—Benjy left his Mummy's bed and went back to his blocks on the floor. Then he built a huge house out of the blocks, way, way up, till it was higher than Benjy himself.
>
> "Benjy's house," he said, giving Mummy another sweet smile. Then his little mouth dropped, and he said, "Poor, poor Benjy. Big house aw faw DOWN!"
>
> And with one little pink shoe he reached out and kicked the house. All the blocks, every single one, came crashing down on the floor with a great CRASH-BANG!
>
> It was a HUGE noise, and it almost scared the life out of Benjy's Daddy, who stayed up late at night, and who had been sound, sound asleep.
>
> "OWP!" he yelled, and he fell out of bed and hit his head, hard, on one of the building blocks that had rolled over near him.
>
> "Goo morning, Daddy dear!" said Benjy, and he ran right across the floor in his little pink shoes and gave Daddy a big kiss, right on the very spot where Daddy's head had hit the building block. "Benjy kiss it and make it aw better," he said (19–20).

On Benjy's first day in school Mummy proudly dons her college cap and gown to escort her son, who is dressed like a pudgy Little Lord Fauntleroy, right down to his velvet suit and hat. Ati Forberg rendered an overstuffed

12. Edwin O'Connor, *Benjy: A Ferocious Fairy Tale* (Boston: Atlantic Monthly Press/Little, Brown, 1957).

version of Reginald B. Birch's illustrations for Frances Hodgson Burnett's mawkish 1886 book. However, Forberg did not work directly from Birch's well-known Fauntleroy get-up, and in fact she is quite sure that it was O'Connor himself who suggested Benjy's outfit.[13] The Fauntleroy outfit may owe something to the horrid English boy at the Shelbourne. At school Benjy imposes himself on the teacher as a super-pet, much to her annoyance, especially when she tries to have time alone with Mr. Man Teacher. In the nasty world of classroom politics, Benjy also becomes that most abhorred of Irish villains—the informer. Even Miss Teacher (Benjy's "School Mummy") seems appalled at Benjy's singular disloyalty when he fingers naughty culprits. Predictably enough, Benjy soon gets a black eye. He then plays with older girls and avoids rough games.

One day Benjy meets his dubious Good Fairy. This emissary from some necessary but ambiguous world of poetic justice is dressed shabbily in a baseball uniform, hat tilted to one side. He smokes cigars to nurse a whopping hangover and his diction would not get Mummy's seal of approval. When asked for the customary wish, Benjy says, "whatever big and marvelous things happen to little Benjy, the very same big and marvelous things will happen to his dear Mummy, too!" (87) The last and longest chapter grants Benjy his wish, in a classic reminder that one should take great care with one's wishes. At a picnic on Daddy's birthday, a thoroughly miserable affair for the browbeaten honoree, Benjy discovers a smaller version of the enormous roc's egg in the *Arabian Nights*. Disobeying Daddy's ineffectual protests not to pick it up (Mummy overrules him anyway), Benjy drops and breaks the mysterious egg, from which issues a "great black yoke." Immediately two gigantic birds swoop from the mountains to carry off Benjy and Mummy. The story ends with Daddy contentedly smoking his cigar and drinking his beer, heretofore proscribed domestic pleasures, while watching television with Sid the Airedale.

When O'Connor submitted the manuscript for publication, there was bafflement and alarm on all sides. What on earth was going on with the author of *The Last Hurrah*, a book that was rapidly turning Edwin O'Connor into the bestselling author in the history of the Atlantic Monthly Press? In January 1957 Helen Strauss wrote O'Connor that Sam Lawrence at Atlantic Monthly Press and Arthur Thornhill at Little, Brown were hesitant at best and confused at worst. Strauss herself pointedly called *Benjy* a very odd book, and pleaded with O'Connor to withdraw it, implying strongly that it would do his career no good at that point. She knew the joint presses would

13. Ati Forberg (Johansen), telephone interviews, March 7, 10, 13, 2001.

publish it, because O'Connor was now in the cockpit. And even though the book might sell 30,000 copies, Strauss thought O'Connor was making a bad mistake.[14] (As it turned out, *Benjy* never sold more than 5,000 copies; the country's bestselling novelist laid an egg indeed.) Charlie Morton wrote a week later that he was much concerned about the book's promotion, and he thought the book needed at least one attractive character. He did like O'Connor's original subtitle, "A Rather Harsh Fairy Tale," but even that involved marketing problems.[15] Peggy Yntema was more open to the book and had tossed it around a good deal with O'Connor while it was in progress. When O'Connor was stumped for an ending—a familiar problem for this writer who seldom planned ahead—Peggy herself thought up the macabre bird scenario.[16]

But what was *Benjy* all about? No doubt some exasperated readers simply branded it a 143-page shaggy dog story. And certainly O'Connor's closing sentences gather shagginess about them: "On the whole, [Daddy] thought, it was very possible that [Mummy and Benjy] would never come back. And they never did." But this vexing finale might only be a red herring; even a shaggy dog can be meaning's best friend.

On one obvious level *Benjy* is a parody of saccharine children's books. In this regard, an early unpublished item by O'Connor sheds some light. Sometime probably in the late 1940s he wrote a five-page sketch entitled "Literary Tea," in which a wretched author finally breaks into print with an illustrated children's book written in a "staccato Esperanto." At an authors' party, he assures a friend, "You don't think I'd go in for any of that Bunny Rabbits and sugar-and-spice stuff, do you?"[17] Such sappy books were staples in England, even if Beatrix Potter's unsentimental calculus was the exception. American children's books were usually less sentimental and in the 1950s they were even getting irreverent toward the genre's sacrosanct traditions. The text of *Benjy*'s dust jacket emphatically ends on that very note: "They [author and illustrator] dedicate [the book] to all readers of all ages who have never, at any time, been *good little boys* or, for that matter, *good little girls*" (their italics). It also bears remembering that O'Connor enjoyed making up long and off-beat stories for the Montgomery and Cutting children, as well as his own nieces and nephews.

But was that all there was to it—a parody of sentimental children's litera-

14. Helen Strauss, letter to Edwin O'Connor, January 30, 1957, EOCP 254.
15. Charles W. Morton, letter to Edwin O'Connor, February 8, 1957, EOCP 203.
16. Peggy Yntema, personal interview, April 10, 1999.
17. EOCP 31.

ture? Five years later O'Connor told Herbert Kenny, book editor for the *Boston Globe*, that after *The Last Hurrah* he needed an interlude: "I felt I had to do something slight before tackling another novel, so I wrote *Benjy*. I had no particular subject in mind."[18] But again one detects a whiff of the red herring. To be sure novelists often rest between big books. But novelists cannot turn off so easily and just write a deliberately "slight" piece. There is more to this puzzle.

Another hint is found in Daddy's job. Although he repairs televisions, nothing is said about television programs until the very end, when Daddy and Sid watch impassionately the news: "Mummy Ballou, college graduate, and her little son, Benjy Ballou, birdnapped . . ." (142). During his years as a television reviewer, O'Connor had more than once spoken out about sitcoms' endless debunking of American fathers, a cheerfully foolish act destructive of society itself. In *Benjy* the mother has usurped all power with the assistance of a college diploma. To compound matters, the merely skilled father has accepted his diminishment. The result is a selfishly warped "nice little boy" of whom his mother thinks: "it was nice to have a man in the house at last!" (113). When it came to the family, O'Connor was a traditionalist by upbringing and conviction in an era when it was so much easier to be one. For centuries Catholicism had taught that the family, not the individual, is the fundamental unit of society, along with the implied corollary that the father is its chief authority. The family was not a democracy, certainly not when it came to children and their parents, but was ideally a microcosmic society of mutual and reciprocating love, rights, and responsibilities. The bizarre family in *Benjy* gets all of this wrong. One could even speculate that *Benjy* partakes of the nature of parable, wherein a theological dimension can be glimpsed. The Good Fairy may be disreputable, but at least he brings with him, by means of his magical and smelly cigar, the bracing odors of a sulphurous realm that awaits disorder in the modern family. And an even deeper theological probe might pause to consider the Catholic insistence that original sin is present even in children, "since conception," as O'Connor hinted. In fiction by Catholics—think only of Greene, Waugh, and Flannery O'Connor—children are usually not sentimentalized by Rousseauvian bunkum.

There are also political overtones in *Benjy*. In school Benjy recites the Pledge of Allegiance "so much louder than anyone else" and not once but

18. Herbert A. Kenny, "How O'Connor Won the Prize," *Boston Sunday Globe*, May 13, 1962.

many times a day: "standing by his desk like a little soldier with his arms shooting out towards his flag." When asked for an explanation, Benjy says, "it's just 'cause I'm proud to be a little American boy!" (56–58). However, Benjy's gesticulating is more reminiscent of a Hitler Youth than the American who calmly puts his palm over his heart on such occasions. All this is preamble to Benjy as informer:

Benjy would point [miscreants] out, one by one, with his little finger. Sometimes Miss Teacher seemed not to see Benjy as he did this, so then he would stand up and tell her right out loud, and then the bad little boys and girls would be kept after school and punished (62–63).

During the McCarthy era O'Connor took the liberal stand that the Wisconsin senator's charges of Reds in the government posed a serious danger to the country. Letters from Professor Roger McHugh in Ireland even joke about O'Connor's uncharacteristic anger over McCarthy and his ilk. O'Connor's sister remembers that her brother had outspoken disagreements with his father over Dean Acheson who, as Truman's Secretary of State, became a special target of some recklessly uninformed Republicans still bent on undoing the New Deal in any way possible. And so superpatriot Benjy, the idolater of the flag, easily becomes Benjy the loathsome informer.

However much the generic, sociological, theological, or political dimensions of *Benjy* suggest themselves, it is the psychological dimension that captures the reader of this children's book which is so obviously written for adults as well. Indeed, as the subtitle warns us, we are in the realm of the "ferocious fairy tale," with its suggestion of unvarnished Grimm instead of "sugar-and-spice stuff." "Ferocious," like its Latin ancestor *ferocitas*, carries ambiguous connotations, like so much else in this odd book. The most savagely ferocious creatures are of course the two cosmic birds of vengeance, but violent disorder was earlier seen when Benjy builds his tall house of blocks, only to kick it down and indirectly hurt Daddy. In that passage quoted earlier lurk all the ingredients for a Freudian stew. Too much so, perhaps. The whole incident—from the bold caps declaration of love for Mummy to Daddy's head injury from those very blocks which "almost scared the life" out of him—has Oedipus complex writ as large as Benjy's alphabet blocks. As in many *New Yorker* cartoons and Thurber stories of the time, O'Connor may very well have been lampooning the half-baked theories of the Doctor from Vienna, most of which are now in the dustbin.

Many autobiographical traces remain, nevertheless. In some obscure way, the death of O'Connor's father had aroused the need to exorcize some private demons. Sorrow and guilt and memory all conspired to bring Benjy, character and book, to birth. Indeed, one reason many people found *Benjy* so baffling was their lack of awareness that it so intensely mirrored the author whose life had been so private. First of all, there is the basic family situation of doting mother and remote father. While both are different from O'Connor's mother and father in many ways, still some familial provenance seems inescapable, especially when the mother as first home educator is considered. The father's conspicuous lack of a college diploma, moreover, could very well be an angular reflection of those Woonsocket rumors about Dr. O'Connor's degrees. Secondly, the overly protected Benjy in his Fauntleroy livery may have been O'Connor's way of killing once and for all that image which he must have realized other children had of him during one phase of his childhood.

Noteworthy too is Benjy's school:

How Benjy enjoyed his trips, early every morning, to The Little Red Schoolhouse! (And here is a little secret: the schoolhouse was *not* little, and it was *not* red! No! It was really a very big building made of grey cement, but both Mummy and Benjy liked to call it The Little Red Schoolhouse.)

Debunking the little red schoolhouse of nostalgia is part of the satire on children's books which romanticized schooldays. But O'Connor's own first three grades *were* spent at a schoolhouse that was both little and red. Beyond doubt Woonsocket's Summer Street School is the model for the "The Little Red Schoolhouse." O'Connor even seems to call attention to the fact that he is deliberately covering his tracks in "here is a little secret." Further, there was no need to call the actual building a cement one; the wooden one of popular imagination had not been mentioned. But the Summer Street School is not only little and red, but has wooden clapboards right out of Winslow Homer. By the slight slip of omission O'Connor has all but called Benjy's school the Summer Street School.

After Benjy's pummeling by the "dirty little boy" in repayment for his squealing, Benjy resolves to play only with the "nice little girls," even though they are a little older. Here O'Connor is undoubtedly remembering the months he spent in the private kindergarten where he was the only boy.

Finally, one two-page illustration in the book is significant. When the Ballou family drives to the fateful picnic in the last chapter (naturally Mummy drives, with Benjy beside her while morose Daddy sits in back), Forberg depicts a 1920s vintage car. True, such jalopies lend themselves to cartooning, but nothing else in the book has a twenties look. The curious effect is to make the Ballous appear as poverty-stricken as Steinbeck's Okies. There was no reason why Forberg could not have used a 1950s station wagon. But a 1920s car would take Benjy back to the time O'Connor was his age: circa 1923. Thus, O'Connor drew on thirty-year-old Woonsocket memories, and not for the last time. The death of a parent undams memories, of course, and in O'Connor's case many of them wound up in this curious book, as he took his own long measure from the schoolyards of Woonsocket to the present.

An interesting complication in the matter of *Benjy* is the illustrator. Ati Forberg was Beate Gropius Forberg.[19] She was the adopted daughter of Walter Gropius, the influential architect who had come to America in 1937 after the Nazis closed the influential Bauhaus he had helped to found. In 1957 Gropius was professor emeritus at Harvard. Bauhaus utilitarian theories were enjoying an Indian summer in the States, as seen in O'Connor's own Wellfleet house, before being dismissed in the 1970s by the whimsies of postmodernism. Ati was born in Germany in 1925 and so was seven years younger than O'Connor. She attended the experimental Black Mountain College in North Carolina and later the Chicago Institute of Design. *Benjy* was the first of almost thirty children's books which she illustrated.[20] Her black, pink and orange drawings for *Benjy* are large, playful caricatures that often spread over two pages (even three in one case) and sometimes dictate the text's layout. For example, the long neck and beak of the gigantic bird dives down the book's spine and shoves the text aside irregularly, while her enormous wings spread over the top of the pages. Benjy cowers in the bottom right corner.

The close cooperation between author and illustrator takes on larger significance when we remember O'Connor's infatuation with attractive German women. Although the artist liked O'Connor, whom she had met in Wellfleet that summer, she did not love him. O'Connor had dated her striking stepsister, Christel, who was a Lufthansa stewardess. When O'Connor heard that Ati was not getting enough work as an artist, he offered his book to her to illustrate. Seen in this light, *Benjy* assumes a somewhat different configuration. O'Connor was widely regarded by the avant garde set in Wellfleet as being "conventional" in his mores and morals. His devout Catholicism, although never advertised, was almost palpable to some.[21] He therefore needed some avenue to advertise the fact that he was not a prig and was independent of Momist control. The result was a "ferocious fairy tale" where the annihilation of Mummy and her spoiled son is illustrated by a woman O'Connor obviously was trying to impress. The author's darker humor, as seen earlier in "Animal Life," was flourishing in a new medium and in a unique collaborative effort.

19. Some information on Ati Forberg can be found in Reginald Isaac, *Gropius: An Illustrated Biography of the Creator of the Bauhaus* (Boston: Little, Brown, 1991), passim.

20. *Contemporary Authors Online:* www.galenet.com

21. Forberg, interviews.

In dispatching the odious Benjy and his mother, O'Connor was putting a side of himself behind him. The Good Fairy, who had seen and approved of the snatching from the sidelines, makes his last notebook entry under the name Ballou: "'Toot finee,' he said, and blew a big cloud of [cigar] smoke" (139). At home that evening Daddy is granted a newly liberated life of sorts, which he celebrates with a "very long and quite expensive cigar" (143). For O'Connor a part of his life was "toot finee" because his father's death had paradoxically released him. And yet he felt it necessary to close the book with Daddy enjoying some contentment at last as he lives on in a strange immortality. Skeffington had died, and at some length, but from then on O'Connor's fathers would stubbornly endure.

In addition to losing his own father in 1956, earlier that year O'Connor had lost two other older men who were important in his life. Fred Allen had died in March, and although the friendship had been brief, the childless Fred and his wife Portland had enjoyed the company of the younger man immensely. In November Portland wrote to thank O'Connor for all his help in bringing out her husband's posthumous autobiography. She closed by saying, "[You] are one of the finest men I have ever met."[22] One of those acts of help was a rare television appearance a few months after Allen's death. To help promote Fred Allen's posthumous *Much Ado About Me,* O'Connor broke his anti-WGBH vow. Boston's educational station had just started *I've Been Reading,* with Professor P. Albert Duhamel of Boston College. Duhamel is a vigorous Renaissance scholar and teacher who was rumored to devour ten books a week. He had known O'Connor for some years at Wellfleet, and so he presumed upon an old, albeit strained, friendship and cajoled O'Connor into talking about Fred Allen. O'Connor stipulated that Duhamel pick him up at 48 Beacon Street one half hour before air time and return him one half hour after the program.[23] O'Connor was determined not to socialize before or after. Unfortunately, tapes from those years were usually not saved. For some years afterwards O'Connor worked with Portland on an edition of Allen's letters, and was doing so as late as 1961.[24] But at some point the project was taken over by the journalist Joe McCarthy and published in 1965 with no mention of O'Connor. When *Fred Allen's Letters* was published, O'Connor wrote a favorable review for the *Boston Globe* on April 23, 1965.

In May Monsignor Holland died. For some years O'Connor's old friend

---

22. Portland Allen, letter to Edwin O'Connor, November 23, 1956, EOCP 83.
23. P. Albert Duhamel, letter to author, March 25, 1999.
24. George Ryan, "For O'Connor It's Not the Last Hurrah," *Information,* December 1961, 20.

had been a pastor in Pawtucket, about ten miles from Woonsocket. An irate O'Connor wrote the bishop of Providence that during Sunday Mass the pastor at St. Charles' had given only cursory mention of the affectionately remembered former pastor. The bishop replied diplomatically. He largely agreed with O'Connor, but he also mused in Skeffingtonian cadences that the newly famous novelist would understand the "many imponderables and inexplicable mysteries of people."[25] In rapid succession, then, three deaths had helped put unusual emotional pressure on O'Connor.

Some of this emotional pressure shows up in the manuscript of *Benjy* which O'Connor sent to the printer. The sixty-eight pages have only a few minor corrections in his hand, but there are several emphatic countercommands to his editor, Peggy Yntema, who had written in a few helpful suggestions. At three places O'Connor writes in thick pencil and with some testiness: "NO REWORD! AUTHOR STET!"; "NO STET"; "NO! STET EOC."[26] This is the first graphic example of his resistance to editorial direction, and stands in contrast to his willingness to be advised on *The Last Hurrah* a year earlier. O'Connor probably felt that he and not his younger editor was now in the position to manage the text. He was hot property and knew it. But beyond that, those defiant "STET" commands—"let it stand"—reveal a singular protectiveness about this work; no other printer's copy of his works has such fiercely posted "Keep Out" signs. *Benjy* was too close to something deeply personal.

Some notice was given to *Benjy* when it was published in October 1957. If O'Connor had not been so recently popular, it probably would have been ignored altogether. *Newsweek* gave it the biggest play, with a review, interview, and photograph. The reviewer saw the book as a "fine fairy tale indoctrination against 'Momism,'" that special Philip Wylie target of the 1950s.[27] A *Time* review called it a "Thurberesque" virtuoso piece, while admitting that "the fun sometimes wears thin." The reviewer nearly gave away the ending while promising not to do so.[28] O'Connor did not take kindly to such pranks.

Perhaps the most incisive commentary on *Benjy* came from a man who knew O'Connor well and who was a past master at probing psychological origins in literature. Edmund Wilson's astute detection of the traumatic experience of twelve-year-old Dickens in the blacking shop as the source of so much of his work is often regarded as a milestone in twentieth-century liter-

25. Bishop Russell J. McVinney, letter to Edwin O'Connor, June 5, 1956, EOCP 194.
26. EOCP 48: 44, 48, 65.
27. "Manhandling Mother," *Newsweek*, October 21, 1957, 118–19.
28. "From Curley to Curlylocks," *Time*, October 21, 1957, 108.

ary criticism.[29] Shortly after O'Connor's death, this is what the elderly Wilson wrote about *Benjy:*

I believe that the explanation of his satirical children's fable *Benjy*—the story of a horrid little prig who makes trouble for everyone else—is that Ed was always on his guard about letting people be conscious of his virtuous habits because he realized how easy it would be for these to become obnoxious. He neither smoked nor drank; he was considerate and incorruptible. . . . [H]e was one of the few educated friends I have who struck me as sincerely attempting to lead the life of a Christian.[30]

O'Connor saved three letters from readers, including one from a seven-year-old girl whose favorite part was the birdnapping, and another from a distraught, humorless mother who scolded: a devout Catholic should know better than to attack motherhood. Perhaps the most engaging readers consisted of seventh graders in Woonsocket Junior High School. In 1965 their English teacher, Miss Ann Marie Plante, read portions of *Benjy* each day. Hers was a difficult class with discipline problems, but somehow *Benjy* calmed their friskiness. She had the class write brief responses to the book. The boys' favorite scene was Benjy's black eye. Both boys and girls relished the ghastly denouement. O'Connor must have enjoyed these responses eight years after the book was published.

In 1996 the Boston fine-book publisher David R. Godine brought out a new edition of *Benjy,* with illustrations by Catherine O'Neill. Mr. Godine reissued the book because he had always liked the "somewhat nasty, misogynistic, dark Irish humor that no politically correct publishing house would ever touch today." The edition has yet to sell a thousand copies, but Mr. Godine has no regrets.[31]

On Thursday September 13, 1956, the day before O'Connor's father died, the *Boston Post* ran a proud announcement on page one: "Edwin O'Connor to Write Weekly." No, O'Connor had not returned to television reviewing for his recent employer; that purgatory on earth would have been unthinkable. Rather, O'Connor performed a characteristic gesture of remarkable loyalty and charity. The *Post* had been ailing for years, and in early September was on the point of expiring. A couple of years earlier the paper had been so mismanaged and desperate that it missed payroll several times; on one of these occasions, O'Connor told the *Boston Globe,* he was down to his last thirty-

---

29. Edmund Wilson, "Dickens: The Two Scrooges," in *The Wound and the Bow* (Boston: Houghton Mifflin, 1941), especially 3–9. Part of the essay had earlier appeared in *Atlantic Monthly.*

30. Edmund Wilson, "'Baldini': A Memoir and a Collaboration," in *BL,* 367.

31. David R. Godine, note to author, July 12, 2000.

five cents.[32] Now the *Post* was strongly rumored to be going under for good. In a desperate move it cut the price of its Sunday edition from twenty cents to a dime. When O'Connor heard the rumors, he unhesitatingly offered his services—gratis. O'Connor had been so grateful to certain *Post* editors for hiring him when he was strapped for money in that fall of 1953 that he now offered to write a weekly column for the Sunday edition. The announcement said "he will select his own topics and will, of course, write as he pleases." In order to boost sales, O'Connor and the *Post* obviously were hoping to trade on what had become a household name in Boston.

As Elliot Norton remembered it, O'Connor spent Thursday afternoons writing his column at his apartment. He then walked over to the *Post*, "delivered it like a copy boy," chatted with old chums, and then left.[33] As it turned out, he only wrote three. The first appeared on September 16, two days after his father's death, and would thus have been written two days before the death. In turn, the column had been prompted by news of the death of an idiosyncratic Notre Dame priest. The second column, written just after his father's death and funeral, recounts the vagaries of the World War I veteran O'Connor served with during his Coast Guard days on Cape Cod. The pattern of the columns is emerging: O'Connor is regaling his readers with tales of eccentricity. His last column ran on September 30. In it he describes a failed, unnamed Boston politico whose undistinguished career was shortened by two fatal habits: he could not remember names (he had five for O'Connor, one of which was "Harvey"), and his punctuality showed an ignorance of the dramatic delayed entrance that Curley had mastered so well. The next day, Monday October 1, was the last for the *Boston Post*. With no announcement or even hint, it published its last edition. O'Connor's efforts had been to no avail, as he probably knew beforehand; he had an Irish fondness for lost causes. A couple of weeks later O'Connor received a letter from an editor at the defunct newspaper. He thanks O'Connor deeply: "I am sure all good *Post* men shall never forget your generous action."[34] To this day O'Connor's gesture that September is remembered in Boston journalism circles as an act of saintliness in a most profane calling.

In October O'Connor took his second annual trip to Notre Dame. This time he gave a more formal talk. Now that he was a celebrity, Notre Dame's man of the hour was asked to do more than simply chat with Frank O'Malley's class. Accordingly, O'Connor methodically worked on a fifteen-page

32. Joe Harrington, "A Success Year," *Boston Globe,* January 13, 1957, A24.
33. Elliot Norton, letter to Veniette O'Connor, March 30, 1968, EOCP 276.
34. Joseph McManus, letter to Edwin O'Connor, October 15, 1956, EOCP 192.

talk on the teaching of writing in college.[35] He was never comfortable giving talks. A certain initial hesitancy is readily apparent in the typescript, as if he is hunting for his subject. But as the talk proceeds, he becomes eloquent about the courage necessary to declare one's ambition as a writer, and about the great value of those gifted teachers (here all present must have glanced at Frank O'Malley) who stimulate and encourage that ambition. He concludes by complimenting most especially the overlooked heroics undertaken by the teacher of freshman English:

The good teacher always walks the wastes in search of the oasis, and when he finds it, works like mad to make it bloom. I speak from personal experience when I say that to meet such a teacher, in this first formative year in college on which so much depends, is to contract a debt which is not easily repaid and which certainly can never be forgotten.

Earlier in his talk O'Connor had hinted at his own father's reaction to his ambition to be a writer when he said:

[T]he young man who wants to be a writer is not apt to meet the same sort of home sympathy and support as other young men. And even when he does get that sympathy and support, it's almost necessarily of a negative order: an understanding parent may go so far to say, "All right, go ahead, I won't stand in your way, and you have my blessing!" but this is . . . all he can do, because he hasn't the faintest idea about writing. . . . So while this kind of support is better, far better, than outright opposition, it doesn't help the young man at all in his chosen career.

This catches Dr. O'Connor's attitude just about right. The passage is as close as the son ever would come to mentioning his father in public, and this just a month after his death.

In late January 1957, with *Benjy* done, O'Connor treated himself to his first luxury vacation. Royalties from *The Last Hurrah* amply funded a few weeks of winter vacation in the Bahamas. There he hoped to plan his next novel, "the Big One," as he called the first known reference to his ambitions for what would become *The Edge of Sadness*.[36]

Harbour Island is a tiny cay three miles long and half a mile wide, just off the northern tip of shoestring Eleuthera Island in the Northern Bahamas. Its long beach is considered one of the best in the region. O'Connor stayed at the exclusive cottage colony at Pink Sands Lodge, a sedate retreat that offered quiet time to write and plenty of space for his favorite pastimes of reading on the beach, tanning, and swimming. He also tried a little fishing, Bahamian style.

35. Untitled speech about teaching writing and English in college, University of Notre Dame, October 1956, EOCP 46.
36. Harrington, "A Success Year."

At daily Mass, O'Connor soon got to know Father John H. McGoey, S.F.M. (the Scarborough Foreign Mission Society of Canada), an energetic missionary at the Blessed Sacrament Church. Father McGoey worked tirelessly in his parish, in spite of frailty from wrenching experiences as a young missionary in wartime China, from cancer later, and more recently from a colostomy. He was a little older than O'Connor. For three years he had organized cooperatives for farmers, had run a school with three Sisters of Charity of Mt. St. Vincent on the Hudson in New York, raised money (O'Connor was a generous benefactor), and even did much of the handyman work around his compound. O'Connor's only encounter with missionary life impressed him. Father McGoey became something of a pest, however, because he also had literary ambitions and quickly latched on to O'Connor, whose fame had apparently reached the Bahamas. With O'Connor's help he got his memoirs, *Nor Scrip Nor Shoes*, published by Little, Brown in 1958. The prolific author went on to publish almost twenty theological and pastoral works. In his later years he had his own small publishing house in Florida.

Toward the end of his stay on Harbour Island, O'Connor received a letter from his brother Jack, who was looking into the tax situation for him. The alarming news was that O'Connor might be in the old 81 percent tax category, a devastating situation for authors who do not ordinarily have steady incomes, but who might hit it big in the odd year or two. Jack's contact was hopeful, however, that O'Connor's tax bracket could be reduced to 50 percent.[37]

In early February O'Connor spent a few days in pre-Castro Havana with Walter Gropius, his wife, daughter Ati, and Ati's cousin. On one occasion O'Connor treated everyone to an evening on the town. O'Connor probably had flown over from Harbour Island, although this is not entirely clear.[38]

O'Connor returned to the Pink Sands Lodge about a half dozen times; along with the Morris Inn at Notre Dame and the Shelbourne Hotel in Dublin, it became a frequent part of his yearly cycle. The tan he picked up there would keep his already deepening complexion dark through the winter until Wellfleet in May. But he told Peter Davison that social life at Harbour Island left something to be desired: there was not enough Jewish wit to enliven the place.

37. John Vincent O'Connor Jr., letter to Edwin O'Connor, January 26, 1957, EOCP 221.
38. Forberg, interviews.

CHAPTER TEN

❧ *The Edges of Sadness*
(1957–1961)

By 1957, at age thirty-nine, O'Connor's routines were firmly set and would remain largely unchanged for the next five years. His yearly cycle consisted of residence in Boston for most of the year; a stay of two or three weeks at Harbour Island in January most years; several trips to Dublin, usually in March; Wellfleet for about four months from late May to mid-September, with many visits through the fall; and almost always an October week at Notre Dame. This measured rhythm appealed to his need for routine gracefully paced by seasonal rituals.

O'Connor's daily rounds became well known in Boston and Wellfleet and are still remembered vividly by many.[1] What follows is a typical day at each locality. First, his Boston day. O'Connor was an early riser, and after brewing coffee by boiling, a simple method he probably picked up during Coast Guard duty, he was at his small typewriter by seven o'clock. He would write steadily with great concentration for about two hours, have some toast, and work for another hour or two. Most of this work was done directly on his old green portable typewriter before it was replaced by a Smith-Corona electric in the early 1960s; sometimes during travel or while at the beach he might do a little work in longhand, but he preferred the neatness and finality of typescript. For his trips he had a tiny, flat Hermes travel typewriter which still has a Nassau sticker attached. Compared to today's wide computer keyboards, the miniature Hermes looks like a toy for such a big-fingered man. Several photographs of O'Connor in his apartment at 48 Beacon Street pose him at or near his typewriter; the typewriter on its fragile-looking table is in marked contrast to O'Connor's hefty size. Often he would have coffee within reach on a tea service.

---

1. For the details of O'Connor's daily life and rounds, I am indebted to the late Phoebe-Lou Adams, Virginia Albee, Barbara O'Connor Burrell, Peter Davison, P. Albert Duhamel, Anna Hamburger, Elliot Norton, Vita Petersen, George Ryan, Arthur Schlesinger Jr., Marian Schlesinger, Robert Taylor, Stephen Weil, Helen Miranda Wilson, and Peggy Yntema.

Writing fiction did not come easily to him. O'Connor was more naturally a talker than a writer, and his written words, so labored over, do not always convey his powers of mimicry and comic invention. His lapidary prose is often better suited to capturing the cadences of melancholy in works like *The Edge of Sadness* and *All in the Family*, both of which were anticipated by the last two chapters of *The Last Hurrah*.

Around nine he would take a break for a few phone calls, as if he couldn't wait to start on his daily socializing. One important call, at 9:15 almost every day, went to Arthur Thornhill at Little, Brown. Years later Thornhill wrote, "We discussed many things pertaining to the industry and it grew into quite a nice relationship."[2]

Midday was for his rounds. In his early Boston years, he often simply made these visits on his old bicycle. Often he had a late breakfast at the Café in the Ritz Carlton Hotel, which was only one block from the offices of *Atlantic Monthly*. With its enviable front onto the Public Gardens, the "Ritz" was Boston's most prestigious hotel. The pithy standard guide to Boston's architecture calls it a "quintessential Boston institution . . . neither glamorous nor imposing."[3] O'Connor liked the small Café, where he often socialized with people from *Atlantic Monthly* and Little, Brown. He especially liked a table under a mural of Boston (since replaced), where he could keep an eye on passersby on adjacent Newbury Street. The Ritz staff affectionately treated O'Connor as a regular, and headwaiter Joe Vitale in particular became fond of the unflappable man who sometimes dropped in three times a day and talked to you as a brother. "Of all the guests that come in here," Vitale said, "with this fellow you get so attached."[4] O'Connor often had lunch there too, which usually consisted of the Ritz hamburger deluxe or a fried egg sandwich, and nothing stronger than a ginger ale.

A highlight of the late morning came around eleven o'clock, when he climbed the stoop at 8 Arlington Street. The offices of the Atlantic Monthly Company were then a large, ivy-covered brownstone. For decades four of its five levels housed inefficiently the offices of both magazine and press in a warren of cut-up rooms and twisting staircases. While it never became quite as peculiar as the offices of *The New Yorker*, where the unlikely could and did happen, these premises had their share of a more muted Boston eccentricity,

---

2. Arthur H. Thornhill Sr., letter to Mrs. Mary E. O'Connor, April 9, 1968. Letter courtesy of Barbara O'Connor Burrell.

3. Susan and Michael Southworth, *The AIA Guide to Boston,* 2nd ed. (Guilford, Conn.: Globe Pequot, 1992), 238.

4. Jonathan Klarfeld, "We All Loved Ed," *Boston Globe,* March 25, 1968, 1 and 78.

O'Connor on Beacon Hill, 1961. Photo by Paul Berg. *Boston Public Library/Rare Books Department—Courtesy of the Trustees.*

which only helped endear the establishment to O'Connor. Today the only reminder of *Atlantic*'s many years in this building is the Neptune logo on the side facing Marlborough Street.

On the ground floor O'Connor would chat with the staff of women who did copy editing. He also looked in on Phoebe-Lou Adams, who, over almost fifty years, until her death in 2001, wrote more than 4,000 concise book reviews for *Atlantic Monthly*. She remembered the vaudeville shuffle, the card tricks, and the jokes. (Adams married Ted Weeks, the editor in chief, fairly late in his life.) Sometimes O'Connor would sing out "Keep Working, Keep Singing, America," a wartime morale tune he picked up at Hartford radio.

With a light trot he then took a narrow staircase to the second floor, where the editors, mostly male, had their offices. After the usual shuffle and maybe a joke, he caught up on gossip with Peter Davison, Sam Lawrence, and especially Charlie Morton, who frequently indulged in his hobby of identifying sports cars passing below his window. Some of the rooms still had elaborate fireplaces and plaster work. The biggest and fanciest room was reserved for the Tuesday morning meetings of the Atlantic Associates, those dozen or so people involved in running the magazine and press; the Associates were evenly divided between men and women. A photo probably from the fall of 1957 shows Ted Weeks presiding at the long table. Through the tall windows appear the trees of the Public Gardens. The scene looks more like a view of the president's office on a leafy campus. On the fireplace mantle behind Ted Weeks four current Atlantic Monthly Press books are displayed. One of them is Fred Allen's *Much Ado About Me.* Two others are by O'Connor: *The Last Hurrah,* the press's biggest seller up to that time, and next to it *Benjy,* apparently there in hopes of catching fire from its predecessor. Today in the newer offices of *Atlantic Monthly* near Boston's North End, two letters from O'Connor in his threadbare years are prominently displayed, as if to encourage struggling writers that they too can succeed by dogged effort.

After a half-hour of office visits, O'Connor would often walk over to the Ritz Carlton Hotel for lunch with some combination of editors, usually including Ted Weeks, Donald Snyder, Charlie Morton, Peter Davison, and Sam Lawrence. To have lunch at the Ritz Café was not to dine cheaply; publishing still attracted people of some means. Charlie Morton kept a wary eye out for flies, inspected the table obsessively, and polished with his napkin the already spotless cutlery. O'Connor enlivened the luncheons with his genial wit and mimicry.

O'Connor's humor served up a mixture of vaudeville zaniness, inside allusions, marvelous vocal imitations, radio-era corniness, and not a little collegian silliness. He was never crude or cruel. Edward Fischer, a Notre Dame classmate and later a professor there, has written one of the best pieces on O'Connor's conversational humor. "Edwin O'Connor, Raconteur" is a distillation of several long talks Fischer had with O'Connor as they strolled the campus during O'Connor's annual visit. "O'Connor could string out vaudeville jokes by the kilometer," Fischer writes. "I have an uncle who is a Southern planter. (Here the pause must be just right.) He is an undertaker in Birmingham." "She was so old that when she lit all the candles on her birthday cake, six people were overcome by the heat."[5] There is a dated quality about these jokes, some of which appear to come from Fred Allen. But O'Connor's delivery, polished by four years in radio, more than made up for the lapsed expiration date.

O'Connor was the only author who had such a close daily relationship

5. *Notre Dame Magazine,* winter 1988–89, 49–50.

The Atlantic Associates, 1957. *Atlantic Monthly* editor Ted Weeks presides at left.
Charlie Morton is to his left. Peter Davison is at lower right with back to camera.
On the mantle are copies of *The Last Hurrah* and *Benjy*. *Photo used with permission of
Atlantic Monthly.*

with the Atlantic Monthly Company. In an important way this was his
Boston family. Several staffers in fact referred to O'Connor in familial terms,
back in an age still unembarrassed by the presence of warm personal relationships in a professional setting. In that family Charlie Morton was O'Connor's principal father figure, as Peter Davison saw it. O'Connor was everlast-
ingly grateful to him for having accepted his first *Atlantic* article. Morton
regularly wrote up his own eccentricities, which were published in 1951 as his
collected essays, *How to Protect Yourself Against Women and Other Vicissi-
tudes.* In 1946, the year he accepted O'Connor's article, he had written the
commentary for a book by the *Boston Herald* cartoonist "Dahl," called simply
Dahl's Boston. Although Morton lived in Cambridge, he was a lively guide
through Boston's eccentricities.

From Arlington Street, O'Connor would retrace his steps across the Public Gardens, a verdant enclosure more meticulously tended than the larger adjacent Common. The Gardens are all flowers, fancy ornamentals, Japanese lanterns, languid willows, swan boats, and cast-iron filigree—effusions of late Victorian pleasures. The much older Common is Spartan in its devotion to military statuary and monuments such as the Boston Massacre Monument, the Commodore John Barry Memorial, the Soldiers and Sailors Monument, and the Shaw Memorial depicting the famous black Civil War regiment. George Ryan of the *Boston Pilot* recounts that an artist friend of O'Connor placed an unidentified (and probably unauthorized) bronze bust of him in the Boston Common directly opposite and facing his apartment building at 48 Beacon Street, where it remained for several years in the late 1950s.[6] O'Connor had thus joined the Common's martial heroes, albeit briefly. The whereabouts of that bust is unknown.

Shortly after passing his own door, O'Connor would arrive at Little, Brown's offices at 34 Beacon Street, almost at the crest of Beacon Hill. At Little, Brown there might be a shortened reprise of the socializing at 8 Arlington Street, and then once a week a walk over to Locke-Ober Café for lunch with Arthur Thornhill.

Sometimes when he had to meet literary people, Arthur Thornhill would take O'Connor to the Somerset Club, Boston's most august men's club. Probably because Thornhill disliked most writers, he needed O'Connor's congenial company. Anthony Powell, England's premier novelist of manners at midcentury, met O'Connor at the club in 1961. He described his Bostonian counterpart as "large, talkative, master of a quiet but lively conversationalist style." Powell rendered the setting, where the voluble O'Connor stood out, in this evocative passage: "Ancient armchairs and sofas underpropped one or two equally antiquated members, ossified into states of Emersonian catalepsy in which shadow and sunlight were not only the same, but had freed them from shame or fame." O'Connor told Powell a story about Evelyn Waugh once ordering three soups for dinner, a story that was news to Waugh. Powell hints that O'Connor enjoyed making up a good story or at least improving greatly upon it.[7]

At some point around midday he would often go to Mass, usually at the

6. My thanks to George Ryan for the untitled original manuscript of a magazine article on O'Connor in *Information*. The published article in December 1961 cut substantial material, including this item. Ryan places the bust in the Public Gardens, but this location would not have faced 48 Beacon Street.

7. Anthony Powell, *The Strangers Are All Gone,* vol. 4 of *The Memoirs of Anthony Powell* (New York: Holt, Rinehart, 1982), 97–99.

Holy Ghost Chapel in the Paulist Center at 5 Park Street, which was just down from the State House. Very few people knew much about this important encounter O'Connor had with God's word and sacrament. To him Mass was more than just a habit. As his agnostic friend Edmund Wilson marveled, O'Connor took his religion with the utmost seriousness. This half-hour at Mass was the quiet center of his life. During the late 1950s the Catholic Church was quickening with talk of liturgical and organizational renewal, and the Paulists were often in the forefront of that renewal. Shortly after becoming pope in late 1958, John XXIII called for the convening of the Second Vatican Council. These were heady years for the American Catholic intelligentsia, many of whom saw their years of chafing under a restrictive and reclusive Church coming to an end. As with politics, O'Connor saw clearly the need for church reform, even as he harbored reservations about the reformers, as evidenced in later works like *All in the Family,* "The Traveler from Brazil," and the "The Cardinal."

Paulists staffed Newman Centers at secular universities and Information Centers in large cities like Boston. They published *Catholic World* and *Information* monthly magazines, the latter of which featured O'Connor on its cover in December 1961. O'Connor was a regular at Boston's Paulist Center. He admired the order for its initiative in the world beyond parochial and ethnic boundaries. Indeed Paulist and Newman centers frequently drew in many educated Catholics disaffected by ingrown tribal parishes in cities and their bland counterparts in suburbs. *The Edge of Sadness* echoes this era, as both Father Hugh Kennedy and his friend Father John Carmody encounter the problems of the Catholic Church in old cities and new suburbs. The Paulist Center prevailed upon O'Connor to give two talks for their lecture series, in 1959 and 1963.

On early afternoons he sometimes dropped in at newspaper offices to visit old chums. But Newspaper Row in downtown Boston was breaking up. The *Post* had folded, the *Globe* had just moved out to a state-of-the-art plant in Dorchester, and the *Herald* would soon follow that exodus from cramped downtown. That eventually left just the *Record-American,* for which Elliot Norton now wrote, and the *Pilot,* the respected archdiocesan newspaper whose editor, Monsignor Francis J. Lally, was O'Connor's friend and confessor for many years. From the *Pilot's* offices on Franklin Street O'Connor would then begin to circle back toward home. At least once a month he stopped in at Jack's Joke Shop, then in Park Square, in order to brush up on the latest magic devices and books. Once O'Connor infiltrated a magicians' convention in Boston. He reported back to Atlantic offices that one illusionist could disappear inside his own hotel room, much to the amusement of his baffled peers. (By luck he had discovered a hidden door in the bathroom.) O'Connor had a childlike fascination with innocent humor containing an element of the bizarre.

From mid to late afternoon O'Connor would go over his morning's work and write a little more. However, the bulk of his daily writing was done during those important morning hours. O'Connor only wrote for four hours at a maximum per day; he sometimes told people that he had an easy life because he worked less than half the standard shift. But of course novelists are always working, in a very real sense; the rest of his day was spent in the kinds of observation, socializing, reading, and contemplation that enriched his stories.

O'Connor sometimes cooked his own dinner in his galley kitchen. Since the near-fatal hemorrhage of 1953, he had to be careful of his diet. Now cooking as a health precaution was turning into an enjoyable hobby. Still, he frequently dined out with old and new friends. In the spring he was sometimes seen in the press box at Fenway Park, courtesy of Rudolph Elie, even though these were lackluster years for the Red Sox. Less often he watched Boston Celtics basketball in the old Boston Garden. Although he was not overly fond of fishing, he did go to a sportsman's exhibition just to see Ted Williams demonstrate his off-season skills with the fly rod.

When he stayed in, evenings were devoted to reading. Besides novels, he read *The New Republic, The New Yorker,* and of course *Atlantic Monthly.* He hardly ever listened to music, although he did own a KLH stereo system, which was, like the Porsche and the Mercedes, state of the art. It was an easy five-minute walk over the crest of Beacon Hill to the Boston Athenaeum, where he selected books and socialized a bit. This venerable private library, almost synonymous with Beacon Hill, has a morose entrance which belies the handsomely arched reading rooms inside. O'Connor still avidly attended plays. Boston had only a few good professional theaters—the Charles, Colonial, Shubert, and Wilbur—names that read like a Boston gazetteer. All are located in Boston's theater district, just to the south of the Common and an easy stroll from 48 Beacon Street. O'Connor told a few people that he once briefly thought of writing a version of *The Last Hurrah* for the theater, but it never even got as far as the aborted version of *The Oracle.* He told others that he never would try his hand at becoming a playwright. However, the theater would tempt him in the end.

These varied stops on O'Connor's rounds were all within a mile of each other in the compact old city, and all were located on or just off the expansive greenery of the Public Gardens and Boston Common. O'Connor found walking a good way to meet people, even though in spite of his size and distinctive appearance he was generally unrecognized as the famous author—which was just as he preferred. By now he knew hundreds of people in the Boston area, from Senator John F. Kennedy to street people who knew his routes just as the London beggars knew of Dr. Johnson's. On one occasion, O'Connor offered his prized Irish tweed coat to a beggar, but since the beggar only wanted money for drink he handed the coat back.

O'Connor's friends formed several distinct circles which usually did not overlap much: Woonsocket chums, O'Malley and others at Notre Dame, colleagues from radio and Fleet Street years, Harvard professors, a few priests, the staffs of his twin publishers, many writers, from Al Capp to Robert Lowell, plus an assortment of neighbors and professional people such as his lawyer, real estate agent, doctor, and dentist, each of whom had to be his friend in that Irish manner wherein a strictly professional relationship is regarded as a cold way to conduct business. O'Connor never more relished his adopted city than during these years. He told one reporter that Boston "is a thoroughly agreeable city in which I feel at home and in which I work well."[8] The old backwater was only beginning to stir with talk of the urban renewal and new construction that began its remarkable transformation in the 1960s and which continues unabated. During the years O'Connor worked on *The Edge of Sadness* (1957–60), the only significant construction, alluded to in the novel, was the disfiguring Central Artery that slashed through the heart of the city. Both *The Edge of Sadness* (1961) and *I Was Dancing* (1964) have a circumscribed, small-city atmosphere that mirrors the author's inner Boston orb.

He stayed clear of politics. When Laurence Winship, editor of the *Boston Globe,* invited him to do a political column for his paper, O'Connor turned him down, although they did become friends.[9] During the 1956 presidential campaign, some friends tried to enlist O'Connor for Adlai Stevenson but were turned away. A letter from O'Connor to Arthur Schlesinger comments on the Democratic convention with breezy humor. Schlesinger was working diligently for Stevenson, but O'Connor's letter shows no serious interest in the issues or in Adlai's "sacrificial lamb" campaign.[10] Like many writers between the 1940s and 1960s, he strongly believed that writers per se had no

8. George Ryan, "For O'Connor It's Not the Last Hurrah," *Information,* December 1961, 19.

9. Elliot Norton, personal interview, June 21, 1999.

10. Edwin O'Connor, letter to Arthur Schlesinger Jr., August 19, 1956, EOCP 279.

special political expertise, and that anyway it was their duty to write, not propagandize. At bottom, he knew he was not really a political novelist anyway, and he would not turn back to political characters for several years. He had new territory to explore. Still, he did ponder politics in serious conversation. His sister remembers that when he did offer a political insight he would typically say, "Look, I've given this a great deal of thought, and this is what I've concluded."[11] He was reluctant to sound off, but when he did he was usually careful and methodical.

If he was not available for the political arena, so too he spurned offers for other kinds of jobs, such as doing a biography of the early Rhode Island industrialist Samuel Slater.[12] He also continued to duck as many interviews as he could, and most speaking invitations as well. After the intense year following publication of *The Last Hurrah*, O'Connor was glad to be given the chance to work quietly on his next big novel.

The summer months at Wellfleet brought some alteration to his work schedule. He still rose early and wrote in the small downstairs study until about 12:30. By tacit mutual agreement the many academics and writers of Wellfleet's tightly knit summer intelligentsia reserve the first half of the day for cerebral pursuits. O'Connor's new house was designed to keep housekeeping down to the bachelor minimum, and tiresome domestic chores were done with dispatch. He did, however, enjoy cooking and specialized in roasts, steaks, and chops done simply. After lunch he would shuffle a half mile on warm sandy roads through the quiet dwarf woods, emerge at the treeless sand dunes, and waddle down to the magnificent beach below the endless tawny bluffs that disappear to the north and south in the summer haze and surf spray. He invariably wore an ancient terry cloth beach jacket and equally battered cap—both much derided, but to no avail. He took along a few books which he spent a couple of hours reading, his head propped on a pillow formed by the terry cloth robe, usually off on his own where no one dared to disturb him. But by midafternoon the little groups at Newcomb Hollow Beach began to form, and the rest of the afternoon was given over to socializing and a couple of plunges into the ocean, where he swam in the rollers with powerful strokes.

At least twice O'Connor rescued people from the surf that can be so dangerous at an outer beach. These people were usually newcomers or the foolhardy, and after his exertions O'Connor would get vehement at their senselessness. He even swore hotly, which was extremely rare for him. Edmund

<hr />

11. Barbara O'Connor Burrell, personal interview, summer 1998.
12. H. N. Slater, letter to Edwin O'Connor, January 4, 1957, EOCP 247.

Wilson once saw him swim far out to rescue two girls on a raft being blown off shore by the wind; O'Connor was exhausted after the strenuous effort.[13] The Apollonian from Boston could not understand such abandonment to the sea's immensity. And as a doctor's son, he had an instinct to save anyone from death. Al Duhamel, who also had a cottage in Wellfleet, remembers one incident:

> One June Saturday, circa 1960, I was down on Newcomb Hollow . . . and Ed was there, reading and obviously wanting to be alone, when this car pulled up, beefy guy white as only a New Yorker can get after a season in the smog, jumped out of his car, ran down to the icy waters, leaped in. We stood and watched the fool, expecting the obvious. Guy got into trouble, and Ed showed signs of going in. I shouted at him, and got him to stop. But those were his impulses, generosity and loyalty.[14]

Arthur Schlesinger has provided a who's who of Wellfleet summer folk.[15] Besides Arthur and his first wife, Marian, there were Edmund Wilson and his wife Elena; Wilson's ex-wife, the acerbic Mary McCarthy (O'Connor once described her as the literary equivalent of a guillotine; she in turn was reported to say that he was nice—almost *too* nice.);[16] Harvard Professors Daniel Aaron and Harry Levin; the architects Serge Chermayeff and Heyward Cutting. From nearby Truro and Provincetown there were frequent visitations to the Wellfleet colony by Norman Mailer, Abe Burrows, Montgomery Clift, Robert Manning, Dwight MacDonald, and Gilbert Seldes. From afternoons on the beach, through extended evening cocktail hours and informal dinners, Wellfleet socializing was lengthy and loud with political and cultural argument. In Boston and at Wellfleet O'Connor refrained from entering these contests; he was more content to sit back and listen. When he did offer food for thought, his affable drollery hushed the noise and soothed the rage.

Saturday mornings were reserved for softball games at several locations. Participants often included Norman Mailer, a shirtless Arthur Schlesinger at first base, and Dwight MacDonald with a bandana knotted on his head. O'Connor often alternated with Schlesinger at first base—a switch from the short to the tall.[17]

Daily Mass was not available for many years in that part of the outer Cape. Even Sunday Mass was for many years celebrated by a priest who

---

13. *BL,* 366.

14. P. Albert Duhamel, letter to author, March 25, 1999.

15. *BL,* 8.

16. Edwin O'Connor, letter to Arthur Schlesinger Jr., August 19, 1956, EOCP 279; the McCarthy quip appears in *BL,* 34.

17. Mary V. Dearborn, *Mailer: A Biography* (Boston: Houghton Mifflin, 1999), 156.

drove fifty miles from New Bedford. This was WASP lower Cape, between the "Irish Riviera" upper Cape and the Portuguese enclave in Provincetown. O'Connor's only co-religionist, as Amos Force might put it, was Al Duhamel. The two of them would attend the seven o' clock Sunday Mass with a dozen other people. Once in the early 1950s the visiting priest reported that the previous month's entire collection was only sixty dollars. The next Sunday he warmly thanked the communicant who in one donation had tripled that sum. That donor was of course O'Connor, long before *The Last Hurrah* could reasonably support such largess.[18] Anna Hamburger remembers that O'Connor stood out as a Roman Catholic curiosity: he was the only person in their set who was known to attend a church at all. When the Sunday Mass schedule changed to a later hour, people were surprised that O'Connor's beach arrival was actually delayed by his attendance at church.[19]

Edmund Wilson's daughter Helen remembers O'Connor as an attentive listener who was quite secure in himself. He was especially close to her mother, Elena, who was quite shy. O'Connor was a hit with children. "Big Ed," as they called him, was a kind of father figure cum big brother—the best possible combination. He was kind, gentle, and generous, and while attractive to many women, he was not at all a predatory male during a time of increasing sexual high jinks on that part of the Cape.[20]

A few times during the summer O'Connor, missing the Boston rounds, would drive the two hours to the city. The drive to Boston is a big inverted "J" and in summer traffic it could be tedious. In Boston he would get a haircut at the Ritz and make some of the usual rounds before driving back, usually the same day.

In early May 1957 the Pulitzer Prizes for 1956 were announced. Many critics and readers, and especially of course Bostonians, felt that *The Last Hurrah* was the odds-on favorite in the fiction category. The *Saturday Review of Literature* had just polled many writers and reviewers, and indeed O'Connor's novel came out on top by a wide margin, beating out John Hersey's *A Single Pebble* and Rebecca West's *The Fountain Overflows*. But the Advisory Board, chaired by Columbia University's president, Dr. Grayson Kirk, decided not to award a prize for fiction that year. This was the fifth time since the award's inception in 1918 that such an impasse had occurred. The otherwise anonymous board never discloses its votes and never discusses publicly the

18. Duhamel, letter to author.
19. Anna Hamburger, telephone interview, September 2, 1999.
20. Helen Miranda Wilson, telephone interview, September 10, 1999.

entrants or the proceedings. Kirk was in fact abrupt with a reporter who queried him on the fiction award. More than eighty novels had been submitted. A jury then typically forwarded two to five novels for the Advisory Board's final decision.[21] Irish Catholics in Boston could be forgiven for noting that the lapsed Catholic Eugene O'Neill posthumously received the Pulitzer in drama that year for *Long Day's Journey Into Night*, in which Catholicism is implicitly presented as the morphine of at least one Irish woman, whereas O'Connor as a practicing Catholic was just one Irish American too many for the Pulitzer panjandrums. But O'Connor was not heard to complain and would eventually receive his due.

In October *Atlantic Monthly* dusted off an old manuscript and published O'Connor's last short story, "A Grand Day for Mr. Garvey."[22] It was his third in that magazine and his fifth and final one to see print; O'Connor wrote no more short stories after he started on *The Last Hurrah*. O'Connor had written the story in early 1951, but Helen Strauss had no luck in placing it; surely *Atlantic* had been approached long before 1957. A biographical note in *Atlantic* mentions that O'Connor's *Benjy* would be out that same October, and that the filming of *The Last Hurrah* was under way. It appears that the magazine ran the story as a way to advertise the children's book and enhance sales of the novel. This "tie-in" with books published by Atlantic Monthly Press would be repeated when his next works were published. That notwithstanding, "A Grand Day for Mr. Garvey" is perhaps O'Connor's best short story.

Martin Garvey is an elderly bachelor who has been sent to a comfortable Catholic nursing home by his niece and "the husband," as Garvey calls him in that Irish way in which "the" can carry an unspecified opprobrium. At first devastated to be exiled from Ellen's house and "abandoned," Garvey soon gets to like the place as he secretly enjoys his new freedom. However, he plays a "little game" with Ellen during her weekly visits. He carries on mournfully, complains of food, decries the broken televison set (which all the old timers detest anyway), all in an effort to make his niece miserably guilty—a skill well honed by certain Irish. But Ellen is catching on to his little game and knows how to fend him off. One day in the midst of this weekly deadlock, Garvey is luckily visited by his neighbor down the hall, an old actor of some fame named Calderone, whose stage name was Edwin Cardew. (He is the only one of O'Connor's characters to carry the author's name, but in context it refers probably to his vaudevillian uncle of the same name.) The

21. *Boston American*, May 8, 1957.
22. *Atlantic Monthly*, October 1957, 46–50.

vain Calderone is not much liked in the place, but Garvey presses him into service as one who can more effectively play the martyr's role. True to form, Calderone histrionically declaims to Ellen that he and his comrades have been banished to die in an "asylum" for "old madmen." A theatrical performance to expose and defeat was also used in "Parish Reunion," written at the same time. As the story ends Garvey relishes his small victory in the lists with his niece.

The story is a good example of O'Connor's preoccupation with generational divides, especially among the Irish. Eccentric elderly cranks in conflict with the young fascinated him, and he sometimes paired or even tripled his cranks for effect, as will be apparent in his next two novels. Two items vary that pattern in "A Grand Day for Mr. Garvey." First, one of the pair of codgers is Italian. Secondly, the younger generation in the conflict is represented by a woman, a rarity for O'Connor. She is easily defeated by her uncle and Calderone; the young are usually no match for the old in O'Connor's work.

When Helen Strauss first received the manuscript back in 1951 she wrote O'Connor twice to say she had had no luck in placing another story, entitled "Dad."[23] She had tried thirteen magazines, including *Atlantic, Argosy,* and *Good Housekeeping*—quite a spread. It seems that O'Connor urged her considerably on this one. However, the manuscript of "Dad" is not with the Edwin O'Connor Papers. There are several possibilities. The manuscript may have been lost; O'Connor may have destroyed it; it may not have been deposited with the Papers. A fourth and remote possibility is that the unpublished "The Coward," about a boy's disillusionment with his father, is in fact "Dad" under a different title. At any rate, this is a frustrating loss in a biographical exploration of an author so absorbed with fathers.

When it appeared in *Modern Irish-American Fiction* in 1989, "A Grand Day for Mr. Garvey" became the only short story by O'Connor to be anthologized.[24]

In January 1958 O'Connor took his second vacation at Harbour Island. From there he wrote John Kelleher the first of several letters as "Bucko Donahue." O'Connor was widely known in his circles as a gifted mimic who practiced this minor art in letters but more often on the telephone. Already famous for his "Curley," he added to his repertoire public figures like Prince

23. Helen Strauss, letters to Edwin O'Connor, April 3, 1951, and April 12, 1951, EOCP 376.
24. Daniel J. Casey and Robert E. Rhodes, eds., *Modern Irish-American Fiction: A Reader* (Syracuse, N.Y.: Syracuse University Press, 1989), 116–26.

Philip, Dean Rusk, and Bishop Fulton J. Sheen, as well as an assortment of more private inventions like Bucko. He would call up someone whose sense of humor he especially enjoyed (an Abe Burrows, say) or those who needed some lightening up (his Harvard professor friends) and then maintain a lengthy monologue ruse as Queen Elizabeth's consort or the television bishop. Of course most people recognized O'Connor's soft bass right away, but most enjoyed the performance, which could be lengthy. Like Dickens, O'Connor seems to have cultivated a lively colony of characters in his imagination, and could release them on the spot.

In the first letter, "Bucko Donahue" is revealed to be a black Bahamian who fills in Kelleher on local gossip while showering the visiting Edwin O'Connor with fawning admiration. He also claims to be the world's expert on ancient Irish annals, sagas, and genealogies.[25] This first letter establishes Bucko's ancestry. "I am a genuine Irishman, even though I am black as the ace of spades." He goes on to imply that his "da" was the "Big Fella" (the nickname of the assassinated Michael Collins of Irish Revolution fame), whom he confuses with the partly Spanish Eamon de Valera of the same era. It is not clear whether the confusion is Bucko's or O'Connor's. Bucko signs off "Erin go ha ha." His script is shaky with the d.t.'s.[26] Today O'Connor's letter might be considered in questionable taste, but it should be remembered that there is in fact a West Indian phenomenon known as the Black Irish (not to be confused with the strictly Hibernian variety, which can consist of a number of shades with respect to skin, hair, or eyes). These people, particularly numerous on Montserrat in the Leeward Islands, are descendants of Irish convicts transported during the slave era who donated their surnames along with their genes. Also, it must be remembered that O'Connor was writing satire, in which the literary strategies should forestall a simplistic response. Thus, O'Connor could be mocking Irish follies magnified in Bucko, while simultaneously presenting an adroit sketch of the subservient attitudes of certain West Indians that were so distressing to encounter in those years.

Three months later O'Connor wrote Kelleher from Dublin, but he quickly drops the Bucko persona.[27] The highlight of the letter is O'Connor's hilarious report on Brendan Behan, who at the time was transforming himself into the most flagrant stage Irishman of the century. O'Connor had met Behan several times. On the first of these occasions, the drunken Behan had

---

25. For more information on Bucko, see John Kelleher's article, "Edwin O'Connor and the Irish-American Process," *Atlantic Monthly*, May 1968, 48–52.

26. Edwin O'Connor, letter to John Kelleher, January 11, 1958, courtesy of John Kelleher.

27. Edwin O'Connor, letter to John Kelleher, April 16, 1958, courtesy of John Kelleher.

vomited on the street. On April 14 O'Connor had gone with the Montgomerys to the Pike, Dublin's most experimental theater. After a gloomy Sartre curtain raiser about the Resistance, the Behan came as comic relief. But even before *The Big House* began, O'Connor and the Montgomerys were alternately appalled and entertained by the elderly woman beside them.

The woman had a great paper sack on her lap which contained bottles of stout, laundry, pieces of bread and probably a soiled child. This proved to be Madame Behan, mother of the distinguished playwright, who was attending the first night in the company of her husband. She kept on expanding, taking her coat off, throwing the paper sack around. . . . Madame Behan made things no better by leaning over to Mr. Montgomery every few minutes, and saying, in stout-filled tones, "Sorry, darlin'," a comment which reduced him to permanent rage. . . . Just before the curtain went up on *The Big House* the theatre was graced with the personal presence of Brendan himself, who was quite rumpled and quite drunk. Throughout the play he kept delivering encouraging cries towards the stage, and when it was all over he delivered a little speech from the stage, in which he asked the audience, "Did my double meanin's get across?" He was assured that they did, but, taking no chances, he proceeded to tell one or two remarkably single-meaninged jokes. So ended the evening.

A few years later Behan encountered O'Connor in Boston. John Kelleher recounts it from O'Connor's telling:

[Behan] kept calling ahead and wiring ahead that the only one he particularly wanted to see was Ed O'Connor. Somebody threw a great welcoming party for him and Ed was dragooned into attending, but when midnight had passed and Behan hadn't turned up Ed firmly departed. Next day he was having lunch at the Ritz, Behan who was stopping there came down to the diningroom, spotted Ed, and at once joined him. Ed said he had an exquisitely embarrassing three quarters of an hour while Behan did his usual performance, obscenities included, and kept sending the food back because it wasn't cooked as in Drumcondra. When Ed finally did get away, he passed two Boston banker types at the entrance, looking into the room. One was saying to the other, "Who do you think that could possibly be?" "Not one of ours," said the other. True observation.[28]

The disparity between the two writers was unimaginably wide: the decorous Irish Bostonian gentleman and the loutishly uninhibited ruffian, former Borstal prisoner for his I.R.A. deeds, up from the slums of Dublin. And yet O'Connor enjoyed Behan's work, and even seems to have overlooked the alcoholism that would kill the diabetic writer in 1964. O'Connor was less censorious about alcohol by this time, even while he remained dry himself.

O'Connor's trip to Dublin in 1958 (with a continuation to London) was apparently delayed by the death of Rudolph Elie on March 11. Elie was in Los

---

28. John Kelleher, letter to author, July 3, 2000.

Angeles on assignment for the *Boston Herald*. When he was stricken by a heart attack, he first called his family and then O'Connor. It is believed that O'Connor helped the widow make the funeral arrangements for one of his oldest Boston friends.

In late August 1958 O'Connor had another brush with the academia he had foresworn since his semester of teaching night school back in 1951. Father Theodore Hesburgh, the new president of Notre Dame, invited O'Connor to accept membership on the university's Advisory Council for the College of Liberal and Fine Arts. The president wrote a gracious letter which began, "Dear Ed." The two had met and corresponded since 1956. Catholic universities were beginning to open up governance and committees to lay people, and they sometimes sought out big names like Edwin O'Connor. Father Hesburgh assured O'Connor that the two annual meetings of the Council would be short.[29] O'Connor politely declined at some length in an October 1 letter now lost. His reason, gleaned from reading between the lines of Father Hesburgh's reply, was concern for precious time away from his work. Father Hesburgh graciously accepted O'Connor's decision and even envied his resolute dedication, which a university president, who must juggle many factors when making a decision, could not so easily enjoy.[30]

The biggest excitement that year for fans of *The Last Hurrah* was the release of the film version in late October. Problems had beset the film in practically all departments and phases. Beforehand, the author had been asked to go to Hollywood as a "consultant," but O'Connor knew how much that meant and stayed away. It is notoriously difficult for novelists to exercise any real control over film versions of their work. He stayed in New England and watched developments from afar with mounting skepticism.

Helen Strauss had been dispatched to Hollywood by the Morris Agency to convince Columbia's Harry Cohn that Spencer Tracy was the only man for the lead role. At the time Morris represented Tracy, who badly wanted the part. Cohn was at first cool to using Tracy, but Strauss was able to convince him in the end—after dutifully unbleaching her hair when Cohn said she looked like a Hollywood tramp. When Cohn then secured John Ford to be director, things went steadily downhill. After a remarkable career in directing

---

29. Rev. T. M. Hesburgh, C.S.C., letter to Edwin O'Connor, August 28, 1958, University of Notre Dame Archives, UPHS 118.

30. Rev. T. M. Hesburgh, C.S.C., letter to Edwin O'Connor, October 20, 1958, University of Notre Dame Archives, UPHS 118.

almost two hundred films going back to the silent era, Ford in his twilight years was not the best choice for an urban political film. His great films, like *The Informer* (1935), *Stagecoach* (1939), *The Grapes of Wrath* (1940), and *How Green Was My Valley* (1941), were behind him. He may have been born John Feeney in an Irish-speaking house, and may have done well with Liam O'Flaherty's *The Informer,* but his more recent John Wayne film, *The Quiet Man* (1952), was an indication that when it came to Irish material Ford was no longer made of sterner stuff. All too often, as Maureen Dezell puts it in a study of Irish Americans, "the director seemed to lose his sense of subtlety and complexity when his subject was Ireland or the American Irish."[31] Delays and script problems compounded matters, and Harry Cohn died during filming. The set, one of the biggest of its day, burned down and had to be rebuilt. And then there was the cast, as described by Helen Strauss:

Ford cast the many juicy character roles in the film with most of his beloved Irish cronies, many of them long absent from the screen and most preserved by a familiar pickling process. There probably never was assembled a larger and more inflammable bunch of hundred-proof carousers.[32]

Helen Strauss relayed these disasters, follies, and vices. O'Connor steeled himself for the worst. It would not be the last time that he would have the "craythur" to blame for slurring his text as it moved off the page and into the bright lights.

According to the *Boston Globe*'s Martin Nolan, a veteran Boston journalist and O'Connor-watcher, in the midst of this mayhem Ford and Columbia had a falling out, and the film that was eventually released suffered from cutting by other hands. Its 121 minutes seem far longer than two hours. Nolan writes: "As a film *The Last Hurrah* is like many an ambitious Irishman of its time, a charming failure."[33]

For at least two years rumors about casting had been blowing around like so much litter on Boston Common. Jack Lemmon, recently catapulted into fame by *Mister Roberts,* was going to be Adam. Speculation for Skeffington ran from James Cagney, who would have been lively at least, to Jackie Gleason, who would have been sorely miscast.[34] Ford did make a serious effort to snag Orson Welles, but apparently Welles's lawyers botched the deal.[35]

31. Maureen Dezell, *Irish America: Coming into Clover: The Evolution of a People and a Culture* (New York: Doubleday, 2001), 29.

32. Strauss, *Talent for Luck,* 169–70.

33. "Larger Than Life," *Boston Sunday Globe,* October 24, 1999, N1 and 8.

34. Unidentified newspaper article, July 20, 1956.

35. Joseph McBride, *Searching for John Ford: A Life* (New York: St. Martin's, Press 2001), 589. McBride often attributes to Ford special touches in the movie which in fact came directly from the novel.

O'Connor's own preference for Skeffington was curious but revealing. According to his sister and several others, O'Connor hoped for Claude Rains, the superb British character actor known for his articulate diction and impeccable carriage. His Captain Louis Renault in *Casablanca* was his defining moment. Whether his role as Job Skeffington (who is Jewish) in the 1944 *Mr. Skeffington* had anything to do with O'Connor's nomination is not known, but preferring the gentleman Britisher as *his* Skeffington speaks volumes about O'Connor's conception of his main character's dignified and sophisticated mien, and also manifests certain of O'Connor's ideals about the direction assimilation might take.

Rumors also surfaced just before shooting in early 1958 that some location work might actually be done in Boston or some other New England locale. There was a small flurry of excitement in January that Gloucester's Annisquam section had been picked.[36] But not a bit of the film was ever shot in New England.

The film opened finally in late October 1958. Tracy turned in a lame performance, a disappointment to his fans, as he came up lamentably short in capturing Skeffington's complexity and depth. The veteran actor patently struggles with his lines. At one point Tracy is clearly heard rattling his coffee cup for no apparent reason. At another point he reaches down to pick up something from the floor—again a baffling gesture. Such scenes should have hit the cutting-room floor. The script writer, Frank Nugent, puts the film's title into Tracy's mouth, where it comes out as "the last *hoo*-ray," the likes of which was never heard in Boston—which, by the way, is also named in the movie, albeit indirectly, when Tracy says "banned in Boston." Jeffrey Hunter, a youthful heartthrob, hardly helped out as Adam Caulfield. John Gorman was played by the perennially untalented Pat O'Brien. Sepulchral Basil Rathbone did a passable job as Norman Cass Sr., as did John Carradine as Amos Force and Edward Brophy as Ditto Boland. Jane Darwell, like Carradine an old trouper in Ford's informal stock company, lifts things with her Delia Boylan. O. Z. Whitehead played Norman Cass Jr. perfectly in one of the best scenes, where Tracy's halting, thick diction finally serves a purpose in explaining the Fire Commissioner's job to the witless yachtsman.

The *Boston Globe*'s Marjorie W. Sherman covered the world premiere on October 23 at the old Loew's Orpheum in downtown Boston. A detail of thirty policemen was required to handle the crowds and escort the guests inside. Mayor John B. Hynes attended, along with Torbert MacDonald and Chub Peabody, who would be governor of the Commonwealth in a few

36. Unidentified newspaper article, January 29, 1958.

years. But in a big disappointment to all who waited for the "star" of the film, James Michael Curley never did arrive. Sherman wrote what everyone knew: "He's been pretty sick for a long time now." Apparently Spencer Tracy did not attend, although Jeffrey Hunter did. She also wrote that O'Connor did not attend, but left it at that.[37]

The fact is that O'Connor was livid. The most detailed account of his re-action comes from his old *Boston Post* friend Elliot Norton, who by the late 1950s was the dean of Boston's half-dozen drama critics. His reviews now were appearing in the tabloid *Record-American,* and he had recently started a weekly theater program for WGBH-TV. Twelve years after the event Norton recalled the movie's premiere. O'Connor first saw the film at a press review. Even though he was prepared for the worst, he was still shocked. The depth of his hatred for the movie surprised many friends, who had never seen the usually bouncy O'Connor so bitter. He even swore mildly, another big sur-prise. According to Norton, O'Connor thought the film a travesty of what he had written, and he was particularly outraged by "Pat and Mike" stereotyp-ing. Norton claims, in contradiction to Marjorie Sherman, that somehow somebody got O'Connor to attend the world premiere a few days later. There he said to one gushing fan, "I was sorry, madam, that movie theater seats don't have the same equipment that airline seats have." (Norton also wrote that O'Connor had talked with some producers, including Lawrence Carr, who had backed *Mame,* about a musical version of *The Last Hurrah;* nothing came of it because O'Connor knew of his own limitations for developing a musical. Later he hoped that his new friend Abe Burrows might try, but O'Connor never pressed him.)[38] Some remember O'Connor actually walk-ing out midway through the showing, while others insisted he stayed to the end. Time and memory may be mixing up the two different showings he may have attended that week. Others heard him say that he would never consider allowing another of his novels to be filmed; his vow was not partic-ularly firm, however. He apparently never did see this film again.

O'Connor probably was upset at the ways Cuke Gillen and to a lesser ex-tent Charlie Hennessey were portrayed. Gillen was played by a veteran char-acter actor, James Gleason, who turned this minor character into a dim-wit-ted hack. Wallace Ford's Charlie Hennessey was tolerable, but not as interesting as O'Connor's. O'Connor had felt deep gratitude toward Louis Brems and Clem Norton, the real-life originals of these two, and he must have felt stung by their diminishment in the film.

37. *Boston Globe,* October 23, 1958.
38. *Boston Record-American,* March 4, 1970, 24.

One underlying problem may have nagged O'Connor: Spencer Tracy's private life. O'Connor said courteous things about Tracy in public, and he visited him at his apartment in New York. But that apartment had been shared for some time now with Katharine Hepburn, after Tracy left his wife. Such liaisons were still not publicly proclaimed in the late 1950s, but theirs was an open secret. For the Irish Catholic Tracy to have abandoned his wife was a serious sin that could not be glossed over. Listen to O'Connor when Skeffington himself dresses down his philandering lieutenant, Johnnie Byrne:

Like the voters who would now turn sharply against the guilty Byrne, Skeffington took a poor view of marital infidelity. Like most of his people, he did not regard it as one of the genial sins. It was perhaps the single offense with which he had never been charged . . . domestically, Skeffington was unassailable (*LH* 238).

Skeffington knows that in politics, at least, adultery was a liability and not merely the "private matter" that Johnnie pleads, and certainly not a "genial" sin. In Catholic morality the line between private and public acts cannot be sharply drawn, because the private act will have its public consequence. Skeffington was a dutiful Catholic, it must be remembered, as was his creator. To see his fictional hero being portrayed by an adulterer may have been more than O'Connor could manage and may account for some of his bitterness. He must have felt that the audience would know all about Tracy and Hepburn and that such knowledge would confuse them about his Skeffington. Nevertheless, he held no personal grudge against Tracy, and for several years he carried on a correspondence with Hepburn. Four of her letters to O'Connor, written in a huge scrawl that is almost a graph of her famous voice, are with his papers.

Reviews of the film were generally tepid. Philip Hartung in the November 14 *Commonweal* did give it high praise, while avoiding specifics. But *Time* on October 27 thought it was much too sentimental, and *Newsweek* called it "pretty naive stuff" the same week. *The New Yorker* for November 1 dismissed it, as might be expected, although not as harshly as Anthony West had denounced the novel in its pages. Tracy expected an Oscar for his role as Skeffington but was sorely disappointed, even though he did receive one for *The Old Man and the Sea* that same year.[39] The movie was not a blockbuster.

In 1977 Carroll O'Connor (no relation) wrote and starred in a made-for-TV version of *The Last Hurrah* that is no longer available. Appearing with him were Burgess Meredith as the Cardinal; Tom Clancy of the Clancy Brothers was Ditto Boland.[40]

---

39. Bill Davidson, *Spencer Tracy: Tragic Idol* (New York: Dutton, 1987), 176.

40. Carroll O'Connor's autobiography, *I Think I'm Outta Here: A Memoir of All My Families* (New York: Pocket Books, 1998), barely mentions this film version.

Curley tried to get into the act, of course. For over a year he had kept his lawyers busy over the movie, and this time they meant business. Curley might have made his peace with the book, but there was no telling how "he" might look on the screen. Here again the private life of Spencer Tracy might have been a factor for the thoroughly monogamous Curley. The facts about the legal action are somewhat murky, but the following is known. In August the Associated Press reported that Curley was suing Columbia Pictures to prevent the Boston showing of the film. Columbia replied that Curley had signed a release and had been paid $25,000. Curley claimed his signature on the document was a forgery and by this outrageous ploy got Columbia to cough up another $15,000. Curley's fame at eighty-four and *The Last Hurrah*'s continuing notoriety caused the *Boston Evening Globe* to put the story in bold headlines on September 12, 1958: CURLEY'S MOVIE SUIT DISMISSED. Curley, it transpires, never did see the film. But his family previewed it in early September and shortly thereafter instructed attorneys to drop the suit. None of the legal maneuvers delayed the premiere.

With a fitting sense of timing, James Michael Curley died, on November 12, while *The Last Hurrah* was still showing in Boston. Curley was given a monster send-off, the likes of which had never been seen in the city. As his body lay in state in the Massachusetts State House where 100,000 people passed by, a photographer snapped a remarkable shot: O'Connor contemplating Curley on the catafalque. The photo catches O'Connor's mixture of ironic detachment and nostalgic wonder. The next day the *Boston American* ran the big tabloid photo on page one with the headline, EPILOGUE TO 'LAST HURRAH.'[41] A big story in *Life* on November 24 ran thirteen photos of Curley and mentioned the movie, but said nothing about the book or the author. It was hard to tell who was eclipsing whom—O'Connor or Curley, Curley or Skeffington, Skeffington or Tracy. Rumor had it that after Curley's death, the weeping rose audibly in Loew's Orpheum theater during Tracy/Skeffington/Curley's extraordinarily long death scene.

A month later O'Connor was in Rome for the elevation of Boston's Archbishop Richard J. Cushing to Cardinal.[42] O'Connor went as a special correspondent for the *Boston Globe*, the third Boston newspaper he wrote for. He

41. Beatty, *Rascal King*, 6–7; 16. The newspaper photo appeared on November 14, 1958.

42. I have drawn on O'Connor's report in his two-part series in the *Boston Globe*, December 14 and 21, 1958; supplementary information is from George Ryan's "For Edwin O'Connor It's Not the Last Hurrah" *Information*, December 1961, 16–20; also, George Ryan, letter to author, July 18, 2000; telephone interview with George Ryan, July 21, 2000.

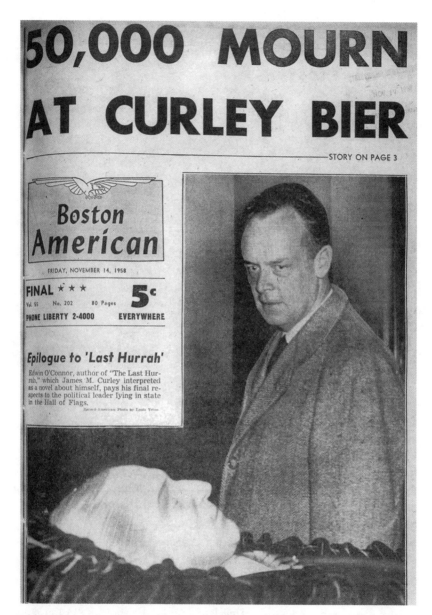

50,000 MOURN AT CURLEY BIER

STORY ON PAGE 3

Boston American

FRIDAY, NOVEMBER 14, 1958

FINAL ★ ★ ★

Vol. 55   No. 202   80 Pages   **5¢**

PHONE LIBERTY 2-4000   EVERYWHERE

Epilogue to 'Last Hurrah'

Edwin O'Connor, author of "The Last Hurrah," which James M. Curley interpreted as a novel about himself, pays his final respects to the political leader lying in state in the Hall of Flags.

Record-American Photo by Louis Tetas

Edwin O'Connor contemplating James Michael Curley lying in state, November 14 1958. *Reprinted with permission of the Boston Herald.*

Rome, December 1958. O'Connor and his confessor, Monsignor Francis J. Lally, editor of *The Pilot*. O'Connor was covering the elevation of Archbishop Richard J. Cushing to Cardinal for the *Boston Globe*. *Courtesy of Barbara O'Connor Burrell.*

was a good friend of the *Globe*'s editor, Laurence Winship, and so he needed little persuading; O'Connor was usually happy to help out friends. There was undoubtedly also an ulterior motive. For over a year O'Connor had been steadily at work on his new novel about a priest. What better way to get some deep background than a trip to Rome and Vatican City? The *Globe* for its part knew that the Edwin O'Connor byline on its front page insured a trusting readership for the big event.

And a big event it was. Cushing had been archbishop of Boston since 1945, when he succeeded Cardinal William O'Connell, who had been crusty, aloof, and pompously defensive to the point of arrogance. He also lived well. Cushing was a refreshingly informal man with a common touch. His pursuit of ecumenism is now widely appreciated as a true witness in improving relations with Protestants and Jews. The raspy, nasal roar of "the Cush" could only come from Boston and was a marvel to hear as it soared to fill any space. O'Connor had heard from relatives a story of Archbishop Cushing driving through a blizzard late at night to Rhode Island in order to be at the bedside of a dying priest friend. Cushing arrived just before the grumpy, unlikable man died—a moment of grace that found its way into *The Edge of Sadness*, when the stricken Charlie Carmody summons Father Kennedy. It was widely rumored in Boston that Pope Pius XII had withheld the red hat for Cushing because of the scandal involving Father Leonard Feeney, who preached a rigidly exclusionary version of "no salvation outside the Church." But now Pope John XXIII wasted no time in naming cardinals like Cushing, whose long years of preaching and working for unity had found an admirer. In 1959 Cardinal Cushing wrote a "Dear Ed" letter to O'Connor in which he thanked him for his gift of a thousand dollars that would be earmarked for the Cardinal's new project: an institution for children who were both blind and handicapped.[43]

For the trip to Rome O'Connor went first to New York for his overseas flight. He spent a few days in London and Dublin, where a friend wrote him a letter of introduction to Cardinal Tisserant, dean of the College of Cardinals. For some reason known only to Vaticanologists, the letter had to be written with a fountain pen. It was totally indecipherable.

O'Connor was overwhelmed by Rome, "this incredible layer-cake of a city." Unlike James Joyce, who lived there briefly some fifty years earlier, O'Connor was willing to be impressed. He stayed at the Hessler Hotel at the top of the Spanish Steps and thoroughly enjoyed his ten days in the Eternal City, with its tiny Vatican City enclave. In fact, his newspaper reporting contains more superlatives than just about anything he ever wrote. He was awestruck by the spectacle in St. Peter's Basilica as the "scarlet line of cardinals began their slow and reverent approach across the green carpet." The broad *galero*, the red hat worn only on that occasion, was bestowed upon each new cardinal. Later O'Connor and the Boston group had a private audience with the pope. Although he spoke in Italian, John XXIII hoped that they would all meet again in heaven, "where of course we will speak English." This was the humorous John XXIII that endeared himself to all but the rigid. O'Connor shared with his readers his favorite story about Cardinal Roncalli before he became pope. Roncalli had been in the Vatican's diplomatic corps where his wit, common sense, and good judgment flourished. One evening at a dinner party he found himself seated next to a skimpily dressed young

43. Richard Cardinal Cushing, letter to Edwin O'Connor, October 6, 1959, EOCP 125.

woman. When the fruit bowl was being passed around, she selected an apple. "Be careful," Roncalli said to her, "it was only when Eve ate the apple that she discovered she was naked." Such a story could raise eyebrows behind Boston's lace curtains, but O'Connor knew he could get away with it.

Although most of the ten-day trip was on the solemn side, there was time for other pursuits. He had lunch with Ignazio Silone, whose 1936 novel *Bread and Wine* O'Connor admired for its vision of social justice infused with religious values. On another occasion, George Ryan of the *Pilot* recalls that at a sedate press dinner attended by many high-ranking American clergy, Pittsburgh's Bishop John Wright asked O'Connor to do an impromptu imitation of Curley. O'Connor complied with an uproarious "Curley" who talked of that "upstart boy" who had turned him into a fictional character. It did not take long for this story to get back to Boston and travel through the clerical grapevine. When Father Francis Curley, S.J., heard that his father, in the grave only a month, had been mimicked in Rome by O'Connor while the hierarchy cheered him on, he understandably became cool toward the writer. Later, after he had left the priesthood, he spread wildly inaccurate stories about the man who mimicked his father.

The next two years were uneventful. O'Connor published nothing between his *Globe* articles in December 1958 and *The Edge of Sadness* in 1961. One could almost call 1959 and 1960 two of the most obscure years of his adult life, were it not for the fact that O'Connor was now a much-sought-after dinner guest in Boston, Cambridge, and Wellfleet. (Later, when New York invitations became numerous, some in Boston feared that O'Connor would jump publishers and cities. They had no cause for alarm, because O'Connor was by now a firmly anchored Bostonian.) O'Connor was a quiet dinner guest and seldom a dominant one. A few people felt he was slightly patronized as a court jester. Those who knew him best never treated him this way. No doubt some efforts were made at these soirees to match up O'Connor with prospective women. But as he entered his forties, his prospects seemed to be fading.

O'Connor's winning manner comes through in an account of a big night at Arthur Schlesinger's Cambridge home in 1961. Luminaries like Edmund Wilson, John Kenneth Galbraith, Hans Morganthau, and Max Lerner filled the house. On top of this charged atmosphere was the added excitement of Secret Service agents roaming the house in preparation for a visit by President Kennedy the next day. A young Brandeis undergraduate found herself cowed into insecure silence until the man next to her sensed her situation and struck up a casual conversation. In contrast to the rest of the company, he was quietly unassuming. The student did not know who he was until he mentioned in passing that he had written one of her favorite novels, *The Last Hurrah*. She was floored and still warmly remembers O'Connor's little act of social kindness.[44]

John Kelleher was alone in Dublin while on a sabbatical from Harvard during the spring semester of 1959. O'Connor had popped into Dublin the preceding December, and so he did not make his usual pilgrimage there in March. When he learned that Kelleher, away from his wife and daughters, was lonely in a city he found irksomely depressing, O'Connor wrote him two letters in April. In the first one he commiserates seriously with his good friend. Yes, he agrees, Dublin can dampen the spirits. "But a backwater is a backwater and Dublin is one and will be one forever and ever, amen. I like it; but then I stay a couple of weeks and go." He also admits he could never again spend months there as he did in 1953 and 1954. He sends along his best to his favorite Irish friends: the Montgomerys, the O'Faolains, and the Sweeneys. A second letter was written shortly afterwards. O'Connor seems alarmed at Kelleher being "down in the dumps," and so he put on his funny hat. In his best deadpan manner he tells Kelleher to worry no more: the arsonist plaguing Kelleher's town of Westwood has been apprehended. "By the way, the police said that it was in the ashes of your house that they found the clue. . . ." But not to worry: Kelleher's family is doing just fine in their new one-room apartment in Roxbury. He then mentions in passing that Harvard's recent abolishment of all Irish studies was a particularly intolerant act. And so forth. O'Connor's humor, some of it racially tinged, seems a bit gauche today, but Kelleher enjoyed O'Connor's offbeat style. He needed the wry cheering up.[45]

In October 1959 O'Connor gave one of his rare talks. As a favor to the Paulists at their center on Park Street, O'Connor inaugurated the 1959–60 annual series called the Christian Culture Lectures. He was introduced by Mayor John B. Hynes, Curley's successor, who had been mayor for a decade. The talk was advertised as "The Writer Who Doesn't Exist."[46] The manuscript of this talk is entitled "The Catholic Writer."[47] The two titles taken together point to O'Connor's thesis, which he sums up at the end: "Do not

---

44. Margo Howard, letter to author, January 18, 2000.
45. Edwin O'Connor, letters to John Kelleher, April 4, 1959, and April (undated) 1959, courtesy of John Kelleher.
46. Unidentified newspaper article, October 7, 1959.
47. EOCP 51.

look for Catholic Novelists—there are none. There are Catholics who write novels—that is all." This sensible talk reminded his audience that, while they may be understandably frustrated at not finding many good novels written by Catholics, they must first demand that literature be done well. Excellence in the craft is the first requirement of a writer. Too often, he gently reminds his hearers, Catholic educators, critics, and reviewers have succumbed to the temptation to put the Catholic writer's religion on display first, as if that automatically produced a good work of art. He remembers one old priest at Notre Dame who lectured badly for years in this fashion on Catholic literature and art. Educated Catholic readers needed to discriminate and admit, for example, that Waugh's *Brideshead Revisited* is not his best work, even if it is his most "Catholic" novel. (Some might demur at O'Connor's judgment here.) He particularly singles out the many third-rate "Catholic" novels in which miracles are imported to resolve conflicts. Such pietistic *dei ex machina* may dupe the simple-minded but cannot engage the increasingly educated Catholic reading public. This comment has a special bearing on *The Edge of Sadness*, which was in its last stages of composition. O'Connor avoids anything smacking of the miraculous in this story about a priest and the difficult care of ornery souls. God's mysterious providence may be at work in his characters' lives, but it does not manifest itself in thunderclaps or contrivances. O'Connor also notes that the best American novel with a Catholic setting and theme came from someone who was not Catholic at all: Willa Cather's *Death Comes for the Archbishop*, a Frank O'Malley favorite. One comment in particular must have made the audience glance at Mayor Hynes, who was notably more honest than Curley had been. O'Connor said that we cannot excuse failed "Catholic" fiction any more than we should excuse corrupt Catholic politicians who only create bad government. This analogy sheds an interesting retrospective light on Skeffington. Was O'Connor having second thoughts about the Robin Hood ethics of his protagonist?

In December O'Connor was mentioned in *Time*, but not for work of his own. *Time* ran a cover story on Anne Bancroft for her performance as Annie Sullivan in the Broadway production of William Gibson's *The Miracle Worker*. After a performance O'Connor was quoted as marveling at Anne Bancroft's convincing Irish brogue. (The real Annie Sullivan was actually American-born.) According to Elliot Norton, O'Connor may have been in the audience for another reason: he thinks O'Connor may have dated her.[48] Miss

48. Elliot Norton, personal interview, June 21, 1999. Barbara Burrell cannot confirm Norton's account, but she does remember that her brother once dated Yvonne DeCarlo, whose movie career was making something of a comeback in the mid-1950s.

Bancroft has not replied to an inquiry. O'Connor did save the copy of the December 21 *Time*.

In 1960 the election of his postwar Boston acquaintance to the presidency heartened O'Connor both as a Democrat, although he was not a straight-ticket voter, and as a Catholic, even if he was not an adulator of Catholic politicians. O'Connor was also glad that a native son brought Boston once again into political prominence. In a way, too, Kennedy's election brought the old Massachusetts backwater alive as did no other effort of that time. After that 1960 election, there was no turning back for Boston. The era of Curley was over at last, and his fame, along with that of his fictional counterpart, began to fade from public view.

O'Connor also had his man in the White House in the person of Arthur Schlesinger Jr. The Harvard professor had been a good friend for over ten years, but after Schlesinger assumed his new duties as Kennedy's special assistant for Latin American affairs, the two saw less of each other in both Boston and Wellfleet. Schlesinger was also storing up material for his Pulitzer Prize-winning account of the Kennedy presidency, *A Thousand Days*. Still, it would appear from a lengthy letter Schlesinger wrote on White House stationary that by March 1961 time was heavy on his hands. Schlesinger's letter tries to imitate O'Connor's mimicry, but it does not come off. He says that he was enjoying reading the galleys of his friend's new novel.[49] O'Connor had finished that novel just before Christmas of 1960.

The Edge of Sadness is O'Connor's best novel.[50] When published on June 5, 1961, it was recognized by discerning readers as a significant advance in content and form over *The Last Hurrah*. In control over the material, in emotional richness, and in memorable characterization, O'Connor was at the height of his powers.

His control was achieved by first-person narration, which he had not used since the unsatisfactory "A Young Man of Promise." (O'Connor was wary of that point of view, and yet the sequence of his novels shows a neat alternation of the first person with the third from *The Oracle* to *All in the Family*: counting "A Young Man of Promise," he completed three of each type.) Father Hugh Kennedy may be colorless as a character, but as a narrator he is superb. His colorlessness may be attributed to his self-effacing role as confessor, just as O'Connor himself was known as a sympathetic ear for

49. Arthur Schlesinger Jr., letter to Edwin O'Connor, March 12, 1961, EOCP 240.
50. Edwin O'Connor, *The Edge of Sadness* (Boston: Atlantic Monthly Press/Little, Brown: 1961).

people's troubles. But Hugh's love of old timers' conversation brings to his own storytelling a wonderful artistry, which fortunately avoids the more erratic crab-like moves of the people he describes.

The interplay of emotions and atmospheres in the novel is unlike anything O'Connor ever achieved. From spiritual aridity and filial bitterness to warm friendships and the mystery of God's grace rekindling hope in the breast, O'Connor covers a lot. He is at his best in rendering loneliness, and so when Charlie Carmody announces at his birthday party, *"I'm lonesome"* (O'Connor's emphasis), the most pervasive mood of the book is struck. Besides Charlie's loneliness, there is of course the narrator's own, which forms the substance of the novel. The edges of loneliness also appear in Charlie's son John and daughter Helen, and in an assortment of minor characters like the pathetic religious-goods merchant. This lonesomeness is personal, social, and spiritual. On the personal level, it also reflects O'Connor's own. Indeed, when Ati Forberg saw the title of her former admirer's new novel, she felt it perfectly fit its author's own inner life.[51] In spite of his large and increasing social circles, he had few close friends and even they were rarely taken into his private worlds. Bob Taylor, John Kelleher, Niall Montgomery, Frank O'Malley, and a few more completed this group. The long years of dedication to his writing had left him oddly isolated from the family life which he wrote so much about and in particular from women, who still appear infrequently. While O'Connor was attracted to beautiful, lively women and they to him, his pursuit of excellence even in this area of life had forestalled serious involvement with any particular woman. He was now in his early forties, with a receding hairline and the fixed habits of the single. His friends were resigned to O'Connor as yet another confirmed Irish bachelor.

If O'Connor had created a busy menagerie in *The Last Hurrah*, he carefully scrutinized only a selected few in this next novel. Father Hugh Kennedy's interaction with the Carmodys is the core of the novel. These characters are portrayed in more depth than anyone in *The Last Hurrah*, Skeffington included. Scenes of soul-baring are particularly noteworthy, especially those by Charlie, Helen, and John on separate occasions, all to Father Kennedy, and all of course outside the confessional.

The world of *The Edge of Sadness* is the city again, but as befits a more intensely focused novel about parishes and families, it is a smaller city than Skeffington's. About its politics we know little, in marked contrast to *The*

---

51. Ati Forberg, telephone interviews, March 7, 10, and 31, 2001. O'Connor never saw Ati after 1959, when he learned she was pregnant with her first child. A mutual friend, John Taaffe, noticed that O'Connor abruptly avoided him also, as if he were a reminder of Ati. John Taaffe, telephone interview, May 12, 2001.

Last Hurrah. The one politician presented, Helen's son Ted O'Donnell, is running not for mayor but for Congress, and as a fully certified A.D.A. liberal. Irish American horizons had changed.[52] One indication of the unnamed city's smaller size comes not from its civilian politics but from the Church hierarchy. Instead of a Cardinal as in *The Last Hurrah,* this city only rates a bishop, and even his office seems downsized, perhaps in an oversight by the author, from the archbishopric of his predecessor. It is a very Irish city with very Irish parishes, although significantly Father Kennedy's Old St. Paul's has long since ceased to be one of them. The Irish there had moved out and up to parishes like Saint Raymond's, "where everyone knew everyone else" (28), just as in Joyce's Dublin.

Although this city is smaller than Skeffington's, it still has touches of Boston. Only two pages into the novel we learn that it is a seacoast city from whose roofs can be seen the "muted bluish outlines of the hills far to the north," just what O'Connor could see from his high windows at 48 Beacon Street. Like almost all of his novels, *The Edge of Sadness* begins in O'Connor's favorite season of summer. As in the opening of *The Oracle,* a refreshing east wind with a Boston sharpness has just blown away a heat wave. Old St. Paul's has long been recognized as having its source in Boston's St. James Church on the edge of Chinatown. (The most attentive listener to Father Kennedy's sermons is Mr. Yee, who knows not a word of English.) More importantly, Old St. Paul's is also just two blocks away from Skid Row, again resembling the old "Combat Zone" not far from St. James Church. O'Connor probably got to know of St. James Church during his newspaper days, when it was known as the "church of the printers" because it had a special Sunday Mass to accommodate typesetters from nearby Newspaper Row.

However, in shrinking the city O'Connor has also made it feel less like Boston and more like some other New England city like Portland, Providence—or even, by not too much of a stretch, Woonsocket itself. While Woonsocket is not on the sea, O'Connor definitely had parts of his home town in mind. The rubber factory, the "car barn," the vaudeville theater, the lover's lane on a hill—these and a dozen other details are Woonsocket's as much as Boston's. Hugh revisits his old neighborhood haunts with the same

---

52. It would appear from Father Kennedy's reaction to Ted's endorsement by the A.D.A. that O'Connor too had misgivings about this left wing of the Democratic Party (*ES* 65–66), even though one of its founders in 1947 had been Arthur Schlesinger Jr. (along with Ronald Reagan!). By the late 1950s, the few Catholics in the organization were already questioning some its stances. For a useful history of the organization see Steven M. Gillon, *Politics and Vision: The ADA and American Liberalism, 1947–1985* (New York: Oxford University Press, 1987).

intense nostalgia O'Connor displayed in "A Love Letter to Woonsocket" in 1951. Here Hugh is looking at a section of his boyhood parish:

[W]hen I was a boy, fields had been here: fields, and a dumping ground. Now fields and dump were gone. It had become a residential area for the well-to-do. . . . [H]ere, for example . . . Helen and Frank O'Donnell lived, in one of the more impressive of the comfortable, conservative, semi-stately brick homes (95).

Right down to the old dump, this is O'Connor's old North End neighborhood. The emphasis on the field recalls O'Connor's love of Hoyle's Field. The house could easily be 247 Gaskill Street, and Frank in fact is, like O'Connor's father, a doctor. However, in 1958 during an early draft of *The Edge of Sadness*, O'Connor's widowed mother moved to Providence's East Side to be next to her daughter and son-in-law. 247 Gaskill, which had been the O'Connor homestead since its construction in 1924, was sold. The unusual nostalgia for family and neighborhoods in this novel stems from the fact that O'Connor no longer could return to Woonsocket to touch base. Like Hugh Kennedy, he was now a man without a family at the homestead.

Even more noteworthy than these localities is the structure of the Carmody family. Charlie Carmody is the autocrat in a family which consists of two sons and two daughters. (His wife, like so many of O'Connor's fictional wives and mothers, had died—decades back, in this case.) If we include O'Connor's cousin Pat Greene, who lived with the family for nineteen years and was called by O'Connor a "sister," this configuration of siblings exactly mirrors the author's own family. There was even a young Carmody whose death in infancy recalls the O'Connors' second child in all but gender. Even the birth orders and personalities are parallel to some extent. John Carmody is the older brother, and like Edwin the more serious one. But his burned-out misanthropy lacks O'Connor's saving and abundant sense of humor—fatally so, as it turns out. In a remarkable act of self-exorcism, O'Connor arranges for John's death by the same massive stomach hemorrhage that nearly killed him in 1953: he bleeds out whatever of John Carmody is in him. Brother Dan, younger by four years, is cut from different cloth. He mirrors some of Jack O'Connor's younger-brother syndrome as he spends his life moving from one deal to the next: "Dan had not been a success. All along the line things had suddenly 'gone wrong'" (*ES* 43). Daughters Helen and Mary do not readily correspond to Barbara O'Connor and Pat Greene, but then this is a novel about fathers and sons primarily. Like the O'Connors, Charlie also employs domestic help in the person of Agnes, a "hardy old household dragon." His granddaughter-in-law employs a cook and a nurse for the children. This marks the first time that O'Connor in his new affluence portrays domestics in his novels.

All of this is not to say that *The Edge of Sadness* is "about" the secret life of the O'Connor family, any more than *The Last Hurrah* is "about" James Michael Curley. But writers have long fallen back with varying degrees of intention on their own families and upbringings in order to prime the energies needed to depict that most fundamental arena of human action. Tolstoy, Dickens, Joyce, Lawrence, and Marquand—from whatever nation, religion, or class—the novelists of families so often re-present their own, with varying and complex degrees of nostalgia and misgiving. In having the principal Carmodys "confess" to their old family friend Father Hugh, O'Connor was making some of his own family their stand-ins so that the fierceness of their love and pain could take on a powerful reality.

Charlie Carmody is an Irish Catholic version of *The Last Hurrah*'s Amos Force and Norman Cass Sr. combined. For decades the mean-spirited skinflint stuffed his moneybags as a slum landlord, as the fathers of Hugh Kennedy and his curate so well remember. Two of his obsessions are Roosevelt and especially playgrounds for poor neighborhoods: "And I just don't mean troubles like Roosevelt and his crazy gang with their big taxes, or the city tearin' down half my lovely tenements to build playgrounds for bums" (79). Just as Norman Cass Sr. had resisted loaning the city money for a playground, so too Charlie cannot stand the thought of an urban version of Hoyle's Field for poor kids. Edenic Hoyle's Field lived on in O'Connor's nostalgia as he made it a minimal requirement of social justice for children. Kindly old Mr. Hoyle from his boyhood was a standard for all adults in their dealings with children. O'Connor's models for virtue sprang from actual people, not abstract ideologies for social engineering. Charlie's swipe at Roosevelt (as in *The Last Hurrah*, the only president named in the book) echoes Dr. O'Connor's fulminations against the New Deal and its president.

Father John Carmody is one of O'Connor's most complex characters. He is intelligent, aware, and dedicated to the point of being driven. He can savage an individual parishioner or his whole parish in blistering satirical outbursts to his boyhood friend and seminary classmate, Hugh Kennedy. All his life he has chafed under his father, who simply looks right past him, that is, when he is not playing exasperating games with him. Charlie Carmody had never really given his blessing when his son entered the priesthood, because after the death of Charlie Jr. in infancy John was supposed to succeed to the family business. At his birthday dinner, a long scene covering several chap-

ters and one of O'Connor's best sustained pieces of writing, Charlie goes
public with his displeasure about his surviving sons:

A man works the whole of his life like a slave, buildin' a grand big business up out of
nothin' at all, just so's he can leave it to some one of his sons, and what happens? Nobody wants it. Nobody cares. John packs up and goes off to the seminary, and I
s'pose there's nothin' to be said against that. We got to have priests. Some of my best
friends are priests. But you can't leave a business like mine to a man that lives in a
rectory. And then there's Dan.

Here Charlie closed his eyes, as if the mere remembrance of Dan's various des-
tinies was too much for him (81).

But as with haughty Roger Sugrue in *The Last Hurrah,* no one has ever stood
up to Charlie—no one save Helen, that is, but that was years ago in college.
John's ferocious outburst against his father is saved for Hugh, an outburst in
which Hugh too gets wounded. It is as if O'Connor has created in John a humorless version of himself, complete with all his pent-up resentments, which
finally get bled out, literally. If John's angers are any indication, O'Connor's
may well have been deep and long lasting.

Charlie Carmody is not the only father O'Connor develops, however. As
he sometimes does in his work, he creates another father who is the ideal version. That father is Hugh's own, Dave Kennedy. Just as John Carmody was
Hugh Kennedy's classmate "of my own age, almost to the day" (12), so too
their fathers were the same age, although they were hardly friends. Like Charlie, Dave had been a widower for decades. O'Connor created with these fathers and sons an unusual case, in pairs, of the literary double, a device increasingly discussed by critics in the 1950s and one found in many of
O'Connor's favorite nineteenth-century authors, Dickens and Dostoevsky
chief among them.[53] As Charlie himself says, Dave Kennedy and he were
"born on the same block and in the very same year. . . . There was people
used to take us for twins" (83). Even their surnames—Carmody/Kennedy—
echo each other, especially to the Boston ear. Dave is the antithesis of Charlie.
He is kind, generous in spirit, and much more accurate and honest in his
assessment of people. He is also funny. Like Dr. O'Connor, Dave Kennedy
contracts a lingering disease at just about the same time in the early 1950s, if
my calculations about the book's hazy time structure are correct. Like Dr.
O'Connor he insists on staying in his sickbed at home, and like Dr. O'Connor he enters into a semi-coma. (He eventually dies, unlike Dr. O'Connor, in

---

53. See Karl Miller, *Doubles: Studies in Literary History* (Oxford: Oxford University Press,
1985); Robert Rogers, *A Psychoanalytic Study of the Double in Literature* (Detroit: Wayne
State University Press, 1970).

a hospital. After his coronary Charlie Carmody also remains at home, in long scenes reminiscent of Skeffington's demise at home.) Dave Kennedy's painful death and the spiritual crisis it brings about precipitates Hugh's rapid spiral into alcoholism. Dave's death was instrumental in beginning the story Hugh tells, just as O'Connor began his novel the year after his own father died. Dave Kennedy even has one of Dr. O'Connor's verbal tics: he often ends a sentence with "indeed," as in his standard "Ah, yes, that's a very good point indeed!" (132). In playing off these two fathers against each other, O'Connor was trying out two versions of fatherhood, in which he used elements both attractive and disheartening in his own father. This is would not be the last time he would stage such a contest. At the novel's crux—Hugh's moral dilemma when Charlie, desperate to find one person who liked him, asks Hugh whether Dave Kennedy ever liked him—O'Connor writes that Charlie wanted a "special pat on the back, to be sure: a pat on the back from my dead father. Passed on by the one possible middleman" (367). Hugh, as son and narrator, must negotiate between his dead father and the seriously ill Charlie Carmody, just as O'Connor had to weigh his own versions of fatherhood, which in the end were parts of his own being.

Father Hugh Kennedy is a compendium of several priests O'Connor knew, but he is not any one of them. O'Connor had encountered many priests at Notre Dame, of course, but now he was concerned more with a parish priest who lives closer to families and whose rectory is analogous to a home. Monsignor Francis Lally, editor of the diocesan newspaper from 1948 to 1972 and O'Connor's confessor, was his closest priest friend during this time and his best resource for parish life. Lally shared his love of books with O'Connor. He was bright and quick, had winning ways suffused with good humor. As editor, he turned the *Pilot* into one of the finest diocesan papers in the country. As a civic leader on many committees, especially the powerful Boston Redevelopment Authority which he directed from 1961 to 1970, he was often the only priest many Brahmins knew.[54] In 1962 Little, Brown published his thoughtful little book, *The Catholic Church in a Changing America.* Many priests were impressed with the accuracy of O'Connor's depiction of rectory life in *The Edge of Sadness;* the details owe a good deal to long chats with Monsignor Lally. Even a British Dominican friar was amazed at the faithful portrayal of a priest's life.[55] But O'Connor was also fond of quoting

54. George Ryan, telephone interview, July 21, 2000.
55. Rev. Evans Illtud, O.P., review of *The Edge of Sadness* in *Blackfriars,* October 1962, 101–3.

Henry James's remark that to write of military life, one need only peek through the barracks windows for a few minutes.

Some of Hugh Kennedy may derive from his old Woonsocket pastor and friend, Father Cornelius Holland. In 1943 Holland had been transferred from St. Charles' to a more blue-collar Pawtucket parish, thus tracing in a general way Hugh's move from St. Raymond's to Old St. Paul's. In 1921 Father Holland had published *His Reverence—His Day's Work,* in which "Father Sperinde" (Father Hope) writes thirty short letters to "Prudenzia" (Prudence) about various aspects of priestly life, from raising money to administering the sacraments. More than likely O'Connor had read this book by his old pastor and friend, and he may have even borrowed some of its homely anecdotes and descriptions such as preparations for a bishop's visit or quiet work alone at night in the rectory. Holland's Victorian prose style may have left its impress on O'Connor's. When the witty Philadelphian essayist Agnes Repplier opened her introduction to Holland's book with the statement, "Laymen seldom write successfully about priests," she could even have been a challenge to him.[56] Monsignor Holland's death in 1956 may have triggered memories. Father John McGoey's life on Harbour Island supplied a few details, especially the mice Hugh hears scuttling through the wall on his first night in Old St. Paul's. In *Nor Scrip Nor Shoes* Father McGoey recounts his first day at his mission church, where he was appalled to find that his predecessor had actually cultivated a whole colony of mice.

Lally, Holland, and McGoey were not alcoholics. But there was no shortage of such priests in the Boston archdiocese; every parishioner had at least heard of them. Not a few Irish Catholic households discreetly kept "Father's bottle" in the china closet for visits from the unfortunate man. The one who comes closest to anything like Father Kennedy was Monsignor Lally's predecessor as editor of the *Pilot,* Father Francis P. Moran. A talented enough man and something of a specialist in Eastern liturgies, Father Moran became jaded and burned out in midlife. Some years later O'Connor visited him as he was dying in a hospital. When O'Connor asked the patient if he could get anything for him, Father Moran asked for bon-bons. O'Connor drove around to several stores before finding the chocolates.[57]

O'Connor knew several tipplers: Sam Lawrence at *Atlantic,* Arthur Thornhill at Little, Brown, and of course Frank O'Malley at Notre Dame. Sometimes these men were drawn to the abstemious younger man because

56. Rev. Cornelius J. Holland, S.T.L., *His Reverence—His Day's Work* (New York: Benziger, 1921).

57. George Ryan, letter to author, July 18, 2000.

they appreciated his clear-eyed view of the world, and they knew he would not be censorious. The one who gave him the most private pain, however, was his old professor, to whom he owed so much. By the time O'Connor started on *The Edge of Sadness,* he had seen O'Malley's advanced alcoholism twice, once in May 1955 and again in October 1956. He continued his annual October visits right through the writing of the novel, or four more times. When the book was published the dedication page said simply: "For Frank O'Malley."

And he even put him in the book. In a remarkable ploy, O'Connor created a minor character who was undoubtedly meant to be recognized by O'Malley as himself. When Father Kennedy is sent to the Cenacle, a center for alcoholic priests in Arizona, he meets there the sad case of a frequent recidivist:

He was a small, pale man with a fragile and strangely gay face; he must have been more than fifty, but there was about him such a persistently youthful air that he might have been in his thirties. Each time he came back he was a washed-out, shaking ruin, but he had an astonishing ability to recover. . . . I talked with him often; never once did he admit to being an alcoholic (148–49).

In almost all respects, this is a sketch of Frank O'Malley. For the next six pages O'Connor develops this minor character, and to make sure O'Malley got the message, he mentions that the priest had been posted to five different places, among them South Bend. O'Connor all but gives O'Malley's campus address at Lyons Hall. O'Connor's final private clue for O'Malley comes when the backsliding priest mentions Claudel's *Le Soulier Satin.* Claudel was one of O'Malley's favorite authors, and in 1959 O'Connor had in fact joked in a letter to him from Harbour Island that he was working on a musical version of *Le Soulier Satin.*[58] All the clues were there for O'Malley to pick up. Clearly, O'Connor was throwing his mentor a lifeline in the best way he could and in a manner O'Malley might appreciate, through a work of literature. Frank O'Malley, like that forlorn priest and like so many alcoholics, would not recognize his problem. When Hugh leaves the Cenacle (he stayed there four years, an unusual length of time, but it does exactly correspond to O'Connor's college years with O'Malley), he thinks of the sad man:

I pray for him regularly, as I'm sure many others . . . do: he's not a man who's difficult to pray for. I hope he's all right, and that wherever he is or wherever he goes someone will be found to take a little care of him now and then, to occasionally do for this poor, engaging, bright-faced wanderer what another man, not necessarily any

58. Edwin O'Connor, letter to Frank O'Malley, February 17, 1959, Frank O'Malley Papers, University of Notre Dame Archives, CFOM 26/06.

better, but maybe just a little more prudent, or even a little more selfish, would by instinct do for himself (154–55).

There is no record that O'Malley recognized himself; in any event there was
no rupture with O'Connor. In 1965 O'Malley did spend six harrowing weeks
at a hospital for alcoholics, but he soon returned to the habit that killed him
in 1974.[59]

Some naive readers of *The Edge of Sadness,* incidentally, formed the hasty
conclusion that O'Connor must have been an alcoholic to write so convincingly about the condition. It comes as quite a surprise when these people are
informed that Edwin O'Connor never drank in his life. It was simply the
case that O'Connor did not advertise his abstemiousness, and so some people never noticed it.

Father Danowski's name may come from a Boston College catalogue, but
his character, one of O'Connor's masterly portraits, very likely stemmed
from a young Polish American priest named Father Matthew Strumski, who
ministered to Dr. O'Connor in his final illness. O'Connor liked the priest in
spite of his prosaic stolidity.[60] The bishop's "severe and autocratic" predecessor, Archbishop Gartland (114), is an inside joke on one of O'Connor's
Boston friends, Arthur Gartland. He was a sociology instructor at Notre
Dame when O'Connor studied there, and now headed Action for Boston
Community Development (ABCD). Roy, the mixed-race janitor-handyman
at Old St. Paul's, may derive from Father McGoey's mission compound in
the Bahamas. Roy's evasive fantasies belong to a type recognized by anyone
familiar with hangers-on at mission stations in the West Indies. A tip-off
here is his Christmas gift of a worn leather key case for Father Kennedy. Roy
claims it was once owned by the Duke of Windsor, King Edward VIII of ab-
dication fame. A mystifying infatuation with the British royals and their
downfalls was widespread in the British West Indies.

The Edge of Sadness is a convincing exploration of Irish family mores, a
thoughtful tract for the changing times in the Catholic Church on the eve of
the Second Vatican Council, and a moving account of a humble man's twilight of the soul. Avoiding Waugh's baroque excesses about Britain's recusant
elites in *Brideshead Revisited,* and refraining from the whiskey-priest's tor-
tured ambiguities in Greene's *The Power and the Glory,* the novel works out
the progression of Hugh Kennedy's soul in a quieter middle-class milieu.

59. Meaney, O'Malley, 206.
60. Burrell, interview. In a telephone interview, June 16, 2001, Father Strumski could not
recall specifically ministering to Dr. O'Connor, but he did admit that it was highly likely; he
does remember coming to the house and meeting Barbara and Edwin.

There are few spiritual histrionics, and certainly none of the Hollywood version of muscular Catholicism that Hugh scorns. Precisely because O'Connor was not a visual novelist, note should be taken of the few arresting images that do occur. One of these, early in the novel, stands as a metaphor for O'Connor's sense of God's grace. When Hugh gives John Carmody the "grand tour" of Old St. Paul's, O'Connor ends one important paragraph thus: "We could hear nothing, and for the first few moments all we could see were dim outlines, the dull red glow of the sanctuary lamp, and, spearing its way across the nave, one single thin shoot of sunlight which came in through a broken stained-glass pane" (28). This muted Caravaggio moment captures the atmosphere of the novel, in which the light of God's grace quietly enters a murky world in unexpected ways and where His Real Presence is abiding.

O'Connor saved three small stenographer's notebooks in which he had made jottings for the novel.[61] These notebooks usually accompanied him on travels or to the beach. What strikes one who studies these notebooks is that O'Connor had to *hear* a character's voice before he could get on with it and write it up. For example, there is a much-worked-over sketch of Father Danowski in which O'Connor is obviously trying to get his voice down to his own satisfaction. At other times he would write a lead-in sentence, such as "The rectory is quiet," several times with slight alterations and embellishments, but in different handwriting, as if to try out the moods of the place. The two manuscripts of the novel reveal nothing of importance; the printer's copy contains mostly small corrections and one unimportant shift of dialogue from one scene to another. O'Connor tired of reading the galleys half way through, and sent them back to Atlantic Monthly Press for someone else to do.[62] The title for the novel only came to him very late, just as he was finishing it. "Edge" was probably meant to be taken primarily as the thin edge of the wedge, as seen in this passage when Father Kennedy thinks of a social invitation "as some sort of thin edge of the wedge. . . . I was not exactly wedge-proof; I knew my own vulnerability" (264).

The book's dust cover was a brown background with white lettering, in the same plain format as *The Last Hurrah* and with no illustration. An impish photo by Hans Namuth appeared on the back. The five dollar price was up a dollar since his last novel five years before.

Once again O'Connor's novel was a main Book-of-the-Month Club selection. Charlie Morton wrote a sketch of his friend for the club's June 1961

61. EOCP 54.
62. Edwin O'Connor, untitled speech discussing his work, 1961?, EOCP 50.

newsletter, in which he emphasized O'Connor's integrity as a writer, as well as his privacy. Morton revealed that after working on his novel for a year, O'Connor started it all over in the spring of 1958. Sports car enthusiast that he was, Morton could not resist mentioning O'Connor's Porsche. *The Edge of Sadness* was also a selection of the Catholic Book Club, the Thomas More Book Club, and the Catholic Literary Foundation. It also became a Reader's Digest Condensed Book.[63]

The *Boston Globe's* reviewer gave the novel a good write-up on June 4, as did the *Herald's* on the same day. No large claims were made for the novel. It was clear that *The Edge of Sadness* was not going to be a publishing phenomenon like *The Last Hurrah*. There were few feature stories. The title never became a catchword like "the last hurrah." The *Boston Herald* Sunday magazine did run a special feature by Clifton Fadiman, along with an extended "bookcerpt" from the novel.

As he had done five years earlier for *The Last Hurrah*, John Kelleher once again wrote the lead review in the *New York Times Book Review*. He calls the "dark and funny novel" not just the definitive novel of Irish American middle-class life, but an important work about God's mysterious grace. He correctly sees that Hugh Kennedy is the main character, but unfortunately the review ends abruptly, before Kelleher can flesh out his thesis.[64] The next day Orville Prescott wrote a follow-up review in the same newspaper. Although he found O'Connor's characters well done, he does find Charlie Carmody tiresome by the end—an understandable reaction. Prescott is the only commentator, by the way, who suspects that Providence may be the locale as much as Boston; he came close to discovering Woonsocket.[65] Over at the *Herald Tribune*, novelist Morris L. West, an Irish Australian, wrote in praise of the "strangely elegiac book" by "an artist of integrity and a craftsman of singular accomplishment." A short passage reveals West's unusual take on the novel:

Its small cast of personages are caught in that *accidia* of middle-age when, for all the high-piled logic of doctrine, for all the assiduous practice of rule and piety, the spirit moves in a twilight of uncertainty, believing desperately in a designing providence, yet forced inexorably towards the final, bleak understanding that the act of faith is, and always must be, a leap into the gathering dark.[66]

The Saturday Review put O'Connor on its cover again, this time a different Hans Namuth informal photo. Granville Hicks gave the novel a favorable

63. Rank, *O'Connor*, 120.
64. "Curious Indeed the Way God Works," *New York Times Book Review*, June 4, 1961, 1.
65. *New York Times*, June 5, 1961, 29.
66. *New York Herald Tribune*, Book Review Section, June 3, 1961, 23.

review, but like many others he errs in calling Charlie Carmody the main character, although he does recognize the importance of Father Kennedy's change.[67] As he had done with *The Last Hurrah,* Gouverneur Paulding of *The Reporter* gave one of the best notices. His last paragraph is worth quoting:

Of course what gives [the novel] depth is the author's awareness that these people live beneath the eye of God. The truth is simply that all lives are of considerably more interest when they are related to a system, any system, that provides a standard of immensity against which to measure them. The system can be Hardy's, somber and disheartening, in which man is despairingly alone beneath the stars. It can also be—why not?—the poetics of Christianity. That is the system Mr. O'Connor employs and it works quite well.[68]

John Kenneth Galbraith wrote a humorous review which upsets with Shavian paradoxes the received version of recent Irish American history. Farm-born, Presbyterian, Ontario immigrant, Harvard professor, Galbraith had just been appointed ambassador to India by Irish American President John Kennedy, which was exactly Galbraith's point: the Irish had thoroughly arrived. Galbraith calls O'Connor the "leading prophet of the acculturation of the Irish." He ignores the religious theme. Galbraith finds that O'Connor's conflict now has shifted from Irish vs. Yankee to Irish vs. Irish, a burden they are always capable of bearing. He thinks Hugh Kennedy's alcoholism unconvincing. While not much happens, O'Connor has made an interesting tale out of "slender" materials. The remarkable thing about this favorable review is its appearance in *The New Yorker,* which finally printed some good words about the Boston author.[69]

The novel got a generally warm reception in the American Catholic press, which was maturing rapidly at that time. Had O'Connor published his novel about an alcoholic priest just a decade earlier, when Greene published his controversial *The End of the Affair,* he would have met with some cries of treason for airing dirty rectory laundry. For some reason, however, the widely read Jesuit magazine *America* did not accord *The Edge of Sadness* a full review, and granted it only a brief but complimentary notice in its roundup of Christmas books on November 25, where the ascending star of Walker Percy was described more warmly. In *Commonweal* Thomas Curley called the novel a good improvement over weaknesses of structure and character in *The Last Hurrah.* He makes two incisive points. First, he correctly notes that Father John Carmody's outburst to Hugh about the maddening, meander-

67. "Behind the Lace Curtains," *The Saturday Review,* June 10, 1961, 20.
68. "A Priest's Return," *The Reporter,* June 22, 1961, 48.
69. "Sadness in Boston," *The New Yorker,* June 24, 1961, 87–94; reprinted in Galbraith's *A Contemporary Guide to Economics, Peace and Laughter* (Boston: Houghton Mifflin, 1971).

ing conversation of the old Irish is an attack on O'Connor's own interests and methods, and that is precisely poor John's problem. He cannot lighten up and connect with that Irish world of pre-Enlightenment discourse as convoluted as designs in the Book of Kells. Curley's second point was an interesting challenge to O'Connor. He argues that in his studious avoidance of autobiographical fiction, O'Connor puts too much distance between himself and his characters, and thus lets them off too easily by not demanding more of them.[70] That avoidance of autobiographical fiction is debatable, as this chapter suggests, but the problem of O'Connor enjoying his characters overmuch has some weight. O'Connor could get away with excusing the deeds of a Frank Skeffington, but he cannot do that so easily with a Charlie Carmody.

Time and *Newsweek* split this time over O'Connor. *Time*'s reviewer found the motivation unconvincing at many points. (The reviewer also failed to get some facts straight.) Furthermore, the long relationship between Charlie Carmody and Hugh Kennedy is dragged out with little to show in the end. The reviewer was pointing up a notoriously difficult problem in novels like this: just how does one dramatize a spiritual conversion convincingly? O'Connor does rush things at this crucial point, just as Flannery O'Connor—*pace* her admirers—often did in her work, and it is easy to miss the moment of insight and grace. *Time*'s reviewer was closer than he realized to something else when he said that the Carmodys reminded him faintly of the Tyrone family in O'Neill's *Long Day's Journey Into Night*.[71] *Newsweek*, by contrast, gave one of the most glowing reviews of the book and author: "the funniest man writing novels in this country." But that funny man had his "arresting seriousness" too. The reviewer, who had interviewed O'Connor at 48 Beacon Street, lets O'Connor have the last word: "[W]e're all made in the image of God. In humanistic terms, I suppose you would put it that we're all co-operating in some great enterprise in which every drop of charity you can feel or give spreads and multiplies more than you can imagine."[72] This was a rare statement by O'Connor on his theological and novelistic aims, and the anonymous reviewer/interviewer must have been talented indeed to open up the author.

O'Connor received far less fan mail for his new novel than for *The Last Hurrah*. Many readers were apparently expecting a sequel to that novel, and

70. "An Irish-American Middle-Class World," *Commonweal*, June 16, 1961, 306–7.
71. "Something About the Irish," *Time*, June 6, 1961, 90.
72. "Meet Old Charlie," *Newsweek*, June 5, 1961, 95.

so a common reaction of the time was that *The Edge of Sadness* was disappointing in its seriousness. Many of these readers forgot how serious *The Last Hurrah* had been, especially as it ended. One reader who took a special professional interest was his editor, Peggy Yntema. Midway in the writing O'Connor may have become unsure of himself, and so he had given her a large portion of the manuscript for her appraisal. She wrote him a personal letter in which she assures him that the first-person point of view is managed well. She exalts the book's characterization, its "autumnal, elegiac mood," and its adroit balancing of the cast. Most remarkably, she as an "outsider" found the novel's presentation of God's presence unique in fiction, more powerful even than in *The Brothers Karamazov.* High praise indeed, and she still maintains this position. She had misgivings over the book's pace, but did not elaborate. Also, she did not quite "feel" the presence of the narrator, although Hugh did have a memorable voice.[73] At least two Protestants wrote to praise the book's affirmative vision. And two famous names wrote complimentary letters. Katharine Hepburn was deeply touched by the book: "Your people *will* haunt me," she wrote.[74] Robert Lowell said that he read the novel "in two long gulps, a day and a night." He found it hard to believe that O'Connor was not a reformed alcoholic. His favorite part was when the "sour priest" died: "Like Dante your Hell is more human than your Heaven." He ends with an unfinished enigma: "Great courage and endurance in not letting you [sic] big talent." Lowell's letter was to "Dear Ed" and he signed with his nickname "Cal." Boston's most famous poet was not known to be a friend of O'Connor; Lowell's several biographers do not mention the novelist. But when "Cal" said that he hoped to see O'Connor soon, we can assume that these two Beacon Hill residents probably knew each other from social gatherings and the Athenaeum. Lowell was of course a fascinating interpreter of Boston himself, especially in poems like "For the Union Dead," in which the Civil War Negro Regiment casts a long shadow over Boston in the early 1960s.

The Edge of Sadness went through several printings and editions in both hardcover and paperback. It made the bestseller lists, but never went as high or for so long as *The Last Hurrah.* There was some talk of stage versions and a film. Karl Malden, who had played a memorable priest in *On the Waterfront,* once had an option.[75] On December 3, 1962, O'Connor recorded two

73. Peggy Yntema, letter to Edwin O'Connor, October 6, 1959, EOCP 270; personal interview, April 10, 1999.

74. Katharine Hepburn, letter to Edwin O'Connor, April 22, 1962?, EOCP 162.

75. Burrell, interview.

sections of the novel. The first is from a scene in which Hugh ruminates in his rectory (101–11), the second when we are introduced to Father Danowski (19–24). O'Connor kept the Carmodys out of the recording. *The Edge of Sadness* had been long out of print when Father Andrew Greeley, an admirer of O'Connor's book and a novelist himself, generously helped in a reprinting by the Thomas More Press in 1990, for which he wrote a short introduction. This edition too is now out of print.

CHAPTER ELEVEN

✣ Annus Mirabilis
(1962)

In October 1961 O'Connor took his customary trip to Notre Dame, where he gave an informal, untitled talk on his work.[1] He was in a retrospective mood, but except for the mystery of the purloined sweater in his senior year, he ruled out nostalgic indulgence in the "good old days" of his alma mater. While talking modestly about the success of *The Last Hurrah,* he alluded to *The Late George Apley* and hoped that he was not destined to be hung like John P. Marquand in that American gallery of one-book authors. He did think that *The Edge of Sadness* was a better novel, because it dug more deeply; that novel would always be his favorite. About the future he was uncertain. He revealed no plans and was in no hurry simply to make money. He concluded: "A serious writer writes primarily not because this is his way of making a living, but because this is his way of *living.*" (O'Connor's emphasis). It was all "a gift from God."

He was also plainly tired. At the outset he talked openly of fatigue from the four years of steady work on *The Edge of Sadness,* and of his inability to finish proofing the galleys. He also hinted at feeling older than his years. As noted earlier, O'Connor began to show signs of aging in his late thirties, and the process only accelerated throughout his forties. Part of the reason was the recurrent stomach problem. Later in 1961 he had a portion of his stomach removed in an effort to contain the ulcer. The operation was successful, but O'Connor still had to be wary of his diet. Some visitors to his hospital room remember seeing a striking blonde with him. . . .

Earlier that year Wheaton College, then a small women's college about thirty miles south of Boston, had invited O'Connor to join its faculty. Once again the academy opened its doors to O'Connor, and once again he stayed outside. The college then offered the position to Bob Taylor, O'Connor's friend from his newspaper days. Taylor took the po-

---

1. Untitled speech at Notre Dame discussing his work, EOCP 50. Although the manuscript is undated, from internal evidence 1961 seems the best year.

sition in September and taught there until his retirement in the mid-1990s. During most of these years he also wore his other hats as book editor and art critic at the *Boston Globe.*[2]

O'Connor took a delayed trip to Harbour Island in February 1962. He had not been down to the Bahamas in two years; the previous year he had taken a West Coast trip instead. He wrote his mother that the weather was wonderful for swimming and that he was "at last working well."[3] This may be the first indication that his next work, *I Was Dancing,* was under way. He sounded renewed.

The first prodigious event of the year came on late Monday afternoon, May 7, 1962. O'Connor was driving down to his summer home, probably for the first time that season. Just as he entered Wellfleet he was listening to the 5:00 news.[4] The Pulitzer Prize awards were to be announced, so O'Connor pulled off the road and listened intently. When he heard that his good friend Abe Burrows got the drama award for *How to Succeed in Business Without Really Trying,* O'Connor said quietly to himself, "Good for Abe." Then for the fiction award he heard the name "Edwin O'Connor" and said, "Good for me."[5]

At 5:34 Columbia University's President Grayson Kirk sent a telegram to O'Connor's Beacon Street address: "I HAVE THE HONOR TO ADVISE THAT COLUMBIA UNIVERSITY TRUSTEES HAVE AWARDED YOU THE PULITZER PRIZE IN FICTION FOR 'THE EDGE OF SADNESS.'"[6] The same day Kirk sent a letter formally announcing that the award was given for "distinguished fiction published in book form during the year by an American author."[7] The award then carried a cash payment of five hundred dollars.

The money hardly mattered to O'Connor, but the award itself was immensely prestigious. (It was also the first time a Bostonian had won a Pulitzer for fiction since Marquand for *The Late George Apley* in 1938.) Many people thought that O'Connor had been unfairly denied the award back in 1957. Now many believed that the 1962 award was actually a retrospective one for *The Last Hurrah.* Similar comments were heard that same year when John Steinbeck received the Nobel Prize. There was also some grumbling that both awards were undeserved.

2. Robert Taylor, personal interview, April 5, 1999.
3. Edwin O'Connor, letter to Mrs. Mary Greene O'Connor, February 9, 1962, EOCP 215.
4. Jonathan Klarfeld, "We All Loved Ed," *Boston Sunday Globe,* March 24, 1968, 1.
5. Abe Burrows, *Honest Abe: Is There Really No Business Like Show Business?* (Boston: Atlantic Monthly Press/Little, Brown, 1980), 325.
6. Grayson Kirk, telegram to Edwin O'Connor, May 7, 1962, EOCP 115.
7. Grayson Kirk, letter to Edwin O'Connor, May 7, 1962, EOCP 116.

Congratulatory telegrams and letters arrived throughout the following days. From the serious to the leg-pull variety, a common note was that the award was well deserved and overdue. One letter was from Niall Montgomery, who begs his friend to visit, with the implication that O'Connor had not been over in a while. He closed with a "Niallogism": "Come and see us Ed before we fall for the grim reaper's scythe-splitting gags."[8]

Just prior to May 7, O'Connor had received the National Catholic Literary Award for 1962. When interviewed by the diocesan newspaper at her home in Providence's East Side, O'Connor's mother said that all the good news was the "best Mother's Day present possible."[9] O'Connor's first teacher of reading swelled with justifiable pride.

And there was still more that month. On May 24, O'Connor was formally presented a Distinguished Achievement Award and a check for $2,000 from the National Institute of Arts and Letters. The citation, delivered by the Institute's president, Malcolm Cowley, read in part: "To Edwin O'Connor . . . who has already shown, in three novels, an unusual range of perception and understanding; and whose uncompromising but generously comedic handling of satire makes an even brighter promise for the future."[10] At the annual New York ceremony, jointly held with the stuffy American Academy of Arts and Letters, Rhode Island was well represented among the seven honorees: the only poet to be recognized that year was Pawtucket's own Galway Kinnell; the novelist John Hawkes, a Brown University professor, also received an award. The Irish were certainly in evidence: Edwin O'Connor, Galway Kinnell, and Frank O'Connor, who had lived in the States for most of the 1950s, all basked. They were in the company of William Faulkner (who died suddenly a few weeks later) and Boston's Samuel Eliot Morison, both of whom received gold awards. Aldous Huxley gave an address, "Utopias, Positive and Negative." It was a heady night for O'Connor.

Even though O'Connor had no family left in Woonsocket, he still returned occasionally to see old friends and stroll along Main Street. On one of these trips, two days before the Pulitzer announcement, he granted an interview to a La Salle Academy junior named Richard Potenza from his own hometown. The two had lunch at the Howard Johnson's in Park Square and talked for an hour. "Boy, was I ever honored," Potenza gushed. "Edwin O'Connor is the most affable and interesting person I have ever met."[11] The

8. Niall Montgomery, letter to Edwin O'Connor, May 11, 1962, EOCP 199.

9. Undated clipping from *The Visitor*, May ?, 1962.

10. National Institute of Arts and Letters, program and award citation, May 24, 1962, EOCP 205.

11. "O'Connor Here on Saturday to Grant Student Interview," *Woonsocket Call*, May 8, 1962.

interview, "Prominent Alumnus," appeared in La Salle's student newspaper in June. Mostly, O'Connor reminisced about his days at the high school. He said that *The Edge of Sadness* was waiting for filming but did not elaborate. The student took note of O'Connor's new Mercedes. At a Communion breakfast at Providence's Sheraton-Biltmore hotel later in the year O'Connor was inducted into the La Salle Academy Alumni Hall of Fame, along with a prominent surgeon and the auxiliary bishop of Providence.

O'Connor took time out from all the honors to write one of his infrequent book reviews. For obvious reasons, he had been asked by the *New York Times* to review John Henry Cutler's *Honey Fitz,* a biography of John F. Fitzgerald. To O'Connor this colorful Boston mayor and Curley opponent was one of a "handful of picturesque and, today, barely credible figures who dominated Boston politics during the first half of this century." In his review O'Connor accuses the tone-deaf Cutler of writing hagiography: "Is this the first citizen of Dorchester? Or of Assisi?" Curiously, however, he lambastes Cutler for softening Fitzgerald, as when Cutler claims that his subject avoided coarse language; that in general is how O'Connor metamorphosed Curley into Skeffington. In the best tradition of Irish suspicion, O'Connor speculates that Cutler wrote with "one eye . . . on the White House," which was then occupied, of course, by John Fitzgerald's grandson. (By an odd irony, Cutler had been "research" assistant, a.k.a. ghost writer, for old Kennedy foe James Michael Curley on *I'd Do It Again.*) The subtext of O'Connor's review appears to be: I did this so much better in a novel.[12]

O'Connor savored the momentous month in his customary quiet manner. Besides, he had something more important on his mind.

The second prodigious event that year was Veniette.

Around women O'Connor had always been on the shy side. Fitting the profile of the oldest male in the Irish family, he had been studious and dutiful—a marked contrast to his younger brother, who was all for parties and girls. In fact, over the years a rumor has spread that O'Connor once contemplated the priesthood, but his sister is sure that O'Connor never was serious in that direction. His family never pressured him, either. He may have written about priests, but that is as far as it went. O'Connor had the barest of financial prospects for sixteen years after college. His pursuit of women was irregular and was mostly conducted on the Cape. By 1961, as Arthur Schlesinger puts it, "Ed's friends had come to suppose him an incorrigible Irish bache-

12. Edwin O'Connor, "Boston Was His Bailiwick," review of *Honey Fitz,* by John Henry Cutler, *New York Times Book Review,* May 27, 1962, 5.

lor."[13] With the possible exception of the friend of his college days named Jean, it seems that few women pursued O'Connor either, although many were initially attracted to him. His reserved manner and his fixed ways were barriers which few seemed willing to surmount. And of course there was the well-known difficulty of living with a writer, a creature known to inhabit his own world for hours on end, all the while living inside the same walls as his partner in life.

O'Connor was courtly and considerate with women. He had been raised and educated in a culture that still paid some homage to the ethos of the "Catholic gentleman." This ideal, a product of centuries of intertwining the Christian view of love and marriage with the conduct required by chivalry, had been spread in an attenuated form by middle-class mores in the Victorian age. James Joyce depicted the notion foundering on the rocks of illogic when Stephen Dedalus's elders tell him to be a gentleman above all things and a good Catholic above all things. In immigrant America, Victorian class ideals had a long run in certain assimilated sectors, ironically even among Irish Americans. A version of the gentleman's code entailing proper respect for women was enunciated widely in Catholic middle-class life until the 1960s, when the code lost its coherence. By temperament and training O'Connor was the last of a line in the particular form of this courtesy shown to women.

Needless to say, courtliness does not always win fair lady. A certain ardor is required, but O'Connor withheld himself too much, and as a consequence he usually failed to take an assertive role. On top of this was the inevitable egoism of the writer who must see the world from his perspective. Additionally, he was the pampered oldest son of a doting Irish American mother. Finally, notwithstanding his public verbal exuberance, many of O'Connor's friends detected an underlying stratum of melancholy, one that surfaces most in *The Edge of Sadness*. This melancholy was certainly not clinical, but these edges of sadness and nostalgia could have been an obstacle for some women.

And then into the incorrigible bachelor's life came Veniette Caswell Weil. No one knows much about how O'Connor met Veniette (pronounced "Ven-*eat*").[14] The very fact that he apparently told few people says something

13. Schlesinger, Introduction to *BL*, 21–22.

14. For reminiscences about Veniette, I am especially indebted to Stephen Weil, Barbara O'Connor Burrell, and Marian Schlesinger; and also to Ruth Bourke, Peter Davison, Jean DeGiacomo, Nina Holton, John Kelleher, James Montgomery, Rose Mary O'Brien, Beatrice O'Connor, Vita Petersen, Arthur Schlesinger Jr., Robert Taylor, Helen Miranda Wilson, and Peggy Yntema. An obituary in the *Boston Globe* on September 12, 1978, was also useful.

about his sense of privacy. It would seem his privacy was respected. All that can be gathered from relatives, friends, and associates is that they met during the summer of 1961 in Wellfleet, where Veniette had summered for a few years. One scenario has them meeting at a party in Edmund Wilson's blue house on Route 6. Vita Petersen recalls that in the late summer of 1961 O'Connor told her that he had just met a stunning blonde; it seems that as Veniette was packing her car to return home from summer vacation, her dalmatian ran off and was captured and returned by O'Connor.[15] Others remember seeing her at his bedside in Boston's Deaconess Hospital after the stomach surgery for ulcers in the fall.

Their "coming out" as a couple occurred in the summer of 1962, after a brief courtship and engagement. One afternoon, to the great surprise and delight of all, O'Connor nervously showed up at Sinkler Beach, books in hand as usual, with a blonde in a big straw hat. She was clearly his junior by some years. Those not of the Irish persuasion have difficulty understanding the excruciating embarrassment during this transition in the life of a sensitive Irish son. So much in that son's life militates against such a moment in the sun. Since O'Connor was turning forty-four that summer, his discomfort must have been all the more acute. But O'Connor's friends warmly accepted Veniette into the tight little circle on the beach. They understood immediately that the two were very much in love. (Around this time O'Connor was invited to the White House by his old Boston friend John F. Kennedy, but he declined because he had an important date with Veniette. Loyalties in the right order were carefully valued by O'Connor.) He felt enormous relief in surviving this introduction of Veniette to his friends. He had also driven over to Providence with his fiancee and introduced to his mother the first woman he had ever brought home. Apparently he survived this hurdle too. But there was one prior hurdle which O'Connor had also methodically cleared.

O'Connor's future wife was born in 1925 as Veniette Caswell in Waltham, just west of Boston. Her father's people were Nova Scotian, her mother's French Canadian. Veniette's father was a jack-of-all-trades, engraving chief among them. Her home life was not happy, and a few years at a parochial school left some scars. The fact that she was valedictorian of her Waltham High School class is an early sign of her intelligence and a desire to move up high. She won a scholarship to Tufts University in nearby Medford, where she majored in government. After that she received a masters in political science from the University of Tennessee and was awarded the university's first

15. Vita Petersen, personal interview, June 10, 2001.

fellowship in history. In spite of her academic accomplishments, most people did not find her particularly intellectual, and around talking heads she usually remained on the sidelines, much like O'Connor himself. After Tennessee she moved to Washington to work for the Democratic National Committee as a campaign organizer in Maryland's sixth congressional district. Later she was executive secretary of the National Council on Agricultural Life and Labor, and was an assistant to the publications director of the Carnegie Endowment for International Peace. Her pronounced liberal views once got her arrested at a hotel in Washington, when she insisted on having a drink at the whites-only bar with a black man.

In her Georgetown neighborhood there lived a physicist named George Leon Weil, who had worked with Enrico Fermi on the Manhattan Project in Chicago and Los Alamos. For some time George Weil had noticed through the window of his basement apartment a snappy pair of legs taking someone to work. One day he approached Veniette at the bus stop. He had been married briefly before, and was nineteen years her senior, but he pursued her relentlessly and wore her down in the end. Against her better judgment Veniette married George Weil in a civil ceremony in December 1950. They were living in Cabin John, Maryland, when their only child, Stephen, was born in March 1952.

The marriage was a failure from the start. George Weil was an aloof and cerebral man, and the age difference with his wife hardly helped. After a divorce in 1960 Veniette lived with her son in Washington and summered on the Cape. She once dated Daniel Patrick Moynihan when he was beginning his long career in the capital. According to her son, O'Connor wanted to be introduced to her when he learned in the summer of 1961 that she was divorced. How long he had been eyeing her before this is unknown.

Herein lay the biggest hurdle of all for O'Connor. Veniette was not only divorced, she had been raised as a Catholic, although she was hardly a practicing one. In a classic case of an author's life following his art, O'Connor was now almost in the position of one of his own characters, Kevin Rowan from "A Young Man of Promise," written some ten years earlier. In that unpublished novel Kevin had to wrestle with his Catholicism and his heart, as well as with his father. O'Connor had fudged that outcome, but now he had a real heart's desire to consult even as he endeavored to adhere faithfully to his religion. He wasted no time. If he was reticent about the circumstances of meeting Veniette, he carefully let it be known to several friends and family that he would never have gone ahead with the marriage if the Church would not countenance it. There was a way, and he had a well-placed friend in his confessor, Monsignor Francis Lally. Accordingly, Lally greased the diocesan bureaucratic wheels. In the end, the problem was not particularly difficult. Since Veniette had married outside the Church, that marriage was not recognized by the Church in the first place. These legalistic ecclesiastical entanglements did not sit well with Veniette, because she assumed, erroneously, that the outcome would make her son an illegitimate child. But she put aside any private resentment.

When O'Connor took out a marriage license in Boston's old City Hall on August 16, 1962, it may have been his first time inside the building Mayor Curley had occupied for sixteen years. Obviously tipped off by a City Hall clerk, Boston newspapers ran the story the next day; they noted that O'Connor could not be reached for comment. O'Connor phoned John Kelleher and said, "I'm going to tell you something. And I don't want any comment. I am going to get married." When Kelleher gasped, "Holy God!" O'Connor snapped back, "I said I didn't want any comment." He was taking Irish male reticence about romance to new lengths.

Edwin and Veniette were joined in matrimony on Sunday, September 2, 1962, in a chapel of the Cathedral of the Holy Cross in Boston.[16] He was seven years older than the thirty-seven-year-old Veniette. Officiating were Monsignor Lally and Father Francis Moran, both important to the making of *The Edge of Sadness.* O'Connor's brother was the best man, and his sister Barbara the maid of honor. Instead of the customary nuptial Mass, there was only a five-minute ceremony. This arrangement, doubtlessly unsatisfactory to the devout O'Connor, was probably the best he could get out of Veniette, who was not prepared to start practicing her religion again. There were only ten invited guests.

O'Connor's light summer suit made his deep tan stand out. Veniette wore a white turban hat with a light veil halfway down her face—a concession to tradition. But as if to defy the veil, her white wool suit sported a faintly incongruous leopard trim at the collar. After the couple paused for press photographs on the cathedral steps, Veniette had to run through the rain to O'Connor's waiting car. The small group adjourned to the Ritz for a quiet celebration. Abe Burrows sent nonsense verse concerning the "point" that the O'Connors were "joint."[17] The newlyweds took a wedding trip to Vermont.

It might seem that the marriage was off to an uncertain start. The wonder is that it turned out to be a happy one for both, to everyone's joy. O'Connor told friends that he could not believe his luck in marrying Veniette. She in

16. Much of the following information about the wedding comes from an unidentified newspaper clipping, dated by hand September 2, 1962.
17. Abe Burrows, "I'm an Optimist," EOCP 107.

Edwin and Veniette on the steps of Holy Cross Cathedral, shortly after their wedding on September 2, 1962. *Courtesy of Boston Public Library, Print Department.*

turn was deeply in love with this man who could make her laugh so heartily and who treated her so considerately. As in his efforts at publishing, success in love came late to O'Connor, but again it was real and deeply satisfying.

Veniette was tall, beautiful, and talented. Her willowy figure was so flawless that other women beheld her with awe. As a teenager she once did a stint as a live model in Filene's window. When O'Connor met her she was more or less a blonde but was graying prematurely, and so she began to frost her hair. She had tawny eyes, dark eyelashes, and a long straight nose. Some snaggle-teeth caused her to smile more than laugh in public. She reminded some of that Irish American icon of the 1950s, Grace Kelly, while others conjured up Botticelli's Venus. Veniette was not struck with her own looks, however, and prized intelligence and hard work. Over the years she had gradually put aside her political interests for her growing interest in painting. She worked in various media and styles, and took courses at Boston University. Although her work never amounted to anything like a career, it was satisfying for her that happiness in love coincided with the development of her own talents.

During their first summer in Wellfleet, O'Connor reluctantly surrendered his downstairs study for use as Veniette's studio. Heyward Cutting designed a "hidey-hole" writer's studio for him about two hundred feet down a hollow through the gnarled pines. O'Connor would repair there for his morning's work and leave the house to Veniette and Stephen.

Veniette was also expensive. She dressed stylishly and impeccably, and had some success in dressing up O'Connor more. On one of her frequent shopping trips to New York, she bought twenty pairs of shoes, only to discover that the sizes were all wrong. Once O'Connor gave her a showy ring, the kind an inexperienced man would buy. She liked to indulge her tastes in antiques, even if her judgment was not always the best. O'Connor seldom liked to accompany her on these hunts, and so he would usually give Veniette cash and wish good luck as she and Stephen went shopping. O'Connor seems to have held the purse strings, but he untied them frequently and generously.

O'Connor's two monastic rooms at 48 Beacon Street would hardly suffice now. Like Gatsby, he was intent on impressing a woman. Accordingly, he secured the services of his neighbor and friend, the Beacon Hill real estate agent John Tosi, who found for them an unusual and impressive townhouse to lease at 107 Chestnut Street, at the western foot of the Hill in a small area known as "the Flat."[18] The townhouse was a stone's throw from Storrow Drive and the Hatch Shell, and was equidistant from the *Atlantic* offices and

18. For information about 107 Chestnut Street, I am indebted especially to John Tosi for his letter of June 23, 1999, and subsequent telephone interview.

The newlyweds' first residence, 107 Chestnut Street on Beacon Hill. *Photo taken by author, 2000.*

Little, Brown. Its light Mediterranean stucco stood in unusual contrast to the older dark bricks of its neighbors, and the cobblestone courtyard in front adds an un-Bostonian air of romance. Its first owner, Grace Nichols, had the house built in 1913 to reflect Fenway Court, the famous Boston "palace" of Isabella Stewart Gardner. Nichols's own "palazzo" had twenty-three rooms.[19] By increasing his living space more than tenfold, in one stroke the man who had been so modest about his living arrangements began a course of living grandly.

No. 107 Chestnut Street was already furnished with numerous Italian antiques, which were a special draw for Veniette. When Edmund Wilson saw an eighteenth-century sedan chair in the spacious front hall, he joked that O'Connor could now be carried past the State House. (Wilson also discloses that the owner of 107 Chestnut Street was an admirer of O'Connor's work and therefore gave O'Connor a substantial discount.)[20] But the impressive house came with a huge drawback. The Flat was aptly named because, as reclaimed land close to the Charles River, it drained badly. With distressing

19. Moore and Weesner, *Beacon Hill,* 36.
20. *BL,* 346.

regularity the Charles flooded many basements of the Flat. Early in their marriage O'Connor and Veniette, along with Stephen, had to do bailing and cleanup, and not for the last time. On one of these occasions O'Connor disappeared from duty for a half hour, much to Veniette's annoyance. He reappeared in tuxedo and top hat, cracking jokes about being dressed at last for work.

Chestnut Street was a prestigious address. It runs parallel to Beacon Street, up from the Esplanade almost to the State House a third of a mile away. Unlike Beacon Street, most of it is quiet and secluded. Many consider it Beacon Hill's most beautiful street. Notables who have lived on or just off Chestnut Street include Edwin Booth, Julia Ward Howe, Richard Henry Dana, James Russell Lowell, Francis Parkman, Robert Frost, and Sylvia Plath. Robert Lowell was born on the street. *Atlantic's* Ted Weeks and Sam Lawrence were living on it in 1962. O'Connor swelled with the knowledge that, as late as 1962, he was one of a tiny number of Irish Americans who had made it to this part of Beacon Hill. Like his father back in the 1920s, he was conscious of making a statement by his presence in an exclusive enclave.

The couple was happy in a way that only those who have been lonely for years can know. In becoming expert in making each other laugh, they were cultivating a crucial ingredient for a good marriage. Even in public, Veniette could be reduced to helpless convulsions when O'Connor was "on." Monsignor Lally, a man who knew O'Connor well, said that after his marriage "happiness shone out of him as if he had swallowed the sun."[21] But if he knew how to tickle Veniette's funny bone, there were instances when small tensions arose. Early in the marriage an incredulous O'Connor confided to John Kelleher that he could not understand how Veniette could run out of gas in the Mercedes, and right in downtown Boston. Kelleher, blessed with a loving family of wife and four daughters, calmed down his steaming friend as he assured him that such things happen and are most definitely not occasions for male gloating. Another problem was Veniette's blue tongue. Somewhere along the line she had learned to swear like the proverbial trooper, and it took some doing for O'Connor to make it clear that he found it offensive. The biggest problem was religion. Veniette had not been a practicing Catholic for years; those who have claimed that she was a devout Catholic like her husband are clearly mistaken. Also, Stephen, whose father was Jewish, had been raised neither as an observant Jew nor as a Catholic. While O'Connor never forced his religion on either of them, he did make it abun-

---

21. Monsignor Francis J. Lally, review of *BL, The Boston Globe,* February 22, 1970, 78.

dantly clear that they were not to interfere with his religious practices or even disparage them.

Veniette's favorite social role was that of hostess. The O'Connors began a vividly remembered tradition of throwing lavish dinner parties for up to forty people. Sometimes O'Connor cooked a few gourmet items at these affairs. Usually the dinners were catered by the Ritz staff, with Joe Vitale there to supervise, and at considerable cost. O'Connor was more than making up for years of enforced frugality and solitary living.

With Veniette came a stepson. To people who didn't know him well, O'Connor could seem indifferent to children. One reviewer of *Benjy* had assumed he actively disliked them. While he certainly did not suffer spoiled brats gladly, the fact is that O'Connor was a hit with children. For all his older-than-his-years demeanor he was like a kid himself in some ways, as many imaginative people are. The endless humor and the magic tricks are just the most obvious signs. Daniel Aaron particularly remembers that this youthful side showed up most at Wellfleet, where children showed their affection for "Big Ed," who was adept at inventing games with old rubber balls or beer cans.[22] Jack O'Connor's family captured "Uncle Sonny" on a few minutes of home movies from the 1950s, which show him eagerly helping his nieces and nephews on an Easter egg hunt; the children show ready affection for him.[23]

Now O'Connor had some responsibility for a ten-year-old boy. With no experience of fathering he set out to be responsive and dedicated, and again his fundamental decency carried him through. Getting a stepfather at Stephen's age can be unpleasant, as O'Connor well knew from his Dickens, but the experience was not so for Stephen. "I *loved* him," is Stephen's simple and heartfelt answer to the inevitable question of his response to O'Connor.[24] Here was the father he had never really had. Stephen was as lightly built as O'Connor was big in the bone; one photo shows Stephen looking up in awe at the giant stooping over him. O'Connor did a lot with Stephen. He took Stephen to his first game at Fenway Park. There was softball at the Cape. (On one occasion Stephen insisted that O'Connor pitch to him as hard as he could; O'Connor gave the old "Allah" windup from his college years, and fired right into Stephen's chest, knocking him out momentarily.) On one Cape expedition he showed Stephen one of the Coast Guard huts he used during the war. During a trip to Harbour Island,

22. Daniel Aaron, "Edwin O'Connor Remembered," *America*, May 4, 1968, 604.
23. My thanks to O'Connor's nephew, Edwin O'Connor, for a videotape conversion of the movies, and to Barbara O'Connor Burrell for lending me her copy of the video.
24. Stephen Weil, personal interview, November 21, 1998.

O'Connor spent a long morning bonefishing Bahamian-style with Stephen, but they had little to show for it. They played Scrabble and Jotto, word games in which O'Connor had the obvious advantage. In the summer of 1963 O'Connor got a phone call from Hyannisport to come over to the Kennedy compound for the day. When the O'Connors arrived, Caroline and John were there but the president had been called away suddenly to Washington. Stephen enjoyed himself anyway, after a suitable swimsuit was found for him. Veniette and Jacqueline Kennedy formed a friendship that continued for some years.

O'Connor was always solicitous about Stephen's room at home. Stephen attended the Browne and Nichols School in Cambridge through the ninth grade. For high school he attended the Holderness School in Plymouth, New Hampshire, a two-hour drive from Boston. O'Connor and Veniette became friendly with the headmaster. O'Connor also dropped in to see his old Coast Guard buddy Louis Samaha at his general store in Plymouth. In Boston Stephen accompanied O'Connor to Christmas midnight Mass a few times.

O'Connor was loyally protective of Stephen. Once over the phone he chewed out the manager of the Coop in Harvard Square, who had, in O'Connor's estimation, treated Stephen rudely for a teenage prank in the store. For Stephen's sixteenth birthday, O'Connor took him to Locke-Ober's as his initiation into Boston manhood. Stephen has an enduring memory of his stepfather as a gentle, soft-spoken giant who dressed casually and smelled of Medaglia D'Oro coffee and toast in the morning.

Stephen would see his father in Washington from time to time, and George Weil would come to Boston and stay in the Copley Plaza Hotel. It seems that the boy had much more fun with O'Connor.

Veniette was not the most domestic of wives and mothers, and she learned a lot about cooking from her new husband. O'Connor joked with Niall Montgomery about her copious use of wine in cooking, which was as close as O'Connor ever got to alcohol. Veniette also came with two dogs, a dalmatian named Gigi and a beagle named Puffy, who was afraid of men and only slowly warmed up to O'Connor. Once she peed into O'Connor's shoe while he stood talking to a friend on the Common. She also liked to howl at night in the dark Wellfleet woods.

His friends say that marriage did not change O'Connor much. Just as he remained the same eminently likeable Ed after the success of *The Last Hurrah,* so too he saw the same friends and made the same rounds.

Toward the end of the year O'Connor began a collaboration with Edmund Wilson on a novel about a magician named Baldini.[25] O'Connor had known Wilson since his earliest summers at Wellfleet in the late 1940s. Their friendship was more personal than literary; O'Connor often admitted that he seldom talked shop with the literati. The friendship with this man twenty-three years his senior was one of those paternal-filial relationships that were so important to him, especially in his early career. O'Connor considered Wilson the "greatest literary critic in the English-speaking world today."[26] Like Skeffington and Charlie Carmody and so many of the fictional elders in O'Connor's imaginative stable, Wilson was the last of a breed. He was a man of letters without academic affiliation, save for some visiting lectureships. Like O'Connor, he wrote extramurally. As a result, he was renowned for his independence of interests and judgment in an impressive series of studies. Whether it was the relationship of Marxist theory to literature or the significance of the Dead Sea Scrolls, Wilson followed wherever his judicious nose led him. He would scour an author or topic until he was satisfied he could write something interesting and intelligent. For his part, Wilson said in an interview on June 2, 1962, that "the only American fiction writers I always read are Salinger, James Baldwin, and Edwin O'Connor."[27] He explained himself on Baldwin but did not elaborate on Salinger and O'Connor. Many have been surprised at Wilson's statement. First of all, it was not meant to be a judgment on contemporary American authors, most of whom he admitted to not keeping up on; the context of the remark makes it clear that he is simply talking of his tastes. Secondly, O'Connor was a friend, even if Wilson found his nonstop humor a tad wearisome.[28]

One bond between the two men was their fascination with magic. Since boyhood Wilson had been taken with the history of the subject, and like O'Connor he frequented magic and joke shops. O'Connor was more interested in magic for its showmanship value. As Rank points out, sleight of hand is an analogue to some of O'Connor's literary maneuvers, wherein a digression can be a clever way to isolate significance elsewhere.[29] Both men

---

25. This date can be ascertained from Wilson's journal, reprinted as *The Sixties: The Last Journal, 1960–1972*, ed. Lewis M. Dabney (New York: Farrar Straus and Giroux, 1993), 182.

26. Edwin O'Connor, "A Meeting on Sunday," *BL*, 388. Wilson is not named, but the context and description clearly point to him.

27. "An Interview with Edmund Wilson," in *The Bit Between My Teeth: A Literary Chronicle of 1950–1965*, by Edmund Wilson (New York: Farrar Straus and Giroux, 1965), 546.

28. Wilson, *The Sixties*, 137.

29. Rank, *O'Connor*, 189. The point is taken, but too often Rank excuses O'Connor's digressiveness by using formalist criticism to rationalize plain lack of economy.

enjoyed performing, and at Wellfleet they even sometimes put on little joint shows for children. It must have been a vaudevillian scene: the tall, glib O'Connor and the short, growly Wilson.

Their collaboration on the story of Baldini was meant, like their protagonist's art, only as a diversion. There is no indication that either man thought seriously of publication. The working rules, described by Wilson in a memoir of O'Connor, stipulated that they would write alternate chapters about the magician, with Wilson leading off.[30] Into a 5-by-7-inch blank book with a hard blue cover each would handwrite a chapter, and then turn it over to the other.[31] Since Wilson was living in Cambridge that year, the exchange could be done easily. It appears Wilson wanted to write a dark comedy while staying within the realm of the possible, while O'Connor was willing to entertain flights of the fantastic. Whether they had laid down additional ground rules is not known; apparently they did not outline any kind of plot. However, according to Wilson the collaboration soon became in O'Connor's mind a game of chess, and when Wilson was checkmated after just four chapters the game ended. Only thirty-nine of the three hundred blank pages had been used. Veniette told Wilson that when O'Connor had dutifully finished chapter four and turned the blue book over to his coauthor, he gloated, "Well, I guess I've got him now."

This unfinished novel done by collaboration was to be about collaboration itself. In the first chapter, Wilson sets up the premise. Jack Baldini wants to extend his range by working on a grand new stunt with the most famous woman magician of the day, Esmeralda the Great. Naturally, there is an ulterior purpose—Baldini is attracted to her. Esmeralda, however, plays coy. In the next chapter, rendered by O'Connor, we see Baldini in his tiny apartment covered with illusionist mirrors to "enlarge" it. He is lonely and longs for love; a year ago he had been humiliated by Esmeralda, when he gave her a private showing of his vanishing elephant trick. Baldini wants to devise a grand trick that necessitates the presence of a woman magician. In Wilson's chapter three, Baldini talks things over with Esmeralda, who is still mysteriously coy. O'Connor wrote the last chapter, in which Baldini is humiliated again when, at Esmeralda's apartment, he finds her with the supercilious Englishman Derek Marchmont, who informs Baldini of his upcoming marriage to Esmeralda, whereupon Baldini faints and the text ends.

In his memoir Wilson indicated that, had they continued "this nonsense,"

---

30. Originally published as "The Great Baldini: A Memoir and a Collaboration" in *Atlantic Monthly*, October 1969, 67–74; "The Great" was left out when it was reprinted in *BL*.
31. The blue book of Baldini is with the Edwin O'Connor Papers, 363.

he would have had Esmeralda turn out to be a vicious man-hater who would try to use her arts to kill Baldini during the grand trick. About four years later O'Connor and Wilson discussed reviving Baldini's adventures, but nothing eventuated. When the harmless "burlesque," as Wilson called it, was published by *Atlantic Monthly* after O'Connor's death, the magazine hyped the piece by putting a picture of a flamboyant magician on the cover. Wilson's accompanying memoir is far more valuable than the unfinished story.

On December 3, 1962, O'Connor made the only recordings of his works. He read passages from *The Last Hurrah* and *The Edge of Sadness*. He delivered Skeffington as someone quite distinct from himself and closer to Curley's mellifluous elocution, but Father Hugh Kennedy's voice is the same as his own. For some reason the recording was released only posthumously, by CMS records of New York. The album jackets depict the same late afternoon Beacon Hill scene, circa 1950. Why Beacon Hill for two novels that barely go there is a minor mystery, but it does say something about the Proper Bostonian myths that were already gathering around the author. Herbert Kenny of the *Boston Globe* wrote a moving appreciation when the records were released. "What is curious," he noticed, "and even poignant, is that both these readings are concerned with death."[32]

In July the perceptive critic Richard Gilman had written one of the earliest surveys of O'Connor's still developing career as a novelist. Gilman described O'Connor as a sound middlebrow author who avoided the stylistic pyrotechnics of a Faulkner but who was certainly not a hack like a Wouk. He stressed O'Connor's grounding in the local, the tribal, and the familial. In assessing the novelist at midcareer he saw that O'Connor's major strength was his evocation of the past challenged by an "encroaching future." But this strength was a double-edged sword, because O'Connor too often nursed his nostalgia. Gilman detected in O'Connor "a refusal to face the fact that the future is upon us and that the dead are truly dead." The result is that only his older characters lead vivid lives, while his younger ones are "bloodless abstractions or stereotyped figures of unpleasant, aggressive contemporaneity." Gilman advised that O'Connor "throw off the seductiveness of the past" and address themes of his own time.[33] Almost as if he were reading Gilman's mind, O'Connor was trying to move in that very direction.

32. Herbert Kenny, "An Emphasis on Death," *Boston Globe,* undated clipping, 1969.
33. Richard Gilman, "Pulitzer Prize Winner: Edwin O'Connor," *Sign,* July 1962, 60–61.

CHAPTER TWELVE

ℬ *Crisis*
(1963–1964)

In early 1962 O'Connor had begun steady work on his first complete play. With stomach problems under control and his interest in Veniette developing, his spirits were considerably lifted. He wrote the play during the year that brought its share of prizes followed by marriage in September, and early the next year he finished it. But he had misgivings, which first surface in 1963 during a radio interview on his work.

The mere fact that O'Connor agreed to a radio interview is significant. Since the success of *The Last Hurrah*, he had refused almost all radio and television offers, giving in on one occasion to promote Fred Allen's posthumous autobiography. O'Connor's sense of privacy was by no means as extreme as J. D. Salinger's, but he did guard it jealously; he also disliked interruptions of his routine. Moreover, ever since the fiasco of the aborted interview with Curley in 1956 he had had an aversion to Boston's WGBH, which was producing this 1963 interview. But after marriage to the outgoing Veniette, O'Connor was more relaxed, and in fact during 1963 he was more publicly active than he had been for some years. Besides, after winning the Pulitzer, he was in demand. The old radio hand succumbed.

A key player in getting O'Connor to be interviewed was Ted Weeks, who was then in his last years as editor of *Atlantic Monthly*. Weeks had known O'Connor for more than fifteen years, and if he often was muddled about the facts of O'Connor's life and was never one of O'Connor's close friends at *Atlantic*, he had nevertheless helped the young author during those difficult years when O'Connor toiled obscurely. When Weeks invited O'Connor to be interviewed for his weekly program, called "Writers of Today," for national educational radio, O'Connor agreed out of loyalty. The interview took place in the library of Boston's Museum of Science, which sits on a dam in the middle of the Charles

River. The two had a magnificent view of the city which the novelist had depicted.[1]

Weeks comes off as a haphazard interviewer. His questions are in no particular order as they leap off the jotting pad. His summations, such as they are, are hurried and sloppy. O'Connor, on the other hand, speaks in measured and thoughtful sentences. In listening to the tape, one detects little camaraderie or intellectual horseplay between the two men. It was not an inspired half-hour.

When asked about the future, O'Connor replied that he had finished a play, but he sounded nervous about it. He briefly mentioned his love of the theater and how he wanted to "get mixed up in theater just for this one experience." That statement reveals a lot about how much O'Connor had stored up: the trip with his father to Los Angeles in 1929; all the visits to vaudeville, plays, and films; his radio scripts and television reviewing; his magic and mimicry. Buried deep inside this private novelist was a dramatist waiting for his chance. Therein lay the recipe for disaster. O'Connor almost sees it coming as early as this interview, when he admits that he wrote the still unnamed play with unusual speed. But haste was not part of his customary method. Furthermore, he admits that during the writing he was not "engaged," a new buzzword of the existentialist early sixties. In context, O'Connor seems to mean by the word that he was not emotionally involved. Moreover, he is frank about his misgivings. Is it really a play? Was he a playwright at all? He sounds unsure.

And so the public learned for the first time of the famous novelist's venture into drama.[2] During most of 1963 and 1964, O'Connor spent considerable time and energy on this venture, to say nothing of pouring himself emotionally into the enterprise. If he was not "engaged" while writing it, he certainly was wedded to *I Was Dancing* for far too long afterwards.

Once the play was done to his satisfaction, in February 1963, O'Connor put it in the hands of the tireless Helen Strauss, whom he valued for her con-

1. The audiotape is EOCP 304. The catalogue to the Papers dates the interview to 1968, but from internal evidence this cannot be correct. For one thing, on the tape Weeks is identified as editor of the *Atlantic*, a position he gave up in 1966. The evidence suggests 1963 as the most probable year. WGBH's records are of no help for this period.

2. On his wedding day, O'Connor had told a reporter that he was working on a play, but he declined to give any details because "giving the public an outline in words is like shoving out a skeleton." He went on to say that the "play will be my kind of stuff, however. Both happy and sad." Unidentified newspaper clipping, dated by hand September 2, 1962.

tacts in the entertainment industry. In the meantime, he had no other big irons in the fire; his next important work did not get started until some time in the summer. In addition to the WGBH interview he gave several talks that year.

The first of these was the McGeary Foundation Lecture at the anniversary ceremonies of the Thomas More Association, a Catholic lay organization in Chicago that promoted Catholic reading through its book club and respected bimonthly magazine, *The Critic,* which reprinted O'Connor's address.[3] O'Connor received the annual Thomas More Medal for distinguished literature by a Catholic. He gave his address in a low-key manner in a large hotel ballroom to about 500 people, probably the biggest live audience he ever addressed.[4] O'Connor developed "For Whom the Novelist Writes" with his usual mixture of humor and seriousness, as he outlined several audiences for the novelist: first, his peers; second, reviewers and critics (he names Edmund Wilson and Alfred Kazin, both friends, as his favorites, and disparages guru-critic Leslie Fiedler, "who writes about Leslie Fiedler"); third, the buying public; and most important of all—the novelist himself. He stressed the importance of never pandering to the public, as did the bestselling Harold Robbins. The novelist's most important public is his smallest. O'Connor's long concluding sentence is an eloquent display of his integrity:

But in the end, when a novelist has finished his book, if he can pick that book up, and if he can begin to read it, and continue to read it with the feeling that this is not so bad, that it might even be pretty good; if he can read it, not with *complete* satisfaction, of course—I think no serious writer has ever felt that—but at least with the satisfaction that he has done as well as he can at this particular time, and that the book he has before him comes fairly close to being the book he had originally intended to write; . . . then he is pleased in a special way, and no matter what else may come to him from others as a result of this book—whether fame, or money, or appreciation—it is quite likely to be this special private pleasure, this special satisfaction which he feels alone, and which he can share with no one, which will be his greatest reward.

O'Connor developed the talk with ease and confidence. If his thesis blazed no new trails, it did show that O'Connor was a thoughtful craftsman who had his literary values in good order.

In October he made his second and last appearance at the Paulist Center

3. Edwin O'Connor, "For Whom The Novelist Writes," *The Critic,* April–May 1963, 13–17; reprinted in *BL,* 269–80.

4. Joel Wells, telephone interview, August 22, 2000. Mr. Wells, who had been with the Association for many years, remembers that when Graham Greene was notified of his own award, Greene said that the severed head of St. Thomas More must be turning in its grave.

lectern on Park Street, for the Christian Culture Lecture Series, which was now in its sixth year. Although their friendship was cooling, Elliot Norton introduced O'Connor for his talk, "A Meeting on Sunday."[5] In this, probably the longest public address he ever gave, O'Connor warmed to a subject close to his heart: the dismal state of the Sunday sermon, a problem "which has been bothering me for some time." As was his wont, he first recalled a figure from a half-century ago. Practically the only one in the parish with some advanced education, the priest back then commanded respect in the pulpit, which trumpeted authority. But the American parish in 1963 was much more educated and diversified, and few lamented the demise of Redemptorist-style bellowing anyway. But now, he said, most sermons were unprepared, sloppy, and dull. O'Connor was particularly alarmed that so few priests preached on the Scriptures. (It should be remembered that O'Connor spoke only one year into the Second Vatican Council, which did redress this grievous situation; today homilies may be still dull, but at least they take as their texts the Old and New Testament readings for the week.) O'Connor was also dismayed that the death in June of Pope John XXIII, whom he obviously admired, was so widely ignored on the Sundays that followed. He goes on to disparage the inordinate time given to reading parish announcements and to fund-raising, although he does admit that, compared to their Protestant brethren, Catholics are notoriously stingy in parish support. He once thought of writing a magazine article critical of pulpit oratory for fund-raising; its title would be "The Second Collection Today Is . . ." What bothers O'Connor most is that too many priests simply do not take the time and care that a well-written sermon requires. Here the wordsmith scolds, and maybe the buried dramatist too. O'Connor wants sermons that live, that are relevant to spiritual concerns, that have a certain flair. The great danger, he sees, is that the Church might lose a whole generation through the sheer apathy generated in this one weekly encounter between the pastor and his flock.

O'Connor was at his best in this talk, which is the most vivacious one he ever gave. It was apparently well received. John Kelleher, who was in attendance, said of the talk: "It rocked, and delighted, the faithful."[6] Unlike his other talks about Catholic novelists or the writer's responsibility, "A Meeting on Sunday" opened up a satirical armory as only Catholics can do, in what O'Connor's opening sentence called "an intra-mural talk." He was in a kind of sanctuary in the Paulist Center, which was not the typical parish by any means. O'Connor made it clear that he was not decrying the Paulist Center,

---

5. Reprinted in *BL*, 381–97.   6. Quoted in *BL*, 17.

but he did hint at churches on the Cape, the suburbs, and his old hometown. Also, after a year of marriage to the less than pious Veniette, O'Connor may have been more willing to get some gripes off his chest. But underlying all the skewering was a serious concern for the future of the Church, and especially for how the Word was preached. This concern had already surfaced in *The Edge of Sadness,* when Father Kennedy realizes only too keenly his own shortcomings in the pulpit.

That same month O'Connor also took his usual trip to Notre Dame. Sometimes on these visits he would read from portions of his work to Frank O'Malley's classes, even if it was only to the fifteen students in that all-important freshman English section he so highly prized. He might also speak to O'Malley's larger Modern Catholic Writers class. Notre Dame English Professor Edward Fischer recalled in a short memoir that O'Connor also enjoyed the company of Professor Thomas Stritch, who claimed that O'Connor was the best raconteur he had ever met. Sometimes O'Connor would also take long campus walks with Professor Fischer, and once he gave a talk to his class.[7] A few times O'Connor gave a formal reading or talk in the basement auditorium of the Law School, where 300 could hear him. This talk was usually not highly publicized, although after winning the Pulitzer, publicity became difficult to avoid. On one of these occasions, around 1964, a snippy undergraduate asked the author whether he would ever write sexually explicit material; apparently the student had noticed its utter absence in O'Connor's two big novels. A witness remembers O'Connor being dumbfounded at the question. The times, even at Catholic universities, were changing. After a pained moment, O'Connor deflected the question and spoke of the writer's integrity and vocation.[8]

During this first full year of marriage, O'Connor kept to most of his usual yearly trips, now accompanied by Veniette, whom he showed off proudly. On the eve of St. Patrick's Day, they flew to Ireland. And of course there were the long summer months in Wellfleet. During that same summer O'Connor's mother and sister took a trip to Ireland, their first, where they met the Montgomerys, about whom they had heard so much for ten years. Niall wrote O'Connor, whom he addressed as "Sonny" for the first time; it was unusual for anyone outside the O'Connor family to do so. Niall was delighted at Mrs. O'Connor's unguarded comments, such as: "One thing I do not like about Europe is those Americans." In referring to President Kennedy's recent trip

---

7. Edward Fischer, "Edwin O'Connor, Raconteur," 49–50.
8. Brian Barbour, personal interview, May 6, 1999.

to Ireland, she said, "His first duty was to visit the Pope," a comment sure to please Protestants and other Americans United for the Separation of Church and State.[9]

In September O'Connor and Veniette received several "telegrams" congratulating them on their first anniversary. Among the alleged well-wishers were the venomous tongues of "Gore Vidal" and "Mary McCarthy."[10] These are the first such congratulatory spoofs O'Connor kept; there would be many more on birthdays and anniversaries, as O'Connor's friends, especially Abe Burrows, began to train his own mimicry on him. (An excerpt from one of Abe's birthday verses: "So here's a gift for a wonderful guy / As Nixon would say, it's from my wife and I.")[11] Apparently O'Connor thoroughly enjoyed the compliments.

November 22, 1963, was a shattering day for O'Connor. There is no account of where he was when he heard the news from Dallas. On an early Friday afternoon, he would probably have been somewhere toward the end of his daily Boston rounds; then again he may have been driving to the Cape. Most likely he would have headed immediately to a church. As many have said, to be Irish and Catholic and Bostonian that day was to experience a triple anguish. The fact that he had known and liked John Kennedy for almost twenty years only intensified his grief and anger. O'Connor generally kept clear of politicians and preferred instead the company of middlemen and advisers like Louis Brems and Arthur Schlesinger who could talk as insiders, and he had never played up his acquaintanceship with the president. No doubt he too had heard of Kennedy's sexual escapades, which were no secret on Beacon Hill and which were even whispered behind Dorchester's lace curtains. Irish attitudes in these matters could be inconsistent: smiling at unfounded folk tales of Daniel O'Connell's philandering (a huge bust of the Liberator sits incongruously in Charlie Carmody's front hall) while pouncing on Parnell's single lapse. In any event, O'Connor overlooked Kennedy's priapism.

The next Monday a distraught O'Connor dropped in as usual at the *Atlantic* offices. No one had ever seen the normally reserved but affable Ed O'Connor like this. He said to Phoebe-Lou Adams, "If those people ever offer to secede again, I'll shoot the man that stops them."[12] It must be remembered

9. Niall Montgomery, letter to Edwin O'Connor, July 30, 1963, EOCP 199. This is the last of fifteen letters O'Connor kept from the Montgomerys. While there is no evidence of a falling out, O'Connor saw less of Ireland after his marriage. Niall and Hop never visited America.

10. EOCP 274.   11. EOCP 108.

12. Phoebe-Lou Adams, telephone interview, April 15, 1999.

that for three days Boston had been in an ugly mood. Wild, irrational charges and rumors flew around almost immediately, as instant assassination experts bore knowledge that Kennedy had been killed by Protestants, blacks, Masons, Mafia, Klan, or Commies—not to mention Nixon, Johnson, Castro, or North (or South) Vietnam. The city that flung rumors around like snow flurries took only days to germinate the paranoid scenarios that infect the country to this day. In many Irish American households solemn pictures and plaques of the slain Chief would be enshrined for decades. O'Connor eventually got over his grief, but it is noteworthy that the only scene of human violence in his work occurs in a novel written after the assassination. The country had begun its rapid implosion when O'Connor caught some of it in the opening chapter of *All in the Family*.

The following year O'Connor finally did get to the White House. The occasion was a state dinner in honor of Ireland's president, Eamon de Valera. "Dev" was old and blind, and it was safe to honor him now that his roles in the Easter Rising of 1916 and his rebellion against the Irish Free State in 1922 had been domesticated and mythologized. He had been Ireland's prime minister many times and now served as the purely ceremonial head of state. President Johnson invited notables to the formal dinner on May 27, 1964. The name Edwin O'Connor had no trouble making the list, because he was still widely considered the foremost Irish American writer. O'Connor and Veniette sat at a table with Pennsylvania Governor David Lawrence, who—obviously not recognizing O'Connor—by chance told everyone that Pittsburgh's Bishop John Wright was the model for Monsignor Killian, the Cardinal's secretary in *The Last Hurrah*. When O'Connor politely disputed this claim, Lawrence insisted all the more. Finally O'Connor said, "I wrote it, so I know."[13] He could delight in toppling Humpty Dumpty.

The rest of this chapter is devoted to O'Connor's long, frustrating, and exhausting struggle with his next work, *I Was Dancing*, which appeared twice in 1964, first as a novel and then in its original form as a play. If this sounds confusing, that's not the half of it, as the Irish say.

The basic conflict and indeed the whole plot of *I Was Dancing* is that familiar one of father and son. But now O'Connor moved this conflict from the wings of subplot, where it had been lurking in his previous work, to center stage. Along with this enlargement came an edgy rawness in both versions of *I Was Dancing* that is found nowhere else in his work, because now

13. Edwin O'Connor, interview with P. C. Brooks, *Boston*, November 1964, 22–23.

father and son confront each other with the gloves off. O'Connor clearly wanted this "showdown," a word emphasized in the novel.

Reduced to its barest outline, the plot of *I Was Dancing* is simple enough. Indeed, the novel would have worked better as a long short story, as Edmund Wilson immediately told him.[14] And the play definitely should have been a one-act. Daniel Considine, known theatrically as Waltzing Daniel Considine, is an old vaudevillian who has been living for a year at his son's home, in a retirement that is wearing thin for both the son and the son's wife of seven years. As the story develops we learn that Daniel had been on the road with various troupes during most of Tom's life. In fact, when Daniel showed up at Tom's door a year back, it was the first time they had seen each other in twenty years. Recently Tom had given his father an ultimatum: he must move out to a retirement center. Old Irish that he is, Daniel will have none of it. Daniel tells three cronies that he has a plan, to be revealed that night, to thwart the treasonous ultimatum. When the deadline comes, however, father and son have a long, knockdown exchange, and Daniel's plan—a faked heart attack—convinces no one. Defeated, he tries to put the best face on things at the end.

Thus, the bare bones of *I Was Dancing* in both of its versions. There are no essential differences between the play and the novel. The predecessors in O'Connor's writing career are many. In "Anthony Cantwell" the father had given his returned veteran son a helpful boot, which is resented. In *The Oracle*, General Blackburn overstayed his welcome at Usher's house and became a problem for husband and wife. More important parallels show up in the 1950s. First, in "A Young Man of Promise," Kevin Rowan's father actually gives his son a gentle ultimatum to leave. In "A Grand Day for Mr. Garvey," we meet an old protagonist in his post-ultimatum life in the nursing home. Skeffington is stuck with the feckless Francis Jr. in *The Last Hurrah*. In *The Edge of Sadness* Charlie Carmody is a trial for his middle-aged sons and daughters, especially Father John, who is driven to the edge. This last work brought the father-son conflict more to the surface than any previous work, and with it a bitterness in places. The quality and tone of the conflict in *I Was Dancing* develops this bitterness from the previous novel, which had been completed just a year or two earlier. It is almost as if O'Connor gave to Tom Considine the opportunity that John Carmody could never muster the courage to engineer. John had to blurt out his soul's agony to his best friend, but Tom faces his father head on. One could speculate how much O'Connor's courtship of Veniette during the writing of the play brought a more as-

---

14. Edmund Wilson, letter to Edwin O'Connor, April 23, 1964, EOCP 265.

sertive O'Connor to the fore. The novel's dedication reads: "To Veniette With Love." This is the only one of his five dedications that has any emotional tenor.

Autobiographical fingerprints are all over this work. Over the years O'Connor told several interviewers that he disliked autobiographical fiction because the novelist used up himself and his material too fast. But he protested too much. Although O'Connor would only try out the more customary personal narrative at the very end of his life, other works, particularly "A Young Man of Promise," *Benjy,* and *The Edge of Sadness,* had indirectly borrowed material from his own life. And now once again O'Connor was, whether he was fully aware or not, brooding on his past.

Once again he arranged a long widowerhood for the father, as he had done for the fathers of Anthony Cantwell and Kevin Rowan, and for Skeffington and Carmody. The son may be married, but we never see his wife; in the novel version she is conveniently out of town. The arena is cleared for father and son to lock horns in the one room of the house where Daniel lives. The play has no other setting than this one room.

For convenience in tracing autobiographical elements, the more available and detailed novel version will be used for *I Was Dancing.*[15] O'Connor wrote this version in the spring of 1963, a few months after finishing the play. He was getting impatient with delays in theatrical production, and so partly at Helen Strauss's bidding he rewrote the play as a novel. Perhaps it was a way to build up publicity, but it was also something he had to get off his chest. He wrote this novel more rapidly than any he had ever done and finished it in a few weeks. Of course, he had the essential story already done, but he did add a few characters and scenes, none of them of importance. The central conflict between father and son remains intact. What puzzles one now is that nobody apparently ever saw this strange story as O'Connor's own. Was he that reticent about his relationship with his father?

First, though, the problem of the biographical or genetic fallacy has to be dealt with. Readers commit this error when they transfer details of the author's life too readily or naively to the author's works. Thus, Ishmael becomes a stand-in for Herman Melville, or in a trickier case, Stephen Dedalus becomes co-extensive with James Joyce. Nevertheless, there are some works, usually failed ones like Thomas Wolfe's, that are indisputably autobiographical to their cores. The better autobiographical work finds some method to distance author from characters and personae. O'Connor attempts such

---

15. Edwin O'Connor, *I Was Dancing* (Boston: Atlantic Monthly Press/Little, Brown, 1964).

strategies in *I Was Dancing,* but still the life comes through, often painfully so. Indeed, toward the end especially it almost seems as though he exposes the Considines, father and son, more as an act of therapy than anything else. Here the "proof" lies in the details, but also in a gauge of the work's emotional "pressure." This very word is emphasized by O'Connor himself, just after Daniel's faked heart attack and before the climactic scene, when he writes of the son: "But now he was conscious of a pressure to talk, a pressure of so many things inside him that had never been said, and that should have been said" (189). It is precisely at this point that O'Connor ratchets up the emotional intensity of the work, and the long, exhausting, and finally tedious dialogue that ensues strikes the reader/viewer as coming more from O'Connor's buried past than from the play itself. Furthermore, this climactic scene marks the third novel in a row in which an elderly man "confesses" in his bedroom in drawn-out scenes, all precipitated by real or faked heart attacks. Skeffington had died from his heart attack, Charlie Carmody had survived his to grumble and gouge for another day, but Daniel Considine faked his. Dr. John O'Connor's heart attacks and drawn-out death hover over this psychodrama.

Tom Considine is forty-four, O'Connor's very age when he completed the play in 1962. We learn that he has attended the best schools, was close to his mother, married late, and has no children. He works in a fairly big city where he walks a lot and uses the telephone a great deal. So far, the author almost to a T. To put some distance between Tom and himself, O'Connor makes him a lawyer. Like so many of O'Connor's younger characters, he is also humorless.

There are deeper connections, most of which surface during the final showdown. At one point Tom tells his father something about friendship:

In this city today there are twenty men, all about your age, who have no family ties with me, who have never given me a cent, who had no special reason and certainly no obligation to help me or even to like me. And yet from every one of them I've gotten more kindness, advice, assistance, and just plain human consideration than I've ever gotten from you (196–97).

O'Connor could be alluding here to that long line of older men toward whom he felt affection and loyalty: Monsignor Holland, Frank O'Malley, Louis Brems, Charlie Morton, Ted Weeks, Sam Lawrence, Edmund Wilson, Elliot Norton, several editors at the *Boston Post,* Monsignor Lally, Sean O'Faolain, Clem Norton, Fred Allen, Arthur Thornhill, Laurence Winship, Abe Burrows, Arthur Gartland, and more. This score of men had befriended, encouraged, educated, hired, informed, entertained, critiqued, and absolved him. This was his larger family that stretched from Boston to Wellfleet and from South Bend to Dublin. When the drama version of *I Was Dancing* was published in 1965, O'Connor had that passage about paternal friendship, which also had been in early versions of the play, removed. Perhaps he realized that its autobiographical provenance was too obvious.

Even more remarkably, O'Connor gives Tom his own family nickname during the showdown, when Daniel accuses his son:

"You're a cold boy and you always were. I knew it the very first time I laid eyes on you. It was in the hospital right after you were born. . . . I looked down at you, and I said . . . , 'Hello, Sonny, I'm your Dad.' And what did you do? I'll tell you what you did, Tom: you gave me a smile. Small as you were, you gave me a smile. But Tom: *d'ye know what kind of a smile?*"
Tom said, "I'll make a guess: a cold smile."
"Right!" Daniel cried. "A cold smile! *It was the coldest smile I ever saw on a child*" (190; O'Connor's italics).

Obviously O'Connor had not looked into too many maternity ward basinets, but in the context of the play the father's words have some force. Laconic Tom definitely is on the cool and calculating side. O'Connor must have heard by this point in his life that he too was known for a seriousness that registered with some as frostiness. And even his friends attested to the famous wintry grin and basilisk stare, those ancient Irish weapons, for people with whom he had little patience. In holding a side of himself up for critique, Edwin O'Connor was examining some part of "Sonny."

Earlier, Tom's Yankee friend, Jack Pomeroy, could talk to Tom about Irish American family complexities with a detachment Tom cannot manage:

"You're a puddle of sentiment. You can't even mention your father without thinking that he should be Dear Old Dad. . . . You start to feel guilty because you don't feel what you think you're supposed to feel. You know what your trouble is? You have no experience: you've never thrown your father out before" (161).

You've never thrown your father out before. Therein lurks the worm eating the heart of *I Was Dancing*, gnawing at the play's Irish conscience. As Al Gottlieb, one of Daniel's cronies, says, "A family is something to punch you in the nose. Hard" (129). Freud reputedly said that the Irish were the one people for whom psychoanalysis was useless. Whether the statement is apocryphal or not, and whatever one may think of Freud's theories, the statement does catch something about the singular nature of Irish emotional life. More recently Colm Toibin has commented on family life in Irish fiction:

[T]here is almost no version of domestic harmony at the end of an Irish novel; there is almost no version of domestic harmony at the beginning of an Irish novel; there is no Irish novel which ends in a wedding, or a match being made. Irish fiction is not like that; Irish fiction is full of dislocation and displacement. . . . Fathers in Irish writing are absent, or angry, or mad, or strangely silent.[16]

One need not construct a crude oedipal paradigm to sense that for years O'Connor had internalized a problem with his father. This problem may not have been highly visible to many, but it lay like the iceberg's bulk beneath so much that he wrote. As Tom had mused earlier, "All roads led to Daniel . . ." (40). Like Tom, O'Connor felt ambivalence, guilt, remorse, resentment, and anger that finally erupted in this work and got the better of it in the process. He tried to banish the father in this work, but Daniel Considine rises from his "deathbed act" (187) and is "still dancing, still shouting" in the last sentence of the novel.

Almost as if he wanted to advertise the roots of *I Was Dancing*, O'Connor early on has Daniel thinking back over his half-century on the road, and of the long, cold waiting "for the train which would bring him to the split-week booking in Valparaiso, Indiana. Or Cardiff, Wales. Or Woonsocket, Rhode Island. Or Paris, France" (12). Just as he had buried "South Bend, Indiana" inside a string of places for Frank O'Malley's detection in *The Edge of Sadness*, he was now burying his own hometown in hopes someone would see. But who? The only explanation that suggests itself is that O'Connor was doing all this for himself. But the inside joke was serious enough.

The city in *I Was Dancing* is even more indeterminate than its predecessors. There is barely a clue about a possible Boston, Providence, or Woonsocket, save the fact that there are Yankees and Irish in all three cities. Because he needed a house that was abstracted from specific local circumstances, the geographical locale of the work is even more vague than in his other novels. But time was another matter. In a move unique for him, O'Connor pinpoints the year of the action. We can infer 1962, the very year O'Connor wrote the first version, because at one point Daniel recalls what he was doing "[t]wenty-one years ago" during the attack on Pearl Harbor in 1941 (69). But why would O'Connor so uncharacteristically provide a date? Perhaps because Daniel's fifty years as vaudeville showman started the very year Dr. O'Connor hung out his shingle in Woonsocket. If this be coincidence, it is a remarkable one.

Another item throws an oblique light on this conjunction of fact and fiction. One of Daniel's three friends (Job's three "comforters"?) is Billy Ryan: "He was a physician. (Or was he?) There was always a doubt, Tom thought,

16. Colm Toibin, introduction to *The Penguin Book of Irish Fiction* (New York: Penguin, 2001), xxiii.

about all his father's friends" (18). By his own admission Billy Ryan has shaky medical credentials. At one point, Father Feeley, another friend, even refers to Billy as a "jungle pharmacist" (135). O'Connor must have heard those rumors about the credentials of his own father, the former pharmacist, and decided to make them real in the case of "Doctor" Billy Ryan, whose questionable status makes Daniel guilty by association. Put another way, Billy is a facet of Daniel's own bogus status as caring father, which Daniel must confess at the end of the play.

And yet: a problem remains, one not easily solved. While it seems beyond question that O'Connor, like so many writers with an Irish pedigree, nursed a father problem, it would appear that the father in question was not Dr. John V. O'Connor. Or at least not all of him. Just as Skeffington was not Curley outright, so too Daniel Considine was not O'Connor's father *in toto*. To be sure Dr. O'Connor was vastly different from his first son. One was as dour as the other was affable. He was a difficult father at times, but there is no evidence that he was a crumb like Daniel Considine. The most we can say is that the young O'Connor never felt that his father fully supported his endeavors in radio, journalism, and fiction, and that as he grew older he magnified the distance between himself and his father. His father may never have stood in his way, but the son was looking for something more encouraging. There was never any kind of open hostility between the two, and certainly no rupture. What went on inside O'Connor beneath the family courtesies is, of course, another matter. At bottom, the conflict appeared to be one within O'Connor himself. The father and son conflict was a way to work out tensions of his own in a way that recalls the two sets of doubles in *The Edge of Sadness*.

Atlantic Monthly Press and Little, Brown published *I Was Dancing* in March 1964. The novel's dust jacket was a departure for O'Connor novels. Gone are the plain, drab covers of his previous two novels. In keeping with the more frantic sixties, the cover featured colored stage spotlights and contemporary lettering. A Literary Guild edition of the novel appeared in April, and a Reader's Digest condensed book came out the same month. A year later, the Bantam paperback depicted Daniel Considine on the cover looking for all the world like a young Frank Sinatra.

The reviews were mostly unenthusiastic. A frequent note was that O'Connor was letting his admirers down. Another was that the weaknesses of his earlier work were now in plain view: garrulity, stereotyping, lack of action, a nearly exclusively male world, unsatisfying resolutions. Perhaps the most glowing review appeared in the March 23 *Newsweek,* where O'Connor could do no wrong. *Book Week* for March 22 was also generous in a review that noted that the father-son business was, if possible, more complex than *Hamlet.* And Arthur Schlesinger praised the novel in the *Boston Globe* on March 24, although he did concede it was a lesser book than its two famous predecessors. This time around the *New York Times Book Review* did not secure the services of John Kelleher for its review, on March 22, which was mixed at best. *Time* came down hard on the novel on April 10, as did *The Saturday Review* on March 21, when it complained that the novel "boxed [O'Connor] into an airless little corner neatly sealed off from any recognizable life." Entitled "The Womanless World of Edwin O'Connor," the review provoked O'Connor to outspoken anger.[17] Even *Atlantic Monthly*'s brief notice in April was restrained, and it picked up O'Connor's surprisingly "harsh" tone. *The New Yorker* for April 4 dismissed the novel for its cold and mediocre characters and "painfully forced" writing. Not since *The Oracle* had there been such an array of hostile reviews, but O'Connor and his producers disregarded this handwriting on the wall and proceeded with the theatrical version for that fall.

To back up a bit. When Helen Strauss first read the manuscript of the play O'Connor sent her in February 1963, she was aghast. Her "sober novelist" had become a "star-struck playwright" who would not be dissuaded. Trusting on instincts long-honed in dealing with the theater, she knew from the outset that disaster loomed. Accordingly, she tried the ploy of getting O'Connor to rework the play into a novel. But when Garson Kanin, the successful Broadway director who did *The Diary of Anne Frank* in 1955 and *Funny Girl* early in 1964, got wind that the famous Edwin O'Connor had written a play, he badgered Strauss into letting him see it. He and his wife, the actress Ruth Gordon, began "bubbling" with delight and enthusiasm over *I Was Dancing.* They quickly sent it to David Merrick, the most successful Broadway producer of the time, who also bubbled. All three sang superlatives. Strauss remained baffled at these goings-on. She wrote of Merrick: "[He] must have been looking for something to do that season."[18] Which was hardly true. Merrick, who reveled in being "the abominable showman," would have anywhere from three to six plays and musicals in a given year back then, when he was at the height of his power. He hardly needed the work.[19] When contracts were

17. Rank, *O'Connor,* 145.
18. Strauss, *Talent for Luck,* 275.
19. Obituary of David Merrick, *Providence Journal,* April 27, 2000, C6.

signed, "Gar" sent a gushy telegram to O'Connor: "I WILL PLEDGE MY UT-MOST FOR THIS BEAUTIFUL PLAY."[20]

The usual production delays ensued, but since the impatient O'Connor had little working knowledge of theatrical complexities, he took Strauss's suggestion and tossed off the novel. Strangely enough, the completed novel took a long year to see print, but O'Connor was not unduly upset. His mind was fixed on the play. The delay between the novel and movie versions of *The Last Hurrah* had taught him little.

There were other stresses and strains. Early on, probably in the spring of 1962, O'Connor stopped Elliot Norton on the Common, took him up to his apartment at 48 Beacon Street, and showed him an early version of the play. Norton was Boston's most respected drama critic, and if he wrote reviews for the low-brow *Record-American,* his weekly drama show on WGBH television more than made up for it. And of course he was O'Connor's longstanding friend, who had been instrumental in getting him on the *Boston Post* in his hour of need. After perusing the manuscript, Norton calmly said that it needed work. From that moment, Norton knew their friendship was strained. The essential problem was that the play needed action. Like so many novelists who turn to the theater—Norton had seen many over the years—O'Connor simply could not dramatize sufficiently. Norton saw novelists as necessarily always looking back to what had happened, once upon a time. But playwrights must make it happen now, on a stage, in front of an audience, all involving considerable knowledge of the craft.[21] O'Connor's penchant for nostalgia was bound to get in the way. Henry James's midcareer flirtation with playwriting that ended so humiliatingly when *Guy Domville* was booed in 1895 should stand as the cautionary tale for all plot-starved novelists lured by the bright lights.

In the summer of 1964, a flurry of Boston rumors had it that O'Connor's forthcoming play was all about Fred Allen: one "Bostonian" on another "Bostonian." But the only connection between Fred Allen and Daniel Considine was vaudeville; the similarity stops there. Daniel's Australian tour may have been suggested by Allen's own Down Under tour, which he described in his memoirs, but as characters they are far removed from each other. O'Connor thought the world of Fred Allen and would never have presented him as vain and manipulative.

Casting was a problem. Kanin wanted the best, and in December of 1963 he nearly snagged John Mills. But this excellent British choice worried that

20. Garson Kanin, telegram to Edwin O'Connor, August 28, 1963, EOCP 172.
21. Elliot Norton, personal interview, June 21, 1999.

he might not be able to portray an American. O'Connor, Kanin, and Mills discussed it over lunch in New York, but hope for Mills fell through.[22] The names of Lee Tracy and Tom Ewell also surfaced briefly.

By midsummer of 1964 Merrick and Kanin had lined up the cast. Burgess Meredith would be Daniel to Orson Bean's Tom. These two principals were not entirely to O'Connor's liking. Back in his days as a televison reviewer, O'Connor had once called Bean seriously miscast in a production of *Arsenic and Old Lace*.[23] David Doyle, known later for his role in television's *Charley's Angels*, was to be Billy Ryan.

O'Connor had an odd relationship with the producer. Merrick was in awe of O'Connor's reputation and could not see how a play by this bestselling author could miss. He was even deferential to O'Connor, a rarity for this man whom many considered a bully. O'Connor in turn found Merrick to be a quietly helpful gentleman. At one point during the play's deadly Boston run, Merrick secretly brought actors up from New York to see whether they could fill in and salvage the play, but these machinations went nowhere. Merrick and O'Connor never became real friends, and eventually Merrick shunned O'Connor.[24]

During the summer of 1964 O'Connor developed one of his stranger friendships. Almost every day he would speak on the telephone at considerable length with Lillian Hellman on Martha's Vineyard. At almost sixty she was enjoying something of a comeback after stormy years in the 1950s defying the House Un-American Activities Committee. The leftist playwright was something of an odd mentor for the more apolitical O'Connor, but he prized her advice on any number of theatrical problems and personalities.[25] Her notorious mendacity apparently did not surface in these talks, and O'Connor trusted her instincts implicitly.

The play went through three-and-a-half weeks of rehearsals in New York in September, and then cast and crew came to Boston for a pre-Broadway tryout at the Wilbur, where O'Connor involved himself in the final preparations. There was a good deal of frantic rewriting in that typical last-minute show-biz manner, which could not have sat well with the painstaking author. These on-the-fly revisions continued long after opening night.

O'Connor kept two prompt copies which show extensive scribbling and nervous wear. These copies, along with several other manuscripts, galley

22. Garson Kanin, telegram to Edwin O'Connor, December 12, 1963, EOCP 172.
23. *Boston Post*, January 7, 1955, 21.
24. Elliot Norton, "Hub Author Made Friends of Stars," *Boston Record-American*, March 5, 1970; Norton, interview.
25. Norton, "Hub Author."

proofs, and the final published version, are the kind of nightmare that only a textual scholar could love.[26] The most telling revisions and variations in all these versions occur toward the end, that part of his work O'Connor always had trouble getting under control. For the drama version of *I Was Dancing* O'Connor had at least four endings. The actors' copy, which presumably was used for the actual production, ends with Daniel doing his old dance routine for his three pals, who had come in to see how the battle with Tom turned out. Daniel yells out joyfully to his pals that he is going back to vaudeville. One earlier manuscript ends with Daniel dancing, but saying only, "I've changed my plans!" as in the novel version. A third manuscript version looks highly tentative and was quickly discarded because it was so clearly unsatisfactory. In this version, Daniel lies to the cronies that his fake heart attack had worked successfully on Tom and his wife, and that he could stay after all. "I knocked them arse over teakettle," he exclaims. In the last version, the published Dramatists Play Service edition, Daniel simply leaves with his pals, but still jaunty and unbowed. This ending was O'Connor's last go at the play after its theater run, and so it presumably represents his final wishes for it. These endings show that this play, out of all O'Connor's works, gave him considerable trouble. To the extent that the play was his showdown with his father's ghost, *I Was Dancing* reveals that O'Connor wrestled to the end. And that struggle was not over yet.

The play was a flop twenty minutes into its opening and everyone knew it. Everyone but the playwright, that is. For almost a decade O'Connor had been habituated to success, and even the cool reviews of the novel six months earlier had not deterred him; besides, the novel had sold reasonably well, even if it was never a bestseller. Elliot Norton kept close tabs on the play and on his friend during this trial. At the Wilbur one day he watched O'Connor in a balcony observing Burgess Meredith during a dress rehearsal. O'Connor was amused at first, but then became angry at Meredith's slipshod handling of his lines. O'Connor tallied up fifty-seven flubs and miscues. When it dawned on O'Connor that Meredith was drinking fairly heavily, he latched on tenaciously to this excuse for the play's failure.[27] He could not admit for the longest time that the failure lay in the character of Daniel Considine in a play that drowned in talkiness.

O'Connor gave an interview to P. C. Brooks of *Boston* magazine in which

26. EOCP 57–61; 308. The Dramatists Play Service edition was published in New York in 1965 and is still available. This acting edition contains a photograph and diagram of the set, along with a detailed inventory of props and costumes.
27. Norton, interview.

an accompanying photo shows O'Connor on stage with Burgess Meredith during a rehearsal. O'Connor has bags under his eyes and could not conceal the worry. His comments to Brooks also reveal a not terribly coherent O'Connor; the strain was taking its toll. He claims to like Burgess Meredith, who "can do anything." At another point he talks about what he sees as the play's theme: what to do with the elderly. O'Connor claims that people do not live in houses any more, only apartments. For some reason, he then abruptly laments the fact that there are no more home wakes. Perhaps the most revealing statement is the following: "[E]ven in the best of families, people for one reason or another, sometimes good, sometimes bad, find themselves as they get older, getting farther and farther from what would be called their home."[28]

The October 5 opening night at the Wilbur turned out to be a very blue Monday. Boston reviewers tried to be polite on behalf of a nice guy. The next day, the *Boston Traveler*'s Alta Mahoney thought the characters were interesting, if only something would happen in what was at most a work in progress. George Ryan wrote a thoughtful, though finally negative review in the *Boston Pilot*. O'Connor told Ryan that he respected the review nonetheless.[29] But the crucial review would be Elliot Norton's. Such was Norton's authority in the 1960s that he was widely believed to make or break a Boston run. And now he was in the unenviable position of writing a review of his friend's play.

Over the years Norton had learned to craft a review of 700 or 800 words in thirty to forty minutes in order to make the press deadline; someone once timed him at twenty-one minutes. In his reminiscences Norton claims that his *Record-American* review on October 6 tried to walk a fine line. But the review he actually wrote was an abruptly dismissive notice that lacked even faint praise. The review opened, "To be brief about it—and blunt—Edwin O'Connor's first play doesn't work on the stage." He went out of his way to blame O'Connor and not the director or the admittedly shaky Burgess Meredith. Norton was clearly scolding his younger friend for not heeding the advice he had given two years earlier. When he read the review, O'Connor was peevish—a word that several people began using about him during this incident and others later. Clearly he felt let down by a friend, almost betrayed. In his obsession with his first theatrical attempt he thought friends should come through for him. The high premium he placed on personal loyalty overruled considerations of objectivity and integrity. The strain with

28. O'Connor, interview with P. C. Brooks.
29. *Boston Pilot,* October 10, 1964, 12; George Ryan, letter to author, July 18, 2000.

Norton deepened by the hour as a new problem presented itself. At 7:30 that evening, Wednesday, O'Connor was scheduled to appear live on Norton's WGBH television program, "Elliot Norton Reviews." An audibly upset but defiant O'Connor phoned Norton that he would appear, but only because people would talk if he did not show up. O'Connor's last television interview, on October 6, 1964, was awkward, to put it mildly.

Over the twenty-two years of his weekly program Norton did more than 1,100 interviews with dramatists, producers, directors, and actors. He would ask straightforward questions, and the salty Bostonian seldom let fame, glitz, or jargon sway his judgment. He could parry deftly with the likes of David Merrick. Because Norton wasted little time on flattery, his sober Bostonian critiques were in marked contrast to television's smiley culture. The interview with O'Connor was strained. Norton tried to be gentle and kept the uninterrupted twenty-eight minutes to a discussion instead of a critique, but at one point O'Connor pointedly told Norton he was upset at his newspaper review. Although a slow rapprochement came about in the ensuing years, the two never regained their old friendship.[30]

O'Connor was in the dumps. Helen Strauss was in Boston, ready to console. She remembered walking around the Common many times with her stubborn client as she urged him to cut his losses and forget the whole thing. She wanted to spare him any more agony on Broadway. But "the stars were still in his eyes," she recalled. He insisted that everything would work out once the play moved to Washington, the last stop before Broadway.[31] An unidentified friend sent him a cheer-up letter; the postscript to the effect that Veniette in the audience was the real star at the Wilbur probably did little to lift O'Connor's sagging spirits.[32] Robert Manning, the new editor at *Atlantic Monthly,* who was fast becoming one of O'Connor's most cherished friends, saw O'Connor openly angry for the first time.[33]

O'Connor threw an opening night party at his Chestnut Street townhouse. It must have been a somber affair. When his old friend Bob Taylor was leaving, O'Connor stopped him near the sedan chair to say that he was still hopeful that a little more work would save the play.[34] As Taylor went

30. Norton, interview; author's personal recollections of Norton's series. The review appeared in the *Record-American* on October 6, 1964, 38. If the videotape even exists, it is a victim of the Boston Public Library flood of 1998 and now is in a freeze-dried condition; the prospects for restoration are uncertain.

31. Strauss, *Talent for Luck,* 275.

32. Larry ?, undated letter to Edwin O'Connor, EOCP 275.

33. Robert Manning, personal interview, April 5, 1999.

34. Robert Taylor, personal interview, April 5, 1999.

down the front steps, O'Connor called out from the darkness above, "Look, it's a flop, isn't it. But it won't stay one." He was trying to summon all the old optimism he could muster. Taylor remembered the moment as epiphanic: "He loomed large in those shadows then, and he still does."[35]

The play limped along for two weeks at the Wilbur, but the October 19 opening in Washington was more painful yet. At one point Helen Strauss was watching from backstage at the National Theater with David Merrick. "The audience, such as it was, sat motionless, absorbent as soundproofing, draining the sounds from the stage and returning a soft rustle of unison coughs and throat clearings." Even Merrick was despondent now. He turned to Strauss and said, "Okay, you're so smart, what would you do if you were the producer?" The ever-sensible Helen replied, "Close it!" But Merrick just walked away to seek out some flattery.[36] O'Connor was there, looking exhausted. An interviewer in his room at the Washington Hotel commented on how tired the playwright looked. O'Connor joked that he had taken the New Haven sleeper train, on which you cannot sleep. He grumbled about finding the theater boring, distracting, and tiring. "Usually I never read my own stuff," he told the interviewer. "Now I have to listen to it every day." The interview trailed off when O'Connor began foreswearing theater. If he ever tried it again, it would be "not very soon."[37]

After two more painful weeks in Washington, the play stumbled onto Broadway for a November 8 opening at the Lyceum Theater on West 45th Street, where some predicted that Burgess Meredith would finally lift the play off the boards. Nothing of the sort happened. In desperation O'Connor hastily scribbled some forgettable lyrics on his hotel stationary for Meredith to sing. The review in the *New York Times* delivered the final blow. Howard Taubman liked some of the characterization and wit, but altogether this play that started slowly talked itself "into limpness." Furthermore, the denouement looked contrived. Meredith never fully realized his character and Bean was pallid. Nevertheless, Taubman saw potential in O'Connor as a dramatist.[38] John McCarten's brief notice in *The New Yorker* on November 21 tried to find a few nice things to say, but he dismissed "Mr. O'Connor's vaudeville" as "full of holes as a lace stocking."

After the first performance O'Connor was finally resigned to the worst. That same night he trudged with John Kenneth Galbraith to Grand Central

35. Robert Taylor, undated (1970?) *Boston Globe* clipping, a review of *BL*.
36. Strauss, *Talent for Luck*, 275.
37. Edwin O'Connor, interview with Leroy F. Aarons, *Washington Post*, October 18, 1964, G1.
38. Howard Taubman, review of *I Was Dancing*, *New York Times*, November 9, 1964, 40.

Station for the Boston train. Galbraith remembers that O'Connor was crushed and profoundly saddened. He also was struck by how much his friend had aged.[39]

I Was Dancing closed after two weeks. For some time O'Connor leveled an acrimonious barrage against Burgess Meredith for sinking his play. Twice now an actor's drinking had marred an adaptation of his work. A few agreed with him; most did not. Edmund Wilson found it tiresome after a while that his friend could not recognize his "lack of sense of scale" in making a long play out of thin stuff.[40] More generously, Abe Burrows chalked the failure up to the solitariness of the novelist who could not release his play to the director and actors.[41]

That was just about the end of *I Was Dancing*. The Dramatists Play Service edition appeared the following year. Except for a Polish television version in the early 1990s, the play was never produced again.

O'Connor had traveled on this detour for far too long. He was distracting himself inordinately from his best talents in an ill-advised reach. One can only guess how his life with Veniette was affected. Fortunately, by year's end he began to put the terrible autumn of 1964 behind him. Best of all, he had not abandoned fiction, and he told several reviewers that he was itching to get his newest project moving along. Just in time to rescue his flagging spirits, the stunning opening chapter of his still unfinished next novel appeared in *Atlantic Monthly*—in late November, as the set of *I Was Dancing* was being dismantled.

39. John Kenneth Galbraith, personal interview, November 12, 1999.
40. Wilson, *The Sixties*, 454–55.
41. Burrows, *Honest, Abe*, 174–75.

CHAPTER THIRTEEN

ॐ *Recovery*
(1965–1966)

The contrast between *I Was Dancing* and the opening chapter of what was to be *All in the Family* is striking. O'Connor never did get a handle on either format of *I Was Dancing,* especially the play's several tentative conclusions. The writing in both play and novel is strained, and the plot, such as it is, grows tedious as the characters quickly become uninteresting. In his most open confrontation with the father figure that absorbed him, O'Connor's writing had suffered a setback. Fortunately, he was beginning to realize that the long line of older characters was taking its toll: Anthony Cantwell's father; General Blackburn in *The Oracle;* Colonel Sinclair in "Animal Life"; Monsignor Sugrue in "Parish Reunion"; Kevin Rowan's father ("YMP"); Frank Skeffington, John Gorman, Charlie Hennessey, Amos Force, Norman Cass Sr., Nathaniel Gardiner, and Roger Sugrue *(LH);* titular Mr. Garvey; Charlie Carmody, Dave Kennedy, Bucky Heffernan, and P. J. Mulcahy *(ES);* Daniel Considine and his three cronies *(D).* This score of men, at least a generation older than both their author and the younger characters against whom they so often do battle, had come to dominate his work over a fifteen-year span. Indeed, O'Connor told several interviewers in late 1964 that they had been his stock in trade, but also that it was time for a new inventory of more contemporary characters. "I'm going to leave the old men alone for a while," he told one interviewer, "[t]hough I may get an old man in there just to establish my trademark. . . ."[1]

The opening chapter of his next novel, published as "One Spring Morning" in the December 1964 *Atlantic Monthly,* marks a refreshing change for O'Connor, even if the Thoreauvian title belies the terrible incident that unfolds. The writing is as crisp and limpid as the mountain air and lake water of the setting, and there is no old man in sight—not yet, anyway. O'Connor accomplishes much of his effect here through the narrator's carefully controlled memory of boyhood. Although O'Connor's penchant for nostalgia is in evidence, for the most part it

1. O'Connor, interview with P. C. Brooks.

does not cloy. In one sense, to be sure, O'Connor has simply shifted down his age categories as the young boy observes his parents who are in their thirties. But boyhood memories form only the opening of the novel; adults with their politics and their families constitute three-fourths of it.

The appearance of "One Spring Morning" could not have come at a better time for O'Connor, and this *Atlantic* issue pulled out all the stops for him. To begin with, O'Connor's portrait appears for the first time on the cover, and not once but three times in overlapping drawings by James Avati that catch O'Connor by turns in bemused, alert, and contemplative moods. Although his lined brow and general aging are prominent, the open jersey collars and deep tan suggest Wellfleet sittings that previous summer, when O'Connor appeared relaxed and confident before the theater tribulations that were to come. The placement of O'Connor on the cover of his home-base magazine was complemented by a boxed announcement in the table of contents that "One Spring Morning" was an "Atlantic Extra," a feature event. Of course, it was also a way to whet readers' appetites for the complete novel later. Finally, the Thomas Nason contemporary wood engraving that accompanied the story captured the dark remoteness of northern New England's pine-fringed lakes.

Between the appearance of "One Spring Morning" in December 1964 and its barely changed reappearance as the opening chapter of *All in the Family* in September 1966, O'Connor worked on completing the novel with his customary discipline. (The chapter also appeared, as "One Still Morning," in *Life*'s international edition of August 23, 1965, along with five illustrations by Richard M. Powers; O'Connor was paid a thousand dollars.)[2] However, pre-publication of the mostly unfinished novel's opening chapter hung like a Damoclean sword over his typing table. Having started so brilliantly with what Arthur Schlesinger calls his best sustained piece of writing, O'Connor was painfully aware that he had to perform up to expectations.[3] This was an unprecedented situation; no other work of his had ever been given a sneak peek. But it put something of a strain on him—just when he did not need another one. He confessed to Bob Taylor that he had painted himself into a corner with that powerful opening chapter, and that he hoped he could fulfill its promise.[4] The Dickensian hazards of writing without a narrative plan would now dog him.

---

2. A. B. C. Whipple, editor of *Life* International Editions, letters to Edwin O'Connor, December 17, 1964, and July 21, 1965, EOCP 264. My thanks also to Pamela T. Wilson of Time Inc. Archives.

3. Schlesinger, Introduction to *BL*, 23–24.

4. Robert Taylor, personal interview, April 5, 1999.

Nevertheless, O'Connor was relieved that *I Was Dancing* was behind him, as he wrote with renewed confidence. Once again he was fusing two of his oldest subjects, politics and families, and he found quickly an important place for his "trademark" old man figure, who would turn out to be yet another problematic, dominant father.

In the meantime O'Connor's natural sociability and Veniette's gregariousness were bringing ever more friends into his varied circles. High on the list were Walter Kerr, the no-nonsense New York drama critic, and his wife, Jean Kerr, the popular playwright and author of *Please Don't Eat the Daisies* and *The Snake Has All the Lines*. O'Connor saved one letter from Jean Kerr which attests to the intensity of the friendship when she says that "you two" (Ed and Veniette) are "our" favorites, along with mutual friends Abe and Carin Burrows.[5] Jean Kerr's knack for domestic comedy and her firm Catholicism were additional bonds. O'Connor also was acquainted with Phyllis McGinley, whose "light" humorous verse carried serious Catholic themes, but nothing about their friendship survives.

O'Connor was devoting more time than ever to his culinary efforts. He befriended a former pianist turned food critic and cookbook author named Michael Field. Although food critics tended to dismiss Field, O'Connor thought enough of his abilities to write a book review of *Michael Field's Cooking School* for *Life* magazine in 1965. "How to Cook Without Baloney" scorns the cute and campy in favor of Field's lucid precision, from which one departs at one's peril. O'Connor clearly prefers a man's by-the-book method of cooking, which allowed little room for spontaneity and invention.[6] He developed another friendship with Ed Giobbe, a painter and cookbook author in the Provincetown artist colony, where the O'Connors bought one of his paintings. Giobbe recalls O'Connor's delight in cooking light meals with a French accent. Like many others, he remembers how easily and naturally O'Connor and Veniette got along. He especially admired O'Connor's open, friendly nature, which "never used intelligence as a weapon."[7]

For a long time O'Connor had been especially close to Robert and Jean DeGiacomo, whom he had met at John Kelleher's home in suburban West-

5. Jean Kerr, undated letter to Edwin O'Connor, EOCP 176.

6. Edwin O'Connor, "How to Cook Without Baloney," review of *Michael Field's Cooking School,* by Michael Field, *Life,* July 16, 1965, 21. By coincidence, this review appeared in the issue that began serializing *A Thousand Days,* Arthur Schlesinger's book on the Kennedy presidency.

7. Ed Giobbe, telephone interview, October 5, 1999.

wood, where Bob served as town counsel.[8] The DeGiacomos came from the blue-collar Dorchester section of Boston and were a hardworking, dedicated, and caring couple. According to several people, Bob DeGiacomo may have been O'Connor's closest friend during these years. They met frequently for breakfast or lunch at the Ritz. The extreme reserve of both men would normally be a hindrance in such friendships, but that was not the case here. Unfortunately, no paper record concerning their friendship survives. Bob De-Giacomo was an unusually conscientious lawyer who rose to assistant attorney general. In the mid-1960s he had a prominent role in investigations into the Boston Common parking garage scandal. This controversial underground garage had been proposed during one of Mayor Curley's terms and had been fought by preservationists and Beacon Hill residents. Even as construction proceeded in the early 1960s all kinds of scandals involving graft erupted. As a Beacon Hill resident for almost a decade, O'Connor must have cheered on Bob DeGiacomo's prosecution of the culprits. Whereas exposing corruption had not figured largely in *The Last Hurrah,* now in the more activist 1960s O'Connor interested himself in the desirability as well as the dilemmas of reform, all of which became important in *All in the Family.* Indirectly, then, his friendship with DeGiacomo may have influenced the novel.

Encouraged by his successful prosecution in a highly publicized case, Bob DeGiacomo ran for state attorney general in 1966. O'Connor took a small but active role in DeGiacomo's campaign, most likely as a speech writer, as ties of friendship and loyalty lured him out of the writer's den. DeGiacomo's was the only political campaign on which O'Connor ever worked, his one overt involvement in the activist decade.[9] But all for naught. DeGiacomo lost badly at the Democratic state convention in June. O'Connor kept a tally in a small notebook of what appear to be votes for the five candidates, but for some reason he put no figure down for his friend. Perhaps the scenario that unfolded reminded him too painfully of Skeffington's "last hurrah" night. Later, Clem Norton sent O'Connor one of his microscopic pages of opinion in which he said, not too kindly, that "DiGiacomo [sic] doesn't know what hit him and can't be told."[10] Bob DeGiacomo eventually became a judge in

8. I wish to thank John Kelleher, John Tosi, and Jean DeGiacomo for information on O'Connor's friendship with Robert DeGiacomo.

9. Unless, that is, one counts his advice to Arthur Schlesinger on a speech at the annual Al Smith Dinner. O'Connor suggested that his friend quote Dr. Johnson on the Irish."[T]he Irish are a FAIR PEOPLE—they never speak well of one another" could stand as a gloss on some of O'Connor's best satire. Edwin O'Connor, letter to Arthur Schlesinger Jr., October 11, 1961, EOCP 279.

10. Clem Norton, letter to Edwin O'Connor, September 17, 1966, EOCP 207.

Massachusetts, before moving to New Mexico, where he also sat on the bench.

In the spring of 1964, O'Connor began one of his most important friendships, when Robert Manning came fresh from the New Frontier to *Atlantic Monthly*.[11] Bob Manning was almost O'Connor's age. In 1949 he began working at *Time,* where he rose to senior editor and later ran *Time-Life*'s London office. His most recent position had been Undersecretary of State for Public Affairs in the Kennedy administration. Manning assumed the title of executive director at *Atlantic* and succeeded Ted Weeks as editor two years later, a position he held until 1980. Given *Atlantic*'s continuing interest in world affairs, it is easy to see why this veteran journalist and old Washington hand was chosen. He quickly became much more of a friend for O'Connor than Ted Weeks had ever been.

The two men met at a welcoming lunch upstairs at the Ritz. O'Connor had to correct Manning's initial mistake about his name. "It's not Edward, it's Edwin," he said, while possibly mimicking Ted Weeks, who was close by. Manning found O'Connor to be cheerful and quippy, but he soon detected a strong seriousness beneath the banter. He also realized early on that O'Connor was getting worried about his writing. Manning quickly saw that his role was to be the encouraging friend that O'Connor needed during an unsure phase. Like several other people, including Bob Taylor and Abe Burrows, Bob Manning called O'Connor his best friend, even though they knew each other only a few years. O'Connor had that kind of quiet personal magnetism.

Editor and author had one interesting encounter in Wellfleet. Once when Manning was staying at Heyward Cutting's house, his Karmann Ghia was rammed by O'Connor, who was driving his big Mercedes much too fast on the winding sandy road. Manning's small car was disabled. The *Boston Globe* ran a small story under the headline, "Author and Editor Collide." But there never was any breach between the men, and the Mannings and O'Connors socialized frequently. Manning sometimes ran in a fast set with other ex-New Frontiersmen, but he admired O'Connor's unusual probity. He never heard O'Connor swear or tell an off-color joke. He, too, like many others, remembers O'Connor's habit of throwing a penny out a window at the *Atlantic,* as if to say, "Who needs money?" On other occasions, O'Connor would modulate the gesture into a kind of shrug, as if throwing something away. Manning appreciated O'Connor's cookery, especially his masterpiece—butterflied leg of lamb on the grill.

11. For the following material I am grateful mostly to Robert Manning for a personal interview on April 5, 1999, and to Peter Davison for supplementary information.

O'Connor's reputation for clean living could never be punctured by the gossip columnists, but in December 1964 he did suffer a bit of embarrassment in a case of mistaken identity. A San Francisco newspaper blabbed that an Edwin O'Connor was a "virtual commuter" from Nevada to San Francisco, where he was seeing a local woman. On Christmas Day Jack Rosenbaum publicly apologized in the *San Francisco News Call Bulletin* for the mix-up with the Boston author.[12]

O'Connor still regularly visited Rhode Island to see his mother and sister on Providence's East Side. If Jack's children were also visiting, O'Connor would treat them to ice cream at the Newport Creamery around the corner on Angell Street, where he still indulged his own weakness. When the Beatles invaded America in 1964, O'Connor worked his connections to secure tickets for his oldest nephew. And he still told Jack's children long, corny stories about characters named Belnaps and Tortonia, which they fondly recall to this day.[13]

By mid-1965 the O'Connors had had enough of the ordeals by water at 107 Chestnut Street, and at any rate after twenty years of renting O'Connor wanted a Boston house of his own. Accordingly, O'Connor again secured the services of John Tosi, who quickly found a handsome and mostly furnished townhouse at 10 Marlborough Street, across from the old rooming house at No. 11 which O'Connor had left ten years earlier.[14] O'Connor would again live next to the *Atlantic* offices.

No. 10 Marlborough Street had been built and owned by the Wolcott family, whose English ancestor Henry Wolcott landed in Boston in its founding year of 1630. His descendants became prominent in banking and public service. A Roger Wolcott had been a colonial governor, and at the end of the nineteenth century the upright public service career of another Roger Wolcott as governor of the Commonwealth of Massachusetts had overlapped the first years of the very different political tenure of one James Michael Curley. This latter Roger Wolcott may very well be the model for J. P. Marquand's quintessentially proper Bostonian George Apley, the author's protestations about not writing *The Late George Apley* as a roman à clef notwithstanding.[15] O'Connor seems to have realized some of the many ironies of coming into the possession of a house with so many Brahmin resonances. He told Ed-

---

12. Newspaper clipping, EOCP 305.

13. Beatrice O'Connor, personal interview, September 10, 1999.

14. Again I am indebted to John Tosi for supplying much of the following information. Peter Davison, Stephen Weil, and Robert Taylor were also helpful.

15. Introduction to the Modern Library edition, 1940.

mund Wilson that the original owner had built the place "with the ambition of being the possessor of the biggest private house in Boston."[16] For someone so steeped in Boston lore, it seems likely that O'Connor was also aware of the house's literary associations. As he showed with his moves to 48 Beacon Street and 107 Chestnut Street, he was determined to stride the acreage and inhabit the mansions of Boston's Four Hundred.

Although O'Connor bought his new house when Boston real estate values were still relatively low, the purchase nevertheless represented a significant and continuing layout that would soon become unsustainable. O'Connor seemed set on owning what some have called the best-built house in Boston. Excellence had always been important to him. It was part of his upbringing, and had been pursued by him in his choice of education, in his selection of an architect for his summer house, in his developing tastes in food, clothes, cars, and hotels, and most of all in his polished writing. Except for a few rare lapses, his pursuit of high standards did not manifest itself as social climbing or ostentatious display. He was no insecure, provincial Silas Lapham from Howells's novel, determined to have a showy townhouse in the Back Bay. But as for O'Connor's financial acumen and foresight—that was another matter.

Like many of Boston's excellences, 10 Marlborough does not call attention to itself. Its pale limestone exterior, sandwiched between two "red bricks," is a chaste and restrained Georgian revival of four stories that could fit easily into Edwardian London. A pair of Ionic columns flank the sidewalk-level entrance under a handsome Palladian window interlaced with iron filigree. The interior had been meticulously maintained by many "white uniforms" during its sixty years in the Wolcott family. A point of pride were the massive interior doors that still fitted meticulously. The basement contained a full kitchen from which food was sent up by dumbwaiter to a spacious butler's pantry and then eventually to the large elegant dining room. The O'Connors had a new kitchen built in the butler's pantry in order to accommodate sensibly their interest in cooking. From the foyer a grand staircase ascended to the spacious living room on the second floor. With its decorative plaster ceiling and niches empty of their busts, this room appeared to some, like Edmund Wilson, as too formal and even cold, but it was perfect for the large parties given by the new owners and still remembered. Often O'Connor invited Barbara and Bill up from Providence for these parties.

Preserved in one of his notebooks is O'Connor's tentative invitation list to his New Year's Eve party in 1965.[17] A special guest of honor was Abe Bur-

---

16. Edmund Wilson, *BL* 346; *Atlantic*, October 1969, 66.
17. EOCP 71.

rows, who was delighted to attend, even if this Boston fete represented something of a sacrifice for a New Yorker. More than forty people were served lavishly by staff from the nearby Ritz, who were also invited to enjoy the food.[18] The roster of invitations reads like a credit scroll of O'Connor's life: besides Abe and Carin Burrows, there were the Davisons, the DeGiacomos, the Mannings, John Tosi, Heyward Cutting, the Nortons, Laurence Winship, Arthur Gartland, the Galbraiths, Peggy Yntema, and a score more.

One item on the guest list is unexpected: the name "Chub Peabody" is entered with a question mark beside it, then entered again, and eventually crossed out. Endicott "Chub" Peabody had been a young governor of Massachusetts for a single two-year term that had recently ended. He had a star-crossed time at the State House. Even though he had forsaken the Republican Party of his blue blood tribe to embrace the party of F.D.R. and J.F.K., Democratic legislators could not quite trust the former Harvard football player known as the "baby face assassin" for his deceptive gridiron ferocity. "Chub" and O'Connor had become acquaintances at some point, possibly through Bob DeGiacomo. His name on the list is a unique occurrence, because O'Connor ordinarily avoided entertaining important politicians of any stripe. However, he was still writing his novel about a reform-minded governor, and for once he may have cultivated a political friendship out of professional motives.

O'Connor lived at 10 Marlborough Street for a little over two years, until financial reality caught up with him. This may have been his favorite Boston house, and to give it up was probably a sad occasion. While to some it may have seemed a pretentious place for a novelist to own, O'Connor kept the place in perspective. He once quipped to Robert Taylor about his two Marlborough Street sojourns: "I lived in a Marlborough Street rooming house where I shared a bathroom with five other persons. Now I live across the street, and I'm in a single house with five bathrooms."[19]

As it had done so often, *Atlantic Monthly* carried a piece by O'Connor just before Atlantic Monthly Press's publication of his next novel, this to keep his name before the reading public. The light satire of "The Book Fair" appeared in the July 1966 issue, where O'Connor was described as a "guest contributor" filling in for Charlie Morton who was ill; the editor's note added that O'Connor's "important new novel" would be out in September. O'Connor's brief article was the lead item in the "Accent on Living" section, where

18. Robert Manning, personal interview, April 5, 1999.
19. Robert Taylor, "The Way I'll Always Remember Ed O'Connor," *Boston Globe,* March 25, 1968.

O'Connor had broken into print with Morton's help in 1946 and where he had last appeared in 1955. Carl Rose, who still furnished the illustrations, depicted a circus barker whose cane points to a gallery of authors and books. O'Connor's column gently ribs the rituals and irrelevancies of the three book fairs he has attended, two of which had featured him as a speaker. He provides not even the barest summary of his remarks at these events, however, and concludes the article with a wry one-sentence paragraph: "I have not since been to any book fairs."[20] These were the last of his own words that O'Connor himself saw in the magazine that had started his writing career.

The structure of *All in the Family* marks something of an innovation for O'Connor.[21] The first quarter of the book (Part I) records the spring and summer, circa 1935, when the narrator, Jack Kinsella, was "eleven—going on twelve," that phase of boyhood that most interested O'Connor. The remaining three-quarters (Parts II–V) covers almost two years some thirty years later, in the mid-1960s.

Part I, whose first chapter had appeared in *Atlantic*, describes the loss of young Jackie's mother and the ensuing trip with his father to Ireland. Jackie's beautiful, talented, but disturbed mother apparently committed suicide—there were no eyewitnesses—on an early spring trip to the family cabin in northern New England by jumping out of a canoe, taking her other young son with her. "Anthony Cantwell" had inaugurated a series of important characters who were widowers in almost every long work O'Connor wrote: Jonathan Cantwell; Kevin Rowan's father ("YMP"), Frank Skeffington *(LH)*, Charlie Carmody *(ES)*, Daniel Considine *(D)*, Uncle Jimmy Kinsella *(F)*, Gerald Caffery *("TB")*. Other secondary characters are also notable widowers: Amos Force (presumably) and Roger Sugrue *(LH)*, Dave Kennedy *(ES)*. In *Benjy*'s ferocious ending we watch in secret glee as Daddy becomes a widower contentedly free of the awesome and awful Mummy. In the gripping opening chapter of O'Connor's new novel, he makes the death of a wife happen within earshot. (The father's strenuous efforts at rescue in the cold water prove fruitless; the author who had rescued people at Wellfleet captures the

20. *Atlantic*, July 1966, 124–25.
21. (Boston: Atlantic Monthly Press/Little, Brown, 1966). The book was dedicated to his publisher, trusted adviser, and good friend, Arthur Thornhill. When the famous television series of the same name appeared in the early 1970s, a legal challenge by O'Connor's publishers to the use of the title came to naught; Rank, *O'Connor*, 151. As late as January 1966 Edwin O'Connor still did not have a title for his novel, which he was struggling to end. According to a letter from Peter Davison, then director of Atlantic Monthly Press, two titles were apparently being tossed around: *The Governor's Ear* and *The Governor's Cousin*; letter to O'Connor, January 10, 1966, courtesy of Peter Davison.

terror convincingly.) To bring father and son closer, the author also arranges for Jackie's only sibling to perish as well. This time O'Connor isolates and intensifies his father-son preoccupation considerably. However, during the thirty-year gap between Parts I and II, Jack's idealized father, whose dreaminess is symbolized by solo flying in his private plane, has died. He is replaced for the rest of the novel by the Kinsella patriarchal ogre, Uncle Jimmy, the father's older brother and a past master of international business realpolitik. O'Connor got his "trademark" old man in there quickly enough.

All in the Family actually opens with a short scene some three years before the drownings. In two pages O'Connor describes how the family factotum, a small but powerful man named Arthur, subdues a house intruder. The purpose of this scene, the most violent in O'Connor's novels, is not clear, unless it was meant as a foreshadowing of the dangers to the Kinsella clan over the next thirty-five years. (O'Connor's novels usually begin gently with someone doing a lot of talking, but not with physical violence.) With this strikingly different opening, O'Connor was also responding to the rising violence, at home and abroad, of the 1960s; the novel makes one indirect allusion to the Vietnam War and several allusions to rising racial tensions, one of them of some importance.

Only three weeks after the drownings, father and son are driving toward Uncle Jimmy's "castle" in Kerry. Shortly before they arrive, a curious incident occurs (51–52). Jackie's father spots a small shallow pool which is ideal for a dip. Having no bathing suits, they simply strip and wade in because there is no one around in the lonely Irish countryside. One would think the "freezing cold" water in April would be a painful reminder of the recent horror, but O'Connor renders the brief scene as an odd bonding; the words are few but a tacit understanding between father and son helps free them from death's grip. The bracing immersion also prepares Jackie to encounter Uncle Jimmy. Indeed, right after this dip Jackie's father gives his son a talk on money properly used—and on money as used by Uncle Jimmy. This short scene, complete with the gestures and symbolic moves that serve to unite males, is the last such scene of Jackie with the ideal father. These contrasting figures of the ideal but dreamy father and the rough-edged despotic father that is Uncle Jimmy owe a lot to O'Connor's nearly continuous reading of Dickens, where such pairings abound.

An earlier scene (10–12) back at the lake, when father and son admit they dislike fishing and thereupon sink their boat deliberately, may owe something to O'Connor's unsuccessful attempts at fishing with his stepson, Stephen, at Harbour Island. Of course it also serves as an ironic foreshadowing of the drowning scene. For the first time, O'Connor was writing from the deepened perspective of a father himself.

Just before arrival at Uncle Jimmy's Ireland retreat, a symbol richly prefigures the novel's events:

On each side of the road were tall smooth trees with green vines like ivy crawling all over their thick trunks. My father told me that sooner or later these vines would kill the trees by just winding around them and slowly strangling them to death. I kept looking back at the trees and wondering why somebody didn't come along and cut off the vines, and just as I was thinking this my father said, unexpectedly but quietly, "Coming up dead ahead: one castle!" (53)

At this "castle" (a place Uncle Jimmy actually dislikes, along with most things Irish) Jackie spends a long idyllic summer with his three cousins: Phil, Charles, and James. Phil becomes a special pal whom Jack will support against Charles many years later. In fact, for the next thirty years Phil carries in his wallet the pact that they signed that Kerry summer, and he produces it at the novel's climax. Nothing in O'Connor's work so clearly stands for boyhood, family, friendship, and loyalty as that "old folded piece of paper" (415), and nothing—neither politics nor patriarchs—can take its place.

At the castle the maternal warmly contrasts with the paternal in the person of the gentle Aunt Mary, who is the antithesis of her brash James Cagney of a husband. If Uncle Jimmy is prefigured by the disappointing hollow ruin of the ancient castle "dead ahead" on his grounds, Aunt Mary is the life-affirming presence within the beautiful nearby house. In a scene of understated warmth (62–66), she welcomes Jackie to her home and is the only one to speak words of consolation for his loss. They embrace in a moving and convincing moment. "Mary" was of course the name of O'Connor's own mother, and the description of Mary Kinsella vaguely resembles Mary O'Connor: "She was tall . . . , with a long smooth quiet face and a rather big mouth" (62). For the first time, Jackie can cry for his lost mother and brother. Like so many of O'Connor's fictional mothers, she will die young, long before the reassertion of widower Uncle Jimmy in Jack Kinsella's adult life.

Near the end of his stay in Ireland Jackie inadvertently overhears his uncle and father talking one night. Uncle Jimmy tries to rouse his younger brother from what he sees as unhealthy moping over his dead wife. When Jimmy demands that his brother leave Jackie to be brought up with his own sons, Jackie's father rouses himself to guard Jackie against this man who can act brutishly toward his sons, both verbally and physically. Then to his amazement, Jackie, who had simply assumed his mother's death was accidental, hears his father talk about the probability that the death was a suicide.[22] Jackie hears for this first time that Chrissie Kinsella had suffered recurring bouts of deep depression that necessitated long periods of hospitalization, which Jackie had thought to be extended trips. All this is almost more than the confused Jackie can handle, and it hints at so much to come, just like those trees and strangling vines:

[I]t seemed to me that all these things . . . were in some way sad and unhappy. It was as if whatever they had done or been through had for some reason not turned out the way they hoped it would but instead had got all tangled up or twisted around, so that in the end almost everybody wound up being disappointed or miserable or in some dreadful kind of trouble (103).

A few days later Jackie is off to boarding school. Part I ends: "I began what I suppose was the business of growing up" (110).

The rest of *All in the Family* is politics, family, and a breakthrough for O'Connor: love. After a ten-year sabbatical from the tumult of elections, O'Connor abruptly opens Part II thus: "On the first Tuesday of November . . . Charles was elected governor of the state" (113). It is now 1965 or so, made clear by a reference to a "Jack" who is no longer president, along with a few other historical allusions. However, as in all of his novels after *The Oracle*, O'Connor eschews the topical, with one notable exception, as he plumbs the familial.

The political story is simple enough. Charles, the youngest of Uncle Jimmy's sons, had been designated by his father to be the family politician who would clear up the mess in city and state government. The city and state are the very turfs Skeffington ruled, and are thus presumably Boston and Massachusetts, mostly. After four years in City Hall, Charles got elected governor by a 1960s post-Skeffington, heterogeneous coalition on a strong liberal/reformist platform. Charles is no parochial Kevin McCluskey from *The Last Hurrah*, however. He is Ivy League, cool and calculating. Older brother Phil acts as Charles's close adviser and point man. (James, the third brother, has become a famous Vatican II-era priest whose ecumenical jaunts around the world excuse him from family councils; for some reason O'Connor is ambivalent about him.) On election night Jack Kinsella spots tensions already developing between the more idealistic Phil and the more pragmatic Charles,

---

22. A crucial piece of evidence is the lack of any water in the canoe: water would have indicated an accidental capsizing, while lack of water would have meant a deliberate jumping out. Rank (167) reports that, in talks with Peggy Yntema, O'Connor wanted to leave the matter ambiguous. But O'Connor seems to have known something about canoes; he was even planning a canoe trip with John Kelleher for the summer of 1968. The water evidence cannot be easily dismissed.

who is already eyeing the Senate and beyond. After only a few months Phil breaks from Charles, who, he believes, has abandoned the cause of reform. When Phil goes semi-public by writing critically of Charles in a newspaper letter signed by "Edmund Burke," a name rich with suggestions of intelligent Irish political reform, Charles warns Phil to stop at once. When Phil refuses, Charles highhandedly arranges for Phil to be committed to a mental institution and thus be thoroughly discredited. As late as 1965 such commitments for insanity could still be done legally with relative ease. After a painful last showdown, Phil is committed for a brief time. There is just enough unbalanced zeal in Phil's actions to make the imputation of derangement plausible. But the Kinsella family is devastated by it all. Uncle Jimmy bows out of the novel with angry, bewildered words: "'What the hell has happened?' he cried. '*What the hell has happened to my family?*'" (416; O'Connor's italics). His plans for a Kinsella dynasty have destroyed his family. By keeping it all in the family, in his controlling patriarchal manner, he loses the very pride of his life in this Irish American tragedy.

This primary narrative of a family's ruination by politics has its counterpoint in the secondary story of Jack Kinsella and his wife, Jean. During the election-night party we learn that their twenty-year marriage, a childless one, is in deep trouble. Several months earlier Jean had abruptly left for Europe with a cad whom she quickly dropped. Late on election night Jack gets a phone call from Jean, who wants to return. Jack is ecstatic, forgiving, but cautious. He has been hurt, but he gradually comes to understand that he had hurt as well. O'Connor neatly introduces the beginning of love's healing precisely at the apex of Kinsella political fortunes, when that family is poised for its fall. In the end love is the victor in this novel in which politics, both civic and familial, only destroys. To round things off, after twenty years of marriage, Jean becomes improbably pregnant during a second honeymoon in Ireland at the novel's conclusion. O'Connor apparently is emphasizing a return to roots for Irish America.

The political scenario struck many readers and critics as a thinly veiled Kennedy saga, complete with domineering tycoon father who had made his shady fortune in the interwar years, a crusading but reckless brother/adviser who smacks of Bobby Kennedy, and the repudiation of the Curley/Skeffington style by the Kennedys/Kinsellas. Although the Atlantic/Little, Brown edition carefully avoided dealing the Kennedy deck on its dust jacket, the shameless Bantam paperback edition of the following year had no such scruples. Bantam's cover depicted a handsome young man striding toward a bank of microphones for a press conference. He radiates Kennedy charisma:

lean build, healthy head of blow-dried hair, handsome face and famous grin, hand inserted into the pocket of a slightly rumpled suit jacket. An accompanying puff from *Book Week* insinuated, "Politics in the Kennedy mode . . . [O'Connor] has all the facts, fit and unfit." Well, yes and no. To be sure, O'Connor could not have been unaware of some striking parallels between Uncle Jimmy's family and Joe Kennedy's, given his acquaintanceship with Jack, and given moreover the obvious fact that by 1966 the post-assassination mythologizing of the Kennedys was already far advanced. Even John Kelleher thought that his novelist friend compromised himself on this one.[23] But while America's premier family no doubt lurked somewhere in O'Connor's mind, *All in the Family* is no more "about" the Kennedys than *The Last Hurrah* is a biography of Curley. Kennedys and Curley were merely catalysts for O'Connor. His special talents were, as should be apparent by now, geared to probing the family dynamics of successful third-generation Irish Americans. To do so, he did not shirk from available material, much in the way that Mario Puzo knew that Mafia crime families were not a figment of the F.B.I.'s imagination. If O'Connor wanted to write about the tensions in ambitious Irish political lives, then the Kennedy connection could serve well. Shakespeare, after all, used real political dynasties for the history plays.

But there is another reason for O'Connor's use of Kennedy material, especially the Joe Kennedy connection. Powerful and colorful Uncle Jimmy is, like his immediate fictional predecessors, one of O'Connor's self-made Irish American codgers who is determined to manipulate his family. In the run-up to this novel, O'Connor had half-heartedly promised not to let this bugbear back in, but back in he came and with a vengeance. And as we also might expect by now, along with him appears the opposing figure of a son (or nephew in this case) with clear autobiographical elements. Jack Kinsella is largely a passive observer of the unfolding family divisions, a sounding board at best. Like Adam Caulfield, John Carmody, and Tom Considine before him, Jack can do little to change the stubborn ways of the clan patriarch. Unlike his predecessors, however, he finds more of his own life to enjoy.

The parallels between Jack Kinsella and O'Connor are so obvious that one suspects that for the first time the author was adopting an autobiographical perspective in spite of his advertised suspicions of the device. Consider: Jack Kinsella comes from comfortably assimilated and well-educated middle-class Irish America, is only about four years O'Connor's junior, was once a vaudeville buff, is married but has not sired. Furthermore, he is a novelist himself. As Greene did in creating Rollo Martins in *The Third Man* and Maurice Ben-

---

23. John Kelleher, personal interview, May 29, 1999.

drix in *The End of the Affair,* O'Connor has created a partial portrait of himself as a minor novelist who is competent in his craft but not outstanding. In fact, Jack Kinsella works in the Greeneian subgenre of the literary thriller. And when Jack looks back on his career (141–42 especially, and passim), we can hear distinct echoes of O'Connor's own: the early desire to write for a living, the long stretch of failure, his noninvolvement in political movements, even a borrowing from O'Connor's frustrating New York lunches with his first publisher. At one point O'Connor lets his guard down when he has Jack admit to a problem that was beginning to bother O'Connor himself: "I found that I was working and reworking the same paragraph over and over again without much happening. I was conscious of far too many words and far too little action" (292). But even more intriguing than Jack as novelist is Jack as confidential secretary to one Frank Skeffington in his last years. Jack Kinsella did not appear in *The Last Hurrah,* and *All in the Family* is not a sequel to the earlier novel. But retrofitting *The Last Hurrah* to make Jack a secretary—a confidential secretary, at that, with connotations of privacy and trust—to a Skeffington he clearly admired: does this not sound like an oblique stand-in for O'Connor as Skeffington's elegist in the famous novel?

Jack's wife is O'Connor's most developed female character. The maturity brought about by late marriage was bearing fruit. As if to pay a disguised tribute to Veniette, with whom he felt so lucky and happy, O'Connor created in Jean Kinsella a partial portrait of his own wife, along with a curious projection of his own insecurities. Some parallels: Jean is beautifully svelte, dresses stylishly, and draws fashion designs—a glance at Veniette's painting. A more pointed allusion to Veniette occurs when the "convent-trained, willful" Jean describes her unhappy childhood: "Growing up . . . I heard only two sounds in our house: screams and prayers. I got a little tired of both" (234). A bit later O'Connor writes: "In the observance of her religious duties she was quite likely to be casual" (235). As a description of Veniette, this was putting the matter somewhat mildly. O'Connor was having his little private amusement here, while sending his wife a gentle chiding on a matter of supreme importance to him. This was not the first time O'Connor had buried a message to someone he cared about in his novels.[24]

If it can be assumed that a Jean Kinsella/Veniette O'Connor parallel operates in some way, then what are we to make of the marital problems in the novel, specifically those seven months when Jean abandoned Jack? No such separation or anything even approaching it ever took place in the O'Con-

24. What to make of the fact that O'Connor gives Jack's wife the name of the "Jean" from his Notre Dame years? Had O'Connor carried some kind of torch that long?

nors' marriage. The easy answer is that O'Connor wanted his subplot of love's renewal issuing in a new family to be the foil to the disintegrating political family run by Uncle Jimmy. A less obvious source can be found in Jean's long explanation to Jack. Over the twenty long years of their marriage she had come to feel lonely and finally neglected. It is not too hard to imagine that Jean's complaint was one that O'Connor heard from Veniette:

The trouble was that I had you part-time, and you had me in pretty much the same way you had your car or your books or some college buddy. . . . [H]alf the time you were a married man living by yourself. In a way you've always been a married bachelor: sometimes I've thought you lived exactly the way you would have lived if I hadn't ever come along (239).

The particular details and language Jean uses, especially "married bachelor," carry a special relevance for O'Connor. From an autobiographical angle, the story of Jean is both a love letter to Veniette and a projection of the author's understandable insecurities in having married late to a divorcee who was tepid at best in her Catholicism.

Then there is the delicate matter of Jean's pregnancy at the end. After twenty years Jack's wife, now apparently in her early forties, is to give birth to her first child. This unlikely event makes for a homecoming ending to a novel of high political tragedy, but was there a Veniette angle here too? When O'Connor was writing the novel, Veniette was in her late thirties. Her only child had been born a dozen years earlier. By the time *All in the Family* was published the O'Connors had been married four years. In Irish American "good Catholic" families of that era, this meant that an unspoken statute of limitations in matters of procreation was running out. To snoop into this matter between the devoutly Catholic O'Connor and the skeptical, independent Veniette would be to act like too many confessors in the not-so-distant past. But it seems plausible at the very least that O'Connor ended his novel with Jean's joyful announcement of her pregnancy and Jack's ecstatic response as a signal to Veniette that he wanted children of his own. Irish American men can be that circuitous. (In a notebook for the novel, O'Connor struggled with this scene's dialogue. Numerous cross-outs and nearly indecipherable handwriting gather to a head as Jack is thunderstruck at Jean's announcement.[25] In his notebooks it is striking how often O'Connor's jottings become excited and blurry when a character close to himself gets emotionally worked up.) In any event, O'Connor and Veniette never did have a child of their own.

Almost at the end of the novel O'Connor writes:

25. EOCP 71.

Mr. Guilfoyle became . . . the first to hear our news. He seemed overjoyed; he talked to us for a long time; the call ended with his last cry in our ears.

"Come back, come back!" he said. "Come back to Holy Ireland! We'll all be waiting for you!"

I waited for the "Ah ha ha ho!" This time it did not come (433).

The kindly hotel manager drops his customary jollity as he is pressed into service as a serious choric commentator: Holy Ireland can give birth in many senses. Right after this, Jack and Jean pay a last visit to Uncle Jimmy's castle. The day is bleak and empty; Uncle Jimmy had left a week earlier with no mention of his plans. His lack of vital roots in a Holy Ireland, it is implied, had doomed his political offspring in America. The novel ends with an implied contrast between the new life about to enter a family and the withering atrophy of another which sadly lost its way.

A final note on Uncle Jimmy. As the dominating father figure, he has the blood of Charlie Carmody and Daniel Considine in his veins. Wealth, connections, and power make Uncle Jimmy far more formidable, however. A loudmouth whose signature expletive is "bushwa" (a euphemistic Canadian variant of "bullshit" heard frequently among French-Canadians in Woonsocket), Uncle Jimmy is a peppery little man who bullies everyone. Only women, Jean and Phil's wife, Flossie, stand up to him, as Helen once did to Charlie Carmody. As we might suspect, O'Connor borrows for Uncle Jimmy some features from his own father. Both detested Roosevelt, both had a touch of the vaudevillian, and both were capable of popping off angrily. O'Connor tries to soften the picture of Uncle Jimmy toward the end, when Jack notices that he was "a deeply troubled man" and even a lonely "pathetic figure." He was "still nominally the boss of the tribe, and yet for the first time he was completely powerless" (377). This time no heart attack, real or feigned, is required to reduce the once powerful patriarch.

Although the city and state are the same as in *The Last Hurrah*, some shrinkage has occurred, as indicated by a bishop's presence instead a cardinal's. Boston and Massachusetts are the most likely candidates, although as usual O'Connor never provides names. Uncle Jimmy's dismissal of "that deadhead burg" with its "cold codfish Yankees" and "cornball Harps" (89) fixes the location vividly enough. But some items indicate that in downsizing his mythological domain from Boston's proportions O'Connor seems to have Providence and Rhode Island partly in mind too. For example, Charles Kinsella enjoys student support from the six colleges in the area, a size which almost exactly fits Providence and environs in 1965 but which is a far cry from the dozens of colleges in metro Boston. And when Jack Kinsella reminisces about his home turf, Rhode Island seems close by:

[I]n a peculiar way I felt a satisfaction of my own, for this state, this city, was after all my home: I had had my childhood there, I had grown up there, and even though in recent years I had gone away often and sometimes stayed away a long time, I was a poor expatriate—I had never really felt at home anywhere else. . . . Politically it was a mess, and close to being a disaster. . . . Someone once said of us that corruption here had a shoddy, penny ante quality it did not have in other states . . . (147).

The personal nostalgia here is considerable, and the depiction of Rhode Island politics all too accurate. Thus, while O'Connor has Boston chiefly in mind, he tends to reduce the scale of the arena to his own home state's proportions.

If the politics and corruption are petty, the scale of hyper-affluent Kinsella life is outsized. Grand houses abound: Jack's own family manse, Uncle Jimmy's "castle" in Ireland, the "gloomily handsome" old Burroughs mansion that Charles owns (a pointed Irish takeover from a dotty Yankee), Phil's winter home on the Georgia coast. Frequent and prolonged international travel is simply assumed by this clan, along with boarding schools and Ivy League degrees, expensive hotels, country seats, and never a shortage of servants. To some extent all this affluence reflects O'Connor's own pattern in Boston/Wellfleet/Dublin/Harbour Island. It was both a way of life to which he aspired and a potential cauldron of troubles. Like Fitzgerald forty years earlier, O'Connor felt both the lure and falsity of riches, but unlike Fitzgerald, O'Connor generally kept a sober perspective.

There are a few additional allusions of some note. As a kind of private joke on himself, O'Connor lent his own nickname, used only by a few intimates and by O'Connor himself, to the minor figure of "Edso" Monahan, who with his sidekick "Walshie" are tiresome vaudevillian leftovers from *The Last Hurrah*. Wiser revision would have cut these clowns. O'Connor drags them into the novel for some kind of presumed comic relief, but they are merely annoying. The bishop is obviously Richard J. Cushing, whose long tenure as archbishop of Boston (1944–1970; cardinal from 1958) was practically the only one that O'Connor ever knew. The two fleeting descriptions of the bishop would have been immediately familiar to Bostonians as their beloved "Cush": "a shrewd, ancient crag of a man, circumspect almost to the point of meaningless in public speech, blunt as a club in private" (113); "a walking granite pillar. . . . he roared an incomprehensible greeting—a blessing?—into the microphone" (254). The "soft-spoken, sharp-minded" lawyer whom Jack consults about the legality of Phil's consignment to the mental institution appears to be the author's compliment to his loyal friend Bob De-Giacomo. And to show Niall Montgomery that his Boston friend could serve up a "Niallogism," O'Connor created a Dr. Anthony Montgomery as Uncle Jimmy's family doctor. The sons refer to him niallogistically as the "Abominable Abdominal" (385).

One unusual topical allusion to Boston politics of the mid-1960s stands out. For the most part, O'Connor avoided specific issues of the day in his two "Boston politics" novels; he preferred to deal in generalities highlighted by the more pointed ethnic and religious differences that were his metier. But by introducing the character of Margaret Lucille Elderberry, he broke his custom. Like the bishop's, her first appearance in the novel would have been quickly recognized by Bostonians:

> She was by profession a schoolteacher: a great grotesque woman with a large marshmallow face and a tiny bright red mouth. . . . She now taught very little, spending most of her time around the state legislature, where she lobbied ceaselessly for higher salaries for married teachers, and just as ceaselessly against the penny milk program for children. For years she had repeated, over and over again, her two slogans: "The teacher was not meant to be a waitress in a Howard Johnson's" and "My one concern is for the child." She was a ludicrous and not entirely ineffective figure (275–76).

This is one Louise Day Hicks, dead on.[26] Hicks had come to prominence in the Boston teachers' union and was grabbing every available microphone, into which she pronounced in cynical code that the de facto racial segregation in Boston's schools was to remain unchanged. She was a massive compendium of all the complacent and self-serving Boston Irish attitudes on race that had been nurtured or winked at over the long decades of Hibernian triumphalism. She also played the phony victim card against the real victim: to her the dominant Irish culture was being persecuted in the name of racial justice. Her massive resistance, weirdly symbolized by her bodily girth, struck a chord in many Irish Bostonians and led eventually to the wrenching South Boston busing fiasco of the 1970s.

---

26. To the best of my knowledge, Arthur Schlesinger was the first in print to point out the Elderberry/Hicks parallel (*BL* 26). Schlesinger also believes that Frank Dooley (*F* 184–85) was a mini-portrait of Massachusetts Attorney General Eddie McCormack, nephew of "Uncle John" McCormack, who as Speaker of the U.S. House of Representatives was for some fourteen months the immediate successor to the presidency following the assassination of President Kennedy. In 1962 the experienced Eddie McCormack ran in the U.S. Senate primary against the inexperienced but highly connected Ted Kennedy. McCormack doomed himself in a television debate by ridiculing in old Irish style his opponent's utter lack of political experience. There was never much love lost between the old-style McCormacks from Dorchester and the coolly telegenic Kennedys from Hyannisport and Harvard. Schlesinger missed one other Massachusetts allusion, however. Dan Cogan, a "primitive . . . politician . . . [who] ruled the state legislature with a firm and rather brutal hand" (*F* 165), is surely a copy of the crude and often inebriated John Thompson, who as speaker of the Massachusetts House delighted in taunting Governor Chub Peabody, who had tried to oust him.

In the novel Jack is dismayed when Charles fails to counter Elderberry's potential threat to civic peace. O'Connor prophetically has the governor allude to potential trouble stemming from Elderberry: "[She] might get the city emotionally stirred up. A gut issue: maybe the Negro thing. Or No More Puerto Ricans. Or The Child in relation to both. She might ride something like that all the way home" (282). The promise of reform suffers a setback as Charles cringes from confronting the Elderberry forces, who could dislodge him from office. Jack realizes at this point that the cause of badly needed reform in racial matters has stymied Charles, who retreats as a matter of "tact." Charles comes off poorly when we remember that the mid-1960s was the heroic age of the civil rights movement. If Kennedy had waffled too much like Charles, Johnson was achieving the long-denied requirements of simple justice. Measured against the real gains of that time, Charles appears cautious to the point of cravenness.

If O'Connor can decry the wall of resistance to needed reform, he does not spare the reformers either. In Charles's unwieldy coalition "the Professors" are the worst, according to Phil: "They don't want their piece of flesh, they want the whole body" (205). Just as he had done with the professors in Jack Mangan's camp in *The Last Hurrah*, O'Connor delights in skewering academics who moonlight in politics. Later Charles says, "[M]y liberal speech-writers keep slipping 'bigot' to me to describe anyone who goes to church and who doesn't agree with them" (282). These asides are noteworthy because they often skirt close to several of O'Connor's own friends. O'Connor saw the horns of the Democratic Party dilemma, still unresolved in the twenty-first century: how can the party of reform enact its agenda without alienating the very constituency from which it draws strength? Charles's words were prophetic indeed: the Democratic Party would never recover from its zenith in the 1960s, in part because its brain trust became arrogantly irreligious, something that clearly gave O'Connor considerable pause.

Reviews of *All in the Family* were mixed, but on the whole they were better than those for *I Was Dancing*. *Newsweek* on September 19 was disappointed that there was no real political story. *Time*'s reviewer on September 30 felt so badly let down by the two apparently unrelated stories that he ranked the novel even lower than *I Was Dancing*. A surprisingly favorable review appeared in the October 15 *New Yorker*, where Edith Oliver found much to like, although like many she thought that Phil's falling out with Charles was unconvincing melodrama. (Surprisingly, no reviewer of O'Connor at this time discerned the pattern of unsatisfactory conclusions in much of O'Connor's work; and certainly no one was aware that these often forced resolutions were caused by the author's lack of careful narrative planning or by simple unawareness of the potential lurking in his own material.) Howard Mumford Jones, an old fan from Harvard, gave the novel high grades in the October *Atlantic*, where the ad for the Atlantic Monthly Book was placed right next to the review. Jones was puzzled, however, about the novel's opening and closing in Ireland. He concluded by heaping high praise on O'Connor's Dickensian industry, which kept him to his task as a writer without grants, fellowships, or academic posts. Fellow novelist Thomas Curley, writing in the October 2 *Book Week*, was dismayed that O'Connor apparently refused to take politics seriously—a literary heresy in the 1960s. Curley's review was marred by errors: he thought that Jack Kinsella had been the narrator of *The Last Hurrah*, and that someone called Jack Warden had done the same in Robert Penn Warren's *All the King's Men*. In its October 1 issue, *America's* critic abruptly pronounced the novel "as bad as *The Last Hurrah* was good." Paul K. Cuneo thought that two botched narrative lines were cobbled to make the final novel even worse than its parts.

Herbert Kenny, humanities editor of the *Boston Globe*, took up in the *New York Times Book Review* where John Kelleher left off five years earlier. On September 25 Kenny profusely hailed the new novel as the potential opening volume of a "monumental chronicle" worthy of a Trollope. (O'Connor could get a good review in the *Times* only as long as the reviewer was a Boston friend; three days after Kenny's review, Eliot Fremont-Smith dismissed the novel in the same newspaper.) Boston's newspapers as usual came through for one of their own. Clark Kinnaird profusely acclaimed the novel in the *Boston Sunday Advertiser* for September 25. Harvard Professor Theodore Morrison wrote a thoughtful and favorable review in the *Globe* on September 27. He thought the "fine, rich, spacious book" hit a new note of tragedy for the author. Unlike *The Last Hurrah*, which had mostly ducked the issue of corruption, this novel points up the seemingly unresolvable dilemmas about the appeal of political idealism and the necessity of political realism. In the October 2 *Herald* John Galvin conceded the book's brilliance, but in parts only, because O'Connor, in trying to do too much, left too many threads dangling. The *Herald's* new literary editor was Professor Albert Duhamel. As Duhamel was sitting down to Sunday dinner, O'Connor called up his erstwhile friend to chew him out at length for letting Galvin give away too much of the plot.[27]

Whatever fan mail there may have been, O'Connor kept little of it. Lillian

---

27. P. Albert Duhamel, letter to author, March 25, 1999.

Hellman wrote from Martha's Vineyard that while she enjoyed reading the novel, it failed to "open up more, to carry me beyond." She admits to being vague, and also to disliking chatter about books in letters.[28] Harry Levin wrote that he devoured the book almost at a sitting. O'Connor's professor friend thought that the depiction of the Kinsellas approached work by Koestler, Kafka, or even the Dostoevsky of *The Brothers Karamazov*.[29] The most poignant letter came from Elliot Norton, in which he pulled out all the stops: "one of your best . . . more tightly controlled, more smoothly plotted, and much 'warmer' than any of the others."[30] But the letter sounds forced, as if Norton was seeking to patch up the strain on their friendship caused by *I Was Dancing*.

O'Connor's ambivalence about political reform did not play well in an increasingly heated decade when there was little time for careful sifting and weighing, or for the measured narrative pace that O'Connor sedulously practiced. The new concerns of the age, as well as its bewildering acceleration, were threatening to pass him by. In February 1967 *All in the Family* was one of six novels nominated for the National Book Award for Fiction, which was won by Bernard Malamud's *The Fixer*. Little else of any note came O'Connor's way for his novel. The country's political agenda, as well as its tastes in literature, was rapidly changing, even among Catholics. O'Connor's challenge now was to find some new avenues to explore, along with some fresh techniques.

He did not wait long. Shortly after completing *All in the Family*, O'Connor broke his promise of two years earlier and took another stab at a play. The bright lights still lured him. Perhaps he wanted redemption after the crushing disappointment of *I Was Dancing*. The new play went through several drafts, and shortly after his novel came out in September 1966 he thought well enough of the play to give it a title and tote it to Notre Dame to get some reactions. O'Connor tended to wait fairly late during the composition of a new work before formally christening it, and when he did so it was usually a sign that he felt it was more or less ready to see the world. The result is an unpublished manuscript known as "The Traveler from Brazil."[31]

28. Lillian Hellman, letter to Edwin O'Connor, September 16, 1966, EOCP 161.
29. Harry Levin, letter to Edwin O'Connor, September 16, 1966, EOCP 373.
30. Elliot Norton, letter to Edwin O'Connor, November 19, 1966, EOCP 208.
31. My thanks to Barbara O'Connor Burrell for letting me examine the manuscript of "The Traveler from Brazil." The manuscript is 102 pages long and is singled-spaced except for the last sixteen pages, where the dialogue is double-spaced and typed on a different typewriter, along with a header "REVISION ACT II." Endings, as usual, gave O'Connor the most difficulty. The manuscript has six small insertions and corrections in O'Connor's

When Elliot Norton said that he found the play mystifying, he understated the case.[32] Like *Benjy* a decade earlier, "The Traveler from Brazil" cries out for elucidation, and as with *Benjy* such elucidation is not readily forthcoming. The most striking novelty about the play is O'Connor's embrace of contemporary stage techniques, whereby the central character's memories and preoccupations are presented through sudden "spotlighted" vignettes involving some twenty minor characters. Such a technique came easily to an author who had dwelled on memories so much. O'Connor manages these rapid shifts between present reality and memory with a deft hand and wry humor. The resulting pace is considerably livelier than the talky claustrophobia of *I Was Dancing*. The dialogue has a more contemporary, crisper sound as O'Connor shortens his long set speeches, although some are still present. The problem of relative lack of action remains, however. O'Connor still takes too long to get to whatever his topic was.

And therein lies the problem with the play. What is it all about? Act One opens with Gerald Caffery, age forty-three, talking with the "Irish" bartender (he's actually Polish) at his mother's establishment: outdoor café? restaurant? saloon?—like so much in the play, the place does not come into sharp focus. On a late áfternoon in summer Gerald has dropped in for a brief visit on his mother's seventieth birthday. Gert Caffery is a harridan of an Irish mother.

Her father, a turn-of-the-century ward boss named Big Charlie Doyle, often pops in as one of Gerald's spotlighted memories. As things develop, we learn that Gert has been raising Gerald's two young children, Chrissie and Charlie, during the eighteen months since Gerald's wife died. For most of that time Gerald has been away in Brazil, he leads us to believe, on some vague mission. Gert grumbles and scolds and insinuates. Enter Annie Gregory, a vivacious widow of thirty-one who is obviously known and liked by Gerald. Controlling Irish Mother meets indecisive Son's Woman. Stiff Gert is suspicious from the outset, and things only go downhill between her and Annie. To complicate matters, we learn that Gerald has never been to Brazil. In fact, as spotlighted memories and obsessions tumble over each other, we realize that "Brazil" was Gerald's refuge from his family and the increasingly inchoate world outside. Act One ends with two questions in the air: will Gerald come back from "Brazil" for good, and what will happen to his two chil-

---

hand. The exact date of this manuscript is uncertain, but since it was with the William Morris Agency at the time of his death, 1967 or 1968 would appear right.

32. Elliot Norton, personal interview, June 21, 1999. After O'Connor's death, Norton wrote a brief summary of the play in the Boston *Record-American* of March 6, 1970, where he called the play imperfect but interesting. Although his friend had still not mastered dramatic techniques, Norton implied that the innovations showed promise.

dren? Gert's closing lines for Act I say it all: "*I want to know:* WHAT'S GO-
ING ON?" (O'Connor's emphases).

Act Two picks up the pace. It is a week later in the same place. Gert is talking with "Doctor" Wilfred Dentremont, who runs a curious sanitorium outside the city where the few inmates—actually perfectly normal people—are
called "employees." This is Gerald's "Brazil": a bucolic utopia far from the
craziness of the times. Annie and a "priest" named Fahey also are residents.
Gert scolds her son for his escapist indulgence when she trots out an Irish
bogey: "No son of mine will ever go to the funny farm! No one in our family
has ever gone to the funny farm!" (II, 11). Gerald suddenly proposes marriage
to Annie in front of Gert, who is mightily annoyed when Annie accepts. Gert
then tries to set Gerald's children against him, but in this deadly showdown
Chrissie and Charlie stick with their father. The final problem now is, where
will Gerald's newly constituted family live? Gerald opts for Dentremont's
sanitorium, but in an ultimatum to Gerald Annie wants to front the world
bravely: "Let's take a chance with the surf!" (II, 35). A phantasmagoria of all
that revolts Gerald passes before him: vapid teenager music, soul-eroding
advertisements, old Irish politics, mindlessly violent black power canceling
the gains of civil rights, smiling but brutal Southern sheriffs, confusion in
the Church, the increasing carnage in Vietnam. Gerald waffles and suggests a
"compromise." Annie meanwhile, in the tradition of O'Connor's women
who stand up to family tyrants, roundly chews out Gert. Gerald announces
his decision: he and his new family should go to Brazil—the real country,
that is—and strike out on a new life. Joyous celebration at a nearby ice
cream shop is to follow as the play ends.

Immediately obvious in this last completed work by O'Connor is an ample inclusion of contemporary allusion. Not since *The Oracle* fifteen years
earlier had O'Connor been so topical. Indeed, "The Traveler from Brazil"
marks an abrupt break from the four works (*The Last Hurrah* to *All in the
Family*) where tiny allusions to national or world events were few and usually buried. O'Connor had wanted *All in the Family* to have a more contemporary feel to it, but he fell short of his aim. Now he was determined to show
that he could incorporate his times and be on the side of the angels to boot,
on civil rights and Vietnam especially. Furthermore, he seemed to be showing the world, through the story of Gerald, that he could break out of his familiar universe, that author Edwin O'Connor could renew himself. He must
have been stung by those reviews of his previous two works which accused
him of staleness, recycling, and plodding workmanship. Unfortunately, no

word from the horse's mouth about origins and intentions survives for this one. We can only conjecture.

Another important change consists in O'Connor's taking on the not-so-hidden secret about matriarchal Irish family life. Only in *Benjy* had O'Connor gone up against this sacred cow, and there it was not an Irish one but the generic American breed. Gert has inherited the mantle of domination from her politico father. Her own husband is long dead, a possible suicide, and Gerald is her only child. O'Connor had transferred to her many of the failings he had laid on Charlie Carmody, Daniel Considine, and Uncle Jimmy Kinsella: manipulation, lack of affection, and an endless stream of vituperative complaining—all done now in maternal voice. Gert Caffery is a destroyer of family happiness, and Gerald's only salvation lies in putting hemispheric distance between himself and her, with the able assistance of the woman he loves.

The inevitable question presents itself: how autobiographical is this odd play? For twenty years O'Connor had been presenting fictional versions of himself in characters as various as Anthony Cantwell, Kevin Rowan, Adam Caulfield, Benjy, Fathers Hugh Kennedy and John Carmody, Tom Considine, and Jack Kinsella. While these characters are not identical to their author by any means, there are nevertheless important autobiographical strains in them, especially in Kevin Rowan, Benjy, Tom Considine, and Jack Kinsella. The phenomenon is hardly surprising when we remember that American authors from Melville to Mailer have mined this vein. After his early attempts at autobiographical fiction in "Anthony Cantwell" and "A Young Man of Promise," O'Connor had tried to swear off the tendency. But he was not entirely successful. The tightly checked inner man would have his say, and in the most personal way he would allow himself—through his own imaginative constructs.

We could begin with iced coffee and ice cream. These two refreshments favored by O'Connor actually frame the play, in a sense. The opening line in the play comes from Chet the bartender to Gerald: "Another iced coffee, Mr. Caffery?" This would be, of course, the strongest drink O'Connor would permit a bartender to serve him. As mentioned earlier, cold coffee drinks of many types were hugely popular in Rhode Island. At the play's conclusion, listen to Gerald's joyful announcement of his new family's celebration at Grover's: "Ice cream. Three hundred and twenty-eight delicious flavors. Plus assorted sundaes and sodas. Plus a banana split which sells for slightly less than a Cadillac El Dorado" (II, 45). This is O'Connor fondly recording his own weakness.

Gerald is forty-three, just four years younger than his author. This pattern wherein O'Connor creates his surrogates to be within five years of his own age is a particularly strong one throughout his work. Gerald is "casually dressed," much like O'Connor, right down to the loafers. (I,1). At one point when Gerald retreats into his private world, the stage directions point to an unmistakable O'Connor gesture: "And now he goes into a little solo dance step, singing softly as he dances" (II, 17). This little soft-shoe is of course the vaudeville shuffle that many remember as part of O'Connor's dramatic entrances. It was one of his several masks. But at this point in the play Annie touches him gently and Gerald snaps out of his reverie and pops the question. He apologizes for his abruptness to Annie when he says, "You wanted tenderness, and I gave you vaudeville" (II, 20).

Gerald's father died a weak, broken alcoholic. As usual, O'Connor needs to clear out one parent in order to focus on the other. But this father has nothing in common with O'Connor's own, just as the loudmouth Gert Caffery is the antithesis of the charming Mary O'Connor. O'Connor created in Gert the eternal biddy who sucks life and love out of everyone around her. Two of her charges against Annie sail particularly close to O'Connor's shore when Gert describes Annie, to her face, as "some little baggage from nowhere who's half his age and who's gone through one husband already!" (II, 21). O'Connor surely knew that tongues clucked when he married Veniette, to whom Annie is a close cousin. Here he gets his revenge, even if Annie is a braver respondent to Gert than Gerald is. And when Annie says, "Let's take a chance with the surf!" it is not too much of a stretch to pick up the Wellfleet allusion—the Wellfleet where O'Connor had rescued people from the surf, where he had done most of his romancing, and where he had found his Veniette at last. In fact, Gerald at forty-three is exactly O'Connor's age when he proposed to Veniette.

There are more intangible traces of O'Connor in Gerald. For one thing, Gerald does not "do" anything in life. We never learn what profession or career he pursues, if any. (In this respect he is strikingly similar to Jack Kinsella's father.) He is simply an observer of life, a counterpart to the novelist. Like O'Connor he is on the reserved side, but when he does talk he is usually witty and sometimes sarcastic. He inhabits a world of his own and has some difficulty in committing himself and making decisions. In front of his only parent he is still the tongue-tied little boy, as seen in his parting words to Gert: "I'm in a position now I've been in only about ten thousand times before. I don't know what to say to you" (II, 46). O'Connor takes care, however, not to whine through Gerald, who admits at one point that "Catastrophe-wise, I'm small potatoes" (II–12).

As usual, the locale is unnamed. At one point Gerald makes a pointed allusion to the "Ritz" hotel's incipient decline. However, shortly afterwards he alludes to Con Edison as the local power company. (Was this a sign that O'Connor was aiming for a Broadway audience?) As in most of his work the ranking prelate's title is given, but here as in his recent works it is a bishop who occupies the see—hardly New York after all. On the other hand, there is less of a specifically Boston feel than in any of his full length works. O'Connor was probably trying to slough off his "Boston author" image.

"The Traveler from Brazil" showed some promise as a play, but O'Connor had a way to go yet. The play's basic problem is that the familial and the topical are not related in any convincing way. The family, as always, remains O'Connor's arena for conflicts, and the intrusion of the unusually heavy dose of the topical does more to distract than illuminate. Arthur Miller's *Death of a Salesman*, which, as Hugh Rank notes, had some influence on O'Connor's techniques, did the job far more effectively by letting the family story speak for itself and thereby enlarge itself as a metaphor for the culture.[33] But one strongly suspects that O'Connor was bound too privately to the personal situation for significant enlargement to take place.

In early October O'Connor read portions of the play at Notre Dame. Although as usual he preferred to have no advance billing, word spread fast and 300 students packed the law auditorium on October 5. O'Connor told an interviewer that he enjoyed his annual visit and the chance to "recharge his batteries." He also visited one of Frank O'Malley's classes.[34]

Through his agent O'Connor offered the play to David Merrick. The "Abominable Showman," remembering the agonies endured with O'Connor's last effort, rudely returned the play to Helen Strauss without comment. When Leland Hayward took it under option, Henry Fonda briefly considered taking a role. (In a notebook O'Connor listed Jason Robards, Gregory Peck, and Arthur Kennedy as his own picks for Gerald.)[35] But Hayward dropped the play eventually, saying that it needed too much work.[36] The play has never been performed. Arthur Schlesinger found it impossible to excerpt for *The Best and the Last of Edwin O'Connor*.

33. Rank, *O'Connor*, 186.
34. *Notre Dame Alumnus*, November–December 1966, 13.
35. EOCP 70.
36. Elliot Norton, Boston *Record-American*, March 6, 1970.

CHAPTER FOURTEEN

❧ Unfinished
(1967–1968)

As 1966 came to a close, the country was unraveling rapidly in ways too well known to require summary here. O'Connor took unusual note of these changes in "The Traveler from Brazil"—in one scene, the new cry of "Black Power" derails civil rights as the angry young black with his violent rhetoric positively delights the Bull Connors sheriff fondling his cattle prod ("TB" I, 44–45). The war in Vietnam, also lamented in O'Connor's play, was deteriorating monthly in spite of the American build-up. To this fundamentally traditionalist Catholic, the Church too seemed to be unraveling; the presence of an imposter priest in the play is an indication of O'Connor's concern.

On the surface of things, however, late 1966 was good to O'Connor. Initially at least, there was a boost to his income from *All in the Family.* At year's end Peter Davison wrote from Atlantic Monthly Press:

Dear Ed:

I am delighted to enclose a postdated check (the largest I have ever seen) for your general account. I look forward to many more such enclosures in the years ahead.

It has been a fine year for us all, and I look back on it with especial pride because during it we published Edwin O'Connor's finest novel yet.[1]

Davison had known O'Connor for ten years, and was now in effect his principal editor at Atlantic Monthly Press. He had tried to guide O'Connor during the difficulties his last novel caused him, especially with its conclusion, and he was convinced that *All in the Family* was indeed O'Connor's best. A few months earlier, when Davison had written O'Connor that his royalties for the first half of 1966 were still "dominated" by *The Last Hurrah,* he hastened to add: "No doubt, when *All in the Family* comes out, all the books will be stimulated."[2] An eddy of appre-

---

1. Peter Davison, letter to Edwin O'Connor, December 30, 1966, courtesy of Peter Davison.

2. Peter Davison, letter to Edwin O'Connor, September 8, 1966, courtesy of Peter Davison.

hension can be detected here that all was not going quite as well as Atlantic Monthly Press had hoped for its star. O'Connor was still an author known for one big book, and in fact the other books never did become "stimulated."

There were other sources of income. For example, O'Connor continued to receive $13,500 a year from Columbia Pictures for *The Last Hurrah*.[3] And there was still some British interest in *The Oracle* as late as 1967, when BBC television inquired about an adaptation, which never did get off the ground.[4]

Social life sailed along in Boston and Wellfleet as the O'Connors entertained and were entertained. On December 10, 1966, they were guests at the Wilsons' twentieth anniversary dinner at the Ritz. Also in attendance were the distinguished literary critic Isaiah Berlin and his wife. Keats's biographer Aileen Ward, later to become a co-owner of O'Connor's summer house, was also there. Edmund Wilson wrote little place cards for everyone. For O'Connor he dittied somewhat inaccurately:

> This is the place for Edwin O'Connor.
> A man of high gifts and impeccable honor;
> Who has passed his whole life in the city of Boston
> And yet remains someone whom nothing is lost on.

Evidently not everyone realized that O'Connor's first sixteen years were spent in Rhode Island. For Veniette's card Wilson wrote:

> This is the place for lovely Venite [*sic*],
> Who inhabits a palace and yet remains sweet.
> She has crowned the career of remarkable Ed
> And would not be deterred if he dwelt in a shed.[5]

Later in the month O'Connor took Veniette and Stephen to Harbour Island. Arthur Schlesinger had just preceded him at the Pink Sands Lodge; O'Connor sent him a complimentary postcard after hearing of his prowess on the tennis courts.[6] Father McGoey, who still served energetically as the island's priest, later wrote O'Connor that he had chosen wisely in Veniette. The industrious author-priest also asked O'Connor to carry a package of galleys for his next book to the States for him.[7] When Veniette came down with a serious rash, they had to return to Boston early.

In March, he and Veniette went to New York for a week, beginning March 16. Even then O'Connor simply had to be out of Boston on St. Patrick's Day.

3. Helen Strauss, letter to Edwin O'Connor, April 14, 1964, EOCP 254.
4. Susan C. Carew, letter to Edwin O'Connor, September 26, 1967, EOCP 370.
5. Wilson, *The Sixties*, 560–61.
6. Edwin O'Connor, postcard to Arthur Schlesinger, December 23, 1966, EOCP 279.
7. Father John H. McGoey, S.F.M., letter to Edwin O'Connor, December 30, 1966, EOCP 187.

This time he had a special reason: he had been invited by the president of the Massachusetts Senate, Maurice Donahue, to accept an award from Holyoke's St. Patrick's Day Parade Committee, which was given annually to "a distinguished citizen of Irish descent."[8] Donahue coyly noted that John F. Kennedy had been the award's first recipient. But obviously O'Connor declined. This interpreter of the Irish American experience never joined Irish organizations and shied away from their honors. His sister and brother-in-law concur emphatically that O'Connor had a well-formed and unmovable dislike of anything that smacked of organized, professional Irishry.[9]

The outwardly rosy financial picture belied the growing reality that O'Connor was simply not selling as he had ten years earlier. To have expected the comet of *The Last Hurrah* to appear again would be to expect too much. That big check Peter Davison sent was a deceptive anomaly. To compound this deepening downward trend, O'Connor was living considerably beyond his prospects. Right to the end of 1966, Peter Davison recalls, both he and O'Connor certainly thought that the novelist was flush.[10] But within months the picture changed alarmingly, as the bills mounted for the "palace" on Marlborough Street, the Mercedes, the summer house at Wellfleet, a stepson at boarding school, dining at the Ritz and Locke-Ober, trips abroad, Veniette's eye for expensive clothes and antiques. Davison also recalls that it took the experienced Arthur Thornhill to begin a series of warnings. The astute head of Little, Brown still met weekly with O'Connor at Locke-Ober's and it was there that O'Connor gradually absorbed the harsh facts about his financial situation. Arthur Thornhill, to whom *All in the Family* was dedicated, had been around publishing long enough to recognize the familiar pattern of the writer who lives off one big book for too long. He also knew of O'Connor's lack of economy during four years of marriage, when he had forsaken his moderate ways. In retrospect, we can note how tightwads like Amos Force, Charlie Carmody, and Jack Kinsella's grandfather incurred O'Connor's special satirical ire. When he had finally reached a position to spend his considerable riches with someone else, he had done so with cheerful abandon and with little planning about the future.

During 1967 financial worries began to besiege O'Connor. Money had been a worry during the long years of apprenticeship when he eked out a living through odd-job journalism, but back then he had retained a deter-

---

8. Maurice A. Donahue, letter to Edwin O'Connor, December 14, 1966, EOCP 129.
9. Barbara and William Burrell, personal interviews, summer 1998.
10. Peter Davison, letter to author, August 3, 1999.

mined confidence about his future. Now his money was receding into his past, while his future was becoming uncertain. In 1967 and 1968, at least twenty separate jottings in notebooks or on the back of manuscript pages show a desperate effort to cut back on expenses. These are the only extant budget calculations by O'Connor. Very likely for the first time in his life he was taking financial planning seriously. As an indication of the gravity of the situation, one notebook entry tries to cut expenses from mortgage to utilities almost in half.[11] A significant feature of these columns of figures (sometimes labeled "Now" and "Desired") is that most of the figures have no labels next to them; only a few columns have labels such as "monthly paym" or "inc tax." These labels are always printed in letters much smaller than the figures beside them. It would appear that O'Connor was afraid of letting Veniette, who is labeled only as "V," oversee his calculations.

The pressure began to show itself. Although O'Connor retained his geniality and sociable ways, at times a testiness could briefly flare up, especially about anything connected to his writing. Peggy Yntema was sometimes on the receiving end of petty outbursts over minor matters, as O'Connor's fussiness with his text became trying. And he could bristle when others caught a tiny slip, as when Peter Davison once noted that in *The Edge of Sadness* the author had used pi inaccurately.[12]

Compounding his worries was a drop in sales of *All in the Family* and the fact that "The Traveler from Brazil" was getting no takers. His two big recent works were not good omens, and it appears that during much of the year O'Connor stalled on new work. He had hinted at a novel about a publisher, but no manuscript evidence remains, unless the curious manuscript about one George Devine was going to be that story.

The unfinished "George Devine" manuscript is a telling one.[13] The folder in which it is contained appears at first to be a hefty sheaf of almost a hundred pages. In fact, O'Connor never got beyond five pages. The folder houses no fewer than fifty-five attempts by the author to get his story going. Some versions are three, four, or five pages, but many more are just a few sentences, or even just one opening sentence. No other manuscript by O'Connor is remotely like this. It may be this very work that Stephen Weil remembers so vividly as an example of O'Connor's methodical, concentrated, but

11. EOCP 71. Similar financial figuring by O'Connor can be found on the back of many manuscript pages from this time.

12. Peggy Yntema, personal interview, April 10, 1999.

13. EOCP 53. The catalogue dates the manuscript as 196–?. However, an allusion to a papal trip to America places "George Devine" after Pope Paul VI's October 1965 visit, the first such trip of any pope.

frustrating working habits. One day Stephen was watching his stepfather at work. O'Connor sat in front of his portable typewriter on the small writing table. From a large carton on the floor to his left, he would take out a fresh piece of typing paper, insert it, and start typing. He would stare at what he written long and hard, and then, if he was displeased, he would simply remove the paper and place it in a similar box on the floor to his right, even if it contained only a sentence. Then he would start over again.[14] Many manuscripts of this time also show doodling patterns of the G clef; another pattern consists of box-like cubes.

The opening sentence of "George Devine" in most attempts is the same: "When the telephone rang it was two o'clock in the morning . . ." Sudden, unexpected telephone calls had been notable in O'Connor's work from *The Oracle* on. They figure prominently in *The Edge of Sadness,* which begins with a strange telephone call to Father Kennedy from Charlie Carmody at six-fifteen in the morning. However, none of the fifty-five versions of "George Devine" ever gets to the phone call itself. After the opening sentence, which trails off with the ellipsis that O'Connor now favored, he immediately begins a description of George Devine. If this is a portrait of the publisher, it also bears a close resemblance to the author. George Devine (another surname that does not appear too Irish) is in his middle years, feels aging coming on, daydreams Walter Mitty-style about rescuing the pope from drowning, was a pitcher in school, and was friends with an old monsignor. These are more than traces of various stages and incidents in O'Connor's life. Only two possibilities for the telephoner's identity come to George: either his father is dying or his son in Vermont is undergoing an appendectomy by a drunken country doctor. We never find out. Apparently O'Connor finally gave up.

Little other writing from 1967 survives. *The Writer* published his last article, "The Publisher and the Pep Talk," in which O'Connor mostly reminisced about his frustrating relations with his first publisher, who is never named but is obviously Harper in New York.[15] *The Writer* does not carry the same cachet as *Atlantic Monthly;* O'Connor was showing signs of resorting to journalism. Also, when Evelyn Waugh had died a year earlier, O'Connor may have been invited to write an appreciation of one of his favorite authors. The only evidence is this innocuous notebook entry, in its entirety: "Evelyn Waugh is dead. He was a writer who was peculiarly English and not, I think, much appreciated in this country."[16] The article was apparently never fin-

---

14. Stephen Weil, personal interview, November 21, 1998.
15. *The Writer,* April 1967, 31–32.
16. EOCP 71.

ished. One possible explanation for his balking may have been a growing concern that his own status as a Catholic writer was slipping. With his favorite Catholic novelist now gone, he may have looked over his shoulder with some concern. Flannery O'Connor was posthumously hot property by 1967, especially among Catholic critics. (Edwin O'Connor was unenthusiastic about her work;[17] she in turn never read him.) Walker Percy and J. F. Powers had recently won National Book Awards in back-to-back years, Percy for *The Moviegoer* in 1962 and Powers for *Morte D'Urban* in 1963. The National Book Award was by then at least as prestigious as the Pulitzer. Before long, O'Connor was aroused to return to a "Catholic" subject, and not once but twice.

More bad luck was visited on O'Connor when he lost his agent in June. For over twenty years O'Connor had been fortunate in being represented by Helen Strauss at the William Morris Agency. But now she was moving to the West Coast to work for Warner Brothers. O'Connor expressed his loss in an apparently incomplete letter, which was very likely never sent, to an otherwise unidentified "Nat." Because she had been the only agent who had ever done anything for him, O'Connor with his characteristic sense of loyalty felt keenly let down: "Now I'm a little up a tree."[18] Women had been important mentors and supports in his life. First his mother and then Helen Strauss and Peggy Yntema had encouraged and guided his writing. (Veniette was not particularly interested in literature.) Some months of anxiety passed while a successor to Strauss as head of Morris's literary department was sought. When O'Connor apparently grew impatient at the delay in getting a replacement, Owen Laster wrote from the Morris Agency to soothe him.[19] In the end, Laster became O'Connor's agent, and remained so for O'Connor's literary estate. Strauss and Laster came to Boston together for a farewell dinner with the O'Connors. This was Owen Laster's only meeting with O'Connor, whom he found to be funny and animated.[20]

There was even a small legal squabble over subsidiary rights to the dramatic version of *I Was Dancing*. The American Arbitration Association handled the case, which was settled in the author's favor and closed on December 19.[21] O'Connor may not have been directly involved, but it was an additional concern he did not need.

In October O'Connor suffered a particularly sad loss when Charles Mor-

17. Edward Fischer, "Edwin O'Connor, Raconteur," *Notre Dame Magazine,* winter 1988–1989, 49–50.
18. EOCP 213.
19. Owen Laster, letter to Edwin O'Connor, September 29, 1967, EOCP 376.
20. Owen Laster, telephone interview, December 21, 1999.
21. EOCP 88.

ton died after some months in ill health. The eccentric from Omaha who became the Bostonian curmudgeon, at the old *Boston Transcript* and then at *Atlantic Monthly*, had been O'Connor's discoverer in 1946 and a cherished friend ever since. O'Connor had immensely enjoyed Morton's eccentricities and conversation over lunch at the Ritz. At the memorial service in the Unitarian Church just off Harvard Square, O'Connor delivered a lengthy nine-page eulogy. He began by evoking those Ritz lunches and Charlie's obsessions with clean cutlery, gum under the table, and flies anywhere in the room. Then O'Connor dwelled on his friend's deep resentments and his even deeper loyalties.[22] O'Connor was unusually warm and lavish in his farewell to one of the oldest father figures in his life. In fact, the man who could not show public grief when his own father died broke down and wept during his reading of the eulogy.[23]

By this time O'Connor had sold 10 Marlborough Street,[24] and in fact may already have been living temporarily on Louisburg Square in the heart of Beacon Hill. For two months in the fall of 1967 the family sojourned at this fashionable address while a new residence was extensively remodeled.[25] These two months at this most exquisite of Boston addresses must have been tinged with bittersweet emotions for O'Connor; for him Beacon Hill was the ultimate Boston location, even if the Back Bay had more spacious mansions. He had lived at three places on the Hill or its "Flat." Now he must have wondered whether he would ever return.

Not that the new move took O'Connor out of his familiar orbit. Once again he turned to John Tosi, who found a suitable place for sale at 191 Commonwealth Avenue on the corner of Exeter Street, four long blocks or about half a mile from *Atlantic* offices and the Ritz.[26] The grand town house had been built in 1872 by Henry Lee Higginson, who later helped to found the

22. Edwin O'Connor, eulogy for Charles Morton, October 1967, Hugh Rank Papers, University of Notre Dame Archives. Once O'Connor wrote an undated spoof letter to Morton from "Albert Griggs, private detective." Griggs's report on O'Connor's eating habits describe a parsimonious Amos Force breakfast and dinner, but a lavish Ritz-style lunch. The occasion for this spoof is unknown, but obviously Charlie had noted O'Connor's trencherman appetite. Letter courtesy of Peter Davison.

23. Peter Davison, personal interview, March 11, 1999.

24. Apart from the economic necessity of the move, there is some evidence that O'Connor was upset that Marlborough Street had recently become a cruising ground for homosexuals.

25. Weil, interview.

26. Again I am in John Tosi's debt for his detailed recollections of O'Connor's new house in his letter to me of June 23, 1999. Additional material came from Stephen Weil and Robert Manning.

Boston Symphony Orchestra. This was to be O'Connor's only residence on what some have called the most beautiful boulevard in the country. No. 191 is on the long segment known as Commonwealth Avenue Mall. Here a wide expanse of grass, walks, park benches, and stately elms advances down the middle of the avenue from the Public Gardens to Kenmore Square. On almost every block of the Mall eminent Bostonians and others are commemorated by statues. William Lloyd Garrison, the Liberator, was close to O'Connor's new address. In years past Boston's Easter Parade promenaded down the Mall under elms frothy with springtime green against long rows of somber maroon townhouses. In December the Mall is sometimes gussied up with tiny tree lights, to the annoyance of the residents. Boston never did quite get over the lifting of the Puritan ban on Christmas.

John Tosi supervised an extensive remodeling of O'Connor's new residence, which occupied most of the sixth floor. Once again, O'Connor had a top-floor view, as he had at least twice before. The 3,000 square feet accommodated eight large rooms, which still preserved a good deal of the original Victorian paneling and hardware. At Veniette's request an old storage room with a huge skylight was converted into a lightsome dining room with a black and white tile floor. All this took time and there were the inevitable delays. But when the O'Connors moved in shortly after Thanksgiving, they were more than pleased with the results.

But not for long. A notebook records worrisome sums owed for the whole move from 10 Marlborough to 191 Commonwealth. The cost—John Tosi's fee, the movers, the remodeling—was over $24,000, or far into six figures in today's money. In trying to save on expenses, O'Connor had only incurred more. To compound matters he also lists ten separate leaks from the roof and skylight; the main fireplace alone was a veritable downspout for heavy winter rains that would flood the room.[27] The family did not need these reminders of the watery floors at 107 Chestnut Street.

Another problem arose in early 1968 when Time Inc. announced that it was buying Little, Brown. The venerable Boston publishing house would now be a subsidiary of the brash New York publisher of quick-cooked news and photojournalism. Some of Little, Brown's authors began jumping ship when other publishers wasted no time and expense luring them. How many tried to snare O'Connor is unknown, but he did keep one letter from Alfred Knopf Jr., who wrote familiarly on the letterhead of Atheneum Publishers. With elaborate politeness Knopf gingerly asked "Ed" to consider publishing

27. EOCP 70.

with Atheneum: "Nothing would please me more." A month later Knopf wrote another friendly letter after O'Connor had refused. "I do indeed understand, and in fact admire your loyalty."[28] In early March O'Connor's new agent wrote in urgent tones to ask him whether the New York rumors about his leaving Little, Brown were true.[29] But Owen Laster need not have worried. O'Connor's loyalty was firm, and for the present at least he was staying with Little, Brown.

In early 1968, now that he was somewhat settled into his new home, O'Connor began writing fiction with renewed energy. Usually he waited until summer to get new work under way, but now in midwinter he began making up for lost time. If we exclude the five pages of "George Devine," it had been almost two years since he had worked on a novel. This longest hiatus in his career as a novelist can be attributed to a number of factors, ranging from financial jitters to writer's block. Getting sidetracked by "The Traveler from Brazil" did not help, either. Fortunately, O'Connor seemed to understand at last that his best talents lay in fiction.

His first sustained effort at a long work is known as "The Cardinal" manuscript.[30] At first, the manuscript evidence looks like another frustrating "George Devine" effort. Over two hundred surviving pages, which in the end amount only to a short opening chapter and a bit of the next, attest to his enduring stutter at the typewriter. This time there are sixty-nine first pages! One of these first pages has this penciled-in doodling:

> On this day the Cardinal
> On this day the Cardinal
> On this day
> > On this
> > On this
> > On this

28. Alfred Knopf Jr., letters to Edwin O'Connor, January 17, 1968, and February 28, 1968, EOCP 178.

29. Owen Laster, letter to Edwin O'Connor, March 8, 1968, EOCP 376.

30. About half of what eventually was published as "The Cardinal" can be found in EOCP 66. When Professor Kelleher collated various manuscripts for inclusion in *BL* 406–22, he was working with more extensive manuscripts now in the possession of Barbara O'Connor Burrell, to whom I am most grateful. The title was surely provisional, because in 1950 Boston-born Henry Morton Robinson had published a popular novel of the same name about an Irish American prelate; in 1963 it had been turned into an Otto Preminger film with some scenes shot in Boston.

If one did not know better, one might suppose O'Connor to be trying his hand at projective verse or some kind of Beckett-like dialogue. But apparently O'Connor was listening to the music and structure that the words would eventually disclose. Only his openings gave him this trouble; endings were a different problem. Finally something began to move. The collation of the manuscripts by John Kelleher in *The Best and the Last of Edwin O'Connor* is probably as close to O'Connor's intentions as anyone can get. Kelleher's reminiscence and introduction is also one of the best insights into O'Connor's tolerant understanding of clergy during that turbulent period (*BL* 401–5).

At first glance "The Cardinal" looks something like a reprise of the tribal chieftain saga in *The Last Hurrah*, as Hugh Rank notes.[31] O'Connor created his second oldest "trademark" character in the title character; in the manuscripts O'Connor actually hikes his age from seventy-five to eighty. He is given no name in the fragment other than the "Joe" used by another octogenarian priest. In the fragment we see some familiar O'Connor patterns: long reminiscences by old men, displeasure with the reformist course of the times, a doddering eccentric friend, a worldly underling.

Before retiring for the night, the Cardinal reviews the day. It was his golden jubilee as a priest and it had been an exhausting whirlwind. Like the seasoned Skeffington, he had made all the necessary rounds, from schools to television interviews to the big hotel banquet in his honor, where the mawkish "Mother Dear, O Pray for Me" was inaccurately introduced as the Cardinal's favorite hymn. A flashback takes us back two weeks to a medical checkup followed by a rushed biopsy on a suspicious lump in the neck and the grim diagnosis the next day. Faced at last with his impending mortality, the Cardinal sifts through possible successors—no easy task during the turbulent post-Vatican II years. If we can assume that this succession was to be the novel's premise, then O'Connor would be melding several of his most cherished subjects: a dying patriarch, political intrigue, destabilizing times, the riddles posed by reform.

The manuscripts end just as the Cardinal is reviewing some possibilities, one of which in particular catches the eye. Although not included by Kelleher in his collation of the several versions of this section, it intrigues by virtue of its remarkably prophetic accuracy. If we can assume that the Cardinal's archdiocese is more or less Boston, then O'Connor was writing when Richard Cushing, whose elevation to Cardinal in 1958 O'Connor had reported, was still archbishop. Cushing was then seventy-three and known to be in

---

31. Rank, *O'Connor*, 190.

declining health. Speculation about a successor was already dinner table talk in Boston, even in the Back Bay, and such talk undoubtedly was part of the genesis of O'Connor's story. Cushing was slowly dying amidst the general upheaval of the sixties and bewildering change in the Church. Recently seminarians right next to his residence in Brighton had staged a vocal protest against what they saw as their overly paternalistic training. As O'Connor's Cardinal mulls over potential successors, he arrives at his own favorite: "[A] man he barely knew. This was the young Bishop Menendez (Spanish? Portuguese?) from the southwest." Less than three years later Cushing would in fact be succeeded by Archbishop Humberto Medeiros, who had been born in the Portuguese Azores and who came to Boston from Brownsville, Texas. One might almost think that O'Connor had some kind of inside source, but of course when he wrote no such succession had been set up. However, it is worth noting that Humberto Medeiros was not a hit with many Boston Catholics, who saw the archbishopric as a permanent Irish seat, like the civil service or the Boston Gas Company. As he had done in *The Edge of Sadness*, where the wise bishop was of Midwest German ancestry, O'Connor recognized the desirability of an ethnic shake-up for the ingrown Irish clergy in Boston and elsewhere. Kelleher's introduction to "The Cardinal" notes O'Connor's forgiving understanding of clerical foibles, which he knew were real enough. However, in a letter to Arthur Schlesinger during the compilation of *The Best and the Last of Edwin O'Connor*, Kelleher wrote that O'Connor "felt that the powers that be in the Church had a lot coming to them."[32] This judgment on the hierarchy may be Kelleher's as much as O'Connor's; in his introduction to "The Cardinal" manuscript Kelleher admits to his own greater impatience. Nevertheless Kelleher did know this side of O'Connor more than anyone else and so his remark carries weight. If O'Connor was getting tired of the Irish in City Hall and the State House, he may very well have grown impatient with their counterparts in Chancery and Cathedral. Like the pre-Vatican II *Edge of Sadness*, this book would be an anatomy of the American Catholic Church, but now in the much more unsettled post-Council era, when critiquing was the order of the day.

Two final observations about "The Cardinal." In a passing moment of rare melancholy, the old Cardinal thinks back forty years to the day his father died, when the Cardinal would have been at about O'Connor's age when his

---

32. John Kelleher, letter to Arthur Schlesinger Jr., November 10, 1968, EOCP 276. In the same letter Kelleher reports that while working on "The Cardinal," O'Connor was reading Cardinal O'Connell's memoirs, which vastly amused him, through no intention of the author.

own father died. "[I]t was a sadness, but a peculiar sadness rolling in fast like one of the great coastal fogs, it was silent, isolating, depthless, and over-whelming" (*BL* 414). The force of this strangely isolated sentence has a personal ring to it. But was O'Connor thinking of his own father? Or Charlie Morton, recently deceased? Whatever the case, this sentence captures the contours of the sudden, though fortunately short-lived, onslaughts of that peculiarly Irish sadness that were visited on O'Connor and noticed by his friends. Secondly, Schlesinger claims that O'Connor's plan was to have the Cardinal's diagnosis turn out to be erroneous after all (*BL* 27). If Schlesinger's statement is accurate then it serves to confirm the pattern following Skeffing-ton's memorable death, wherein O'Connor's fathers—even Church fathers—do not die within the narrative.

Recollections differ on exactly when and why, but some time in late February or early March O'Connor abruptly stopped "The Cardinal," which was moving ahead with customary slowness, in order to work exclusively on a manuscript now known as "The Boy."[33] John Kelleher, who was much more interested in "The Cardinal" than in "The Boy," believed that O'Connor could never have returned to the first story because the swift changes in the Church were just too bewildering to his friend. In any case, Kelleher reports that O'Connor surprised himself in the way the new story came "with un-precedented ease and sureness" (*BL* 404). Peggy Yntema thought that this new novel had great promise: "In it, all sorts of inhibitions and adhesions had come unstuck. He was writing very fast and happily . . . ; and he had a fresh consciousness of his powers." She also said that the book was to have a "*baffling* dark place in it" (quoted in *BL* 28 and 35; Yntema's emphasis). In under a month O'Connor wrote more than twice the amount in "The Cardinal," and that had taken almost two months. Something unusual was happening in this burst of a creative energy not seen since "One Spring Morning" four years earlier. And therein may lie the clue: both writings are about a boyhood which, in varying degrees, is based on his own. In the case of "The Boy," very much so.

The three and a half chapters of the unfinished manuscript constitute one of the most autobiographical documents from O'Connor. Concerning his boyhood, three other writings are of importance: the opening chapter of the

---

33. Like "The Cardinal," this is only a provisional title, and as in the case of "The Cardinal," the longest version of the manuscript is in the possession of Barbara O'Connor Burrell, who kindly lent it to me. The manuscripts of "The Boy" in EOCP 67 are each only several pages long. The complete extant manuscript was published in *BL* 423–65.

"Coast Guard" manuscript from 1943; "A Love Letter to Woonsocket" in 1951; and, more fictively, the first three chapters of *All in the Family*. Like most Irish-influenced authors, O'Connor tried to shy away from direct autobiography and the first-person point of view, but in fact he was irresistibly drawn to self-dramatization in spite of himself. And while he was repeatedly fascinated by—some might say obsessed with—portraying old men, he could write with unusual freshness and delight about youth, while recording its peculiar mysteries and terrors too. The beginning of *All in the Family* had pointed the way in this regard, and there are hints that his new novel would copy the previous novel's structure of opening boyhood scenes followed by adult chapters set in contemporary times.

The first chapter introduces the family of nine-year-old Joey Dunphy, an only child with loving parents who have means enough to employ a live-in maid. As usual the father is described in more detail than the mother. For some reason, Joey's father travels all over the country and is thus away most of the time. Joey is led to believe that his father is a traveling magician, but magic tricks seem to be more of an avocation for the father, as they were for O'Connor himself, and hardly his occupation. There are echoes of Daniel Considine from *I Was Dancing* here, but unlike that father, Joey's is affectionate and caring and thus more like the father of young Jack Kinsella in *All in the Family*. Chapter Two describes some of Joey's school days and pals. Alma, the elderly live-in maid, gets considerable attention in one of those portrait miniatures that O'Connor could do so well but which also risk being digressive.

Chapter Three, the strongest, gets back on track and introduces complexity with two additional fathers: Joey's maternal grandfather, known only as "P.J.," and the elderly but ramrod-straight Father Sheridan, who is something of a returned regular customer in P.J.'s drugstore. The old men put in their appearance early on and it seems that Father Sheridan was destined to be an important player. The chief locale here is the back room of the drugstore where P.J.'s Irish American cronies gather to deliver half-baked opinions of the catechism variety. Father Sheridan sardonically refers to them as the "Theology Club." Joey loves to listen to the "Old Sod pharmacy talk," as his father calls it (*BL* 455), but he soon learns that his grandfather and his cronies detest Father Sheridan for some mysterious priestly violation which had driven him from the parish years ago. Why Father Sheridan is back in town remains as unknown as his great sin. Alcoholism ("old John Barleycorn") had definitely been part of the picture, but apparently only as a result of some earlier fall; surely O'Connor would not have tried to write of another priest's alcoholism again. When Joey meets Father Sheridan, he discovers that the courteous old gentleman knows his own father quite well. Later, Joey's irascible grandfather warns the boy not to have anything to do with Father Sheridan. (Pedophilia, by the way, is one sin O'Connor rules out when P.J. himself implies that Father Sheridan was guiltless on that count.) Baffled, Joey that night asks his father what the mystery is all about. Joey's father is evasive, but he is quick to defend the old priest as a man more sinned against than sinning: "'What a town,' he said. 'All heart'" (*BL* 452). It is fairly clear to the reader, though not necessarily to the boy, that old Father Sheridan has an unusual relationship with Joey's father. The last chapter is unfinished. In it O'Connor begins to digress about Joey's schooldays again, almost as if he did not want to pick up the thread about the unusual relationship right away.

How the novel would have evolved remains a big "what if"; if his past practice is any guide, O'Connor probably did not have it worked out. For what it is worth, here is what Peggy Yntema, who was privy to O'Connor's daily progress and plans more than anyone, wrote to Arthur Schlesinger:

The scheme was slight. Ed never did stick with his schemes anyway. The boy's father's mysterious absences, the boy's separation from his father, were the interesting part, to Ed. He thought of various ways of accounting for them: the latest was to make the father be a crook, a professional gambler, maybe card-shark. The climax would be the boy's discovery of this. Then the book would end with the father being shot down by the big criminals in whose power he had been, and whom he had decided to defy.[34]

Peggy Yntema does make it clear how tentative were O'Connor's working plans. But this scheme, even with the disclaimers, simply does not ring true. Apart from "Anthony Cantwell," O'Connor never showed interest in writing thrillers, even if Jack Kinsella was such an author. O'Connor was probably just tossing out possibilities in order to arrive by a fictional *via negativa* at a more believable plot. He liked to set up a teaser of a premise and see where it might lead. More importantly, this scheme leaves out Father Sheridan entirely, and it is clear from what we do have that this complication was going to be crucial.

Again, for what it is worth, my own speculation is that O'Connor was going to take a big risk with this one. Following in Greene's footsteps in *The Power and the Glory*, he might have made Father Sheridan, in one of those moments of clerical loneliness which O'Connor had earlier described so well, to be the biological father of Joey's Dad, and thus be Joey's other grand-

34. Quoted in *BL* 27.

father. (One clue is that O'Connor was quick—too quick?—to point out that Joey had been told that his paternal grandfather had lived far away and was dead anyway.) Rumors, ostracism, reassignment, and alcoholism for the priest would then have resulted. To be sure, there are big holes in this hypothesis, not least of which are those absences of Joey's father. Still, there is something about the way P.J. and his cronies refer to the priest that catches the hysteria of the Irish when confronted with the subject of sexuality in clerical ranks—the "worst" conceivable sin committed by the "best" of men—a notion wrong-headed on two counts, as Dante well knew. And for his part, the kindly respect Joey's father accords the old priest hints at much more than meets the eye. Joey's father had obviously forgiven Father Sheridan his sins; he even had him officiate at his wedding. But clearly he now keeps a discreet distance. If such was to be O'Connor's scenario, it would have been an unusually intense presentation of his father-son motif. Such were the times in 1968, even in the Church, that O'Connor could afford to take a risk in this direction, whereas in 1961's *The Edge of Sadness* it would have been all but impossible. Had O'Connor pursued this line, he might very well have achieved a remarkable novel about transgression and redemption.

Almost every page of the story has Woonsocket in it. The opening sentence about growing up "on the outskirts of the small and rather ugly mill city" establishes the tale's unusually strong personal dimension. The train station where Joey often sees his father off is clearly modeled on Woonsocket's own. Several colorful French Canadians such as Mr. Lacasse, the taxi driver, and "Ongo" Saint Onge, the music teacher, appear to be drawn from personal memory too. The old Doremus canal where Joey and his pals like to play is obviously the Blackstone Canal that brought the first Irish to the area as laborers. The three public schools O'Connor attended appear practically undisguised in the opening of the last chapter. It is even possible that his old pastor Father Holland may have lent some of his good character to of Father Sheridan: Joey's crabby grandfather disdainfully refers to him as "His Reverence." Was O'Connor thinking of Father Holland's book, *His Reverence—His Day's Work?* Most intriguing of all is that drugstore. Pharmacy had been in the O'Connor tradition: there was the Blackstone drugstore owned by O'Connor's uncle, supposedly the stingiest man he ever knew. And of course there had been the early career of O'Connor's own father as a pharmacist in Woonsocket. Joey's pharmacist grandfather, a fictional descendant of truculent Uncle Jimmy of *All in the Family,* appears to be a composite of both men. O'Connor had to establish in Joey's father and in Father Sheridan the counterbalancing ideal fathers of intelligent forgiveness and Christian mercy.

We will never know why O'Connor was writing his most autobiographical novel that March, but something was taking him to his boyhood forty years back. The Woonsocket that had resided in some deeply buried stratum of his work was coming to the surface, where Boston was no longer the setting and politics no longer the industry. To the extent that writing is personal therapy, O'Connor may have been taking on unresolved conflicts that followed hometown contours. But what of the "baffling dark place" that Peggy Yntema said would be the book's enigmatic center? And what did it have to do with Woonsocket? O'Connor had never journeyed deep into hearts of darkness because he was too Dickensian to believe the worst about his characters. Perhaps he was now on the verge of that descent. The unfinished novel remains silent.

On the morning of March 22, 1968, O'Connor wrote the following unfinished start of a new paragraph: "But one day, about a month or so after school started, instead of going to Dewey's or playing after school, I went down—Hethering's store on Main Street. . . ." Thus reads the manuscript. The published version removed the dash and the ellipsis (*BL* 465). The dash, although frequently used by O'Connor, is odd here for such a deliberate writer because O'Connor only needed to substitute "to" for clarity. Was O'Connor distracted or was his perception somehow marred that morning? The ellipsis had been a punctuation signature ever since *The Edge of Sadness*, where it often ended a meditative paragraph and signaled a new development. On the other hand, the ellipsis could have indicated indecision. The page was left in his typewriter. It was the last sentence Edwin O'Connor ever wrote.

Death came swiftly to Edwin O'Connor. Around noon on March 22, a Friday, O'Connor fell loudly to the floor at his home. Some accounts claim that he was at his typewriter when he fell; if true, this might account for the peculiarities of that last sentence. Others say he was dressing in his bedroom for lunch at the Ritz.[35] The morning had been raw and gloomy as only a March day in Boston can be. According to one newspaper account, a few hours earlier O'Connor had breakfasted alone at the Ritz on croissants, honey, and coffee while he read his morning paper.[36] For O'Connor to appear at the Ritz twice in one day was not unusual. Just before noon he told Veniette that he was not feeling well, but he was set on going out to lunch anyway;

---

35. Unless otherwise noted, most of the details of O'Connor's death come from Barbara and Bill Burrell, and from Stephen Weil.

36. Jonathan Klarfeld, "We All Loved Ed," *Boston Sunday Globe*, March 24, 1968, 1 and 78.

routine was difficult to break. Accounts differ too on whom he was meeting at the Ritz that day: most say it was Arthur Thornhill, some say Bob DeGiacomo, while others say that he was simply taking Veniette there. Veniette and Mrs. Bilmeyer, a housekeeper who came in most days, heard the fall and ran to O'Connor, who was unconscious. An ambulance rushed him to New England Baptist Hospital, where it quickly became obvious that he had suffered a massive stroke. He was placed on a respirator, but the lifelines on the monitor were running flat.

Veniette called Barbara and Bill to deliver the grim news. They hurried up from Rhode Island. Barbara remembers the incongruity of her brother's bared chest showing his tanned skin against the white sheets. After a frantic search, Stephen, who was on school vacation, was located by telephone in a Harvard Square sub shop where he was playing pinball with friends. Veniette told him to take a taxi to the hospital. When he arrived, his desolate mother was sitting by herself in a long corridor. Stephen did not want to see his stepfather; the bewildered boy, who just days earlier had been taken by O'Connor to Locke-Ober's for his sixteenth birthday, wanted to remember only the living man he loved.

For the second time in his life O'Connor was given the Last Rites. Monsignor Lally, his confessor, administered the sacrament that O'Connor had described at some length in *The Last Hurrah* and *The Edge of Sadness.* In the early morning hours of Saturday, March 23, 1968, after her husband had been on extraordinary life support for over twelve hours, Veniette accepted the inevitable. Monsignor Lally was there when he was taken off the respirator and declared dead shortly afterwards. Edwin O'Connor was forty-nine.

An autopsy was performed. O'Connor's death certificate lists causes of death as "cerebral hemorrhage" and "hypertension." Some newspapers and magazines hastily declared that O'Connor had suffered a heart attack.

Any number of factors may have brought on a stroke. O'Connor was generally careful about his health and had seen his physician, Dr. Robert Foley, three months earlier for a complete checkup. There were few warning signs as recognized by medical science in those years. To many it seemed devastating that someone who never smoked or drank should die in this manner. To the extent that stresses may have been a factor, there was no shortage for O'Connor. First to mind come those mounting financial worries and the problematic course of his career. Anxiety over the remodeling at 191 Commonwealth Avenue, the most extensive he had ever overseen, may have contributed, as did the two house moves in as many months. The numerous roof leaks in the middle of winter could not have helped. And of course there were his continuing responsibilities for a new family which had come in midlife and which he took with complete conscientiousness, if not always with the greatest prudence.

There were many people to contact quickly. On that Friday afternoon Arthur Thornhill reached Bob Manning in Connecticut at Wesleyan College, which he and his son were visiting as a prospective school. Manning was talking with Paul Horgan, the writer, when the news came and caused him to burst into tears. Manning cut the trip short and raced back to Boston in time to see O'Connor in the hospital. Veniette gently told him that his best friend "may never wake up."[37] Several people tried to reach Helen Strauss but failed to get her in time, and so when she heard it out on the West Coast on the eight o'clock morning news, she was shaken: "Big, strapping, bursting with life Ed O'Connor—dead."[38] Peter Davison was visiting Sean O'Faolain in Ireland when the news came; O'Faolain delayed telling Davison until later in the day so as not to spoil the visit.[39] John Kelleher was at home in Westwood when Veniette called on Friday afternoon, and he too was able to see O'Connor in the hospital for the last time.[40] Bob DeGiacomo came to Veniette's aid quickly and handled many of the funeral arrangements.

The two-day wake on Sunday and Monday was fittingly held at J. S. Waterman & Sons Funeral Home, whose rounded triangle noses into the wide expanse of Kenmore Square. Here Beacon Street and Commonwealth Avenue, those most Bostonian of addresses on which O'Connor had lived, cross at a diagonal. As the western terminus to O'Connor's "neighborhood," Waterman's front displays many of its icons: red bricks, bay windows, iron railings. On summer nights the roars from nearby Fenway Park can be heard.

It was a large wake (over 240 people signed the book) and the inevitable comparisons to scenes in *The Last Hurrah* were frequently heard. But apart from its size, it was not any kind of an Irish wake. The atmosphere in the wainscotted rooms was quiet and composed. On one wall a seventy-eight-year-old clock ticked loudly, as if to remind the living.[41] Among the touching entries in the book: Joe Vitale from the Ritz; Clem Norton, who printed his name for all to read; three nuns from Cumberland, Rhode Island; Francis Carroll, the Woonsocket boyhood friend who had gone off to Notre Dame with him. Boston's new reformist mayor, Kevin White, paid his respects, as

37. Robert Manning, personal interview, April 5, 1999.
38. Strauss, *Talent for Luck*, 171.
39. Peter Davison, personal interview, March 11, 1999.
40. John Kelleher, personal interview, May 29, 1999.
41. Jonathan Klarfeld, "A Different Wake from His Novels," *Boston Globe*, March 25, 1968.

did Michael Dukakis and Daniel Patrick Moynihan. Frank O'Malley made the sad journey from Notre Dame. George Curley, son of the late and famous mayor, offered his condolences. Some tulips near the coffin were dying, a symbolic touch not lost on several people.

The funeral was held at 10:00 on Tuesday, March 26, in the Cathedral of the Holy Cross in Boston's South End. O'Connor sometimes had worshiped there, especially at midnight Mass on Christmas. Six years earlier he had been married there. On a windy day of weak Lenten sunshine an estimated five hundred people attended the funeral Mass. A chartered bus transported the Atlantic staff to the cathedral. A few people arrived in chauffered limousines. Photographs in the papers that evening depicted Veniette with downcast eyes behind a thin veil. Stephen looks startled and still bewildered; today he remembers little of the service. O'Connor's brother Jack, who wept for days, was too distraught to attend. Active pallbearers, those "awkward hands of the amateurs" (*LH* 403), were Abe Burrows, Heywood Cutting, Bob De-Giacomo, Arthur Gartland, John Kelleher, Bob Manning, Frank O'Malley, and Arthur Schlesinger. Honorary pallbearers included Paul Aaron, Clem Norton, Stephen Schlesinger (Arthur's son), Arthur Thornhill, and Laurence L. Winship. In later years Clem Norton liked to remind people of the honor bestowed on him. As the pallbearers were negotiating the steps, Abe spoke to Arthur Schlesinger: "'If O'Connor knew you and I were carrying him, he'd get up and walk.' That was not meant to be frivolous; it was just another way of expressing my sadness. O'Connor would have understood."[42]

In attendance were the current and former mayors of the city, Kevin White and John B. Hynes; the mayor of Galway, who was visiting Boston; New Frontiersmen Richard Goodwin and Daniel Patrick Moynihan; Boston journalists Herbert Kenny, Christopher Lydon, and old friends Elliot Norton and Bob Taylor; professors Howard Mumford Jones, Leo Marks, and Samuel Eliot Morison; Lillian Hellman; the Irish Consul in Boston; several waiters from the Ritz.[43]

Monsignor Lally was the celebrant and eulogist. "[E]ulogy was not the custom of the Church, yet . . . in the case of the exceptional man, one was sometimes given" (*LH* 406). Monsignor Lally's short eulogy moved many.

Our hearts are heavy as we bring to the door of the house of the Lord the mortal remains of our dear friend Edwin O'Connor. We cannot yet believe that he is gone, that we will not see again the wrinkled smile, or hear the kindly voice; that wit has

---

42. Burrows, *Honest, Abe*, 106.
43. Boston Globe, March 27, 1968, 43.

passed, and wisdom too, and nothing now will ever change "the eternal Sabbath of his rest." Taken from among us at the summit of his life, the pain of our loss will not be lightly borne, and our sadness tells more eloquently than words all that he has meant to us. . . .

Edwin O'Connor was more than a writer of rare gifts, he was a man of rare goodness. Each one of us can remember the ways in which that goodness touched us, the ways in which we were better for having known him. As he had an instinct for happiness, so too he had an instinct for friends. His was not a friendship lightly given, but, once given, one could not imagine it being withdrawn. The strength of his will, like the vigor of his pen, was prodigious, but it stood always in the service of his ideals. Without sham and without pretense, he was always himself before the world. "He was a man, take him for all in all, we shall not look upon his like again."

We cannot, today, say goodbye in tears to the happiest man we have ever known. From wherever in eternity men look out upon this world of ours, he smiles on us now. And so we part, until we meet again in God's own time and God's own place.[44]

Burial was a few miles away on Cushing Knoll in Holyhood Cemetery located in Brookline, birthplace of John F. Kennedy. The affluent garden-city enclave of Brookline is almost entirely surrounded by the city of Boston. Joseph P. Kennedy's family burial plot is about fifty yards from O'Connor's last resting place. Richard Cardinal Cushing, Joseph P. Kennedy, Edwin O'Connor: these names of the assimilated Irish and their families who had risen high in Church, politics, and literature say much about the avenues to Irish success in America.

Some official tributes would have amused O'Connor. For example, on March 26 Rhode Island Congressman Ferdinand St. Germain addressed the House of Representatives on O'Connor's death; it was hard to tell which was more in evidence—the Congressman's pomposity or his asininity. Even more ludicrous was a resolution of the Rhode Island Senate.[45] In an incomprehensible gaffe, someone who had a passing acquaintance with O'Connor's work actually quoted Skeffington's praise of the Eddie McLaughlin who, Sam Weinberg reminded Skeffington, was the "drunken smush with the squint eye that kept spitting on your lapel" (*LH* 122). Thus, Skeffington's ironic rhetoric for a souse—"[a] tragic thing indeed that this young man was taken from us in so untimely a fashion" (*LH* 124)—was used to memorialize an utterly abstemious man! A more sensible assessment came from Boston City Councilman John L. Saltonstall Jr. He wrote Veniette concerning the City Council's resolution of March 25, which spoke of O'Connor as "a devot-

44. Typescript courtesy of Barbara O'Connor Burrell.
45. EOCP 276.

ed admirer of Boston and a witty yet sympathetic connoisseur of the Boston political scene."[46]

More bearable were tributes from the press. The *Woonsocket Call*'s Edgar J. Allaire, who had followed the hometown author assiduously over the years, put together an article for the evening paper on the very day of O'Connor's death. He concluded: "Success did not turn his head. . . . To old friends, in Woonsocket and elsewhere, he remained the same modest, unassuming, witty Ed O'Connor."[47] The next day the *Boston Globe* printed a moving piece entitled "We All Loved Ed," which reported the reactions of a half-dozen people ranging from Senator Ted Kennedy, who issued a bland statement, to Joe Vitale at the Ritz, whose affection shines through. Al Capp, whose summation of O'Connor became the title of the article, said of his fellow sometime satirist, "He was delighted by idiots, thrilled by stupidity."[48]

On Monday, the second day of his wake, the *Globe* published Bob Taylor's lengthy and touching piece, "The Way I'll Always Remember Ed O'Connor." He noted that O'Connor disliked the eulogist's art, unless it was comical, in which cases he took a special delight. He also remembered how Clem Norton, during his cockeyed political campaigns, would bellow out a big greeting to O'Connor from his sound truck.[49] On the same day the *Globe* also ran a story by Bud Collins, who emphasized O'Connor's unassuming ways and moderate living habits. "He needed only people to turn him on. And he was the same guy with all of them. Always."[50] The *Boston Herald Traveler* took the unusual step of eulogizing O'Connor on the top of its editorial page. Accompanying the tribute was a drawing of a mildly sad O'Connor. "Boston and her people knew themselves better because of O'Connor's writings," said the paper that had abruptly fired him sixteen years earlier. Three weeks later Ralph McGill of the *Atlanta Constitution*, who seems not to have known O'Connor all that well (he refers to him as Edwin J. O'Connor, and states that he had a daughter), called O'Connor "a human being who restored faith in man himself. . . . He was, by any measurement, a very special man."[51]

Bob Manning wrote as "The Editor" in the May *Atlantic* about O'Connor's unusually close relationship with the offices at 8 Arlington Street, where he dropped in sometimes twice a day. "Boston became his spiritual home," Manning wrote, "and the *Atlantic*, we are proud to say, became his

---

46. John L. Saltonstall Jr., letter to Veniette O'Connor, March 29, 1968, EOCP 276.
47. *Woonsocket Call*, March 23, 1968, 4.
48. Klarfeld, "We All Loved Ed."
49. *Boston Globe*, March 25, 1968.
50. *Boston Globe*, March 25, 1968, 13.
51. *Boston Globe*, April 14, 1968.

club." He concluded by saying that "his death . . . was a death in this family."[52]

Old friend Daniel Aaron, then at Smith College, wrote a reminiscence for *America*. He was struck by some similarities between Holy Cross Cathedral and the Old Saint Paul's of *The Edge of Sadness*. Aaron predicted that "[s]ocial historians in time will appreciate how perceptively O'Connor documents the acculturation of the Boston Irish, how he records what one of his characters calls 'the sheer *speed* of the polishing process.'"[53]

The most moving tribute came from Frank O'Malley. Writing in the Notre Dame alumni magazine, the English professor who had inspired his student thirty-two years earlier now recalled that O'Connor's mixture of humor and compassion could be detected as early as that lone short story in *Scrip* back in 1938. O'Malley also emphasized O'Connor's deep attachment to his alma mater:

> Notre Dame meant much to him. I have often thought that it might one day be the central background of a novel. For he retained a remarkable affection for the school and its people. It was his place, the place of his growing up. He genuinely enjoyed his student life, laughing at its inconveniences or restraints, at any aspect that seemed untoward.

O'Malley concluded by recalling O'Connor's annual week-long visits to Notre Dame. Just before O'Connor's death, some students had asked O'Malley whether Edwin O'Connor would come again soon.[54]

In July John Kelleher published the first important article on O'Connor's work. Blandly entitled "Edwin O'Connor and the Irish-American Process," the article still commands respect.[55] After some fond memories, Kelleher assesses O'Connor's work as a whole. It should be remembered that, with the possible exception of Frank O'Malley, John Kelleher probably had the deepest and most wide-ranging conversations with O'Connor. The two met once a month for lunch and talked on the telephone frequently. In fact, while *The Last Hurrah* was a work in progress the author had read from the manuscript over the phone, "bit by bit," to his professor friend. Kelleher's article emphasizes O'Connor's careful and penetrating thinking on a wide spectrum of topics: "in part it was the fruit of his preoccupation with moral theology." He describes O'Connor as a "very sane writer" concerned with stan-

---

52. "Edwin O'Connor 1918–1968," *Atlantic*, May 1968, 55.

53. Daniel Aaron, "Edwin O'Connor Remembered," *America*, May 4, 1968, 604.

54. Frank O'Malley, "ND Mourns Loss of an Author," *Notre Dame Alumnus*, May/June 1968, 18.

55. John V. Kelleher, "Edwin O'Connor and the Irish-American Process," *Atlantic*, July 1968, 48–52.

dards and norms. And while it might appear that O'Connor too often found those standards and norms in a romanticized past, Kelleher insists that O'Connor did not sentimentalize that past because "no generation escapes the consequences of original sin"—although it remains true that O'Connor lamented the passing of a colorful generation. Kelleher also underscored O'Connor's unassailable Christian faith, even though the rush of liturgical reform in the Church perturbed him. A good and happy man, the humorist in O'Connor did not disclose a facile optimist underneath.

Not everyone remembered O'Connor fondly. In late 1969 his old radio colleague and erstwhile friend Walter Hackett wrote that fame and money had changed O'Connor into an arrogant, cynical snob who dumped his old pals.[56] Clearly Hackett was enlarging his own falling out with O'Connor, because no one corroborates this claim. Of course O'Connor moved on in life from some of his earlier circles, as we all do. At any rate, Hackett's unfavorable review of *All in the Family* had been the final straw in what was left of their friendship.

From an unexpected quarter there came another less than gracious memory. In an otherwise friendly memoir, Edmund Wilson wrote that money worked its inexorable influence on his friend: "He developed a slight impatience of a kind characteristic of the rich with the tiresome, the incompetent and the undesirable" (*BL* 346). To argue against Wilson's perceptions takes some doing, but when Niall Montgomery read Wilson's words, he was angry enough to take him to task in a letter to Veniette. Montgomery thought that Wilson was dead wrong about his friend, who had an "inexhaustible humanity" and for whom grand houses and cars were merely toys.[57]

Veniette and the O'Connor family received scores of sympathy letters. Common to many of these were fond memories of O'Connor's unique synthesis of humor, seriousness, friendship, and honesty. Many spoke of how certain locales and groups, especially at Wellfleet, would never be the same again without him. Ted Weeks wrote Veniette on the day O'Connor died: "Your Eddie walked into our lives and into our hearts at 8 Arlington St. as no author has done in forty years."[58] Father John Ryan, a Jesuit at Fairfield University who had known O'Connor since the 1953 hospitalization, wrote

---

56. Walter Hackett, "Criticism Broke Long Friendship," *Providence Journal*, December 15, 1969.

57. Niall Montgomery, letter to Veniette O'Connor, November 2, 1969, EOCP 276.

58. Ted Weeks, letter to Veniette O'Connor, March 23, 1968, EOCP 431.

Veniette that on the day after O'Connor's death he had scrapped his Sunday sermon to talk instead of O'Connor "as the finest Catholic layman I have known."[59] Elliot Norton reminisced in a long letter. Toward the end he disclosed that his wife Florence had worked hard at marrying off O'Connor. But one day O'Connor had let his guard down and told Elliot that the fearsome rate of divorce dismayed him. Norton concluded by noting that O'Connor made "battalions" of his friends' lives "brighter and better."[60] Jacqueline Kennedy recalled the O'Connors' visit to Hyannisport. She urged Veniette, "Please let everyone who wants to—help you now—"[61] Father John McGoey wrote some months later to O'Connor's mother that her son's visits to Harbour Island "were a joy to me." He often remembers him at Mass.[62]

Within a few weeks of O'Connor's death his publishers proposed an anthology of O'Connor's work. The task of editor fell to Arthur Schlesinger, who by then held the Albert Schweitzer Chair in the Humanities at City University of New York. John Kelleher and Edmund Wilson were also asked to lend their names to the project. Wilson, however, soon proved to be a problem. The man who had urged O'Connor to sign with Reader's Digest Books now was huffy about a book which would consist largely of excerpts. In a letter to Peggy Yntema, who was doing much of the grunt work as usual, Wilson said sharply that he would have nothing more to do with the project.[63] But just as Schlesinger was bringing Wilson around, in January of 1969, he too began having serious misgivings about excerpting. At a minimum, short introductions would be needed. Then Wilson began to drag his feet again.[64] And so it went, to the annoyance of Veniette, who quarreled with Wilson.[65] In February Peggy Yntema wrote Schlesinger that she would supply him with notes for the necessary introductions.[66] She also made the selections. (Peggy surely deserved more prominent credit in the anthology; publishing was still a man's world.) By summer Peggy informed Veniette of the title, which Peter Davison had devised: *The Best and the Last of Edwin O'Connor.*

59. Rev. John Ryan, S.J., letter to Veniette O'Connor, March 25, 1968, EOCP 421.

60. Elliot Norton, letter to Veniette O'Connor, March 30, 1968, EOCP 276.

61. Jacqueline Kennedy, letter to Veniette O'Connor, March 26, 1968, EOCP 417.

62. Rev. John McGoey, S.F.M., postcard to Mrs. John V. O'Connor, January 20, 1969, courtesy of Barbara O'Connor Burrell.

63. Edmund Wilson, letter to Peggy Yntema, September 5, 1968, EOCP 276.

64. Arthur Schlesinger Jr., letters to Robert Manning, January 27, 29, 31, 1969, EOCP 276.

65. Veniette O'Connor, letter to Frank O'Malley, October 27, 1969, Frank O'Malley Papers, University of Notre Dame Archives.

66. Peggy Yntema, letter to Arthur Schlesinger Jr., February 5, 1969, EOCP 276.

About one quarter of the book would be "entirely new."[67] These new items consisted of mostly unpublished material: "Baldini"; his two lectures, "For Whom the Novelist Writes" and "A Meeting on Sunday"; "The Cardinal" and "The Boy." For some reason, excluded were O'Connor's newspaper television reviews and his media articles in *Atlantic Monthly;* apparently these were considered not appropriate to O'Connor's memory—a shame because some of this writing crackles with wit and insight. John Kelleher wrote a fine introduction to the last two selections. Edmund Wilson wrote a brief memoir and introduction to the "Baldini" on which he had collaborated. Arthur Schlesinger's thirty-two page introduction was then the nearest thing to a biography of O'Connor. He concluded: "He saw life steadily, without sentimentality of illusion and with an invincible gaiety, joyousness and grace of spirit. He penetrated to the edge of sadness and beyond, but he always returned with a new and exhilarating sense of the absurdity and possibility of life" (*BL* 35).

The 465-page anthology was published in February 1970.[68] Two preview pieces had already appeared: Wilson's memoir along with the Baldini collaboration in the October 1969 *Atlantic,* and a slightly abridged version of "The Boy," re-titled "The Magic Man," in *McCall's* in February 1970. In an effort to capitalize on O'Connor's still considerable fame, the anthology's dust jacket was a near clone of the dark green one for *The Last Hurrah.*

Reviews were sharply divergent. One of the most favorable reviews came from Monsignor Lally, who wrote glowingly of the man more than the works in the February 22 *Boston Sunday Globe.* More penetrating was Victor Burg's in *The Christian Science Monitor* of April 23. He noted how in O'Connor's work "family leads to family, all peopling the same streets." Burg strikes a few condescending notes, but at its best the review succinctly summarizes the man and his work:

For O'Connor there were good men and wise decisions; at the opposite pole, fools and mistakes, never horror, never evil. Despair was a fall from life's potential and God's grace, never the condition of life itself. And perhaps in a time when these negative perceptions begin to parody themselves, O'Connor's gentle optimism shines.

In the March 16 *Washington Star,* Mary McGrory dismissed the book as a sentimental memorial by friends to a man who was less than a major writer. It is difficult to understand why she calls Kelleher and Wilson sentimental. But the most negative review of the anthology came from Denis Donoghue

---

67. Peggy Yntema, letter to Veniette O'Connor, July 25, 1969, EOCP 276.
68. *The Best and the Last of Edwin O'Connor,* ed. Arthur Schlesinger Jr., with contributions by Edmund Wilson and John V. Kelleher (Boston: Atlantic Monthly Press/Little, Brown, 1970).

in the newly hatched *New York Review of Books* on June 16. Donoghue's review needs to be set beside all uncritically glowing accounts of the author. Although Donoghue has impressive critical credentials, this astute critic from Northern Ireland seems not to have remembered O'Connor's works very well. While he does have important things to say about O'Connor's tendency to stereotype and his reluctance to take risks, Donoghue can be confounding, to say the least. Thus, he actually claims that Father Hugh Kennedy in *The Edge of Sadness* is a warmed-over version of Bing Crosby in *Going My Way.* Donoghue also faults O'Connor for excessive use of italics for emphasis. But even a cursory glance at O'Connor's works clearly shows that Donoghue is plainly wrong, because O'Connor rarely resorted to that gimmick. Toward the end of his review Donoghue tries to make lame amends by praising O'Connor's honesty and claiming that "The Boy" showed promise. Donoghue concludes, "His world seems already to have died by its own hand, passing into history at once, abstract and allegorical." An interesting assessment, altogether, but one wonders how well Donoghue understood the Irish American experience to be able to give O'Connor adequate attention.

As the anthology was being assembled, the more important work of collecting and cataloguing O'Connor's papers got under way. Once again Peggy Yntema played an important role as she helped Veniette, who found it difficult to deal with the sad task. School notebooks and term papers, letters and telegrams, a great deal of unpublished material mostly from his early career, manuscripts and proofs, cartoons and photographs, magazines he appeared in or which mentioned him, assorted memorabilia: altogether enough to fill 441 folders. There is even a small souvenir box from Ireland, which still contains tiny dried leaves of shamrock.

The Edwin O'Connor Papers were formally presented to the Department of Rare Books and Manuscripts of the Boston Public Library as a gift from Mrs. Edwin O'Connor on September 22, 1971. There was to have been a special library exhibit honoring O'Connor within a year or two, but the man who had made the verbal assurance was killed in an automobile accident before plans went forward, and so the exhibit died with him.[69]

O'Connor's mother died in 1974 in Rhode Island. Jack O'Connor died two years later; he was just a little older than Sonny when he died. Jack and his

69. Eugene Zepp, Rare Books and Manuscripts Department of the Boston Public Library, conversation with author, summer 1999.

wife Betty raised six children, one of whom, by O'Connor's request, is named Edwin. Barbara and Bill Burrell began raising two children shortly after O'Connor's death.

Veniette could not bear to stay at 191 Commonwealth Avenue. Shortly after her husband's death, in a move that must have puzzled some, she simply moved across the broad expanse of Commonwealth Avenue Mall to 192, from which, of course, 191 is clearly visible. Later she moved to Cambridge near the Galbraiths and Marian Schlesinger, who was a good friend. Only a few months after O'Connor's death, the Mercedes caught fire and was totally destroyed. Veniette was pained by this loss of an important reminder of her husband, because the Mercedes had been the only car they ever had together. Sadder yet was the farewell to the Wellfleet house which, after a few more summers, Veniette had to sell. At some point in the 1970s Veniette and Stephen sold O'Connor's library to Bryn Mawr College.[70] Life had not been made any easier for her after O'Connor's estate was estimated at only $135,000, a considerable falling off from his earlier affluence. He had left no will.[71]

Many people thought that some life went out of Veniette after March 23, 1968. Four years later she was diagnosed with a serious form of cancer. Although she put up a brave fight for several years and suffered much, she steadily slipped. Nevertheless during these years of illness Veniette kept busy. She had already spent a year as coordinator of the Massachusetts committee of the National Health Agencies, and from 1970 to 1972 she had helped to organize and then direct the Independent Study Project, through which high school seniors in Boston could engage in study projects beyond the usual curriculum. When her illness developed, she worked as executive director of the Boston unit of the American Cancer Society; during the last three years of her life she held the same position at the Massachusetts chapter of the National Multiple Sclerosis Society, which underwent impressive growth under her leadership. She also did volunteer work for several institutions such as the Boston Public Library and the campaign for Notre Dame.[72] Although most of her salaried positions paid poorly, Veniette characteristically performed her duties with remarkable verve, even during bouts of illness and treatment.

70. Weil, interviews. The loss of O'Connor's books is less serious than it appears, because he never underlined or made notes; nevertheless, it was a large library and its contents would have provided some idea of his range of interests.

71. *Woonsocket Call*, April 19, 1968.

72. Details from obituary in the *Boston Globe*, September 12, 1978, 30.

In early 1978 Veniette began her final decline. She succumbed on September 11. The wake was from the Waterman Funeral Home in Kenmore Square, where her husband had been waked ten years earlier, and her funeral Mass was also in Holy Cross Cathedral.[73] She is buried next to O'Connor in Holyhood Cemetery, where her name, below her husband's on the tilted black onyx stone, reads as Veniette C. O'Connor.

Within a month of her husband's death, Veniette had made inquiries to Monsignor Lally about instruction in the Catholic faith. Since she was already a baptized Catholic, albeit a lapsed one, it is unclear what her request entailed. Monsignor Lally had suggested that she contact Father Francis Sweeney at Boston College, who had known her husband. She never followed up on her initial inquiry.[74] Nevertheless, it seems that something about O'Connor's life and death had awakened her.

O'Connor's stepson became an angry teenager following the death of a man who meant so much to him. At a time of general student rebellion, Stephen Weil had his own personal reasons as well. He later went through a phase of being a rejected young poet. But while a student at American University he discovered the Judaism that his father's family had left behind; embracing the ancient faith was a homecoming.

Denis Donoghue's observation that O'Connor's world seemed to pass away even as it unfolded was a prescient comment on O'Connor's later reputation. To put it mildly, during the 1970s and 1980s Edwin O'Connor simply fell from view. The reasons for any author's neglect after death are many, but the phenomenon is common enough. Irish American rediscovery was to take many new and unexpected roads in those years. O'Connor's dismissal, in *The Last Hurrah,* of a major conflict in Northern Ireland as utterly improbable is just one indication of how much of the Irish experience he overlooked or avoided. Anything about Irish America—from the surging popularity of the Clancy Brothers to the nascent phase of Irish studies in American universities—which did not pass through his sense of a Bostonianism proper to an assimilated and highly successful writer was beyond his ken.

Nevertheless, some renewed interest in Edwin O'Connor appeared in the 1990s, when so many things Irish American enjoyed a considerable vogue, assisted as they were by the dubious triumphs of Riverdance and *Angela's Ashes.* There was a reprinting of *The Edge of Sadness,* an implausible second

73. Death notice, *Boston Globe,* September 13, 1978, 36.
74. Rev. Francis Sweeney, S.J., telephone interview, March 26, 1999; Rt. Rev. Msgr. Francis J. Lally, letter to Veniette O'Connor, May 6, 1968, Archives of the Archdiocese of Boston.

edition of *Benjy,* a stage adaptation of *The Last Hurrah.* Although scholarship still tends to neglect O'Connor, perhaps Charles Fanning's generous
survey of his career in his authoritative book, *The Irish Voice in America,*[75]
will encourage a fresh look at his works.

Other kinds of posthumous recognition took some time. There had been
a tree planting with a commemorative plaque on Boston Common in 1969,
when a flowering crab was donated by the Atlantic staff.[76] As chairman of the
Boston Tree Memorial Commission, Ted Weeks no doubt had any easy time
recommending this honor for his protégé. The tree, however, died some
years ago. O'Connor was inducted into the Greater Woonsocket Hall of
Fame in 1987, but it took his home state thirty years to honor its most famous native-born novelist. Thanks largely to the efforts of a colorful Rhode
Island historian, Patrick Conley, the Rhode Island Heritage Hall of Fame, in
existence since 1965, inducted Edwin O'Connor posthumously at its annual
ceremony in Providence on May 9, 1998. Barbara Burrell accepted the award
for the brother she admired so much. When she started to speak, emotion
overcame her for a few moments. She then quietly described her brother's
accomplishments; a faulty sound system in the huge convention hall failed to
project adequately. Edwin O'Connor might have been touched and amused
at these last hurrahs with their edges of sadness.

Edwin O'Connor's life was short. His literary yield was relatively small,
and of this only *The Last Hurrah, The Edge of Sadness, All in the Family,* a few
short stories, and some journalism constitute his enduring work. He never
did fulfill his aim to be the Faulkner of the Irish in America, largely because
he restricted his attention to its upper strata, whereas Faulkner presented his
South more comprehensively, from Sartoris to Snopes. But O'Connor's novels certainly helped to interpret important parts of Irish America, especially
its difficult family life following upon a remarkable assimilation. At his best
he wrote with great ethical integrity, with an unusual warmth toward his
characters, with elegant wit.

As his eulogist said, Edwin O'Connor was a man of rare personal gifts
that touched and lifted so many people. If his unusual capacity for enduring
friendships sometimes clouded some friends' judgment of his work, that was
understandable. His genuineness and his delight in life were sorely needed
qualities in the drab fifties and cynical sixties. He may have lacked what Gra-

---

75. Charles Fanning, *The Irish Voice in America: 250 Years of Irish-American Fiction,* 2nd
ed. (Lexington, Ky.: University Press of Kentucky, 2000), especially 316–24.
76. Undated newspaper clipping, 1969?

ham Greene somewhere called the chip of ice in the heart needed by novelists of the first order. Perhaps he found it appalling, to use a Greenian term, to find the human heart too dark. The worlds he knew and wrote about—pre-television journalism, endless Irish conversation, political bosses, family patriarchs, the pre-Vatican II Church—were receding quickly into the American past from which few travelers return. Edwin O'Connor entertained and instructed us for too short a time, but at his best he left us those memorable families of his own.

❧ Bibliography

Published Works By Edwin O'Connor

Novels

All in the Family. Boston: Atlantic Monthly Press/Little, Brown, 1966.
The Edge of Sadness. Boston: Atlantic Monthly Press/Little, Brown, 1961.
I Was Dancing. Boston: Atlantic Monthly Press/Little, Brown, 1964.
The Last Hurrah. Boston: Atlantic Monthly Press/Little, Brown, 1956.
The Oracle. New York: Harper & Brothers, 1951.

Children's Book

Benjy. Boston: Atlantic Monthly Press/Little, Brown, 1957.

Short Stories

"Animal Life." *Flair* (July 1950): 34–35, 96–97.
"Friends Are Made in McCabe's." *Scrip: The University of Notre Dame Quarterly* (November 1938): 2–5.
"The Gentle, Perfect Knight." *Atlantic Monthly* (September 1947): 59–63.
"A Grand Day for Mr. Garvey." *Atlantic Monthly* (October 1957): 46–50.
"The Inner Self." *Atlantic Monthly* (April 1950): 64–65.
"Parish Reunion." *The Yale Review* (September 1950): 59–69.

Unfinished Published Fiction

"The Boy." *The Best and the Last of Edwin O'Connor.* Ed. Arthur Schlesinger Jr. Boston: Atlantic Monthly Press/Little, Brown, 1970: 423–65; abridged version, "The Magic Man," *McCall's* (February 1970): 90–91, 127–32.
"The Cardinal." *The Best and the Last of Edwin O'Connor.* Ed. Arthur Schlesinger Jr. Boston: Atlantic Monthly Press/Little, Brown, 1970: 406–22.
"The Great Baldini." In collaboration with Edmund Wilson. *Atlantic Monthly* (October 1969): 64–75; published as "Baldini" in *The Best and the Last of Edwin O'Connor.* Ed. Arthur Schlesinger Jr. Boston: Atlantic Monthly Press/Little, Brown, 1970: 344–76.

Drama

I Was Dancing. New York: Dramatists Play Service, 1966.

Journalism

Untitled two-part article on the elevation of Archbishop Richard J. Cushing to Cardinal. *Boston Globe* (December 14 and 21, 1958).
"Author of 'Hurrah' Declares He Knows Only One Politician." *Boston Sunday Post* (September 30, 1956): 1 and A3.

"Author Tells All About Curley and Skeffington." *Boston Evening Globe* (June 5, 1961): 1 and 5.

"The Book Fair." *Atlantic Monthly* (July 1966): 124–25.

"The Case of the Sober Shamus." *Atlantic Monthly* (June 1953): 88–89.

"Do British TV Fans Want It Dull?' *Life* (November 2, 1953):109–16.

"The Fairly Merry Widow." *Atlantic Monthly* (October 1946): 134–35.

"Fighting Words." *TV Program Week* (February 26–May 4, 1955): 27.

"For Whom the Novelist Writes." *The Critic* (April–May 1963): 13–17.

"Gold Among the Boo-Hoos." *Atlantic Monthly* (February 1954): 85–86.

"Halls of Ivy." *Atlantic Monthly* (November 1952): 118–19.

"Here in the Studio . . ." *Atlantic Monthly* (October 1946): 137–38.

"The Indirect Approach." *Atlantic Monthly* (June 1955): 87–88.

"It's Spontaneous!" *Atlantic Monthly* (January 1951): 88–90.

"James Michael Curley and *The Last Hurrah.*" *Atlantic Monthly* (September 1961): 48–50.

"A Love Letter to Woonsocket." *Providence Sunday Journal Magazine* (October 7, 1951): 12–15.

"The Meet at Cabinteely." *Atlantic Monthly* (July 1954): 94–96.

"No Laughing Matter." *Atlantic Monthly* (September 1946): 130–32.

"Prove You're Human." *Atlantic Monthly* (February 1947): 113–14.

"The Publisher and the Pep Talk." *The Writer* (April 1967): 31–32.

"Spy Hunt Buddy Turns Up with Wartime Trick." *Boston Sunday Post* (September 23, 1956): 1–2.

"What Night Does to Baseball." *Atlantic Monthly* (August 1950): 48–50; abridged version in *Reader's Digest* (September 1950): 123–25.

"Wise Old Priest Disdained Ways of Worldly Men." *Boston Sunday Post* (September 16, 1956): 1 and 4.

"Words Without Music." *Atlantic Monthly* (November 1951): 104–5.

Lectures

"A Meeting on Sunday." Delivered at the Paulist Center, Boston, October 1963; reprinted in *The Best and the Last of Edwin O'Connor.* Ed. Arthur Schlesinger Jr. Boston: Atlantic Monthly Press/Little, Brown, 1970: 381–97.

"For Whom the Novelist Writes." McGeary Foundation Lecture. Delivered at the Thomas More Association, Chicago, 1963. Reprinted in *The Critic* (April–May 1963): 13–17; reprinted in *The Best and the Last of Edwin O'Connor.* Ed. Arthur Schlesinger Jr. Boston: Atlantic Monthly Press/Little, Brown, 1970: 369–80.

Book Reviews

"Boston Was His Bailiwick." Rev. of *Honey Fitz,* by John Henry Cutler. *New York Times Book Review* (May 27, 1962): 5.

"How to Cook Without Baloney." Rev. of *Michael Field's Cooking School,* by Michael Field. *Life* (July 16, 1965): 21.

"Fred Allen's Letters Make Ideal Reading." Rev. of *Fred Allen's Letters,* ed. Joe McCarthy. *Boston Globe* (April 23, 1965): 45.

Television Reviews

Approx. 150 television reviews for the *Boston Herald* (December 1950–December 1952).

Approx. 300 television reviews for the *Boston Post* (October 1953–January 1956).

Bohlin, Virginia. "Traveler Visits Author Edwin O'Connor's Summer Home." *Boston Traveler* (August 25, 1959): B42.

Breit, Harvey. "In And Out of Books." *New York Times Book Review* (March 18, 1956): 8.

Brault, Gerard J. *The French Canadian Heritage in New England.* Hanover, N.H.: University Press of New England, 1986.

Burns, Robert E. *Being Catholic, Being American: The Notre Dame Story,* 2 vols. Notre Dame, Ind.: University of Notre Dame Press, 1999, 2000.

Burrows, Abe. *Honest, Abe: Is There Really No Business Like Show Business?* Boston: Atlantic Monthly Press/Little, Brown, 1980.

Capp, Al. "A Molasses-Mouthed Radio 'Thinker.'" *New York Herald Tribune Book Review* (July 15, 1951): Section 6, 6.

————. "When Al Capp Met O'Connor." *Boston Sunday Globe* (May 27, 1962): A3.

Claffey, Charles E. "Life & Times of a Political Chronicler." *Boston Sunday Globe* (May 22, 1983): A17, 19.

Cullen, Kevin. "Irish Ex-Premier Stars in Trial of Corruption." *Boston Globe* (July 21, 2000): 1.

Curley, James Michael. "A Hurrah for Curley by Curley." *Life* (September 10, 1956): 120–38.

————. *I'd Do It Again: A Record of All My Uproarious Years.* Englewood Cliffs, N.J.: Prentice-Hall, 1957.

Curley, Thomas. "An Irish-American Middle Class World." Rev. of *The Edge of Sadness. Commonweal* (June 16, 1961): 306–7.

Davidson, Bill. *Spencer Tracy: Tragic Idol.* New York: Dutton, 1987.

Davison, Peter. *Half Remembered: A Personal History.* New York: Harper & Row, 1973.

Delbanco, Andrew. *Writing New England: An Anthology from the Puritans to the Present.* Cambridge, Mass.: Belknap Press of Harvard University Press, 2001.

Dever, Joe. Rev. of *The Last Hurrah. Commonweal* (May 9, 1956): 601–2.

Dezell, Maureen. *Irish America: Coming Into Clover: The Evolution of a People and a Culture.* New York: Doubleday, 2001.

Dineen, Joseph. "A Radio 'Gabber.'" Rev. of *The Oracle. Boston Sunday Globe* (May 13, 1951): A59.

Doblier, Maurice. "'The Oracle,' a Radio Phony." Rev. of *The Oracle. Providence Sunday Journal* (April 29, 1951).

Donovan, Fred J. Rev. of *The Last Hurrah. The Providence Visitor* (February 23, 1956): 5.

Elie, Rudolph. Rev. of *The Oracle. Boston Sunday Herald.* (April 29, 1951): B4.

Fallon, Brian. *An Age of Innocence: Irish Culture 1930–1960.* New York: St. Martin's Press, 1998.

Fanning, Charles. *The Irish Voice in America: 250 Years of Irish-American Fiction,* 2nd ed. Lexington, Ky.: University Press of Kentucky, 2000.

Farrell, James T. "Hurrah! A Good Novel." Rev. of *The Last Hurrah. New York Post* (February 5, 1956): M10.

Fischer, Edward. "Edwin O'Connor, Raconteur." *Notre Dame Magazine* (Winter 1988–89): 49–50.

Fortin, Marcel, ed. *Woonsocket, Rhode Island: A Centennial History, 1888–1988.* Woonsocket, R.I.: Woonsocket Centennial Committee, 1988.

"From Curley Locks to Goldy Locks." Rev. of *Benjy. Time* (October 21, 1957): 108.

Funchion, Michael F. "The Political and Nationalist Dimensions." *The Irish in Chicago.* Ed. Lawrence J. McCaffrey. Urbana, Ill.: University of Illinois Press, 1987.

Fussell, Paul. *Wartime: Understanding and Behavior in the Second World War.* New York: Oxford University Press, 1989.

Galbraith, John Kenneth. "Sadness in Boston." Rev. of *The Edge of Sadness. The New Yorker* (June 24, 1961): 87–94.

Gillon, Steven M. *Politics and Vision: The ADA and American Liberalism, 1947–1985.* New York: Oxford University Press, 1987.

Gilman, Richard. "Pulitzer Prize Winner: Edwin O'Connor. *Sign* (July 1962): 60–61,

———. Rev. of *The Last Hurrah. Jubilee* (March 1956): 48.

Hackett, Walter. "Criticism Broke Long Friendship." *Providence Journal* (December 15, 1969).

Harrington, Joe. "A Success Year." *Boston Sunday Globe* (January 13, 1954): A24.

Harvey, Joseph M. "Hurrah for Whom." *Boston Sunday Globe* (May 13, 1956).

Hassett, Robert L. "Clem Norton Speaks, and Jim Curley Comes Alive." *Boston Herald Traveler* (April 18, 1969): 3.

Hicks, Granville. "Behind the Lace Curtains." Rev. of *The Edge of Sadness. Saturday Review* (June 10, 1961): 20.

Holland, Cornelius J. *His Reverence—His Day's Work.* New York: Benziger, 1921.

Hope, Arthur J. C.S.C., *Notre Dame: One Hundred Years.* Rev. ed. South Bend, Ind.: Icarus Press, 1978.

Hutchins, John. Rev. of *The Oracle.* Unidentified newspaper clipping. June 2, 1951.

Illtud, Evans, O.P. Rev. of *The Edge of Sadness. Blackfriars* (February 1962): 101–3.

Isaacs, Reginald. *Gropius: An Illustrated Biography of the Creator of the Bauhaus.* Trans. Henry Isaacs. Boston: Little, Brown, 1991.

Jones, Howard Mumford. Rev. of *The Last Hurrah. Saturday Review* (February 4, 1956): 12.

Kelleher, John V. "Curious Indeed the Way God Works." Rev. of *The Edge of Sadness. New York Times Book Review* (June 4, 1961): 1 and 33.

———. "Edwin O'Connor and the Irish-American Process." *Atlantic Monthly* (July 1968): 48–52.

———. "The Hero as Irish-American." Rev. of *The Last Hurrah. New York Times Book Review* (February 5, 1956): 1.

———. Introduction to "The Cardinal" and "The Boy" fragments in *The Best and the Last of Edwin O'Connor.* Boston: Atlantic Monthly Press/Little, Brown, 1970: 401–6.

———. "Mr. Dooley and the Same Old World." *Atlantic Monthly* (June 1946): 119–25.

Kenny, Herbert. "An Emphasis on Death." Rev. of Edwin O'Connor's recordings of *The Last Hurrah* and *The Edge of Sadness.* Undated clipping from *Boston Globe* (1969?).

———. "How O'Connor Won the Prize." *Boston Sunday Globe* (May 13, 1962): A5.

Klarfeld, Jonathan. "A Different Man from His Novels." *Boston Globe* (March 25, 1968).

———. "We All Loved Ed." *Boston Sunday Globe* (March 24, 1968): 1 and 78.

Lally, Francis J. Rev. of *The Best and the Last of Edwin O'Connor. Boston Globe* (February 22, 1970): 78.

"Last Hurrah Wins 'Maggie' of Paper-backs." *Woonsocket Call* (October 7, 1958).

Lawrence, William. *Roger Wolcott.* Boston: Houghton Mifflin, 1902.

"Literary Fame Comes Early to Young Woonsocket Author." *Woonsocket Sunday Star* (April 22, 1951), 1–2.

Lowe, Maury. "The Golden Age of Radio." *1971 Rhode Island Yearbook.*

"Manhandling Mother." Rev. of *Benjy. Newsweek* (October 21, 1957): 118–19.

Marquand, John P. *The Late George Apley.* New York: Random House, 1940.

McBride, Joseph. *Searching for John Ford: A Life.* New York: St. Martin's Press, 2001.

McGill, Ralph. "Edwin J. [sic] O'Connor: One of the Really Great Ones." *Boston Globe* (April 14, 1968).

McGoey, John H., S.F.M. *Nor Scrip Nor Shoes.* Boston: Atlantic Monthly Press/Little, Brown, 1958.

Meaney, John W. *O'Malley of Notre Dame.* Notre Dame, Ind.: University of Notre Dame Press, 1991.

"Meet Old Charlie." Rev. of *The Edge of Sadness*. *Newsweek* (June 5, 1961): 95.

Miller, Karl. *Doubles: Studies in Literary History*. Oxford, England: Oxford University Press, 1985.

Moore, Barbara W., and Gail Weesner. *Beacon Hill: A Living Portrait*. Boston: Centry Hill Press, 1992.

Nolan, Martin. "Larger Than Life." *Boston Sunday Globe* (October 24, 1999): N1 and 8.

Norton, Elliot. Four-part series on Edwin O'Connor. Boston *Record-American* (March 3–6, 1970).

———. Rev. of *I Was Dancing* (play). Boston *Record-American* (October 7, 1964): 38.

O'Brien, Daniel J. "Our 'Irish' Politicians." Rev. of *The Last Hurrah*. *Boston Sunday Globe* (February 6, 1956).

O'Connell, Shaun. *Imagining Boston: A Literary Landscape*. Boston: Beacon Press, 1990.

O'Connor, Carroll. *I Think I'm Outta Here: A Memoir of All My Families*. New York: Simon & Schuster, 1998.

"O'Connor Denies Curley 'Hero' in Novel, Tells Ex-Mayor So." *Woonsocket Call* (August 7, 1956).

"O'Connor Here on Saturday to Grant Student Interview." *Woonsocket Call* (May 8, 1962).

O'Connor, Thomas H. *The Boston Irish: A Political History*. Boston: Northeastern University Press, 1995.

———. *Building a New Boston: Politics and Urban Renewal, 1950–1970*. Boston: Northeastern University Press, 1993.

O'Malley, Frank. "ND Mourns Loss of an Author." *Notre Dame Alumnus* (May–June 1968): 18.

O'Sullivan, Michael, and Bernardine O'Neill. *The Shelbourne and Its People*. Dublin: Blackwater, 1999.

"Outrageous Old Crook." Rev. of *The Last Hurrah*. *Time* (February 13, 1956): 94.

Paulding, Gouverneur. "—And He Was Always Good to the Poor." Rev. of *The Last Hurrah*. *The Reporter* (February 23, 1956).

———. "A Priest's Return." Rev. of *The Edge of Sadness*. *The Reporter* (June 22, 1961): 48.

Phelps, Robert. "Radio Rogue." Rev. of *The Oracle*. *New York Times* (June 10, 1951): 22.

Pickerel, Paul. Rev. of *The Last Hurrah*. *Harper's* (February 1956): 86 and 88.

Pierce, David, ed. *Irish Writing in the Twentieth Century: A Reader* (Cork, Ireland: Cork University Press, 2000).

Powell, Anthony. *The Strangers Are All Gone*. Vol. 4 of *The Memoirs of Anthony Powell*. New York: Holt, Rinehart & Winston, 1982.

Prescott, Orville. Rev. of *The Edge of Sadness*. *New York Times* (June 5, 1961): 29.

Quintal, Claire, ed. *Steeples and Smokestacks: A Collection of Essays on the Franco-American Experience in New England*. Worcester, Mass.: Assumption College Institute francais, 1996.

Rank, Hugh. *Edwin O'Connor*. New York: Twayne Publishers, 1974.

Rhodes, Anthony. Rev. of *The Last Hurrah*. *The Listener* (July 5, 1956): 29.

Rogers, Robert. *A Psychoanalytic Study of the Double in Literature*. Detroit, Mich.: Wayne State University Press, 1970.

Rolo, Charles J. "The Great Skeffington." Rev. of *The Last Hurrah*. *Atlantic Monthly* (February 1956): 80–81.

Ryan, George. "For O'Connor It's Not the Last Hurrah." *Information* (December 1961): 16–20.

———. Untitled manuscript on Edwin O'Connor, shortened for article in *Information* (December 1961).

St. Charles—Old and New. Pamphlet for Parish Centennial of St. Charles Borromeo Church, Woonsocket, RI.: n.p., 1928.

Schlesinger, Arthur, Jr. Introduction to *The Best and the Last of Edwin O'Connor.* Boston: Atlantic Monthly Press/Little, Brown, 1970: 3–35.

———. Rev. of *I'd Do It Again* by James Michael Curley. *Saturday Review* (May 27, 1957).

Schlesinger, Marian. "That Rarity—A Merry Man—Remembered." *Boston Sunday Globe* (March 23, 1969): A6.

Shand-Tucci, Douglass. *Built in Boston: City and Suburb 1880–1950.* Amherst, Mass.: University of Massachusetts Press, 1988.

Shaughnessy, Edward L. *Down the Nights and Down the Days: Eugene O'Neill's Catholic Sensibilities.* Notre Dame, Ind.: University of Notre Dame Press, 1996.

Smith, Andy. "On the Air: A Century of Radio and TV in RI." *Providence Sunday Journal* (October 24, 1999): K1, 6, 7.

"Something About the Irish." Rev. of *The Edge of Sadness. Time* (June 9, 1961): 90.

Strauss, Helen. *A Talent for Luck.* New York: Random House, 1979.

Taubman, Howard. Rev. of *I Was Dancing* (play). *New York Times* (November 9, 1964): 40.

Taylor, Robert. *Fred Allen: His Life and Wit.* Boston: Little, Brown, 1989.

———. Rev. of *The Best and the Last of Edwin O'Connor. Boston Globe* (January 28, 1970).

———. "The Way I'll Always Remember Ed O'Connor." *Boston Globe* (March 25, 1968).

Toibin, Colm. Introduction to *The Penguin Book of Irish Fiction* (New York: Penguin, 2001).

Trout, Charles H. *Boston, The Great Depression, and The New Deal.* New York: Oxford University Press, 1977.

"A Vote for O'Connor." Rev. of *The Last Hurrah. Newsweek* (February 6, 1956): 88–89.

Weeks, Edward. Rev. of *The Oracle. Atlantic Monthly* (May 1951): 79.

———. *Writers and Friends.* Boston: Little, Brown, 1981.

West, Anthony. "When in Rome . . ." Rev. of *The Last Hurrah. The New Yorker* (February 11, 1956): 113–16.

West, Morris L. Rev. of *The Edge of Sadness. New York Herald Tribune* (June 3, 1961): Book Review Section, 23.

Wilson, Edmund. "The Great Baldini: A Memoir and a Collaboration." *Atlantic Monthly* (October 1969): 64–75; reprinted in *The Best and the Last of Edwin O'Connor.* Boston: Atlantic Monthly Press/Little, Brown, 1970: 344–67.

———. *The Bit Between My Teeth: A Literary Chronicle of 1950–1965.* New York: Farrar, Straus and Giroux, 1965.

———. *The Sixties: The Last Journal, 1960–1972.* Ed. Lewis M. Dabney. New York: Farrar, Straus and Giroux, 1993.

Winn, Jim. "O'Connor Remained Down to Earth Despite Fame." Woonsocket *Call* (March 29, 1987): D4.

Woodward, Kenneth. "The Life of a Great Teacher." *Newsweek* (October 21, 1991): 60.

❧ Index

A Family of His Own: A Life of Edwin O'Connor was designed and composed in Minion by Kachergis Book Design of Pittsboro, North Carolina. It was printed on 60-pound Sebago 2000 Eggshell and bound by The Maple-Vail Book Manufacturing Group of York, Pennsylvania.